MW01174084

Thackray's 2009 Investor's Guide

THACKRAY'S
2009
INVESTOR'S GUIDE

Brooke Thackray MBA, CIM, CFP

Published in 2008 by: MountAlpha Media:

alphamountain.com

ISBN13: 978-0-97822-001-3

Printed and Bound by Webcom

10 9 8 7 6 5 4 3 2 1

To my wife Jane

Acknowledgements

This book is the product of many years of research and could not have been written without the help of many people. First, I would like to thank my wife, Jane Steer-Thackray, and my children Justin, Megan, Carly and Madeleine, for the help they have given me and their patience during the many hours that I have devoted to writing this book. Second, I would like to thank the proofreaders and editors, Amanda ODonnell and Jane Stiegler. Special mention goes to Jane for the countless hours she spent helping with writing, formatting and editing. This book could not have been written without her help.

Special mention also goes to Don Vialoux. Don has a Chartered Market Technician (CMT) accreditation and many years investment experience with RBC Investments. He is a past president of the Canadian Society of Technical Analysts, a columnist for the Financial Post and a frequent presenter on Report on Business Television. Don currently runs a very popular and highly regarded investment website www.timingthemarket.ca. Over the years Don and I have kept in contact and shared many investment strategies. His advice has always been appreciated and many of his ideas have helped influence the strategies in this book.

INTRODUCTION

THACKRAY'S 2009 INVESTOR'S GUIDE

You can choose great companies to invest in and still underperform the market. Unless you are in the market at the right time and in the best sectors, your investment expertise can be all for naught.

Successful investors know when they should be in the market. Very successful investors know when they should be in the market, and the best sectors in which to invest. *Thackray's 2009 Investor's Guide* is designed to provide investors with the knowledge of when and what to buy, and when to sell.

The goal of this book is to help investors capture extra profits by taking advantage of the seasonal trends in the markets. This book is straightforward. There are no complicated rules and there are no complex algorithms. The strategies put forward are intuitive and easy to understand.

It does not matter if you are a short-term or long-term investor, this book can be used to help establish entry and exit points. For the short-term investor, specific periods are identified that can provide profitable opportunities. For the long-term investor best buy dates are identified to launch new investments on a sound footing.

The stock market has its seasonal rhythms. Historically, the broad markets, such as the S&P 500, have a seasonal trend of outperforming during certain times of the year. Likewise, different sectors of the market have their own seasonal trends of outperformance. When oil stocks tend to do well in the springtime before "driving season," health care stocks tend to underperform the market. When utilities do well in the summertime, industrials do not. With different markets and different sectors having a tendency to outperform at different times of the year, there is always a place to invest.

Until recently, investors did not have access to the information necessary to analyze and create sector strategies. In recent years there have been a great number of sector Exchange Traded Funds (ETFs) and sector indexes introduced into the market. For the first time, investors are now able to easily implement a sector rotation strategy. This book provides a seasonal road map of what sectors tend to do well at different times of the year. It is a first of its kind, revealing new sector-based strategies that have never before been published.

In terms of market timing there are ample strategies in this book to help determine the times when equities should be over or underweight. During a favorable time for the market, investments can be purchased to overweight equities relative to their target weight in a portfolio (staying within risk tolerances). During an unfavorable time, investments can be sold to underweight equities relative to their target.

A large part of the book is devoted to sector seasonality – the underpinnings for a sector rotation strategy. The most practical rotation strategy is to create a core part of a portfolio that represents the broad market and then set aside an allocation to be rotated between favored sectors from one time period to the next.

It does not makes sense to apply any investment strategy only once with a large investment. Seasonal strategies are no exception. The best way to apply an investment strategy is to use a disciplined methodology that allows for diversification and a large enough number of investments to help remove the anomalies of the market. This reduces risk and increases the probability of a long term gain.

Following the specific buy and sell dates put forth in this book would have netted an investor large, above market returns. To "turbo-charge" gains, an investor can combine seasonality with technical analysis. As the seasonal periods are never exactly the same, technical analysis can help investors capture the extra gains when a sector turns up early, or momentum extends the trend.

IMPORTANT:
The beginning date of every strategy period in this book represents a full day in the market; therefore, investors should buy at the end of the preceding market day, i.e. The Biotech Summer Solstice June 23rd to September 13th, would require an investor to enter the market before the closing bell on June 22nd.

What is Seasonal Investing?

In order to properly understand seasonal investing in the stock market, it is important to look briefly at its evolution. It may surprise investors to know that seasonal investing at the broad market level, i.e. Dow Jones or S&P 500, has been around for a long time. The initial seasonal strategies were written by Fields (1931, 1934) and Watchel (1942), who focused on the *January Effect*. Coincidentally, this strategy is still bantered about in the press every year.

Yale Yirsch Senior has been largely responsible for the next stage in the evolution, producing the Stock Trader's Almanac over the last forty years. This publication focuses on broad market trends such as the best six months of the year and tendencies of the market to do well depending on the political party in power and holiday trades.

Recently, Brooke Thackray and Bruce Lindsay (1999) wrote, Time In Time Out: Outsmart the Market Using Calendar Investment Strategies. This work focused on a comprehensive analysis of the six month seasonal cycle and other shorter seasonal cycles in the broad markets such as the S&P 500.

Don Vialoux, considered the patriarch of seasonal investing in Canada, has written many articles on seasonal investing. His writings on this topic have developed a large following, via his free newsletter available at www.timingthemarket.ca.

Seasonal investing has changed over time. The focus has shifted from broad market strategies to taking advantage of sector rotation opportunities – investing in different sectors at different times of the year, depending on their seasonal strength. This has created a whole new set of investment opportunities. Rather than just being "in or out" of the market, investors can now always be invested by shifting between different sectors and asset classes, taking advantage of both up and down markets.

Definition – Seasonal investing is a method of investing in the market at the time of the year when it typically does well, or investing in a sector of the market when it typically outperforms the broad market such as the S&P 500.

The term seasonal investing is somewhat of a misnomer, and it is easy to see why some investors might believe that the discipline relates to investing based upon the seasons of the year – winter, spring, summer and autumn. Other than with agricultural commodities, generally, seasonal investment strategies only use the calendar as a reference for buy and sell dates. It is usually a specific event, i.e. Christmas sales, that occurs on a recurring annual basis that creates the opportunity.

The discipline of seasonal investing is not restricted to the stock market. It has been used successfully for a number of years in the commodities market. The opportunities in this market tend to be based upon changes in supply and/or demand that occur on a yearly basis. Most commodities, especially the agricultural commodities, tend to have cyclical supply cycles, i.e., crops are harvested only at certain times of the year. The supply bulge that occurs at the same time every year provides seasonal investors with profit opportunities. Recurring increased seasonal demand for commodities also plays a major part in providing opportunities for seasonal investors. This applies to most metals and many other commodities, whether the end-product is industrial or consumer based.

Seasonal investment strategies can be used with a lot of different types of investments. The premise is the same, outperformance during a certain period of the year based upon a repeating event in the markets or economy. In my past writings I have developed seasonal strategies that have been used successfully in the stock, commodity, bond and foreign exchange markets. Seasonal investing is still relatively new for most markets with a lot of new opportunities waiting to be discovered.

How Does Seasonal Investing Work?

Most stock market sector seasonal trends are the result of a recurring annual catalyst: an event that affects the sector positively. These events can range from a seasonal spike in demand, seasonal inventory lows, weather effects, conferences and other events. Mainstream investors very often anticipate a move in a sector and incorrectly try to take a position just before an event takes place that is supposed to drive a sector higher. A good example of this would be investors buying oil just before the cold weather sets in. Unfortunately, their efforts are usually unsuccessful as they are too late to the party and the opportunity has already passed.

By the time the anticipated event occurs, a substantial amount of investors have bought into the sector – fully pricing in the expected benefit. At this time there is little potential left in the short-term. Unless there is a strong positive surprise, the sector's outperformance tends to slowly roll over. If the event produces less than its desired result, the sector can be severely punished.

So how does the seasonal investor take advantage of this opportunity? "Be there" before the mainstream investors, and get out before they do. Seasonal investors usually enter a sector two or three months before an event is anticipated to have a positive effect on a sector and get out before the actual event takes place. In essence, seasonal investors are benefiting from the mainstream investor's tendency to "buy in" too late.

Seasonality in the markets occurs because of three major reasons: money flow, changing market analyst expectations and the *Anticipation-Realization Cycle*. First, money flows vary throughout the year and at different times of the month. Generally, money flows increase at the end of the year and into the start of the next year. This is a result of year end bonuses and tax related investments. In addition, money flows increase at month end from money managers "window dressing" their portfolios. As a result of these money flows, the months around the end of the year and the days around the end of the month, tend to have a stronger performance than the other times of the year.

Second, the analyst expectations cycle tends to push markets up at the end of the year and the beginning of the next year. Stock market analysts tend to be a positive bunch – the large investment houses pay them to be positive. They start the year with aggressive earnings for all of their favorite companies. As the year progresses, they generally back off their earnings forecast, which decreases their support for the market. After a lull in the summer and early autumn months, they start to focus on the next year with another rosy forecast. As a result, the stock market tends to rise once again at the end of the year.

Third, at the sector level, sectors of the market tend to be greatly influenced by the *Anticipation-Realization Cycle*. Although some investors may not be familiar with the term "anticipation-realization," they probably are familiar with the concept of "buy the rumor – sell the fact," or in the famous words of Lord Rothschild "Buy on the sound of the war-cannons; sell on the sound of the victory trumpets."

The *Anticipation-Realization Cycle* as it applies to human behavior has been much studied in psychology journals. In the investment world, the premise of this cycle rests on investors anticipating a positive event in the market to drive prices higher and buying in ahead of the event. When the event takes place, or is realized, upward pressure on prices decreases as there is very little impetus for further outperformance.

A good example of the *Anticipation-Realization Cycle* takes place with the "conference effect." Very often large industries have major conferences that occur at approximately the same time every year. Major companies in the industry often hold back positive announcements and product introductions to be released during the conference.

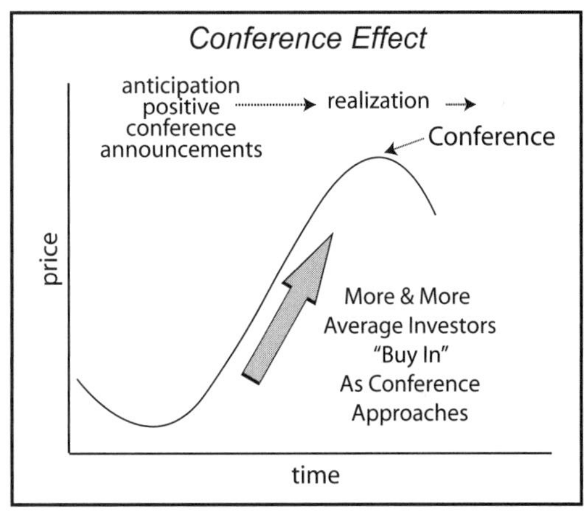

Two to three months prior to the conference, seasonal investors tend to buy into the sector. Shortly afterwards, the mainstream investors anticipate "good news" from the conference and start to buy in. As a result, prices are pushed up. Just before the conference starts, seasonal investors capture their profits by exiting their positions. As the conference unfolds, company announcements are made (realized), but as the potential good news has already been priced into the sector, there is little to push prices higher and the sector typically starts to rolls over.

The same *Anticipation-Realization Cycle* takes place with increased demand for oil to meet the "summer driving season", increased sales of goods at Christmas time, increased demand for gold jewellery to meet the autumn and winter demand, and many other events that tend to drive the outperformance of different sectors.

Does Seasonal Investing ALWAYS Work?

The simple answer to the above question is "No." There is not any investment system in the world that works all of the time. When following any investment system, it is probability of success that counts. It has often been said that "being correct in the markets 60% of the time will make you rich." Investors tend to forget this and become too emotionally attached to their losses. Just about every investment trading book states that investors typically fail to let their profits run and cut their losses quickly. I concur. In my many years in the investment industry, the biggest mistake that I have found with investors is not being able to cut their losses. Everyone wants to be right, that is how we have been raised. Investors feel that if they sell at a loss they have failed, and as a result, often suffer bigger losses by waiting for their position to trade at profit.

With any investment system, investors should let probability work for them. This means that investors should be able to enter and exit positions capturing both gains and losses without becoming emotionally attached to any positions. Emotional attachment clouds judgement, which leads to errors. When all of the trades are put together, the goal is for profits to be larger than losses in a way that minimizes risks and beats the market.

If we examine the winter oil stock trade, my favorite seasonal trade, we can see how probability has worked in an investor's favor. This trade is based upon the premise that at the tail end of winter, the refineries drive up demand for oil in order to produce enough gas for the approaching "driving season" that starts in the spring. As a result, oil stocks tend to increase and outperform the market (from February 25th to May 9th).

The oil stock sector, represented by the Amex Oil Index (XOI), has been very successful at this time of year, producing an average return of 8.6% and beating the S&P 500 by 6%, from 1984 to 2008. In addition it has been positive 92% of the time. Not all seasonal trades are created equal:

XOI / S&P 500 1984 to 2008

Feb 25 to May 9	XOI	S&P 500	Diff (shaded = positive)
1984	5.6 %	1.7 %	3.9 %
1985	4.9	1.4	3.5
1986	7.7	6.0	1.7
1987	25.5	3.7	21.8
1988	5.6	-3.0	8.6
1989	8.1	6.3	1.8
1990	-0.6	5.8	-6.3
1991	6.8	4.8	2.0
1992	5.8	0.9	4.9
1993	6.3	0.3	6.0
1994	3.2	-4.7	7.9
1995	10.3	7.3	3.1
1996	2.2	-2.1	4.3
1997	4.7	1.8	2.9
1998	9.8	7.5	2.3
1999	35.4	7.3	28.1
2000	22.2	4.3	17.9
2001	10.2	0.8	9.4
2002	5.3	-1.5	6.9
2003	5.7	12.1	-6.4
2004	4.0	-3.5	7.5
2005	-1.0	-1.8	0.8
2006	9.4	2.8	6.6
2007	10.1	4.2	5.8
2008	7.6	2.6	5.0
Avg	8.6 %	2.6 %	6.0 %

this strategic sector trade is at the top of the list. Investors should always evaluate the strength of seasonal trades before applying them to their own portfolios. Above is a table of the results.

If an investor started using the seasonal investment discipline in 1984 and chose to invest in the winter-oil trade, they would have been very happy with the results. If they had chosen almost any other year in the last 25 years, they would have also been very pleased with the results. The exception to this occurs in the years 1990 and 2005. These years produced nominal losses of 0.6% and 1.0%, respectively.

Does this mean the system does not work? No. An investor can start any methodology of trading at the "wrong time," and be unsuccessful for a particular trade. In fact, if the investor started in 1990 and had given up in the same year, they would have missed the following successful twelve years. They would have also missed all of the other successful seasonal trades that took place in the year. Investors have to remember that it is the final score that counts, after all of the gains have been weighed against the losses.

In practical terms, investors should not put all of their investment strategies in one basket. If one or two large investments were made based upon seasonal strategies, it is possible that the seasonal methodology might be inappropriately evaluated and its use discontinued. A much more prudent strategy is to use a larger number of strategic seasonal investments with smaller investments. The end result will be to put the seasonal probability to work with a much greater chance of success.

Measuring Seasonal Performance

How do you determine if a seasonal strategy has been successful? Many people feel that ten years of data is a good sample size, others feel that fifteen years is better, and yet others feel that the more data the better. I tend to fall into the camp that, if possible, it is best to use fifteen or twenty years of data for sectors and more data for the broad markets, such as the S&P 500. Although the most recent data in almost any analytical framework is the most relevant, it is important to get enough data to reflect a sector's performance across different economic conditions. Given that historically the economy has performed on an eight year cycle, four years of expansion and then four years of contraction, using a short data set does not provide for enough exposure to different economic conditions.

A data set that is too long can run into the problem of older data having too much of an influence on the numbers when fundamental factors affecting a sector have changed. It is important to look at trends over time and assess if there has been a change that should be considered in determining the dates for a seasonal cycle. Each sector should be judged on its own merit. The analysis tables in this book illustrate the performance level for each year in order to provide the opportunity for readers to determine any relevant changes.

In order to determine if a seasonal strategy is effective there are two possible benchmarks, absolute and relative performance. Absolute performance measures if a profit is made and relative performance measures the performance of a sector in relationship to a major market. Both measurements have their merits and depending on your investment style, one measurement may be more valuable than another. This book provides both sets of measurement in tables and graphs.

It is not just the average percent gain of a sector over a certain time period that determines success. It is possible that one or two spectacular years of performance skew the results substantially (particularly with a small data set). The frequency of success is also very important: the higher the percentage of success the better. Also, the fewer large drawdowns the better. There is no magic number (percent success rate) per se of what constitutes a successful strategy. The success rate should be above fifty percent, otherwise it would be better to just invest in the broad market. Ideally speaking a strategy should have a high percentage success rate on both an absolute and relative basis. Some strategies are stronger than others, but that does not mean that the weaker strategies should not be used. Prudence should be used in determining the ideal portfolio allocation.

Illustrating the strength of a sector's seasonal performance can be accomplished through either an absolute yearly average performance graph, or a relative yearly average performance graph. The absolute graph shows the average yearly cumulative gain for a set number of years. It lets a reader visually identify the strong periods during the year. The relative graph shows the average yearly cumulative gain for the sector relative to the benchmark index.

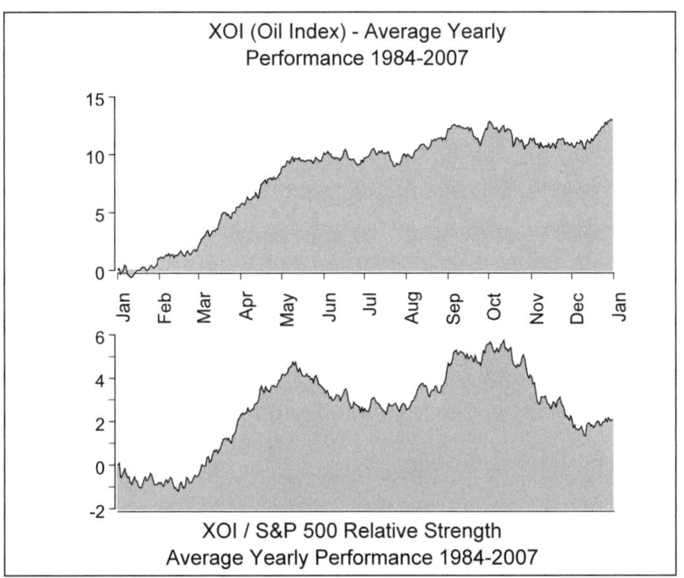

Both graphs are useful in determining the strength of a particular seasonal strategy. In the above diagram, the top graph illustrates the average year for the XOI (Oil Index) from 1984 to 2007. Essentially it illustrates the cumulative average gain if an investment were made in the index. The steep rising line starting in January/February shows the overall price rise that typically occurs in this sector at this time of year. In May the line flattens out and then rises very modestly starting in July.

The bottom graph is a ratio graph, illustrating the strength of the XOI Index relative to the S&P 500. It is derived by dividing the average year of the XOI by the average year of the S&P 500. When the line in the graph is rising, the XOI is outperforming the S&P 500, and vise versa when it is declining. This is an important graph and should be used in considering seasonal investments because the S&P 500 is a viable alternative to the energy sector. If both markets are increasing, but the S&P 500 is increasing at a faster rate, the S&P 500 represents a more attractive opportunity. This is particularly true when measuring the risk of a volatile sector relative to the broad market. If both investments were expected to produce the same rate of return, generally the broad market is a better investment because of its diversification.

Who Can Use Seasonal Investing?

Any investor from novice to expert, from short-term trader to long-term investor can benefit from using seasonal analysis. Seasonal investing is unique because it is an easy to understand system that can be used by itself or as a complement to another investment discipline. For the novice it provides an easy to follow strategy that makes intuitive sense. For the expert it can be used as a stand-alone system or as a complement to an existing system.

Behind the scenes money managers use seasonal analysis a lot more than they let on. I have talked to money managers who have extolled the virtues of making investments based upon seasonal trends. Because of its simplicity, they tend not to emphasize the methodology in public. They fear that the investing public will question why they are getting paid the "big bucks" if they are using such a simple system.

Seasonal investing is easily understood by all levels of investors, which allows investors to make rational decisions. This may seem obvious, but it is very common for investors to listen to a "guru of the market", be impressed and blindly follow his advice. When the advice works there is no problem. When the advice does not work investors wonder why they made the investment in the first place. When investors do not understand their investments it causes stress, bad decisions and a lack of "stick-to-it ness" with any investment discipline. Even expert investors realize the importance of understanding your investments. Michael Lynch of Fidelity Investments used to say "Never invest in any idea that you can't illustrate with a crayon." Investors do not need to go that far, but they should understand their investments.

Novice investors find seasonal strategies very easy to understand because they are intuitive. They do not have to be investing for years to understand why seasonal strategies work. They understand that an increase in demand for gold every year at the same time causes a ripple effect in the stock market pushing up gold stocks at the same time every year.

Most expert investors use information from a variety of sources in making their decisions. Even experts that primarily use fundamental analysis can benefit from using seasonal trends to get an edge in the market. Fundamental analysis is a very crude tool and provides very little in the way of timing an investment. Using seasonal trends can help with the timing of the buy and sell decisions and produce extra profit.

Seasonal investing can be used by both short-term and long-term investors, but in different ways. For short-term investors it provides a complete trade – buy and sell dates. For long-term investors it can provide a buy date for a sector of interest.

Combining Seasonal Analysis with other Investment Disciplines

Seasonal investing used by itself has historically produced above average market returns. Depending on an investor's particular style, it can be combined with one of the other three investment disciplines: fundamental, quantitative and technical analysis. There are two basic ways to combine seasonal analysis with other investment methodologies – as the primary or secondary method. If it is used as a primary method, seasonally strong time periods are established for a number of sectors and then appropriate sectors are chosen based upon fundamental, quantitative or technical screens. If it is used as a secondary method, sector selections are first made based upon one of three methods and then final sectors are chosen based upon which ones are in their seasonally strong period.

Technical analysis is an ideal mate for seasonal analysis. Unlike fundamental and quantitative analysis, which are very blunt timing tools at best, seasonal and technical analysis can provide specific trigger points to buy and sell. The combination can turbo-charge investment strategies, adding extra profits by fine-tuning entry and exit dates.

Seasonal analysis provides both buy and sell dates. Although a sector in the market can sometimes bottom on the exact seasonal buy date, it more often bottoms a bit early or a bit late. After all, the seasonal buy date is based upon an average of historical performance. Depending on the sector, buying opportunities start to develop approximately one month before and after the seasonal buy date. Using technical analysis gives an investor the advantage of buying into a sector when it turns up early or waiting when it turns up late. Likewise, technical analysis can be used to trigger a sell signal when the market turns down before or after the sell date.

The sell decision can be extended with the help of a trailing stop-loss order. If a sector has strong momentum and the technical tools do not provide a sell signal, it is possible to let the sector "run." When a trailing stop-loss is used, a profitable sell point is established. If the price continues to run, then the selling point is raised. If, on the other hand, the price falls through the stop-loss point, the position is sold.

Thackray Sector Thermometer

January

Info Tech
Con Disc.
Financials
Health Care
Telecom
Industrials
Materials
Energy
Utilities
Con Staples

The *Thackray Sector Thermometer* ranks sectors by average monthly gains for the current month. The sector at the top of the thermometer has the largest gain and the sector at the bottom has the smallest gain. The box at the top of the thermometer encloses the favored sectors for the month. These sectors have generally outperformed the S&P 500 for the month and on average have produced a positive gain.

Although all ten of the S&P Global Industry Classification Standard sectors are on the thermometer, some sectors have much better longer term trends than others. This book, in its month to month pages, focuses on multi-month trends with the best performance. Investors should concentrate their efforts on these trends rather than looking at each monthly return in isolation.

Although a lot of analysts refer to seasonal trends starting and ending at the beginning of the month for simplicity's sake, statistically the actual trends seldom occur exactly at month end. The argument for using the first day of the month to start seasonal investments is that sector performance does not change precisely on any particular day. The counter argument is that the average buy date is reflective of a "natural turning point" and it is not a coincidence that many of the dates are a few days before or after the end of the month. The position in this book is that it is more profitable to use the average "natural turning point" dates.

Other than being positive and generating greater gains than the broad market, and outperforming the market more than 50% of the time, there are two other factors in deciding whether or not a sector should be chosen for the favored sector box. First, consideration must be given to the frequency of outperformance relative to the S&P 500. It is possible for a sector to be selected if it has underperformed by a small margin, but it is still positive and has outperformed the broad market more than 50% of the time. In this case the value of outperformance makes up for the small return underperformance. Also, a sector can be selected if it has outperformed the broad market by a significant amount, but it has beaten the market less than 50% of the time. In this case, the value of the extra return outweighs the lack of frequency of outperformance. Second, a sector can be included with a minor negative performance if it outperforms the S&P 500 and the sector is in the middle of its seasonally strong time. If the favored sector has historically outperformed the market in a certain month, been relatively flat in the next month, and strongly outperformed in the following month, it makes sense for the average investor to hold the sector in the relatively flat middle month.

Global Industry Classification Standard (GICS)

Source: www.standardandpoors.com

Energy Sector - The GICS Energy Sector comprises companies whose businesses are dominated by either of the following activities: the construction or provision of oil rigs, drilling equipment and other energy related services or equipment, including seismic data collection, companies engaged in the exploration, production, marketing, refining and/or transportation of oil and gas products, coal and other consumable fuels.

Materials Sector – The GICS Materials Sector encompasses a wide range of commodity-related manufacturing industries. Included in this sector are companies that manufacture chemicals, construction materials, glass, paper, forest products and related packaging products, and metals, minerals and mining companies, including producers of steel.

Industrials Sector – The GICS Industrials Sector includes companies whose businesses are dominated by one of the following activities: the manufacture and distribution of capital goods, including aerospace & defense, construction, engineering & building products, electrical equipment and industrial machinery; the provision of commercial services and supplies including printing, employment, environmental and office services; the provision of transportation services including airlines, couriers, marine, road & rail and transportation infrastructure.

Consumer Discretionary Sector – The GICS Consumer Discretionary Sector encompasses those industries that tend to be the most sensitive to economic cycles. Its manufacturing segment includes automotive, household durable goods, textiles & apparel and leisure equipment. The services segment includes hotels, restaurants and other leisure facilities, media production and services, and consumer retailing and services.

Consumer Staples Sector – The GICS Consumer Staples Sector comprises companies whose businesses are less sensitive to economic cycles. It includes manufacturers and distributors of food, beverages and tobacco and producers of nondurable household goods and personal products. It also includes food & drug retailing companies as well as hypermarkets and consumer super centers.

Health Care Sector - The GICS Health Care Sector encompasses two main industry groups. The first includes companies who manufacture health care equipment and supplies or provide health care related services, including distributors of health care products, providers of basic health care services, and owners and operators of health care facilities and organizations. The second regroups companies primarily involved in the research, development, production and marketing of pharmaceuticals and biotechnology products.

Financials Sector - The GICS Financial Sector contains companies involved in activities such as banking, mortgage finance, consumer finance, specialized finance, investment banking and brokerage, asset management and custody, corporate lending, insurance, and financial investment, and real estate, including REITs.

Information Technology Sector - The GICS Information Technology Sector covers the following general areas: firstly, Technology Software & Services, including companies that primarily develop software in various fields such as the Internet, applications, systems, database management and/or home entertainment, and companies that provide information technology consulting and services, as well as data processing and out sourced services; secondly, Technology Hardware & Equipment, including manufacturers and distributors of communications equipment, computers & peripherals, electronic equipment and related instruments; and thirdly, Semiconductors & Semiconductor Equipment Manufacturers.

Telecommunications Services Sector - The GICS Telecommunications Services Sector contains companies that provide communications services primarily through a fixed-line, cellular, wireless, high bandwidth and/or fiber optic cable network.

Utilities Sector - The GICS Utilities Sector encompasses those companies considered electric, gas or water utilities, or companies that operate as independent producers and/or distributors of power.

Sectors of the Market

Standard & Poor's has done an excellent job in categorizing the U.S. stock market into its different parts. Although the demand for this service initially came from institutional investors, many individual investors now seek the same information. Knowing the sector breakdown in the market allows investors to see how different their portfolio is relative to the market. As a result, they are able to make conscious decisions on what parts of the stock market to overweight based upon their beliefs of which sectors will outperform. It also helps control the amount of desired risk.

Standard & Poor's uses four levels of detail in its Global Industry Classification Standard (GICS©) to categorize stock markets around the world. From the most specific, it classifies companies into sub-industries, industries, industry groups and finally economic sectors. All companies in the Standard & Poor's global family of indices are classified according to the GICS structure.

This book focuses on the U.S. market, analyzing the trends of the venerable S&P 500 index and its economic sectors and industry groups. The following diagram illustrates the index classified according to its economic sectors.

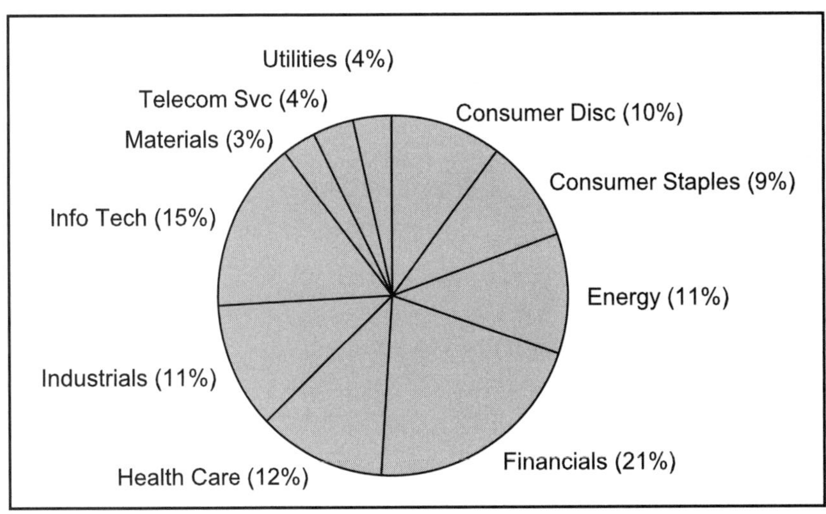

Standard and Poor's, Understanding Sectors, June 30, 2007

For more information on Standard and Poor's Global Industry Classification Standard (GICS©), refer to www.standardandpoors.com

Investment Products – Which One Is The Right One?

There are many ways to take advantage of the seasonal trends at the broad stock market and sector levels. Regardless of the investment products that you currently use, whether exchange traded funds, mutual funds, stocks or options, all can be used with the strategies in this book. Different investments offer different risk-reward relationships and return potential.

Exchange Traded Funds (ETFs)

Exchange Traded Funds (ETFs) offer the purest method of seasonal investment. The broad market ETFs are designed to track the major indices and the sector ETFs are designed to track specific sectors without using active management. Relatively new, ETFs are a great way to capture both market and sector trends. They were originally introduced into the Canadian market in 1993 to represent the Toronto stock market index. Shortly afterward they were introduced to the U.S. market and there are now hundreds of ETFs to represent almost every market, sector, style of investing and company capitalization. Originally ETFs were mainly of interest to institutional investors, but individual investors have fast realized the merits of ETF investing and have made some of the broad market ETFs the most heavily traded securities in the world.

An ETF is a single security that represents a market, such as the S&P 500; a sector of the market, such as the financial sector; or a commodity, such as gold. In the case of the S&P 500, an investor buying one security is buying all 500 stocks in the index. By investing into a financial ETF, an investor is buying the companies that make up the financial sector of the market. By investing into a gold commodity ETF, an investor is buying a security that represents the price of gold.

ETFs trade on the open market just like stocks. They have a bid and an ask, can be shorted and many are option eligible. They are a very low cost, tax efficient method of targeting specific parts of the market.

Mutual Funds

Mutual funds are a good way to combine market or sector investing with active management. In recent years, many mutual fund companies have added sector funds to accommodate an increasing appetite in this area.

As the seasonal strategies put forward in this book have a short-term nature, it is important to make sure that there are no fees (or a nominal charge) for getting into and out of a position in the market.

Stocks

Stocks provide an opportunity to make better returns than the market or sector. If the market increases during its seasonal period, some stocks will increase dramatically more than the index. Choosing one of the outperforming stocks will greatly enhance returns; choosing one of the underperforming stocks can create substantial loses. Using stocks requires increased attention to diversification and security selection.

Options

> Disclaimer: Options involve risk and are not suitable for every investor. Because they are cash-settled, investors should be aware of the special risks associated with index options and should consult a tax advisor. Prior to buying or selling options, a person must receive a copy of Characteristics and Risks of Standardized Options and should thoroughly understand the risks involved in any use of options. Copies may be obtained from The Options Clearing Corporation, 440 S. LaSalle Street, Chicago, IL 60605.

Options, for more sophisticated investors, are a good tool to take advantage of both market and sector opportunities. An option position can be established with either stocks or ETFs. There are many different ways to use options for seasonal trends: establish a long position on the market during its seasonally strong period, establish a short position during its seasonally weak period, or create a spread trade to capture the superior gains of a sector over the market.

THACKRAY'S 2009 INVESTOR'S GUIDE

CONTENTS

JANUARY

	MONDAY	TUESDAY	WEDNESDAY
WEEK 01			
WEEK 02	**5** 26	**6** 25 USA ISM Non-Manufacturing Report on Business (10:00 am ET)	**7** 24
WEEK 03	**12** 19	**13** 18	**14** 17 USA Federal Reserve Board's Beige Book
WEEK 04	**19** 12 USA Market Closed-Martin Luther King Day	**20** 11	**21** 10
WEEK 05	**26** 5 USA UBS Index of Investor Optimism (8:30 am ET)	**27** 4 USA FOMC Meetings USA Consumer Confidence Index 10:00 am ET	**28** 3 USA FOMC Meetings

THURSDAY	FRIDAY
1 30 USA Market Closed - New Year's Day CAN Market Closed - New Year's Day	**2** 29 USA The Employment Situation (8:30 am ET) USA ISM Manufacturing Report on Business (10:00 am ET)
8 23 USA Federal Reserve Bank of Philadelphia: Business Outlook Survey - Historical Revisions (12:00 pm ET)	**9** 22
15 16 USA Federal Reserve Bank of Philadelphia: Business Outlook Survey (12:00 pm ET) USA Empire State Manufacturing Survey - Federal Reserve Bank of New York (8:30 am ET)	**16** 15
22 9	**23** 8
29 2 USA Help-Wanted Advertising Index (10:00 am ET) USA Employment Cost Index	**30** 1 USA Strike Report (8:30 am ET) USA Chicago Purchasing Managers Index (Business Barometer) 9:45 am ET

FEBRUARY

M	T	W	T	F	S	S
						1
2	3	4	5	6	7	8
9	10	11	12	13	14	15
16	17	18	19	20	21	22
23	24	25	26	27	28	

MARCH

M	T	W	T	F	S	S
						1
2	3	4	5	6	7	8
9	10	11	12	13	14	15
16	17	18	19	20	21	22
23	24	25	26	27	28	29
30	31					

APRIL

M	T	W	T	F	S	S
		1	2	3	4	5
6	7	8	9	10	11	12
13	14	15	16	17	18	19
20	21	22	23	24	25	26
27	28	29	30			

MAY

M	T	W	T	F	S	S
				1	2	3
4	5	6	7	8	9	10
11	12	13	14	15	16	17
18	19	20	21	22	23	24
25	26	27	28	29	30	31

JANUARY SUMMARY

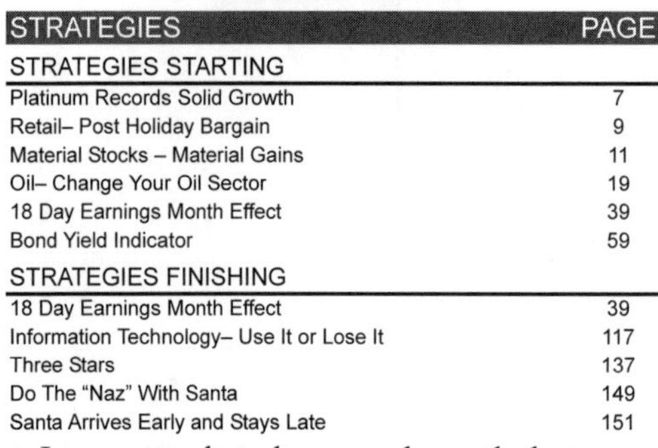

STRATEGIES	PAGE
STRATEGIES STARTING	
Platinum Records Solid Growth	7
Retail– Post Holiday Bargain	9
Material Stocks – Material Gains	11
Oil– Change Your Oil Sector	19
18 Day Earnings Month Effect	39
Bond Yield Indicator	59
STRATEGIES FINISHING	
18 Day Earnings Month Effect	39
Information Technology– Use It or Lose It	117
Three Stars	137
Do The "Naz" With Santa	149
Santa Arrives Early and Stays Late	151

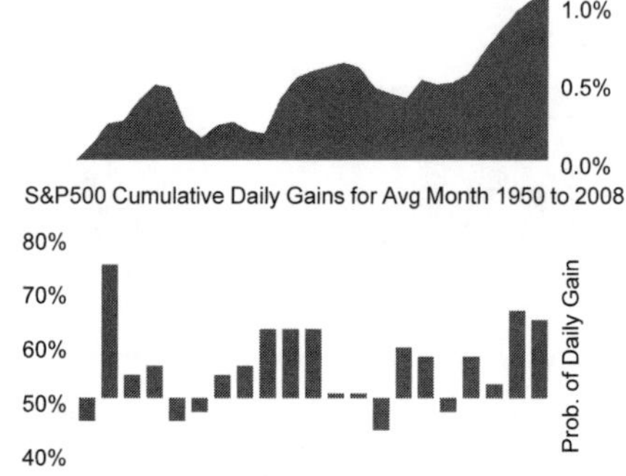

♦ January tends to be a good month, but over the last decade the S&P 500 has only been positive 50% of the time ♦ Information Technology tends to do well, particularly until the Las Vegas Consumer Electronics Show (see *Information Technology- Use It Or Lose It* strategy). ♦ Small companies also benefit as they are the main recipients of tax loss selling (see *Small Cap Effect* strategy). ♦ January acts as a predictor for the rest of the year (see *January Predictor* strategy).

BEST / WORST JANUARY BROAD MKTS. 1999-2008

BEST JANUARY MARKETS

- Nasdaq (1999) 14.3%
- Nasdaq (2001) 12.2%
- Russell 2000 (2006) 8.9%

WORST JANUARY MARKETS

- Nasdaq (2008) -9.9%
- Russell 3000 Gr (2008) -8.0%
- Russell 2000 (2008) -6.9%

Index Values End of Month

	1999	2000	2001	2002	2003	2004	2005	2006	2007	2008
Dow	9,359	10,941	10,887	9,920	8,054	10,488	10,490	10,865	12,622	12,650
S&P 500	1,280	1,394	1,366	1,130	856	1,131	1,181	1,280	1,438	1,379
Nasdaq	2,506	3,940	2,773	1,934	1,321	2,066	2,062	2,306	2,464	2,390
TSX	6,730	8,481	9,322	7,649	6,570	8,521	9,204	11,946	13,034	13,155
Russell 1000	1,280	1,415	1,389	1,147	873	1,163	1,219	1,341	1,507	1,444
Russell 2000	1,064	1,235	1,263	1,201	925	1,443	1,551	1,822	1,989	1,773
Russell 3000 Growth	2,554	3,069	2,654	1,944	1,378	1,872	1,871	2,066	2,238	2,214
Russell 3000 Value	2,001	2,013	2,213	2,051	1,668	2,229	2,450	2,717	3,151	2,883

Percent Gain for January

	1999	2000	2001	2002	2003	2004	2005	2006	2007	2008
Dow	1.9	-4.8	0.9	-1.0	-3.5	0.3	-2.7	1.4	1.3	-4.6
S&P 500	4.1	-5.1	3.5	-1.6	-2.7	1.7	-2.5	2.5	1.4	-6.1
Nasdaq	14.3	-3.2	12.2	-0.8	-1.1	3.1	-5.2	4.6	2.0	-9.9
TSX	3.8	0.8	4.3	-0.5	-0.7	3.7	-0.5	6.0	1.0	-4.9
Russell 1000	3.5	-4.2	3.2	-1.4	-2.5	1.8	-2.6	2.7	1.8	-6.1
Russell 2000	1.3	-1.7	5.1	-1.1	-2.9	4.3	-4.2	8.9	1.6	-6.9
Russell 3000 Growth	5.7	-4.4	7.0	-1.9	-2.5	2.2	-3.5	2.4	2.5	-8.0
Russell 3000 Value	0.4	-3.3	0.4	-0.8	-2.6	1.7	-2.1	4.1	1.1	-4.2

January Market Avg. Performance 1999 to 2008 (1)

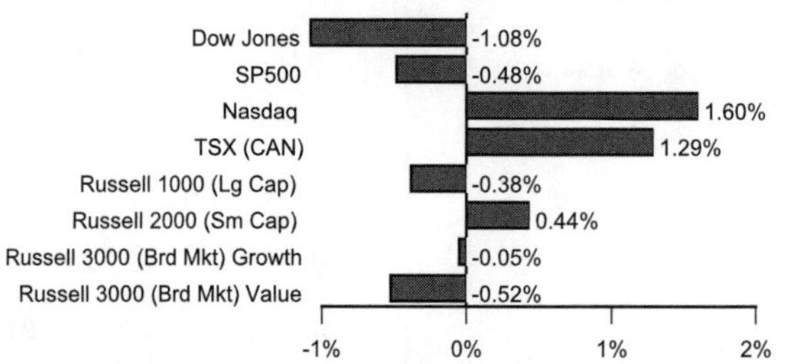

Interest Corner Jan(2)

	Fed Funds % (3)	3 Mo. T-Bill % (4)	10 Yr % (5)	20 Yr % (6)
2008	3.00	1.96	3.67	4.35
2007	5.25	5.12	4.83	5.02
2006	4.50	4.47	4.53	4.74
2005	2.25	2.51	4.14	4.64
2004	1.00	0.92	4.16	5.00

(1) Russell Data provided by Russell (2) Federal Reserve Bank of St. Louis- end of month values (3) Target rate set by FOMC (4)(5)(6) Constant yield maturities.

JANUARY SECTOR / SUB-SECTOR PERFORMANCE

THACKRAY SECTOR THERMOMETER

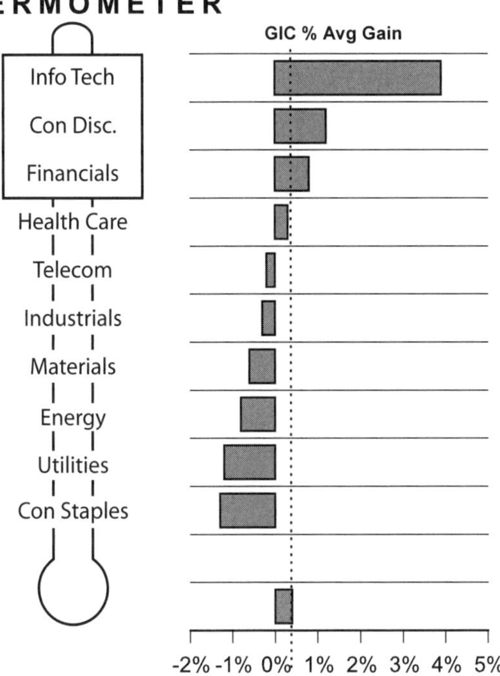

GIC[2] % Avg Gain	Fq % Gain >S&P 500	SP GIC SECTOR 1990-2008[1]
3.9 %	79 %	Information Technology
1.2	53	Consumer Discretionary
0.8	63	Financials
0.3	58	Health Care
-0.2	53	Telecom
-0.3	26	Industrials
-0.6	42	Materials
-0.8	37	Energy
-1.2	32	Utilities
-1.3	21	Consumer Staples
0.4 %	N/A %	S&P 500

GIC % Avg Gain	Fq % Gain >S&P 500	SELECTED SUB-SECTORS 1990-2008[3]
7.3 %	57 %	Semiconductor (SOX) (95-2008)
3.2	68	Software & Services
2.6	53	Autos & Components
1.3	53	Banks
1.2	41	Biotech (92-2008)
0.8	41	Transportation
0.3	41	Retailing
0.2	53	Metals & Mining
0.1	53	Pharmaceuticals
-0.2	42	Gold (XAU)
-0.9	42	Oil Integrated
-1.0	47	Insurance
-1.5	35	Airlines
-3.3	42	Oil & Gas Exploration & Production

Sector

♦ January has been the month for Information Technology, returning an average 3.9% and beating the S&P 500, 79% of the time from 1990 to 2008. ♦ Information Technology has been the best sector in November, the worst sector in December and then the best sector in January. Overall this has presented a good strategy for short-term investors willing to trade the volatility of the market ♦ The Consumer Discretionary and Financials sectors have also made the list by turning in solid performances. ♦ The Consumer Discretionary sector is right in its seasonal sweet spot ♦ Up until 2006 the Financial sector responded well to the year end reports of the major banks. Watch for banks to perform well at this time of year when the sub-prime debacle has fully worked its way through the system.

Sub-Sector

♦ The Semiconductor sector is a turbo charged version of Information Technology. It has produced a return of 7.3% since 1995 and beaten the S&P 500 57% of the time. Although the percentage outperformance of the S&P 500 is not stellar, the average gain is substantially better. ♦ The Software and Services sector has outperformed the S&P 500 by a healthy 68% of the time.

(1) Sector data provided by Standard and Poors (2) GIC is short form for Global Industry Classification (3) Sub Sector data provided by Standard and Poors, except where marked by symbol.

SMALL CAP (SMALL COMPANY) EFFECT

January Effect Starts Early - Ends Late
Small Companies Outperform - Dec 19th to Mar 7th

At different parts of the business cycle, small capitalization companies (small caps represented by the Russell 2000), perform better than the large capitalization companies (large caps represented by the Russell 1000). Evidence shows that the small caps relative outperformance also has a seasonal component as they typically outperform large caps from December 19th to March 7th.

3.7% extra & 21 times out of 29 better than the S&P 500

From 1979 to 2008, being invested in small caps during their seasonally favorable period has paid off 72% of the time and produced an extra 3.7% return.

The core part of the small cap seasonal strategy occurs in January and includes what has been described as the January Effect (Wachtel 1942, 184). This well documented anomaly of superior performance of stocks in the month of January is based upon the tenet that investors sell stocks in December for tax loss reasons, artificially driving down prices, and creating a great opportunity for astute investors. The January Effect is more pronounced for small caps as their prices are more volatile than large caps, providing a greater opportunity to take advantage of tax loss selling.

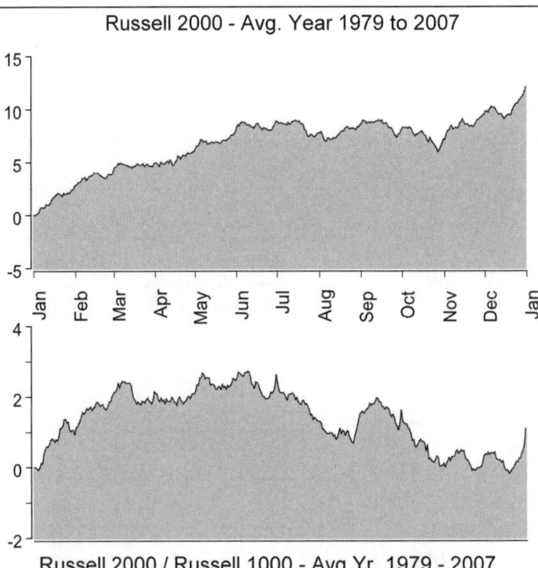

Wachtel, S.B. 1942. Certain observations on seasonal movements in stock prices. The Journal of Business and Economics (Winter): 184.

Russell 2000 vs. Russell 1000 Gains
Dec 19th to Mar 7th 1979 to 2008
Positive

Dec 19 - Mar7	Russell 2000	Russell 1000	Diff
79 / 80	-0.4	-1.3	0.9
80 / 81	4.0	-2.	6.8
81 / 82	-12.1	-12.4	0.3
82 / 83	19.8	11.8	8.0
83 / 84	-7.5	-6.4	-1.1
84 / 85	17.1	7.7	9.4
85 / 86	11.7	8.2	3.5
86 / 87	21.5	17.2	4.3
87 / 88	16.8	8.3	8.5
88 / 89	9.1	6.9	2.2
89 / 90	-1.8	-2.0	0.2
90 / 91	28.8	14.7	14.2
91 / 92	16.8	6.0	10.8
92 / 93	5.1	1.5	3.7
93 / 94	5.6	0.6	5.1
94 / 95	5.5	5.3	0.1
95 / 96	7.9	8.3	-0.4
96 / 97	3.5	9.5	-6.0
97 / 98	10.1	10.2	-0.2
98 / 99	0.1	7.3	-7.2
99 / 00	27.7	-1.7	29.4
00 / 01	4.7	-5.2	9.8
01 / 02	1.9	1.6	0.3
02 / 03	-7.8	-6.7	-1.0
03 / 04	9.6	6.4	3.3
04 / 05	0.3	2.8	-2.5
05 / 06	5.6	0.8	4.7
06 / 07	-0.8	-1.6	0.9
07 / 08	-12.5	-10.9	-1.5
Avg.	6.6 %	2.9 %	3.7 %

Over the years as more and more investors have caught on to the idea, the buy date for stocks has been pushed back to mid-December.

Small caps have outperformed during their seasonal time period fairly consistently. Their underperformance is largely clumped into the mid and late 90s when the markets were in a large cap frenzy. In the years since the large-small cap relationship has moved back to its historical norm.

Russell 2000 (small cap index): The 2000 smallest companies in the Russell 3000 stock index (a broad market index). Russell 1000 (large cap index): The 1000 largest companies in the Russell 3000 stock index

For more information on the Russell indexes, see www.Russell.com

29 MONDAY

30 day	Wednesday January 28
60 day	Friday February 27
90 day	Sunday March 29
180 day	Saturday June 27
1 year	Tuesday December 29

30 TUESDAY

30 day	Thursday January 29
60 day	Saturday February 28
90 day	Monday March 30
180 day	Sunday June 28
1 year	Wednesday December 30

31 WEDNESDAY

30 day	Friday January 30
60 day	Sunday March 1
90 day	Tuesday March 31
180 day	Monday June 29
1 year	Thursday December 31

1 THURSDAY 001 / 364

30 day	Saturday January 31
60 day	Monday March 2
90 day	Wednesday April 1
180 day	Tuesday June 30
1 year	Friday January 1

2 FRIDAY 002 / 363

30 day	Sunday February 1
60 day	Tuesday March 3
90 day	Thursday April 2
180 day	Wednesday July 1
1 year	Saturday January 2

* Weekly avg closing values- except Fed Funds Rate & CAN overnight tgt rate which are weekly closing values.

WEEK 01

Market Indices & Rates
Weekly Values*

Stock Markets	2007	2008
Dow	12,451	13,041
S&P500	1,415	1,444
Nasdaq	2,437	2,592
TSX	12,664	13,879
FTSE	6,284	6,425
DAX	6,660	7,889
Nikkei	17,223	14,691
Hang Seng	20,240	27,445

Commodities	2007	2008
Oil	57.76	98.17
Gold	630.14	853.53

Bond Yields	2007	2008
USA 5 Yr Treasury	4.65	3.29
USA 10 Yr T	4.66	3.94
USA 20 Yr T	4.84	4.43
Moody's Aaa	5.31	5.35
Moody's Baa	6.27	6.49
CAN 5 Yr T	3.93	3.77
CAN 10 Yr T	4.03	3.93

Money Market	2007	2008
USA Fed Funds	5.25	4.25
USA 3 Mo T-B	5.05	3.27
CAN tgt overnight rate	4.25	4.25
CAN 3 Mo T-B	4.15	3.78

Foreign Exchange	2007	2008
USD/EUR	1.31	1.47
USD/GBP	1.95	1.98
CAN/USD	1.17	0.99
JPY/USD	119.12	109.84

JANUARY

M	T	W	T	F	S	S
			1	2	3	4
5	6	7	8	9	10	11
12	13	14	15	16	17	18
19	20	21	22	23	24	25
26	27	28	29	30	31	

FEBRUARY

M	T	W	T	F	S	S
						1
2	3	4	5	6	7	8
9	10	11	12	13	14	15
16	17	18	19	20	21	22
23	24	25	26	27	28	

MARCH

M	T	W	T	F	S	S
						1
2	3	4	5	6	7	8
9	10	11	12	13	14	15
16	17	18	19	20	21	22
23	24	25	26	27	28	29
30	31					

PLATINUM RECORDS SOLID RESULTS
January 1st to May 31st

Most investors focus on gold in the precious metals sector, some look at silver, but few notice platinum. Platinum outperforms gold starting at the beginning of the year and lasting until the end of May.

A large portion of the platinum produced each year is consumed by catalytic converters mainly used in automotive sector to control exhaust emissions. Approximately 40% of platinum is used for jewellery, 37% for catalytic converters and the rest used for other industrial purposes.

7.4% extra and 82% of the time better than Gold

Platinum does well at the beginning of the year as it benefits from positive worldwide economic forecasts that dominate the market at the time. Strong economic forecasts translates into healthy worldwide auto production, which in turn translates into healthy platinum demand. Later in the year as economic forecasts are curtailed, platinum tends to loose its upwards momentum.

Platinum (Metal) - Avg. Year 1987 to 2007

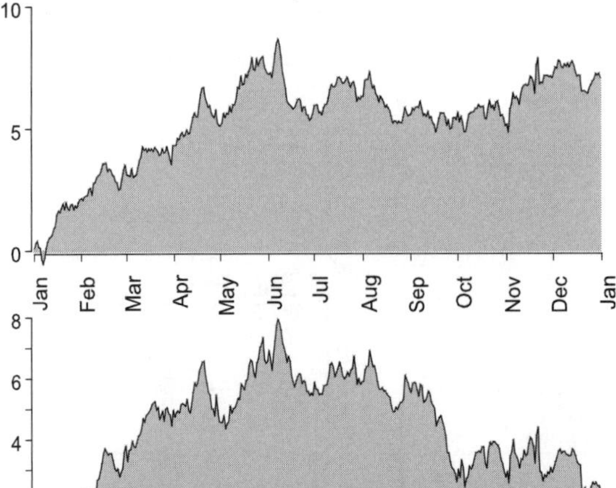

Platinum / Gold Relative Strength - Avg Yr. 1987 - 2007

In recent years, platinum has been in a strong bull market because of increasing inflation expectations, increasing jewellery usage, more stringent automotive emission requirements and supply problems in the South African mines.

Platinum vs. Gold 1987 to 2008*

Positive (shaded)

Jan 1 to May 31	Platinum	Gold	Diff
1987	22.1 %	16.0 %	6.1 %
1988	13.8	-5.9	19.7
1989	-2.6	-11.8	9.2
1990	-0.9	-8.9	8.0
1991	-4.9	-6.7	1.8
1992	4.5	-4.4	9.0
1993	9.0	12.6	-3.6
1994	2.0	-1.1	3.1
1995	3.5	0.3	3.2
1996	-0.2	0.9	-1.2
1997	10.5	-6.4	16.9
1998	0.1	1.2	-1.0
1999	0.4	-6.7	7.1
2000	23.4	-6.2	29.6
2001	-0.6	-2.5	2.0
2002	14.8	18.1	-3.4
2003	7.6	4.1	3.5
2004	2.9	-5.5	8.4
2005	0.5	-4.9	5.3
2006	32.6	27.3	5.3
2007	13.7	4.3	9.4
2008	31.2	6.2	24.9
Avg.	8.3 %	0.9 %	7.4 %

Although palladium, a cheaper metal in the Platinum Group of Metals (PGM) can be substituted for platinum in auto catalyst usage, platinum is a more effective agent with diesel emissions. Currently, approximately 50% of Europe's automobiles are diesel powered. As higher fuel prices change North American driving patterns (a small fraction of autos are powered by diesel), it is expected that the automotive industry will respond by offering a greater selection of diesel powered autos. This should help increase overall platinum demand.

From a macro perspective, there is a risk that a much cheaper alternative to platinum will be introduced to the auto catalyst market and alternative fuel vehicles will rapidly gain market share. Regardless, those investors looking to invest in platinum would be wise to concentrate their efforts in the seasonally strong time period from January to May.

* *Platinum data based upon Bloomberg closing prices & Gold data based upon London PM price.*

5 MONDAY 005 / 360

30 day	Wednesday February 4
60 day	Friday March 6
90 day	Sunday April 5
180 day	Saturday July 4
1 year	Tuesday January 5

6 TUESDAY 006 / 359

30 day	Thursday February 5
60 day	Saturday March 7
90 day	Monday April 6
180 day	Sunday July 5
1 year	Wednesday January 6

7 WEDNESDAY 007 / 358

30 day	Friday February 6
60 day	Sunday March 8
90 day	Tuesday April 7
180 day	Monday July 6
1 year	Thursday January 7

8 THURSDAY 008 / 357

30 day	Saturday February 7
60 day	Monday March 9
90 day	Wednesday April 8
180 day	Tuesday July 7
1 year	Friday January 8

9 FRIDAY 009 / 356

30 day	Sunday February 8
60 day	Tuesday March 10
90 day	Thursday April 9
180 day	Wednesday July 8
1 year	Saturday January 9

* Weekly avg closing values- except Fed Funds Rate & CAN overnight tgt rate which are weekly closing values.

WEEK 02

Market Indices & Rates Weekly Values*

Stock Markets	2007	2008
Dow	12,471	12,722
S&P500	1,419	1,407
Nasdaq	2,466	2,469
TSX	12,535	13,603
FTSE	6,204	6,278
DAX	6,636	7,776
Nikkei	17,019	14,425
Hang Seng	19,699	27,201

Commodities	2007	2008
Oil	54.11	94.76
Gold	611.85	877.00

Bond Yields	2007	2008
USA 5 Yr Treasury	4.70	3.13
USA 10 Yr T	4.70	3.85
USA 20 Yr T	4.88	4.40
Moody's Aaa	5.34	5.36
Moody's Baa	6.29	6.53
CAN 5 Yr T	3.99	3.61
CAN 10 Yr T	4.08	3.85

Money Market	2007	2008
USA Fed Funds	5.25	4.25
USA 3 Mo T-B	5.09	3.21
CAN tgt overnight rate	4.25	4.25
CAN 3 Mo T-B	4.16	3.71

Foreign Exchange	2007	2008
USD/EUR	1.30	1.47
USD/GBP	1.94	1.96
CAN/USD	1.18	1.01
JPY/USD	119.66	109.26

JANUARY

M	T	W	T	F	S	S
			1	2	3	4
5	6	7	8	9	10	11
12	13	14	15	16	17	18
19	20	21	22	23	24	25
26	27	28	29	30	31	

FEBRUARY

M	T	W	T	F	S	S
						1
2	3	4	5	6	7	8
9	10	11	12	13	14	15
16	17	18	19	20	21	22
23	24	25	26	27	28	

MARCH

M	T	W	T	F	S	S
						1
2	3	4	5	6	7	8
9	10	11	12	13	14	15
16	17	18	19	20	21	22
23	24	25	26	27	28	29
30	31					

RETAIL - POST HOLIDAY BARGAIN

Ist of **II** Retail Strategies for the Year
SHOP Jan 21st and RETURN Your Investment Apr 12th

A few weeks after the Christmas holidays retail stocks go on sale, representing a good buying opportunity in mid to late January.

The opportunity coincides with the earnings season. Historically, the retail sector has outperformed from January 21st until April 12th - the start of the next earnings season. During these two and half months the retail sector has averaged 7.6%, compared with the S&P 500 which has averaged 1.6%. Not only has the retail sector had greater gains than the broad market, but it has also outperformed it on a fairly regular basis: 79% of the time.

6.0% extra & 79% of the time better than the S&P 500

It is important for a seasonal investor to be cognizant that most investors do not like to hang around in a sector that is considered dead money (a sector that has little chance of going up).

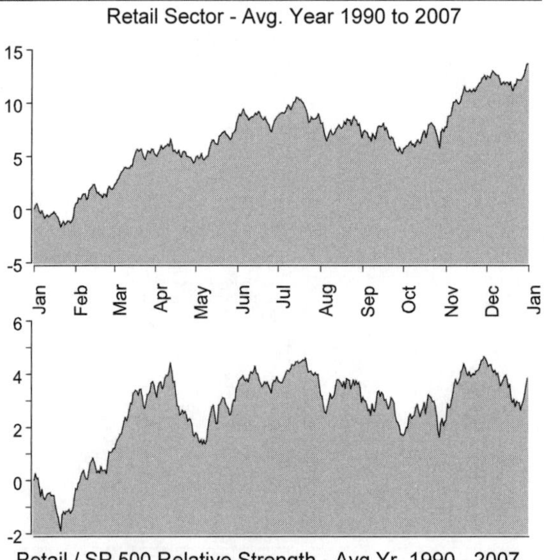

Retail / SP 500 Relative Strength - Avg Yr. 1990 - 2007

With spring and summer being a relatively slow period for retail stores, there is little to drive up retail stock prices. Investors prefer to come back to the retail sector before the busy Christmas holiday season that starts on Thanksgiving. As a result, the retail sector outperforms the broad market from the end of October to the end of November. Investors buy retail stocks anticipating strong Christmas sales and take profits as the holiday season gets underway.

S&P Retail Sector vs. S&P 500 1990 to 2008

Jan 21 to Apr 12	Retail	S&P 500	Diff (Positive shaded)
1990	9.7 %	1.5 %	8.1 %
1991	29.9	14.5	15.4
1992	-2.7	-2.9	0.1
1993	-0.6	3.5	-4.0
1994	2.0	-5.8	7.8
1995	7.4	9.1	-1.8
1996	19.7	4.1	15.7
1997	6.0	-5.0	11.0
1998	20.1	13.5	6.6
1999	23.4	8.1	15.2
2000	5.8	1.5	4.3
2001	-0.5	-11.8	11.3
2002	6.7	-1.5	8.2
2003	6.5	-3.7	10.3
2004	6.7	0.6	6.1
2005	-1.6	1.1	-2.7
2006	3.4	2.1	1.3
2007	-0.7	1.2	-1.9
2008	3.5	0.6	3.0
Avg.	7.6 %	1.6 %	6.0 %

The second part of the cycle is the *Post Holiday Bargain* period. After a pull back from the Christmas holiday seasonal, retail stocks become a good bargain. The timing coincides with the "rosy" stock market analysts' forecasts that tend to occur at the beginning of the year. These forecasts generally rely on healthy consumer spending as it makes up approximately 2/3 of the GDP. The retail sector benefits from the optimistic forecasts and tends to outperform.

Retail SP GIC Sector # 2550: An index designed to represent a cross section of retail companies

For more information on the retail sector, see www.standardandpoors.com.

12 MONDAY 012 / 353

30 day	Wednesday February 11
60 day	Friday March 13
90 day	Sunday April 12
180 day	Saturday July 11
1 year	Tuesday January 12

13 TUESDAY 013 / 352

30 day	Thursday February 12
60 day	Saturday March 14
90 day	Monday April 13
180 day	Sunday July 12
1 year	Wednesday January 13

14 WEDNESDAY 014 / 351

30 day	Friday February 13
60 day	Sunday March 15
90 day	Tuesday April 14
180 day	Monday July 13
1 year	Thursday January 14

15 THURSDAY 015 / 350

30 day	Saturday February 14
60 day	Monday March 16
90 day	Wednesday April 15
180 day	Tuesday July 14
1 year	Friday January 15

16 FRIDAY 016 / 349

30 day	Sunday February 15
60 day	Tuesday March 17
90 day	Thursday April 16
180 day	Wednesday July 15
1 year	Saturday January 16

* Weekly avg closing values- except Fed Funds Rate & CAN overnight tgt rate which are weekly closing values.

WEEK 03

Market Indices & Rates
Weekly Values*

Stock Markets	**2007**	**2008**
Dow	12,573	12,401
S&P500	1,430	1,366
Nasdaq	2,468	2,395
TSX	12,713	13,125
FTSE	6,226	5,998
DAX	6,717	7,500
Nikkei	17,271	13,780
Hang Seng	20,153	25,415
Commodities	**2007**	**2008**
Oil	51.51	91.51
Gold	628.91	895.00
Bond Yields	**2007**	**2008**
USA 5 Yr Treasury	4.76	2.97
USA 10 Yr T	4.77	3.72
USA 20 Yr T	4.96	4.32
Moody's Aaa	5.41	5.29
Moody's Baa	6.35	6.52
CAN 5 Yr T	4.04	3.48
CAN 10 Yr T	4.14	3.80
Money Market	**2007**	**2008**
USA Fed Funds	5.25	4.25
USA 3 Mo T-B	5.12	3.09
CAN tgt overnight rate	4.25	4.25
CAN 3 Mo T-B	4.15	3.57
Foreign Exchange	**2007**	**2008**
USD/EUR	1.29	1.47
USD/GBP	1.97	1.96
CAN/USD	1.17	1.02
JPY/USD	120.93	107.27

JANUARY

M	T	W	T	F	S	S
			1	2	3	4
5	6	7	8	9	10	11
12	13	14	15	16	17	18
19	20	21	22	23	24	25
26	27	28	29	30	31	

FEBRUARY

M	T	W	T	F	S	S
						1
2	3	4	5	6	7	8
9	10	11	12	13	14	15
16	17	18	19	20	21	22
23	24	25	26	27	28	

MARCH

M	T	W	T	F	S	S
						1
2	3	4	5	6	7	8
9	10	11	12	13	14	15
16	17	18	19	20	21	22
23	24	25	26	27	28	29
30	31					

MATERIAL STOCKS (Rocks, Paper, Trees, Steel & Chemicals) MATERIAL GAINS – Jan 29 to May 6

The materials sector of the market was shunned during the 90s as being too "old economy." The general belief was that there was minimal, if any, return possibility for companies that worked with "stuff" that came out of the ground.

Even though this sector underperformed the broad market on an average yearly basis during the 1990s, it still managed to outperform from January 29th to May 6th. Over the last few years the materials sector has produced very good results.

> ***4.0% extra & 13 times out of 19 better than the S&P 500***

There are some well known analysts and investors that believe we are at the start of a ten to fifteen year bull run in commodities, the major driving force in the materials sector. Notably, Jim Rogers, co-founder of the legendary Quantum hedge fund with George Soros, has written a book titled Hot Commodities, which presents a long term positive outlook for commodities. If these pundits are correct and the materials sector outperforms in a similar fashion to the tech stocks of the 90s, not only will the overall average yearly performance of the materials sector be superior to the broad market, but there is a good chance that the real sweet spot of this performance will be in the seasonally favorable time (January 29 to May 6th).

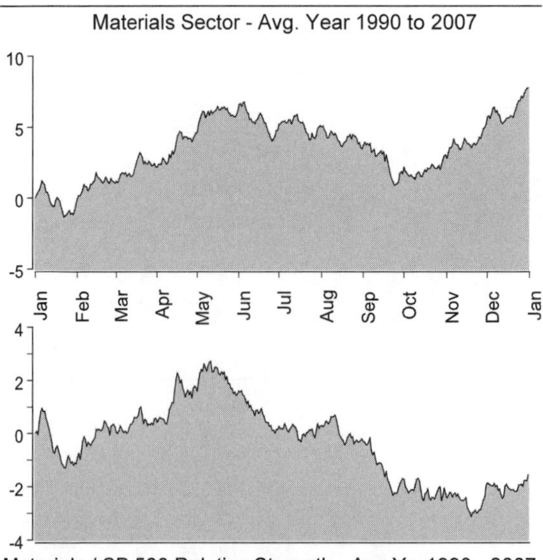

Materials / SP 500 Relative Strength - Avg Yr. 1990 - 2007

Materials Sector vs. S&P500 1990 to 2008

Jan 29 to May 6	Materials	S&P 500	Diff (shaded = Positive)
1990 %	-1.4 %	3.9 %	-5.3 %
1991	12.2	13.1	-0.9
1992	4.7	0.4	4.2
1993	2.4	1.0	1.3
1994	-6.2	-6.5	0.2
1995	10.7	10.6	0.1
1996	10.5	3.1	7.4
1997	5.0	8.2	-3.2
1998	15.5	13.0	2.4
1999	33.4	5.3	28.1
2000	-2.3	5.3	-7.6
2001	14.7	-6.5	21.2
2002	7.4	-7.1	14.5
2003	6.4	8.8	-2.5
2004	-2.1	-1.3	-0.8
2005	0.6	0.0	0.6
2006	9.4	3.3	6.1
2007	8.6	5.9	2.7
2008	11.3	4.7	6.5
Avg.	7.4 %	3.4 %	4.0 %

In recent years the materials sector has performed very well in its favorable seasonal period. In 1999 it beat the overall market by 28.1%, in 2001 by 21.2% and in 2002 by 14.5%. The 1999 outperformance was the result of the world bouncing back from the affect of the Asian Financial Flu, when several Asian currencies plummeted and economies crumbled. At the time, investors drove the price of commodities down because of the fear that Asian demand for commodities would dry up. How the world has changed! Today, every second financial article reminds us of the insatiable Asian appetite for commodities.

Regardless, if you believe there is a fifteen year commodity boom, check-out the materials sector from the end of January to the beginning of May.

> *The SP GICS Materials Sector # 15 encompasses a wide range of commodity-related manufacturing industries. Included are companies that manufacture chemicals, construction materials, glass, paper, forest products and related packaging products and metals, minerals and mining companies, including producers of steel.*
>
> *For more information on the materials sector, see www.standardandpoors.com*

19 MONDAY 019 / 346

30 day	Wednesday February 18
60 day	Friday March 20
90 day	Sunday April 19
180 day	Saturday July 18
1 year	Tuesday January 19

20 TUESDAY 020 / 345

30 day	Thursday February 19
60 day	Saturday March 21
90 day	Monday April 20
180 day	Sunday July 19
1 year	Wednesday January 20

21 WEDNESDAY 021 / 344

30 day	Friday February 20
60 day	Sunday March 22
90 day	Tuesday April 21
180 day	Monday July 20
1 year	Thursday January 21

22 THURSDAY 022 / 343

30 day	Saturday February 21
60 day	Monday March 23
90 day	Wednesday April 22
180 day	Tuesday July 21
1 year	Friday January 22

23 FRIDAY 023 / 342

30 day	Sunday February 22
60 day	Tuesday March 24
90 day	Thursday April 23
180 day	Wednesday July 22
1 year	Saturday January 23

* Weekly avg closing values- except Fed Funds Rate & CAN overnight tgt rate which are weekly closing values.

WEEK 04

Market Indices & Rates Weekly Values*

Stock Markets	2007	2008
Dow	12,524	12,207
S&P500	1,427	1,333
Nasdaq	2,440	2,324
TSX	12,907	12,647
FTSE	6,252	5,734
DAX	6,705	6,727
Nikkei	17,444	13,090
Hang Seng	20,663	23,666

Commodities	2007	2008
Oil	53.57	89.41
Gold	644.17	892.40

Bond Yields	2007	2008
USA 5 Yr Treasury	4.82	2.74
USA 10 Yr T	4.83	3.58
USA 20 Yr T	5.01	4.28
Moody's Aaa	5.47	5.30
Moody's Baa	6.39	6.54
CAN 5 Yr T	4.08	3.46
CAN 10 Yr T	4.17	3.84

Money Market	2007	2008
USA Fed Funds	5.25	3.50
USA 3 Mo T-B	5.13	2.31
CAN tgt overnight rate	4.25	4.00
CAN 3 Mo T-B	4.16	3.43

Foreign Exchange	2007	2008
USD/EUR	1.30	1.46
USD/GBP	1.97	1.97
CAN/USD	1.18	1.02
JPY/USD	121.27	106.54

JANUARY

M	T	W	T	F	S	S
			1	2	3	4
5	6	7	8	9	10	11
12	13	14	15	16	17	18
19	20	21	22	23	24	25
26	27	28	29	30	31	

FEBRUARY

M	T	W	T	F	S	S
						1
2	3	4	5	6	7	8
9	10	11	12	13	14	15
16	17	18	19	20	21	22
23	24	25	26	27	28	

MARCH

M	T	W	T	F	S	S
						1
2	3	4	5	6	7	8
9	10	11	12	13	14	15
16	17	18	19	20	21	22
23	24	25	26	27	28	29
30	31					

JANUARY PREDICTOR

Predicting the Rest of the Year

January has an uncanny trait of predicting the rest of the year. "As January goes, the rest of the year goes." In other words, if January is positive, the rest of the year tends to be positive, and if January is negative, the rest of the year tends to be negative.

74% accuracy predicting S&P 500 direction 1950 to 2007

There have been quite a few different theories as to why January is a good predictor for the rest of the year. Generally speaking, the explanation that makes the most sense is that investors and money managers are setting up their expectations for the rest of the year. If money managers are expecting a good year, they are more inclined to move more money into the market in January, boosting the performance of January and the rest of the year. If money managers are expecting a sub-performance year, they are more inclined to hold back on funds in January, producing a negative January and rest of the year.

In the past there have been different pundits that have included January's performance with the full year performance, which overstates the success of January's predictive ability. Nevertheless, January has predicted the rest of the year with an accuracy rate of 74% (43 times out of 58) for the S&P 500 from 1950 to 2007.

A positive January is a much more successful predictor than a negative January. Positive January months have had an accuracy of 89% predicting a positive rest of year (33 correct predictions out of 37). Negative January months have had much less success with an accuracy rate of 48% (10 correct predictions out of 21).

Basing a yearly investment decision on one month's returns is not considered to be a reasonable portfolio investment strategy and large returns can be missed. For example, in 2003 the barometer predicted a negative rest of year return. The market returned an astonishing 30%.

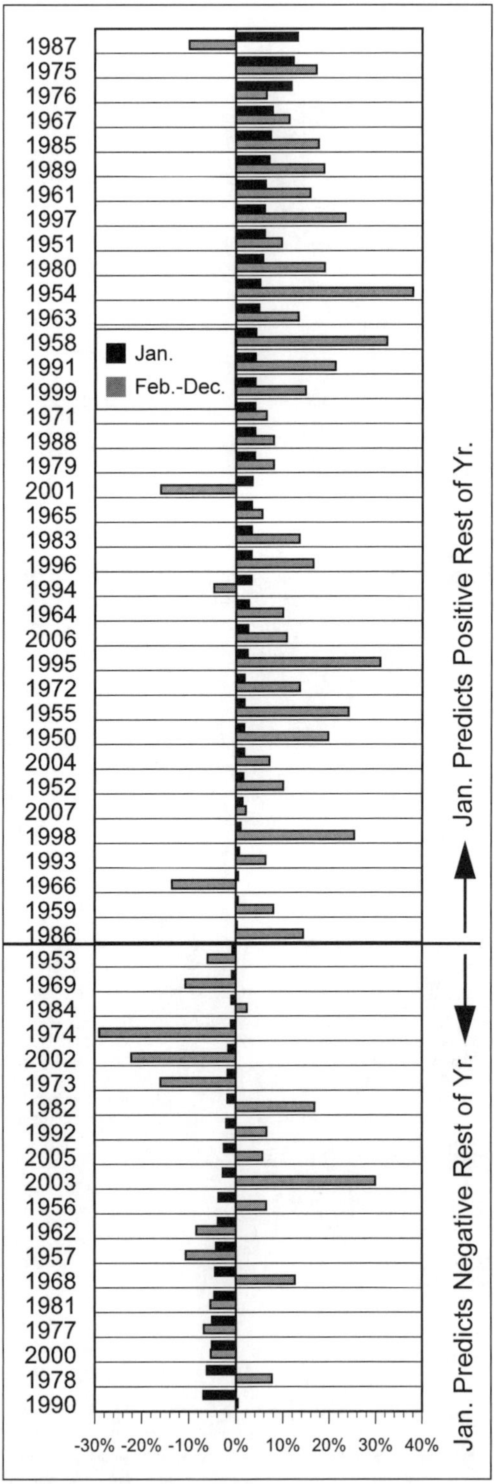

Jan.
Feb.-Dec.
1987
1975
1976
1967
1985
1989
1961
1997
1951
1980
1954
1963
1958
1991
1999
1971
1988
1979
2001
1965
1983
1996
1994
1964
2006
1995
1972
1955
1950
2004
1952
2007
1998
1993
1966
1959
1986
1953
1969
1984
1974
2002
1973
1982
1992
2005
2003
1956
1962
1957
1968
1981
1977
2000
1978
1990
-30% -20% -10% 0% 10% 20% 30% 40%
Jan. Predicts Positive Rest of Yr.
Jan. Predicts Negative Rest of Yr.

26 MONDAY 026 / 339

30 day	Wednesday February 25
60 day	Friday March 27
90 day	Sunday April 26
180 day	Saturday July 25
1 year	Tuesday January 26

27 TUESDAY 027 / 338

30 day	Thursday February 26
60 day	Saturday March 28
90 day	Monday April 27
180 day	Sunday July 26
1 year	Wednesday January 27

28 WEDNESDAY 028 / 337

30 day	Friday February 27
60 day	Sunday March 29
90 day	Tuesday April 28
180 day	Monday July 27
1 year	Thursday January 28

29 THURSDAY 029 / 336

30 day	Saturday February 28
60 day	Monday March 30
90 day	Wednesday April 29
180 day	Tuesday July 28
1 year	Friday January 29

30 FRIDAY 030 / 335

30 day	Sunday March 1
60 day	Tuesday March 31
90 day	Thursday April 30
180 day	Wednesday July 29
1 year	Saturday January 30

* Weekly avg closing values- except Fed Funds Rate & CAN overnight tgt rate which are weekly closing values.

WEEK 05

Market Indices & Rates Weekly Values*

Stock Markets	**2007**	**2008**
Dow	12,593	12,540
S&P500	1,436	1,369
Nasdaq	2,460	2,372
TSX	13,050	13,101
FTSE	6,256	5,884
DAX	6,808	6,882
Nikkei	17,482	13,400
Hang Seng	20,359	23,864

Commodities	**2007**	**2008**
Oil	57.11	91.14
Gold	649.27	920.65

Bond Yields	**2007**	**2008**
USA 5 Yr Treasury	4.85	2.85
USA 10 Yr T	4.86	3.67
USA 20 Yr T	5.04	4.35
Moody's Aaa	5.50	5.38
Moody's Baa	6.42	6.63
CAN 5 Yr T	4.11	3.49
CAN 10 Yr T	4.20	3.86

Money Market	**2007**	**2008**
USA Fed Funds	5.25	3.00
USA 3 Mo T-B	5.13	2.22
CAN tgt overnight rate	4.25	4.00
CAN 3 Mo T-B	4.17	3.39

Foreign Exchange	**2007**	**2008**
USD/EUR	1.30	1.48
USD/GBP	1.96	1.98
CAN/USD	1.18	1.00
JPY/USD	121.24	106.80

JANUARY

M	T	W	T	F	S	S
			1	2	3	4
5	6	7	8	9	10	11
12	13	14	15	16	17	18
19	20	21	22	23	24	25
26	27	28	29	30	31	

FEBRUARY

M	T	W	T	F	S	S
						1
2	3	4	5	6	7	8
9	10	11	12	13	14	15
16	17	18	19	20	21	22
23	24	25	26	27	28	

MARCH

M	T	W	T	F	S	S
						1
2	3	4	5	6	7	8
9	10	11	12	13	14	15
16	17	18	19	20	21	22
23	24	25	26	27	28	29
30	31					

FEBRUARY

	MONDAY	TUESDAY	WEDNESDAY
WEEK 06	**2** 26 USA ISM Manufacturing Report on Business (10:00 am ET)	**3** 25	**4** 24 USA ISM Non-Manufacturing Report on Business (10:00 am ET)
WEEK 07	**9** 19	**10** 18	**11** 17
WEEK 08	**16** 12 CAN Market Closed - Family Day USA Market Closed - President's Day	**17** 11 USA Empire State Manufacturing Survey - Federal Reserve Bank of New York (8:30 am ET)	**18** 10
WEEK 09	**23** 5 USA UBS Index of Investor Optimism (8:30 am ET)	**24** 4 USA Consumer Confidence Index 10:00 am ET	**25** 3
WEEK 10	2	3	4

THURSDAY	FRIDAY
5 23	**6** 22 USA The Employment Situation (8:30 am ET)
12 16	**13** 15
19 9 USA Federal Reserve Bank of Philadelphia: Business Outlook Survey (12:00 pm ET)	**20** 8
26 2 USA Help-Wanted Advertising Index (10:00 am ET)	**27** 1 USA Chicago Purchasing Managers Index (Business Barometer) 9:45 am ET
5	**6**

MARCH

M	T	W	T	F	S	S
						1
2	3	4	5	6	7	8
9	10	11	12	13	14	15
16	17	18	19	20	21	22
23	24	25	26	27	28	29
30	31					

APRIL

M	T	W	T	F	S	S
		1	2	3	4	5
6	7	8	9	10	11	12
13	14	15	16	17	18	19
20	21	22	23	24	25	26
27	28	29	30			

MAY

M	T	W	T	F	S	S
				1	2	3
4	5	6	7	8	9	10
11	12	13	14	15	16	17
18	19	20	21	22	23	24
25	26	27	28	29	30	31

JUNE

M	T	W	T	F	S	S
1	2	3	4	5	6	7
8	9	10	11	12	13	14
15	16	17	18	19	20	21
22	23	24	25	26	27	28
29	30					

FEBRUARY
SUMMARY

STRATEGIES	PAGE
STRATEGIES STARTING	
Oil– Winter/Spring Strategy I of II	21
Presidents' Day Negative Trio (Bearish)	23
STRATEGIES FINISHING	
Presidents' Day Negative Trio (Bearish)	23

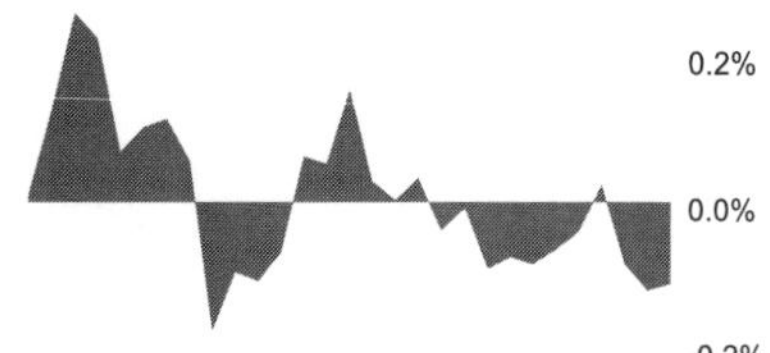

S&P500 Cumulative Daily Gains for Avg Month 1950 to 2008

♦ On average, February has been a fairly flat month. The beginning of February tends to be stronger than the rest of the month. ♦ Typically January's positive momentum spills over into February. ♦ Although on average the month has been flat, there have been some large ups and downs, particularly the Nasdaq market. ♦ From 1997 to 2002, the Nasdaq either had gains or loses of more than 5% and for several years in a row oscillated back and forth between positive and negative returns. ♦ On average, the Nasdaq has not fared well this month.

BEST / WORST FEBRUARY BROAD MKTS. 1999-2008

BEST FEBRUARY MARKETS

- Nasdaq (2000) 19.2%
- Russell 2000 (2000) 16.4%
- TSX (2000) 7.6%

WORST FEBRUARY MARKETS

- Nasdaq (2001) -22.4%
- Russell 3000 Gr (2001) -16.8%
- TSX (2001) -13.3%

Index Values End of Month

	1999	2000	2001	2002	2003	2004	2005	2006	2007	2008
Dow	9,307	10,128	10,495	10,106	7,891	10,584	10,766	10,993	12,269	12,266
S&P 500	1,238	1,366	1,240	1,107	841	1,145	1,204	1,281	1,407	1,331
Nasdaq	2,288	4,697	2,152	1,731	1,338	2,030	2,052	2,281	2,416	2,271
TSX	6,313	9,129	8,079	7,638	6,555	8,789	9,668	11,688	13,045	13,583
Russell 1000	1,238	1,410	1,258	1,122	858	1,178	1,244	1,341	1,478	1,396
Russell 2000	976	1,438	1,179	1,166	896	1,455	1,576	1,816	1,972	1,705
Russell 3000 Growth	2,427	3,259	2,208	1,858	1,367	1,880	1,889	2,059	2,195	2,165
Russell 3000 Value	1,960	1,877	2,152	2,051	1,619	2,272	2,522	2,725	3,094	2,755

Percent Gain for February

	1999	2000	2001	2002	2003	2004	2005	2006	2007	2008
Dow	-0.6	-7.4	-3.6	1.9	-2.0	0.9	2.6	1.2	-2.8	-3.0
S&P 500	-3.2	-2.0	-9.2	-2.1	-1.7	1.2	1.9	0.0	-2.2	-3.5
Nasdaq	-8.7	19.2	-22.4	-10.5	1.3	-1.8	-0.5	-1.1	-1.9	-5.0
TSX	-6.2	7.6	-13.3	-0.1	-0.2	3.1	5.0	-2.2	0.1	3.3
Russell 1000	-3.3	-0.4	-9.4	-2.1	-1.7	1.2	2.0	0.0	-1.9	-3.3
Russell 2000	-8.2	16.4	-6.7	-2.8	-3.1	0.8	1.6	-0.3	-0.9	-3.8
Russell 3000 Growth	-5.0	6.2	-16.8	-4.4	-0.7	0.5	1.0	-0.3	-1.9	-2.2
Russell 3000 Value	-2.0	-6.7	-2.8	0.0	-3.0	1.9	2.9	0.3	-1.8	-4.5

February Market Avg. Performance 1999 to 2008 (1)

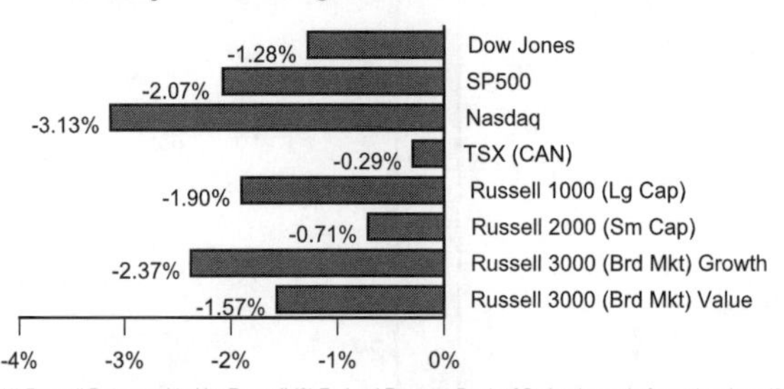

Interest Corner Feb(2)

	Fed Funds % (3)	3 Mo. T-Bill % (4)	10 Yr % (5)	20 Yr % (6)
2008	3.00	1.85	3.53	4.37
2007	5.25	5.16	4.56	4.78
2006	4.50	4.62	4.55	4.70
2005	2.50	2.76	4.36	4.79
2004	1.00	0.96	3.99	4.85

(1) Russell Data provided by Russell (2) Federal Reserve Bank of St. Louis- end of month values (3) Target rate set by FOMC (4)(5)(6) Constant yield maturities.

FEBRUARY SECTOR / SUB-SECTOR PERFORMANCE

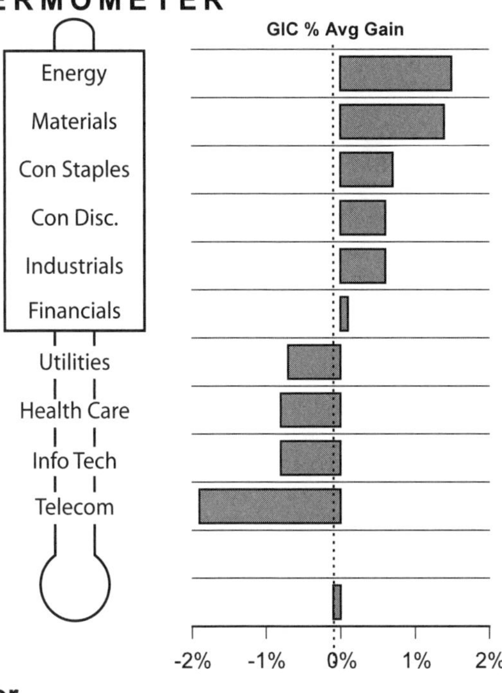

GIC[2] % Avg Gain	Fq % Gain >S&P 500	SP GIC SECTOR 1990-2008[1]
1.5 %	53 %	Energy
1.4	63	Materials
0.7	53	Consumer Staples
0.6	68	Consumer Discretionary
0.6	58	Industrials
0.1	68	Financials
-0.7	26	Utilities
-0.8	42	Health Care
-0.8	47	Information Technology
-1.9	37	Telecom
-0.1 %	N/A %	S&P 500

		SELECTED SUB-SECTORS 1990-2008[3]
3.6 %	63 %	Oil & Gas Exploration & Production
2.7	50	Semiconductor (SOX) (1995-2008)
1.5	58	Metals & Mining
1.5	68	Gold (XAU)
1.4	76	Retailing
1.2	53	Oil Integrated
1.2	53	Airlines
0.8	71	Banks
0.5	53	Transportation
0.0	41	Autos & Components
-0.1	59	Insurance
-0.7	47	Software & Services
-0.8	42	Pharmaceuticals
-1.7	59	Biotech (92-2008)

Sector

♦ Although February is a mediocre month, there are six sectors that have produced positive results from 1990 to 2008. The big winners are the Energy Sector, up 1.5%, and the Materials Sector, up 1.4%. ♦ Information Technology has produced a negative number, along with the three defensive sectors: Health Care, Utilities and Telecom ♦ Information Technology is the big surprise as it drops from a solid #1 in January to the bottom half of the ranking, producing a negative average return.

Sub-Sector

♦ The aggressive part of the energy sector, The Oil & Gas Exploration & Production, produces a strong average 3.6% gain and has beaten the S&P 500 63% of the time from 1990 to 2008. ♦ The SOX index follows closely with an average 2.7%, but it must be noted that the index has only beaten the S&P 500, 50% of the time, illustrating the volatility of the index. ♦ The frequency rate of beating the S&P 500 jumps up to 76%, with the Retailing sector which has produced an average gain of 1.4%. ♦ Of the sub-sectors listed, it is the Health Care sub-sectors that are at the bottom of the barrel.

(1) Sector data provided by Standard and Poors (2) GIC is short form for Global Industry Classification (3) Sub Sector data provided by Standard and Poors, except where marked by symbol.

CHANGE YOUR OIL SECTOR

Exploration & Production (E&P) Jan 30 to Apr 13
Equipment and Services (E&S) Apr 14 to May 17

Periodically, drivers change their oil to extend the life of their car. Investors that have changed their oil sectors at the right time have extended their profits. The energy seasonal cycle has taken place from February 25th to May 9th (see *Oil-Winter/Spring Effect* strategy). This cycle has been extended on both sides by investing in exploration and production stocks at the end of January (January 30), and then switching to equipment and services stocks in mid-April (April 13) and holding until mid-May (May 17).

15.3% extra & 17 out of 19 times better than the S&P 500

Oil E&P and E&S Sector Switch 1990 to 2008* Positive

	E&P Jan 30 to Apr 13	E&S Apr 14 to May 17	E&P & E&S Jan 30 to May 17**	S&P 500 Jan 30 to May 17	Diff
1990	12.7%	10.8 %	24.9 %	9.0%	15.9%
1991	11.2	2.0	13.5	10.9	2.6
1992	4.8	10.4	15.8	-0.1	15.8
1993	27.0	3.7	31.7	0.4	31.4
1994	-11.4	8.3	-4.1	-6.1	2.0
1995	14.3	9.7	25.3	12.0	13.2
1996	7.7	-0.7	7.0	7.2	-0.2
1997	-16.3	13.9	-4.6	7.4	-12.1
1998	9.0	7.9	17.5	12.5	5.0
1999	35.7	9.7	48.8	4.7	44.1
2000	17.9	22.2	44.0	6.4	37.6
2001	5.4	17.8	24.2	-5.5	29.8
2002	14.3	4.1	19.0	0.5	18.5
2003	1.2	15.3	16.7	9.2	7.4
2004	8.9	-5.1	3.3	-4.4	7.7
2005	14.6	-3.8	10.3	0.2	10.1
2006	-4.0	4.0	-0.2	-1.0	0.9
2007	12.4	7.3	20.6	6.5	14.1
2008	29.9	16.8	51.7	4.6	47.1
Avg.	10.3%	8.1 %	19.2 %	3.9 %	15.3%

* Buy date uses close value from day before
** Cumulative Gain - E&P Jan 30 to Apr 13 and E&S Apr 14 to May 17

Very often when a sector seasonally outperforms, such as energy, it is the more speculative sub-sector that starts the outperformance and the more conservative sub-sector that outperforms at the end of the cycle. Intuitively, this makes sense: money managers attempt to generate extra gains in the more speculative area and then rotate into the more conservative area to lock in their profits when the sector becomes "long in the tooth." Oil E&P stocks tend to be more speculative compared with the Oil E&S stocks, which are not as dependent on the price of oil for profits.

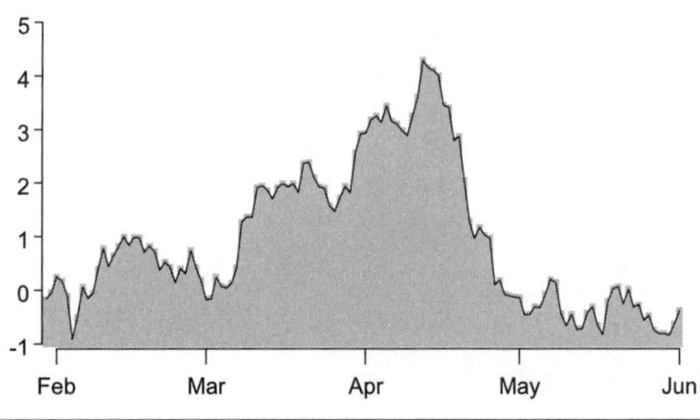

Exploration and Production- S&P GIC sector Equipment and Services 10102020 & S&P GIC Oil Integrated sector 10102010. For more information please see www.standardandpoors.com

Alternate Strategy- The cumulative gain graph for the three major sub-sectors of the energy market has been included to illustrate a possible strategy for money managers to maintain an equity position in the energy sector throughout the year. The Oil Integrated companies (major oil companies involved in all aspects of oil production and sales), provide a good alternative to the Oil E&P sector during less favorable times for oil stocks.

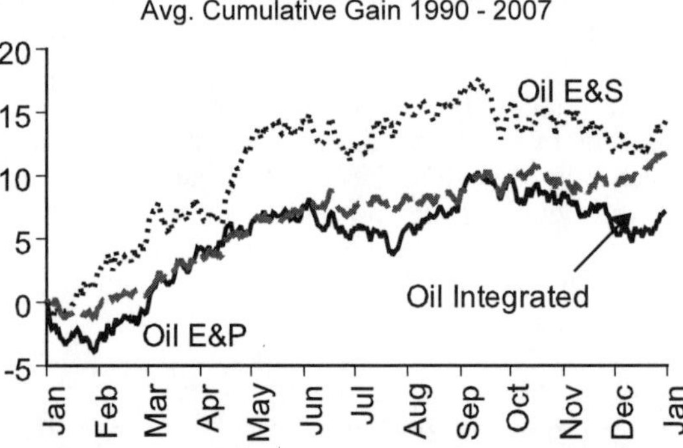

2 MONDAY 033 / 332

30 day	Wednesday March 4
60 day	Friday April 3
90 day	Sunday May 3
180 day	Saturday August 1
1 year	Tuesday February 2

3 TUESDAY 034 / 331

30 day	Thursday March 5
60 day	Saturday April 4
90 day	Monday May 4
180 day	Sunday August 2
1 year	Wednesday February 3

4 WEDNESDAY 035 / 330

30 day	Friday March 6
60 day	Sunday April 5
90 day	Tuesday May 5
180 day	Monday August 3
1 year	Thursday February 4

5 THURSDAY 036 / 329

30 day	Saturday March 7
60 day	Monday April 6
90 day	Wednesday May 6
180 day	Tuesday August 4
1 year	Friday February 5

6 FRIDAY 037 / 328

30 day	Sunday March 8
60 day	Tuesday April 7
90 day	Thursday May 7
180 day	Wednesday August 5
1 year	Saturday February 6

* Weekly avg closing values- except Fed Funds Rate & CAN overnight tgt rate which are weekly closing values.

WEEK 06

Market Indices & Rates Weekly Values*

Stock Markets	2007	2008
Dow	12,643	12,306
S&P500	1,446	1,342
Nasdaq	2,476	2,314
TSX	13,152	12,994
FTSE	6,353	5,856
DAX	6,891	6,823
Nikkei	17,368	13,386
Hang Seng	20,641	24,358
Commodities	**2007**	**2008**
Oil	58.99	89.08
Gold	655.38	900.05
Bond Yields	**2007**	**2008**
USA 5 Yr Treasury	4.76	2.72
USA 10 Yr T	4.77	3.66
USA 20 Yr T	4.96	4.39
Moody's Aaa	5.42	5.40
Moody's Baa	6.32	6.69
CAN 5 Yr T	4.05	3.39
CAN 10 Yr T	4.13	3.81
Money Market	**2007**	**2008**
USA Fed Funds	5.25	3.00
USA 3 Mo T-B	5.15	2.19
CAN tgt overnight rate	4.25	4.00
CAN 3 Mo T-B	4.17	3.31
Foreign Exchange	**2007**	**2008**
USD/EUR	1.30	1.46
USD/GBP	1.96	1.96
CAN/USD	1.18	1.00
JPY/USD	120.82	106.92

FEBRUARY

M	T	W	T	F	S	S
						1
2	3	4	5	6	7	8
9	10	11	12	13	14	15
16	17	18	19	20	21	22
23	24	25	26	27	28	

MARCH

M	T	W	T	F	S	S
						1
2	3	4	5	6	7	8
9	10	11	12	13	14	15
16	17	18	19	20	21	22
23	24	25	26	27	28	29
30	31					

APRIL

M	T	W	T	F	S	S
		1	2	3	4	5
6	7	8	9	10	11	12
13	14	15	16	17	18	19
20	21	22	23	24	25	26
27	28	29	30			

(Stocks)

OIL - WINTER/SPRING STRATEGY

Ist of **II** Oil Stock Strategies for the Year

February 25th to May 9th

The *Oil- Winter/Spring Strategy* is one of the strongest seasonal outperformance trends. From 1984 to 2008, for the two and half months starting on February 25th and ending May 9th, the energy sector (XOI) has outperformed the S&P 500 by an average 6.0%. What is even more impressive are the positive returns 23 out of 25 times, and the outperformance of the S&P 500, 23 out of 25 times.

6.0% extra and 23 out of 25 times better than the S&P 500 in just over two months

The table to the right shows the year by year results. The chart gives a picture of oil versus the broad market for the average year. When the line is increasing, energy stocks are outperforming the broad market. When it is declining, the broad market is outperforming. Notice that there is not only one period of oil stock outperformance, but two. The second period starts in July and ends in September/October. Although the second cycle is strong, the February to May cycle is stronger.

XOI / S&P 500 1984 to 2008

Feb 25 to May 9	XOI	S&P 500	Diff (positive)
1984	5.6 %	1.7 %	3.9 %
1985	4.9	1.4	3.5
1986	7.7	6.0	1.7
1987	25.5	3.7	21.8
1988	5.6	-3.0	8.6
1989	8.1	6.3	1.8
1990	-0.6	5.8	-6.3
1991	6.8	4.8	2.0
1992	5.8	0.9	4.9
1993	6.3	0.3	6.0
1994	3.2	-4.7	7.9
1995	10.3	7.3	3.1
1996	2.2	-2.1	4.3
1997	4.7	1.8	2.9
1998	9.8	7.5	2.3
1999	35.4	7.3	28.1
2000	22.2	4.3	17.9
2001	10.2	0.8	9.4
2002	5.3	-1.5	6.9
2003	5.7	12.1	-6.4
2004	4.0	-3.5	7.5
2005	-1.0	-1.8	0.8
2006	9.4	2.8	6.6
2007	10.1	4.2	5.8
2008	7.6	2.6	5.0
Avg	8.6 %	2.6 %	6.0 %

Oil Sector (XOI) - Avg. Year 1984 to 2007

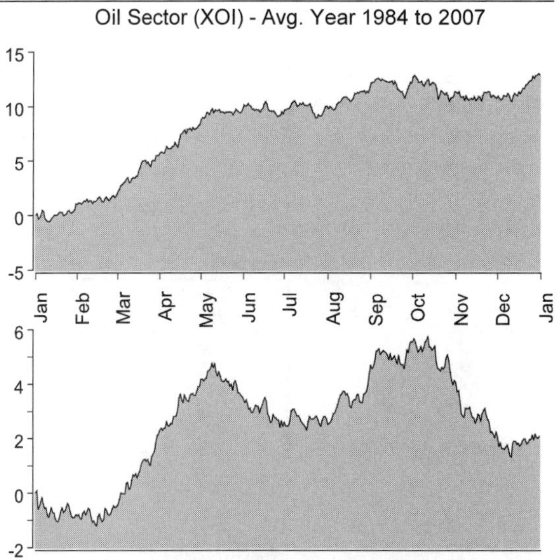

Oil Sector / SP 500 Relative Strength - Avg Yr. 1984 - 2007

A lot of investors assume that the time to buy oil stocks is just before the winter cold sets in. The rationale is that oil will climb in price as the temperature drops. The results in the market have not supported this assumption. The dynamic of the price for a barrel of oil has more to do with oil inventory. Refineries have a choice: they can produce either gasoline or heating oil. As the winter progresses, refineries start to convert their operations from heating oil to gasoline. During this switch-over time, low inventory levels of both heating oil and gasoline can drive up the price of a barrel of oil and oil stocks. In early May, before the kick-off of the driving season (Memorial Day in May), the refineries have finished their conversion to gasoline. The price of oil and oil stocks tend to decline.

> **i** *Amex Oil Index (XOI):*
> *An index designed to represent a cross section of widely held oil corporations involved in various phrases of the oil industry.*
> *For more information on the XOI index, see www.cboe.com*

9 MONDAY 040 / 325

30 day	Wednesday March 11
60 day	Friday April 10
90 day	Sunday May 10
180 day	Saturday August 8
1 year	Tuesday February 9

10 TUESDAY 041 / 324

30 day	Thursday March 12
60 day	Saturday April 11
90 day	Monday May 11
180 day	Sunday August 9
1 year	Wednesday February 10

11 WEDNESDAY 042 / 323

30 day	Friday March 13
60 day	Sunday April 12
90 day	Tuesday May 12
180 day	Monday August 10
1 year	Thursday February 11

12 THURSDAY 043 / 322

30 day	Saturday March 14
60 day	Monday April 13
90 day	Wednesday May 13
180 day	Tuesday August 11
1 year	Friday February 12

13 FRIDAY 044 / 321

30 day	Sunday March 15
60 day	Tuesday April 14
90 day	Thursday May 14
180 day	Wednesday August 12
1 year	Saturday February 13

* Weekly avg closing values- except Fed Funds Rate & CAN overnight tgt rate which are weekly closing values.

WEEK 07

Market Indices & Rates Weekly Values*

Stock Markets	2007	2008
Dow	12,696	12,378
S&P500	1,449	1,351
Nasdaq	2,478	2,334
TSX	13,203	13,187
FTSE	6,402	5,833
DAX	6,926	6,896
Nikkei	17,730	13,335
Hang Seng	20,408	23,375

Commodities	2007	2008
Oil	58.41	94.13
Gold	666.09	910.50

Bond Yields	2007	2008
USA 5 Yr Treasury	4.74	2.73
USA 10 Yr T	4.75	3.72
USA 20 Yr T	4.95	4.49
Moody's Aaa	5.41	5.54
Moody's Baa	6.30	6.83
CAN 5 Yr T	4.07	3.39
CAN 10 Yr T	4.15	3.84

Money Market	2007	2008
USA Fed Funds	5.25	3.00
USA 3 Mo T-B	5.17	2.28
CAN tgt overnight rate	4.25	4.00
CAN 3 Mo T-B	4.18	3.26

Foreign Exchange	2007	2008
USD/EUR	1.31	1.46
USD/GBP	1.95	1.96
CAN/USD	1.17	1.00
JPY/USD	120.51	107.57

FEBRUARY

M	T	W	T	F	S	S
						1
2	3	4	5	6	7	8
9	10	11	12	13	14	15
16	17	18	19	20	21	22
23	24	25	26	27	28	

MARCH

M	T	W	T	F	S	S
						1
2	3	4	5	6	7	8
9	10	11	12	13	14	15
16	17	18	19	20	21	22
23	24	25	26	27	28	29
30	31					

APRIL

M	T	W	T	F	S	S
		1	2	3	4	5
6	7	8	9	10	11	12
13	14	15	16	17	18	19
20	21	22	23	24	25	26
27	28	29	30			

PRESIDENTS' DAY NEGATIVE TRIO

Markets Not Very Patriotic 2 Days Before and 1 Day After

You may like the current president, but that does not mean that you have to invest on either side of Presidents' Day. Two days before and one day after Presidents' Day, have produced results that are less than formidable and have often been back to back negative days. These three days are aptly called the Presidents' Day Negative Trio.

Day before Presidents' Day is the worst day of the Trio- an average negative return and down 66% of the time

From 1971 to 2008, all three days of the trio have produced an average negative return. The two days before have been negative most of the time. The day after has just scraped by with an even chance at being positive or negative.

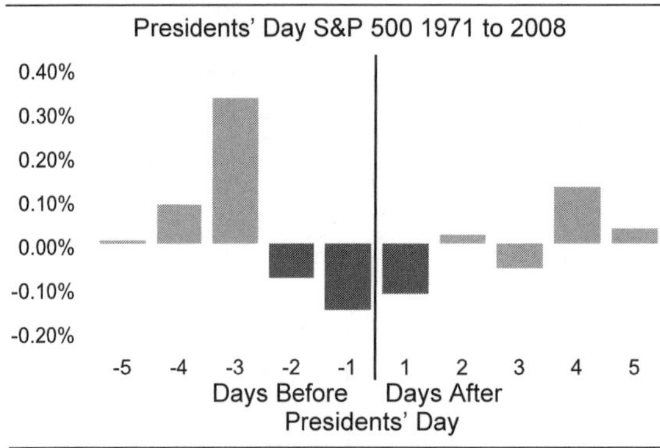

The average negative returns may have more to do with the part of the month the holiday falls on rather than the holiday itself. Presidents' Day occurs, in most cases, right after the third Friday, which tends to be the most negative day of the month. This Friday is the day that the options and futures contracts expire and is commonly referred to as Witching Day. The Friday and the day after, tend to be very volatile and produce negative returns (see *Witches' Hangover* strategy). As Presidents' Day falls in between these two days, it tends to be surrounded by poor performance.

The day after Presidents' Day tends to be a good buying opportunity. First, February tends to provide a bottom around Presidents' Day. Second, the market tends to do well in the beginning of March. Put the two together and you have a good opportunity.

(Shaded = Negative)

S&P500	2 Days Before	1 Day Before	PRESIDENTS' DAY	1 Day After
1971	0.53	0.53 %		0.23 %
1972	-0.03	-0.29		0.01
1973	-0.56	0.46		0.37
1974	-0.03	1.45		-0.16
1975	1.36	0.60		-0.70
1976	-0.52	-0.58		-0.62
1977	-0.57	-0.43		0.00
1978	-0.84	-0.14		-0.42
1979	-0.14	-0.06		0.76
1980	-1.45	-1.12		-0.70
1981	-0.59	-0.39		0.65
1982	-0.20	-0.04		-0.28
1983	0.01	0.38		-1.70
1984	-0.08	-0.25		-0.71
1985	-0.51	-0.44		-0.15
1986	0.66	1.09		1.22
1987	-0.69	1.48		2.07
1988	-0.28	0.66		0.85
1989	0.19	0.66		-0.26
1990	0.87	-0.65		-1.42
1991	-1.30	1.33		0.09
1992	-0.82	-0.29		-1.24
1993	0.32	-0.69		-2.40
1994	-0.52	-0.56		0.81
1995	0.14	-0.67		0.16
1996	-0.65	-0.51		-1.13
1997	1.13	-0.41		0.97
1998	0.40	-0.40		0.26
1999	2.49	-1.91		0.95
2000	0.04	-3.04		0.45
2001	0.81	-1.89		-1.74
2002	-0.18	-1.10		-1.89
2003	-0.16	2.14		1.95
2004	-0.49	-0.55		0.98
2005	-0.79	0.07		-1.45
2006	0.73	-0.17		-0.33
2007	0.10	-0.09		0.28
2008	-1.34	0.08		-0.09
Avg	-0.08	-0.15 %		-0.11 %
Fq > 0	39.47 %	34.21 %		50.00 %

Presidents' Day was originally set aside to honor George Washington's birthday, and later incorporated Abraham Lincoln's birthday which also fell in February. To stem the confusion about which day to celebrate, legislation was enacted in 1971, setting the date to the third Monday in February. The day is now commonly used to celebrate all past American Presidents.

16 MONDAY 047 / 318

30 day	Wednesday March 18
60 day	Friday April 17
90 day	Sunday May 17
180 day	Saturday August 15
1 year	Tuesday February 16

17 TUESDAY 048 / 317

30 day	Thursday March 19
60 day	Saturday April 18
90 day	Monday May 18
180 day	Sunday August 16
1 year	Wednesday February 17

18 WEDNESDAY 049 / 316

30 day	Friday March 20
60 day	Sunday April 19
90 day	Tuesday May 19
180 day	Monday August 17
1 year	Thursday February 18

19 THURSDAY 050 / 315

30 day	Saturday March 21
60 day	Monday April 20
90 day	Wednesday May 20
180 day	Tuesday August 18
1 year	Friday February 19

20 FRIDAY 051/ 314

30 day	Sunday March 22
60 day	Tuesday April 21
90 day	Thursday May 21
180 day	Wednesday August 19
1 year	Saturday February 20

* Weekly avg closing values- except Fed Funds Rate & CAN overnight tgt rate which are weekly closing values.

WEEK 08

Market Indices & Rates Weekly Values*

Stock Markets	2007	2008
Dow	12,726	12,357
S&P500	1,456	1,351
Nasdaq	2,518	2,309
TSX	13,321	13,524
FTSE	6,399	5,920
DAX	6,976	6,903
Nikkei	18,018	13,564
Hang Seng	20,685	23,660

Commodities	2007	2008
Oil	59.57	99.61
Gold	671.10	927.05

Bond Yields	2007	2008
USA 5 Yr Treasury	4.69	2.89
USA 10 Yr T	4.70	3.85
USA 20 Yr T	4.91	4.58
Moody's Aaa	5.37	5.62
Moody's Baa	6.24	6.93
CAN 5 Yr T	4.03	3.47
CAN 10 Yr T	4.10	3.90

Money Market	2007	2008
USA Fed Funds	5.25	3.00
USA 3 Mo T-B	5.19	2.23
CAN tgt overnight rate	4.25	4.00
CAN 3 Mo T-B	4.19	3.25

Foreign Exchange	2007	2008
USD/EUR	1.31	1.48
USD/GBP	1.96	1.95
CAN/USD	1.16	1.01
JPY/USD	120.87	107.51

FEBRUARY

M	T	W	T	F	S	S
						1
2	3	4	5	6	7	8
9	10	11	12	13	14	15
16	17	18	19	20	21	22
23	24	25	26	27	28	

MARCH

M	T	W	T	F	S	S
						1
2	3	4	5	6	7	8
9	10	11	12	13	14	15
16	17	18	19	20	21	22
23	24	25	26	27	28	29
30	31					

APRIL

M	T	W	T	F	S	S
		1	2	3	4	5
6	7	8	9	10	11	12
13	14	15	16	17	18	19
20	21	22	23	24	25	26
27	28	29	30			

PRESIDENTIAL ELECTION CYCLE

1st Year – Not a Great Year

As this year is the first year for the new President, it is important to note that the first year of the presidential election cycle tends to be the second weakest year of the four year cycle. The theory is built upon the tenet that the president makes tough decisions to bring the economy back on track in the first and second years of his term. In the third and fourth years, the president creates policies that help get him re-elected.

5.2% return and 50% of the time positive

The first year of the cycle has produced some large up and down years. Overall, it has produced an average return of 5.2% from 1901 to 2004. This is in comparison to the average of the other years of the election cycle where the S&P 500 has returned an average of 2.3% in the second year, 12.9% in the third year and 9.0% in the fourth year.

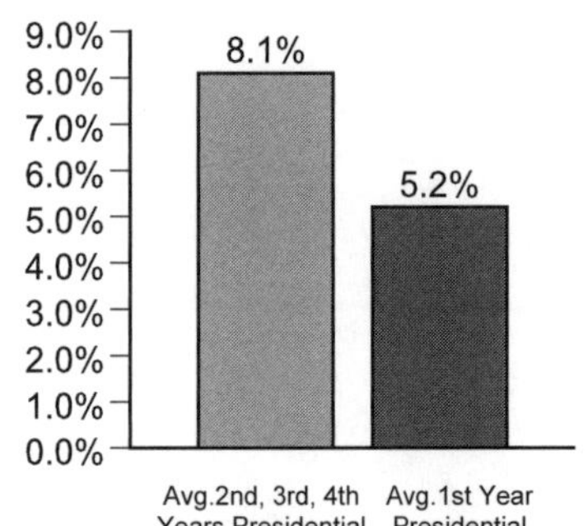

4 Year President Cycle- Dow Jones

	President	1st Year	2nd Year	3rd Year	4th Year
1901	McKinley (R)	-8.7 %	-0.4 %	-23.6 %	41.7 %
1905	T. Roosevelt (R)	38.2	-1.9	-37.7	46.6
1909	Taft (R)	15.0	-17.9	0.4	7.6
1913	Wilson (D)	-10.3	-30.7	81.7	-4.2
1917	Wilson (D)	-21.7	10.5	30.5	-32.9
1921	Harding (R)	12.7	21.7	-3.3	26.2
1925	Coolidge (R)	30.0	0.3	28.8	48.2
1929	Hoover (R)	-17.2	-33.8	-52.7	-23.1
1933	Roosevelt (R)	66.8	4.1	38.6	24.8
1937	Roosevelt (R)	-32.8	28.0	-3.0	-12.7
1941	Roosevelt (R)	-15.3	7.6	13.8	12.1
1945	Roosevelt (R)	26.7	-8.1	2.3	-2.2
1949	Truman (D)	12.9	17.6	14.4	8.4
1953	Eisenhower (R)	-3.8	44.0	20.8	2.3
1957	Eisenhower (R)	-12.8	34.0	16.4	-9.3
1961	Kennedy (D)	18.7	-10.8	17.0	14.6
1965	Johnson (D)	10.9	-18.9	15.2	4.3
1969	Nixon (R)	-15.2	4.8	6.1	14.6
1973	Nixon (R)	-16.6	-27.6	38.3	17.9
1977	Carter (D)	-17.3	-3.2	4.2	14.9
1981	Reagan (R)	-9.2	19.6	20.3	-3.7
1985	Reagan (R)	27.7	22.6	2.3	11.9
1989	G. H. Bush (R)	27.0	-4.3	20.3	4.2
1993	Clinton (D)	13.7	2.1	33.5	26.0
1997	Clinton (D)	22.6	16.1	25.2	-6.2
2001	G.W. Bush (R)	-7.1	-16.8	25.3	3.1
	Average Return	5.2	2.3	12.9	9.0
	% Positive Year	50 %	54 %	81 %	69 %

Not only has the first year had mediocre performance, it has only been positive 50% of the time.

Given the weak state of the economy, large government deficits and the sub-prime crisis, the current President will have his work cut out for him. The situation is particularly difficult because of the lack of resources that the government has at its disposal. With the last government lowering taxes and increasing spending to stimulate the economy, there is little left in the cupboard to be used.

Both the Republicans and the Democrats have provided negative first years while in power. Out of the eighteen times that the Republicans were in power, ten of their first years were negative. Out of the eight times the Democrats were in power, three were negative.

Putting it all together, the first year of the Presidential Cycle has been challenging: and this year will probably prove to be no different.

The Presidential Cycle is closely aligned with the well known and closely followed 4 Year Cycle. In this cycle the market tends to bottom approximately every four years. The bottom is typically predicted to occur towards the end of the 2nd year in the Presidential Cycle at the time of mid-term elections.

23 MONDAY 054 / 311

30 day	Wednesday March 25
60 day	Friday April 24
90 day	Sunday May 24
180 day	Saturday August 22
1 year	Tuesday February 23

24 TUESDAY 055 / 310

30 day	Thursday March 26
60 day	Saturday April 25
90 day	Monday May 25
180 day	Sunday August 23
1 year	Wednesday February 24

25 WEDNESDAY 056 / 309

30 day	Friday March 27
60 day	Sunday April 26
90 day	Tuesday May 26
180 day	Monday August 24
1 year	Thursday February 25

26 THURSDAY 057 / 308

30 day	Saturday March 28
60 day	Monday April 27
90 day	Wednesday May 27
180 day	Tuesday August 25
1 year	Friday February 26

27 FRIDAY 058 / 307

30 day	Sunday March 29
60 day	Tuesday April 28
90 day	Thursday May 28
180 day	Wednesday August 26
1 year	Saturday February 27

* Weekly avg closing values- except Fed Funds Rate & CAN overnight tgt rate which are weekly closing values.

WEEK 09

Market Indices & Rates
Weekly Values*

Stock Markets	2007	2008
Dow	12,293	12,560
S&P500	1,409	1,366
Nasdaq	2,420	2,326
TSX	13,067	13,746
FTSE	6,225	6,003
DAX	6,761	6,895
Nikkei	17,722	13,860
Hang Seng	19,819	24,078

Commodities	2007	2008
Oil	61.64	100.84
Gold	669.69	953.10

Bond Yields	2007	2008
USA 5 Yr Treasury	4.51	2.80
USA 10 Yr T	4.55	3.78
USA 20 Yr T	4.78	4.56
Moody's Aaa	5.25	5.60
Moody's Baa	6.15	6.91
CAN 5 Yr T	3.94	3.35
CAN 10 Yr T	4.02	3.78

Money Market	2007	2008
USA Fed Funds	5.25	3.00
USA 3 Mo T-B	5.15	2.01
CAN tgt overnight rate	4.25	4.00
CAN 3 Mo T-B	4.19	3.18

Foreign Exchange	2007	2008
USD/EUR	1.32	1.50
USD/GBP	1.96	1.98
CAN/USD	1.17	0.98
JPY/USD	118.42	106.36

FEBRUARY

M	T	W	T	F	S	S
						1
2	3	4	5	6	7	8
9	10	11	12	13	14	15
16	17	18	19	20	21	22
23	24	25	26	27	28	

MARCH

M	T	W	T	F	S	S
						1
2	3	4	5	6	7	8
9	10	11	12	13	14	15
16	17	18	19	20	21	22
23	24	25	26	27	28	29
30	31					

APRIL

M	T	W	T	F	S	S
		1	2	3	4	5
6	7	8	9	10	11	12
13	14	15	16	17	18	19
20	21	22	23	24	25	26
27	28	29	30			

MARCH

	MONDAY	TUESDAY	WEDNESDAY
WEEK 10	**2** 29 USA ISM Manufacturing Report on Business (10:00 am ET)	**3** 28	**4** 27 USA Federal Reserve Board's Beige Book USA ISM Non-Manufacturing Report on Business (10:00 am ET)
WEEK 11	**9** 22	**10** 21	**11** 20
WEEK 12	**16** 15 USA Empire State Manufacturing Survey - Federal Reserve Bank of New York (8:30 am ET)	**17** 14 USA FOMC Meetings	**18** 13
WEEK 13	**23** 8 USA UBS Index of Investor Optimism (8:30 am ET)	**24** 7	**25** 6
WEEK 14	**30** 1	**31** USA Chicago Purchasing Managers Index (Business Barometer) 9:45 am ET Consumer Confidence Index 10:00 am ET	1

THURSDAY	FRIDAY
5 26	**6** 25
	USA Strike Report (8:30 am ET) USA Employment Situation (8:30am ET)
12 19	**13** 18
	c
19 12	**20** 11
USA Federal Reserve Bank of Philadelphia: Business Outlook Survey (12:00 pm ET)	
26 5	**27** 4
USA Help-Wanted Advertising Index (10:00 am ET)	USA Strike Report (8:30 am ET)
2	**3**

APRIL

M	T	W	T	F	S	S
		1	2	3	4	5
6	7	8	9	10	11	12
13	14	15	16	17	18	19
20	21	22	23	24	25	26
27	28	29	30			

MAY

M	T	W	T	F	S	S
				1	2	3
4	5	6	7	8	9	10
11	12	13	14	15	16	17
18	19	20	21	22	23	24
25	26	27	28	29	30	31

JUNE

M	T	W	T	F	S	S
1	2	3	4	5	6	7
8	9	10	11	12	13	14
15	16	17	18	19	20	21
22	23	24	25	26	27	28
29	30					

JULY

M	T	W	T	F	S	S
		1	2	3	4	5
6	7	8	9	10	11	12
13	14	15	16	17	18	19
20	21	22	23	24	25	26
27	28	29	30	31		

MARCH SUMMARY

STRATEGIES	PAGE
STRATEGIES STARTING	
Beware the Tech Ides of March (Bearish)	31
Pre-Tax Date - Yield Effect	37
STRATEGIES FINISHING	
Small Cap (Small Company) Effect	5

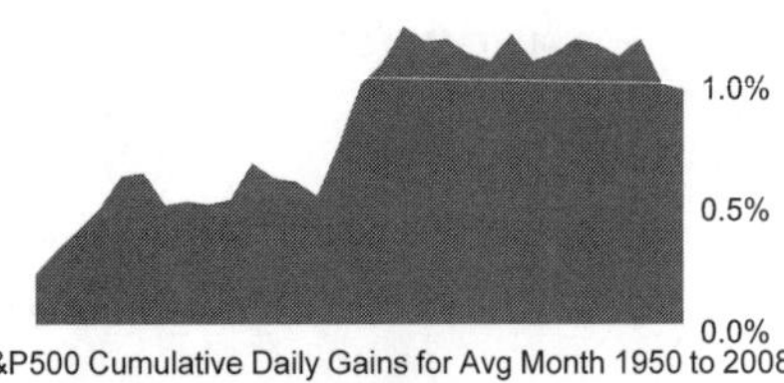

S&P500 Cumulative Daily Gains for Avg Month 1950 to 2008

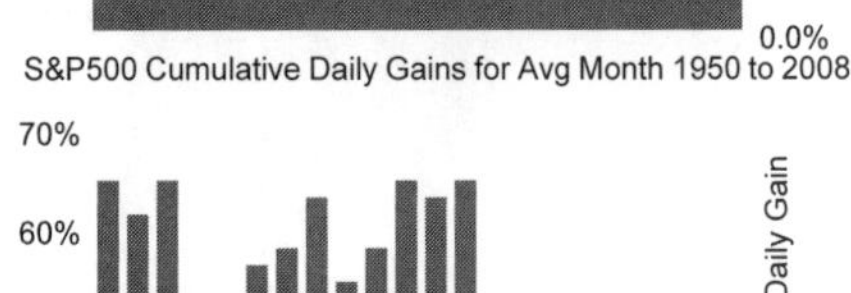

♦ The value sector has been the best performer at both the small cap and large cap level (see *8 'n' 4* and *V&G* strategies) ♦ From 1999 to 2008, the value sector Russell 3000 Value (small and large caps) has been in the top three sectors six out of ten times and has produced a return of 1.4%. ♦ The Nasdaq has a reputation for turning down shortly after the month starts (see *Beware of the Tech Ides of March* strategy) with the most infamous peak in 2000.

BEST / WORST MARCH BROAD MKTS. 1999-2008

BEST MARCH MARKETS

- Russell 3000 Val (2000) 11.1%
- S&P500 (2000) 9.7%
- Russell 1000 (2000) 9.0%

WORST MARCH MARKETS

- Nasdaq (2001) -14.5%
- Russell 3000 Gr (2001) -10.8%
- Russell 1000 (2001) -6.7%

Index Values End of Month

	1999	2000	2001	2002	2003	2004	2005	2006	2007	2008
Dow	9,786	10,922	9,879	10,404	7,992	10,358	10,504	11,109	12,354	12,263
S&P 500	1,286	1,499	1,160	1,147	848	1,126	1,181	1,295	1,421	1,323
Nasdaq	2,461	4,573	1,840	1,845	1,341	1,994	1,999	2,340	2,422	2,279
TSX	6,598	9,462	7,608	7,852	6,343	8,586	9,612	12,111	13,166	13,350
Russell 1000	1,284	1,536	1,173	1,167	866	1,160	1,222	1,359	1,492	1,385
Russell 2000	990	1,341	1,120	1,259	906	1,467	1,529	1,902	1,990	1,710
Russell 3000 Growth	2,550	3,441	1,970	1,928	1,391	1,847	1,850	2,094	2,206	2,149
Russell 3000 Value	1,994	2,086	2,076	2,150	1,620	2,252	2,481	2,765	3,137	2,733

Percent Gain for March

	1999	2000	2001	2002	2003	2004	2005	2006	2007	2008
Dow	5.2	7.8	-5.9	2.9	1.3	-2.1	-2.4	1.1	0.7	0.0
S&P 500	3.9	9.7	-6.4	3.7	0.8	-1.6	-1.9	1.1	1.0	-0.6
Nasdaq	7.6	-2.6	-14.5	6.6	0.3	-1.8	-2.6	2.6	0.2	0.3
TSX	4.5	3.7	-5.8	2.8	-3.2	-2.3	-0.6	3.6	0.9	-1.7
Russell 1000	3.7	9.0	-6.7	4.0	0.9	-1.5	-1.7	1.3	0.9	-0.8
Russell 2000	1.4	-6.7	-5.0	7.9	1.1	0.8	-3.0	4.7	0.9	0.3
Russell 3000 Growth	5.0	5.6	-10.8	3.7	1.7	-1.8	-2.1	1.7	0.5	-0.7
Russell 3000 Value	1.7	11.1	-3.5	4.8	0.0	-0.9	-1.6	1.5	1.4	-0.8

March Market Avg. Performance 1999 to 2008 (1)

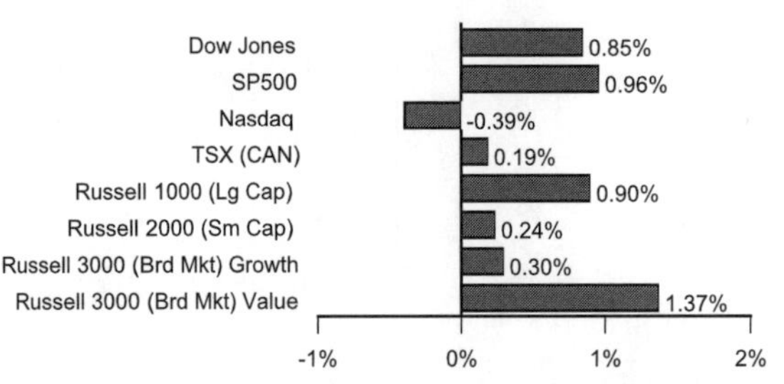

Interest Corner Mar(2)

	Fed Funds % (3)	3 Mo. T-Bill % (4)	10 Yr % (5)	20 Yr % (6)
2008	2.25	1.38	3.45	4.30
2007	5.25	5.04	4.65	4.92
2006	4.75	4.63	4.86	5.07
2005	2.75	2.79	4.50	4.88
2004	1.00	0.95	3.86	4.77

(1) Russell Data provided by Russell (2) Federal Reserve Bank of St. Louis- end of month values (3) Target rate set by FOMC (4)(5)(6) Constant yield maturities.

MARCH SECTOR / SUB-SECTOR PERFORMANCE

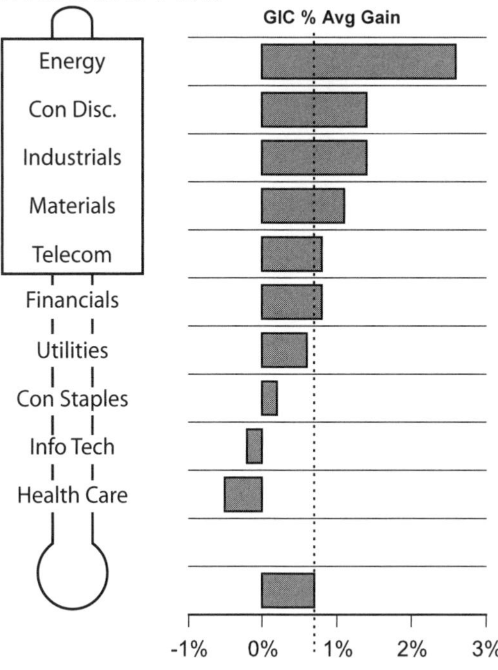

GIC[2] % Avg Gain	Fq % Gain >S&P 500	
SP GIC SECTOR 1990-2008[1]		
2.6 %	68 %	Energy
1.4	74	Consumer Discretionary
1.4	68	Industrials
1.1	47	Materials
0.8	63	Telecom
0.8	53	Financials
0.6	53	Utilities
0.2	53	Consumer Staples
-0.2	37	Information Technology
-0.5	26	Health Care
0.7 %	N/A %	S&P 500

Sector

♦ In March, it is the Energy sector that is on top again. This is the seasonal sweet spot for the sector (see *Oil-Winter/Spring Effect*). ♦ Consumer Discretionary is once again close to the top as the positive beginning of the year forecasts for consumer spending still have an uplifting affect. ♦ Industrials, which usually track the market closely are for the second month in a row a solid performing sector. ♦ Although Materials has fallen down the list, its performance is still solid. As a result it is still on the favored list. ♦ The defensive Consumer Staples sector falls from the favored list and turns in a slightly negative performance and beats the market less than half of the time.

Sub-Sector

♦ The two ends of the selected sub-sectors ranking have not changed from last month. Oil E&P is still at the top and Biotech is still at the bottom. ♦ What has changed are the sectors in between, particularly, the Semiconductor index (SOX) which has fallen significantly from beating the S&P 500 by 2.8% to underperforming by 0.3%. The beginning of March is often the peak of the technology sector.

SELECTED SUB-SECTORS 1990-2008[3]		
5.1 %	79 %	Oil & Gas Exploration & Production
3.3	71	Airlines
3.1	76	Retailing
2.4	63	Oil Integrated
1.6	71	Transportation
1.1	63	Software & Services
0.7	35	Insurance
0.4	43	Semiconductor (SOX) (95-2008)
0.3	47	Banks
0.3	53	Autos & Components
0.2	37	Metals & Mining
-0.5	21	Pharmaceuticals
-0.6	37	Gold (XAU)
-1.6	29	Biotech (92-2008)

(1) Sector data provided by Standard and Poors (2) GIC is short form for Global Industry Classification (3) Sub Sector data provided by Standard and Poors, except where marked by symbol.

BEWARE THE TECH IDES OF MARCH

Market Does Not Favor Tech Stocks – Mar 10 to Apr 15

"Beware the Ides of March"
(Shakespeare, *Julius Ceasar*, Act I, Scene II)

Julius Ceasar is not the only one that has ignored the Ides of March and paid the price. Many investors have been caught in the seasonal downdraft that tends to occur in the beginning of March for Information Technology stocks. In the investment industry, investors have known for a long time that technology stocks tend to peak in March. In March 2000, the technology sector did its thing once again and turned down. The difference this time was that the carnage was devastating.

2.4% less &10 out of 19 times underperformed the S&P 500

The technology sector tends to "go south" in March as a reaction to its typically strong performance from the beginning of October to the end of January (see *Information Technology - Use It Or Lose It* strategy). As this is the real sweet spot for the technology sector for the year, it can get ahead of itself, making it an ideal candidate for a correction in March.

Info Tech & Nasdaq vs S&P 500 - Mar 10 to Apr 15, 1990-2008

(Negative values shaded)

	Info Tech	Nasdaq	S&P 500	Diff IT to S&P	Diff Nas to S&P
1990	0.9 %	-0.1 %	1.9 %	-1.0 %	-2.0 %
1991	-8.5	5.4	1.7	-10.2	3.8
1992	-0.8	-2.6	2.7	-3.5	-5.3
1993	-5.6	-2.7	-1.3	-4.3	-1.4
1994	-13.3	-8.2	-4.5	-8.8	-3.7
1995	6.8	4.6	5.4	1.4	-0.8
1996	3.7	4.4	1.4	2.3	3.0
1997	-4.3	-7.5	-6.2	2.0	-1.3
1998	11.3	8.0	6.4	4.9	1.6
1999	4.4	5.4	3.4	1.0	2.0
2000	-20.2	-34.2	-3.2	-17.0	-31.0
2001	-2.6	-4.5	-4.0	1.4	-0.4
2002	-15.5	-9.1	-5.3	-10.2	-3.8
2003	4.9	6.6	7.5	-2.6	-0.9
2004	0.6	0.4	-1.0	1.6	1.4
2005	-8.7	-7.4	-5.3	-3.4	-2.1
2006	2.7	3.4	1.3	1.3	2.1
2007	4.0	4.4	3.6	0.4	0.8
2008	2.2	3.3	3.2	-1.0	0.1
Avg	-2.0 %	-1.6 %	0.4 %	-2.4 %	-2.0 %

The sector has produced a return that is 2.4% less than the S&P 500 from March 10th to April 15th, 1990 to 2008. It has also underperformed the S&P 500, 10 out of 19 times. Yes, a large part of the average takes into account the March 2000 devastation, but even with 2000's results removed, the numbers still do not add up to a wise investment in the sector at this time.

Tech Sector - Avg. Year 1990 to 2007

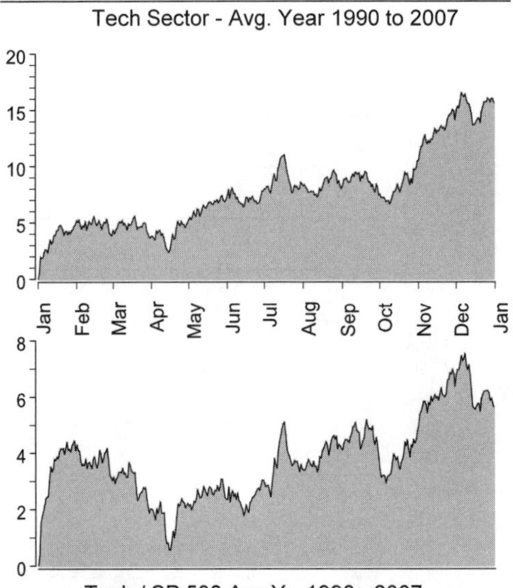

Tech / SP 500 Avg Yr. 1990 - 2007

Alternate Strategy:
The information technology market often peaks late January (January 23rd). An alternative strategy is to start switching assets at this point from the information technology market to the broad market, especially if the information technology market has outperformed during its seasonally strong time, October 9th to January 17th.

The saying "Beware the Ides of March" achieved notoriety in Shakespeare's, Julius Ceasar. In the play, Julius Ceasar ignored the warning of a soothsayer, warning him of the Ides of March and went on to meet his death. In the ancient Roman calendar, every month had an "ides" This Latin word means to divide and was used to divide the month. The Ides of March falls on the 15th.

2 MONDAY 061 / 304

30 day	Wednesday April 1
60 day	Friday May 1
90 day	Sunday May 31
180 day	Saturday August 29
1 year	Tuesday March 2

3 TUESDAY 062 / 303

30 day	Thursday April 2
60 day	Saturday May 2
90 day	Monday June 1
180 day	Sunday August 30
1 year	Wednesday March 3

4 WEDNESDAY 063 / 302

30 day	Friday April 3
60 day	Sunday May 3
90 day	Tuesday June 2
180 day	Monday August 31
1 year	Thursday March 4

5 THURSDAY 064 / 301

30 day	Saturday April 4
60 day	Monday May 4
90 day	Wednesday June 3
180 day	Tuesday September 1
1 year	Friday March 5

6 FRIDAY 065 / 300

30 day	Sunday April 5
60 day	Tuesday May 5
90 day	Thursday June 4
180 day	Wednesday September 2
1 year	Saturday March 6

* Weekly avg closing values- except Fed Funds Rate & CAN overnight tgt rate which are weekly closing values.

WEEK 10

Market Indices & Rates Weekly Values*

Stock Markets	**2007**	**2008**
Dow	12,197	12,132
S&P500	1,393	1,318
Nasdaq	2,375	2,245
TSX	12,935	13,453
FTSE	6,165	5,781
DAX	6,635	6,605
Nikkei	16,901	12,991
Hang Seng	18,990	23,133
Commodities	**2007**	**2008**
Oil	60.85	103.44
Gold	646.68	979.35
Bond Yields	**2007**	**2008**
USA 5 Yr Treasury	4.48	2.51
USA 10 Yr T	4.53	3.61
USA 20 Yr T	4.76	4.48
Moody's Aaa	5.25	5.54
Moody's Baa	6.19	6.89
CAN 5 Yr T	3.90	3.03
CAN 10 Yr T	3.99	3.60
Money Market	**2007**	**2008**
USA Fed Funds	5.25	3.00
USA 3 Mo T-B	5.11	1.55
CAN tgt overnight rate	4.25	3.50
CAN 3 Mo T-B	4.18	2.73
Foreign Exchange	**2007**	**2008**
USD/EUR	1.31	1.53
USD/GBP	1.93	2.00
CAN/USD	1.18	0.99
JPY/USD	116.88	103.20

MARCH

M	T	W	T	F	S	S
						1
2	3	4	5	6	7	8
9	10	11	12	13	14	15
16	17	18	19	20	21	22
23	24	25	26	27	28	29
30	31					

APRIL

M	T	W	T	F	S	S
		1	2	3	4	5
6	7	8	9	10	11	12
13	14	15	16	17	18	19
20	21	22	23	24	25	26
27	28	29	30			

MAY

M	T	W	T	F	S	S
				1	2	3
4	5	6	7	8	9	10
11	12	13	14	15	16	17
18	19	20	21	22	23	24
25	26	27	28	29	30	31

WITCHES' HANGOVER

Day After Witching Day – Worst Day of the Month

Double, double toil and trouble;
Fire burn and cauldron bubble.
(Shakespeare, *Macbeth*, Act IV, Scene 1)

Looking for a negative day to establish a long position, or even short the market? In our book Time In Time Out, Outsmart the Market Using Calendar Investment Strategies, Bruce Lindsay and I coined the term "Witches' Hangover" (WH) to describe the most negative day of the month. It is aptly coined because it is the trading day after Witching Day (WD).

WH avg. gain -0.1% & negative 64% of the time

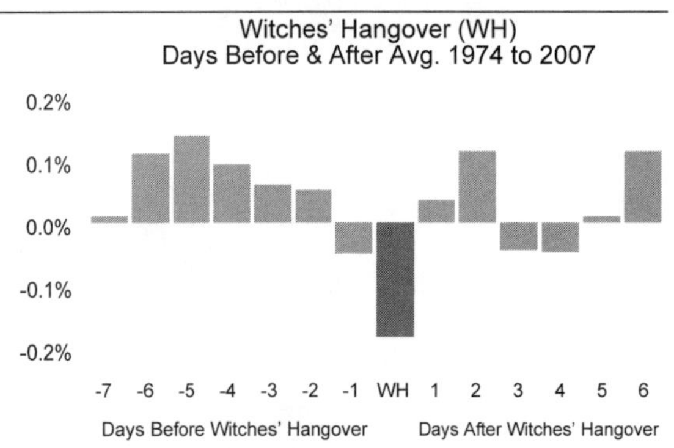

Witching Day (WD), the third Friday of the month, has a track record of volatility and negative performance. This is the day that stock options and futures expire.

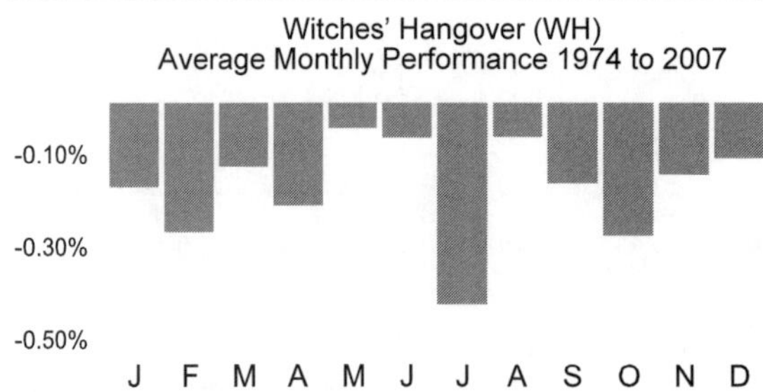

Although investors have been lead to believe that Witching Day is the worst day of the month, Witches' Hangover has produced a bigger negative performance. This may be a result of investors, after a Friday of volatility and poor performance, suffering a stock market hangover and selling into the market on the Monday. In the graph "Witches' Hangover (WH) - Days Before & After Avg" the average daily performance of Witches' Hangover is marked WH and is the darker column.

Daily Avg. Gains for WD & WH
1974 to 2007
Negative [shaded]

	WD	WH
1974	-0.54 %	-0.64 %
1975	-0.13	-0.23
1976	-0.01	0.03
1977	-0.07	-0.26
1978	-0.35	-0.04
1979	-0.16	0.03
1980	-0.14	-0.13
1981	0.16	-0.19
1982	0.32	0.24
1983	-0.09	-0.07
1984	-0.33	-0.20
1985	0.04	0.27
1986	0.23	0.07
1987	-0.02	-1.81
1988	0.62	-0.27
1989	0.22	-0.56
1990	0.02	-0.69
1991	-0.11	-0.33
1992	0.15	-0.24
1993	-0.13	-0.12
1994	-0.19	-0.34
1995	-0.02	0.08
1996	0.27	0.09
1997	-0.46	0.10
1998	0.37	0.55
1999	0.06	0.07
2000	-0.81	-0.44
2001	-0.72	0.45
2002	-0.26	-0.55
2003	0.30	-0.86
2004	-0.03	-0.12
2005	-0.05	-0.08
2006	-0.13	-0.02
2007	0.28	0.00
Avg.	-0.05 %	-0.18 %

Witching Day (WD) is the previous day. WH is clearly the worst day. Together they make a wicked pair. On average, no month has been spared the wrath of the witch…although some months have suffered more than others.

From 1974 to 2007, WH has been negative more than half of the time. Other than 2001, in the years when WH has been positive, the year has performed above average. This is particularly true for the sweet spot of the 90s bull market, from 1995 to 1999.

9 MONDAY 068 / 297

30 day	Wednesday April 8
60 day	Friday May 8
90 day	Sunday June 7
180 day	Saturday September 5
1 year	Tuesday March 9

10 TUESDAY 069 / 296

30 day	Thursday April 9
60 day	Saturday May 9
90 day	Monday June 8
180 day	Sunday September 6
1 year	Wednesday March 10

11 WEDNESDAY 070 / 295

30 day	Friday April 10
60 day	Sunday May 10
90 day	Tuesday June 9
180 day	Monday September 7
1 year	Thursday March 11

12 THURSDAY 071 / 294

30 day	Saturday April 11
60 day	Monday May 11
90 day	Wednesday June 10
180 day	Tuesday September 8
1 year	Friday March 12

13 FRIDAY 072 / 293

30 day	Sunday April 12
60 day	Tuesday May 12
90 day	Thursday June 11
180 day	Wednesday September 9
1 year	Saturday March 13

* Weekly avg closing values- except Fed Funds Rate & CAN overnight tgt rate which are weekly closing values.

WEEK 11

Market Indices & Rates
Weekly Values*

Stock Markets	2007	2008
Dow	12,160	12,021
S&P500	1,390	1,301
Nasdaq	2,375	2,229
TSX	12,877	13,269
FTSE	6,132	5,684
DAX	6,591	6,505
Nikkei	16,951	12,545
Hang Seng	19,107	22,732

Commodities	2007	2008
Oil	57.94	109.35
Gold	648.70	982.65

Bond Yields	2007	2008
USA 5 Yr Treasury	4.46	2.47
USA 10 Yr T	4.54	3.51
USA 20 Yr T	4.78	4.39
Moody's Aaa	5.27	5.53
Moody's Baa	6.23	6.91
CAN 5 Yr T	3.92	2.95
CAN 10 Yr T	4.01	3.52

Money Market	2007	2008
USA Fed Funds	5.25	3.00
USA 3 Mo T-B	5.07	1.37
CAN tgt overnight rate	4.25	3.50
CAN 3 Mo T-B	4.16	2.30

Foreign Exchange	2007	2008
USD/EUR	1.32	1.55
USD/GBP	1.93	2.02
CAN/USD	1.17	0.99
JPY/USD	116.97	101.57

MARCH

M	T	W	T	F	S	S
						1
2	3	4	5	6	7	8
9	10	11	12	13	14	15
16	17	18	19	20	21	22
23	24	25	26	27	28	29
30	31					

APRIL

M	T	W	T	F	S	S
		1	2	3	4	5
6	7	8	9	10	11	12
13	14	15	16	17	18	19
20	21	22	23	24	25	26
27	28	29	30			

MAY

M	T	W	T	F	S	S
				1	2	3
4	5	6	7	8	9	10
11	12	13	14	15	16	17
18	19	20	21	22	23	24
25	26	27	28	29	30	31

SUPER SEVEN DAYS
7 Best Days of the Month

The end of the month tends to be an excellent time to invest: portfolio managers "window dress" (adjust their portfolios to look good for month end reports), investors stop procrastinating and invest their extra cash, and brokers try to increase their commissions by investing their client's extra cash. All of these factors tend to produce above average returns for the market.

From 1950 to 2007
All 7 days better
than market average

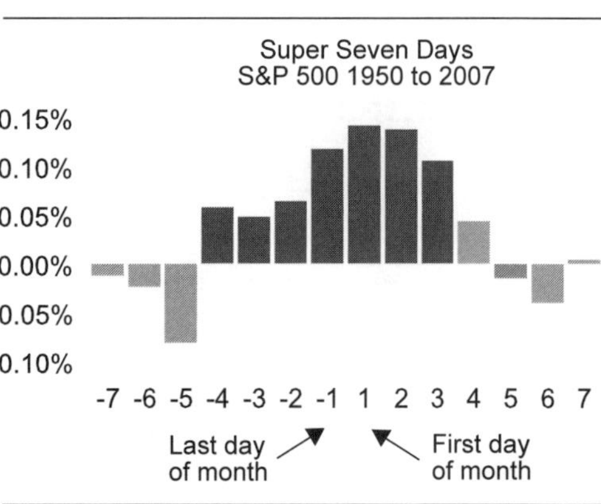

The above diagram illustrates the strength of the Super Seven days. The Super Seven days are the last four days of the month and the first three of the next month represented by the dark columns starting at day -4 to day 3. All of the Super Seven days have daily average gains above 0.03% which is the daily market average gain for the entire year.

% Gain Super Seven Day Period From 1998 to 2007

	1998	1999	2000	2001	2002	2003	2004	2005	2006	2007	Avg.
Jan	5.2 %	3.1 %	1.1 %	-0.2 %	-3.8 %	-1.1 %	-2.5 %	1.8 %	-0.1 %	1.6 %	0.5 %
Feb	0.9	-3.5	3.6	-0.9	5.2	-0.3	0.9	2.2	-0.4	-5.6	0.2
Mar	1.9	2.2	-2.4	-4.3	-2.0	0.2	3.7	0.9	0.8	0.1	0.1
Apr	0.7	-0.9	-1.0	3.2	-1.8	1.7	-1.2	1.2	0.0	1.5	0.3
May	-2.5	-0.5	4.9	-0.7	-3.1	5.7	1.9	0.2	0.5	1.6	0.8
Jun	2.2	5.5	0.1	0.1	-3.6	0.2	-2.1	0.3	1.9	1.8	0.6
Jul	-5.7	-3.1	-1.5	2.0	-0.5	-3.3	1.3	1.3	0.9	-5.6	-1.4
Aug	-10.1	-1.8	-0.9	-6.2	-7.3	3.4	0.8	1.7	0.4	0.8	-1.9
Sep	-5.2	1.9	-0.3	6.9	0.0	2.0	2.9	-1.6	1.8	1.4	1.0
Oct	4.3	4.7	4.5	0.2	2.0	2.0	4.4	2.0	-1.3	-0.8	2.2
Nov	-3.2	2.0	2.6	1.1	-2.6	2.8	1.2	-0.3	1.0	5.5	1.0
Dec	3.8	-3.8	2.1	2.4	4.1	2.7	-1.8	0.4	-0.1	-5.7	0.4
Avg.	-0.7	0.5	1.1	0.3	-1.1	1.3	0.8	0.8	0.0	0.0	0.3

Historically it has been best not to use the Super Seven for the months of July and August. Both of these months have negative average performances and have been negative more often than positive over the last ten years.

Although the Super Seven has done extremely well, there have been two trouble spots of negative performance. First, in 1998 when the Asian Financial Flu currency crisis struck the market, the market had three separate declines of more than 10%, which in turn resulted in three negative performances of the Super Seven greater than 5% at month ends. The months affected were July, August and September. Second, 2002 was a disastrous year for the market. The first major decline started on March 12 and pushed the market down more than 30%. The second major decline started on August 22 and pushed the market down more than 15%. Both of these declines had a large affect on the results of the Super Seven for the year. Despite these negative periods, the Super Seven has outperformed the broad market over the last ten years since 1950.

16 MONDAY 075 / 290

30 day	Wednesday April 15
60 day	Friday May 15
90 day	Sunday June 14
180 day	Saturday September 12
1 year	Tuesday March 16

17 TUESDAY 076 / 289

30 day	Thursday April 16
60 day	Saturday May 16
90 day	Monday June 15
180 day	Sunday September 13
1 year	Wednesday March 17

18 WEDNESDAY 077 / 288

30 day	Friday April 17
60 day	Sunday May 17
90 day	Tuesday June 16
180 day	Monday September 14
1 year	Thursday March 18

19 THURSDAY 078 / 287

30 day	Saturday April 18
60 day	Monday May 18
90 day	Wednesday June 17
180 day	Tuesday September 15
1 year	Friday March 19

20 FRIDAY 079 / 286

30 day	Sunday April 19
60 day	Tuesday May 19
90 day	Thursday June 18
180 day	Wednesday September 16
1 year	Saturday March 20

* Weekly avg closing values- except Fed Funds Rate & CAN overnight tgt rate which are weekly closing values.

WEEK 12

Market Indices & Rates Weekly Values*

Stock Markets	2007	2008
Dow	12,381	12,206
S&P500	1,424	1,309
Nasdaq	2,432	2,228
TSX	13,104	12,874
FTSE	6,265	5,539
DAX	6,768	6,314
Nikkei	17,268	12,124
Hang Seng	19,505	21,361

Commodities	2007	2008
Oil	58.26	105.28
Gold	658.40	975.56

Bond Yields	2007	2008
USA 5 Yr Treasury	4.48	2.34
USA 10 Yr T	4.58	3.39
USA 20 Yr T	4.82	4.22
Moody's Aaa	5.32	5.44
Moody's Baa	6.31	6.82
CAN 5 Yr T	3.98	2.86
CAN 10 Yr T	4.09	3.45

Money Market	2007	2008
USA Fed Funds	5.25	2.25
USA 3 Mo T-B	5.06	0.82
CAN tgt overnight rate	4.25	3.50
CAN 3 Mo T-B	4.17	1.83

Foreign Exchange	2007	2008
USD/EUR	1.33	1.56
USD/GBP	1.96	1.99
CAN/USD	1.16	1.01
JPY/USD	117.67	98.53

MARCH

M	T	W	T	F	S	S
						1
2	3	4	5	6	7	8
9	10	11	12	13	14	15
16	17	18	19	20	21	22
23	24	25	26	27	28	29
30	31					

APRIL

M	T	W	T	F	S	S
		1	2	3	4	5
6	7	8	9	10	11	12
13	14	15	16	17	18	19
20	21	22	23	24	25	26
27	28	29	30			

MAY

M	T	W	T	F	S	S
				1	2	3
4	5	6	7	8	9	10
11	12	13	14	15	16	17
18	19	20	21	22	23	24
25	26	27	28	29	30	31

POST-TAX DATE YIELD EFFECT AVOID BONDS

10 Year Treasury Yield Increases Apr 16th to May 9th

Rising bond yields means falling bond prices.

Bond yields tend to rise from *Post-Tax Day* (last day to file taxes in mid-April). This increase in yield is the reverse of the decrease in yield leading up to tax day. Yields tend to increase as the liquidity in the money market dries up. After paying taxes, there is not a lot of money floating in the system, pushing up the price of money (raising interest rates), and pushing down the price of bonds.

66% of the time the 10 year government bond yield has increased from April 16th to May 9th

The upward trend is significant not necessarily in the magnitude, but in the frequency of the trend. From 1962 to 2008, from April 16 to May 9, the 10 year yield has increased 66% of the time. The magnitude of the opportunity may not be large for the average investor, as the percentage gain shown in the table below is not a change in the yield, but a percentage change in the yield. As more and more investors are using futures for leverage to profit from interest rate movements, monitoring the direction of interest rate changes is becoming more important.

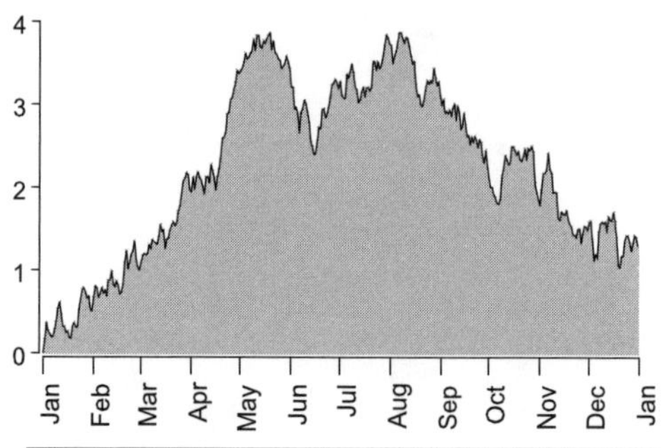

* Figures represent % of change, not actual interest rates.
Source: Federal Reserve - 10 Year Constant Maturity % Yield

CAUTION:
The figures used in this analysis are based upon the % change of the 10 year constant maturity government bond. The % change should not be used as a proxy for the actual yield of bonds.

Source: Federal Reserve Bank of St. Louis
The Federal Reserve has a vast database of free financial information that is updated on a regular basis. The yield for the 10 year government bond: http://research.stlouisfed.org/fred2/categories/47

10 Year Gov Yield % Change April 16 to May 9 (1962 to 2008)* — Positive (shaded)

Year	%	Year	%	Year	%	Year	%	Year	%
		1970	7.02 %	1980	-10.98 %	1990	2.78 %	2000	11.62 %
		1971	7.76	1981	3.57	1991	0.88	2001	0.58
1962	-0.78 %	1972	-0.80	1982	-3.09	1992	0.54	2002	0.97
1963	-2.00	1973	2.56	1983	-0.77	1993	0.68	2003	-7.29
1964	-0.71	1974	3.77	1984	5.09	1994	7.46	2004	8.37
1965	0.00	1975	-0.98	1985	-1.50	1995	-5.97	2005	0.47
1966	-0.42	1976	5.35	1986	3.60	1996	5.72	2006	1.58
1967	6.80	1977	3.45	1987	4.07	1997	-3.05	2007	-1.89
1968	3.39	1978	2.71	1988	3.32	1998	1.96	2008	4.72
1969	1.96	1979	1.74	1989	-0.33	1999	6.95		

* Source: Federal Reserve - 10 Yr. Bond Constant Maturity Yield

23 MONDAY 082 / 283

30 day	Wednesday April 22
60 day	Friday May 22
90 day	Sunday June 21
180 day	Saturday September 19
1 year	Tuesday March 23

24 TUESDAY 083 / 282

30 day	Thursday April 23
60 day	Saturday May 23
90 day	Monday June 22
180 day	Sunday September 20
1 year	Wednesday March 24

25 WEDNESDAY 084 / 281

30 day	Friday April 24
60 day	Sunday May 24
90 day	Tuesday June 23
180 day	Monday September 21
1 year	Thursday March 25

26 THURSDAY 085 / 280

30 day	Saturday April 25
60 day	Monday May 25
90 day	Wednesday June 24
180 day	Tuesday September 22
1 year	Friday March 26

27 FRIDAY 086 / 279

30 day	Sunday April 26
60 day	Tuesday May 26
90 day	Thursday June 25
180 day	Wednesday September 23
1 year	Saturday March 27

* Weekly avg closing values- except Fed Funds Rate & CAN overnight tgt rate which are weekly closing values.

WEEK 13

Market Indices & Rates
Weekly Values*

Stock Markets	**2007**	**2008**
Dow	12,374	12,405
S&P500	1,425	1,337
Nasdaq	2,430	2,307
TSX	13,228	13,344
FTSE	6,297	5,690
DAX	6,864	6,538
Nikkei	17,339	12,671
Hang Seng	19,730	22,428

Commodities	**2007**	**2008**
Oil	64.18	104.49
Gold	663.30	938.63

Bond Yields	**2007**	**2008**
USA 5 Yr Treasury	4.51	2.58
USA 10 Yr T	4.63	3.52
USA 20 Yr T	4.89	4.32
Moody's Aaa	5.40	5.51
Moody's Baa	6.38	6.93
CAN 5 Yr T	4.00	2.96
CAN 10 Yr T	4.11	3.47

Money Market	**2007**	**2008**
USA Fed Funds	5.25	2.25
USA 3 Mo T-B	5.06	1.29
CAN tgt overnight rate	4.25	3.50
CAN 3 Mo T-B	4.17	1.76

Foreign Exchange	**2007**	**2008**
USD/EUR	1.33	1.57
USD/GBP	1.97	2.00
CAN/USD	1.16	1.02
JPY/USD	117.56	99.91

MARCH

M	T	W	T	F	S	S
						1
2	3	4	5	6	7	8
9	10	11	12	13	14	15
16	17	18	19	20	21	22
23	24	25	26	27	28	29
30	31					

APRIL

M	T	W	T	F	S	S
		1	2	3	4	5
6	7	8	9	10	11	12
13	14	15	16	17	18	19
20	21	22	23	24	25	26
27	28	29	30			

MAY

M	T	W	T	F	S	S
				1	2	3
4	5	6	7	8	9	10
11	12	13	14	15	16	17
18	19	20	21	22	23	24
25	26	27	28	29	30	31

18 DAY EARNINGS MONTH EFFECT

Markets Outperform 1st 18 Calendar Days of Earnings Months

Earnings season occurs every three months, the first month of every quarter. At this time, public companies report their financials for the previous quarter and often give guidance on future expectations. The reports are generally released after the second week in the month, giving companies time to compile their data after quarter end.

Earnings are a major driver of stock market prices as investors generally like to get in the stock market early in anticipation of favorable results, which helps to run up stock prices in the first half of the month.

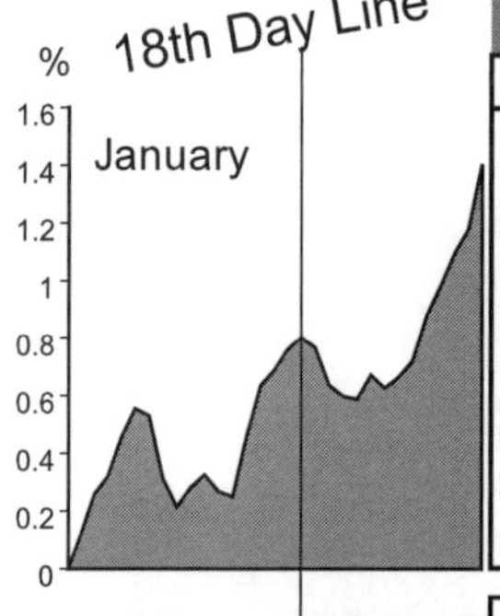

1st to 18th Day 1950-2007

Avg Gain 0.82%	Fq Pos 64%

The first month of the year generally has a good start. Investors and money managers generally push the market upward as they try to lock in their new positions for the year. The result is that the market tends to increase for the first eighteen days, pause, and then accelerate through the end of the month.

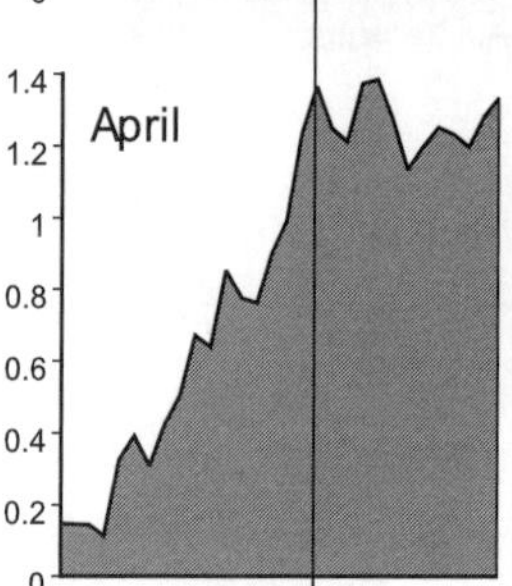

Avg Gain 1.38%	Fq Pos 71%

This month has a reputation of being a strong month. If you look at the graph you can see that almost all of the gains have come in the first half of the month. It is interesting to note that the month returns tend to peak just after the last day to file tax returns.

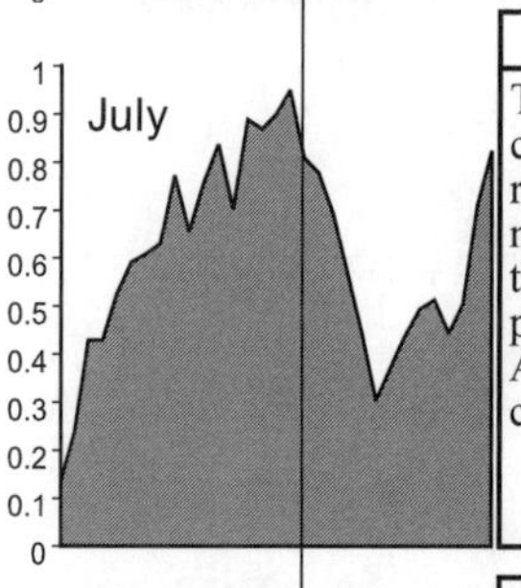

Avg Gain 0.76%	Fq Pos 64%

This is the month in which the market can peak in strong bull markets. The returns in this month, once again, are mostly derived in the first half. Although the first half of July can be positive, the time period following in August and September has a tendency towards negative returns.

Avg Gain 0.97%	Fq Pos 64%

This is the month with a bad reputation. Once again, the first part of the month tends to do well. It is the middle segment, centered around the notorious Black Monday, that brings down the results. Toward the end of the month investors realize that the world has not ended and start to buy stocks again, providing a strong finish.

1st to 18th Day Gain S&P500

	Jan	Apr	Jul	Oct
1950	0.54 %	4.28 %	-3.56 %	2.88 %
1951	4.85	3.41	4.39	1.76
1952	2.02	-3.57	-0.44	-1.39
1953	-2.07	-2.65	0.87	3.38
1954	2.50	3.71	2.91	-1.49
1955	-3.28	4.62	3.24	-4.63
1956	-2.88	-1.53	4.96	2.18
1957	-4.35	2.95	2.45	-4.93
1958	2.78	1.45	1.17	2.80
1959	1.09	4.47	1.23	0.79
1960	-3.34	2.26	-2.14	1.55
1961	2.70	1.75	-0.36	2.22
1962	-4.42	-1.84	2.65	0.12
1963	3.30	3.49	-1.27	2.26
1964	2.05	1.99	2.84	0.77
1965	2.05	2.31	1.87	1.91
1966	1.64	2.63	2.66	2.77
1967	6.80	1.84	3.16	-1.51
1968	-0.94	7.63	1.87	2.09
1969	-1.76	-0.27	-2.82	3.37
1970	-1.24	-4.42	6.83	-0.02
1971	1.37	3.17	0.42	-1.01
1972	1.92	2.40	-1.22	-2.13
1973	0.68	0.02	2.00	1.46
1974	-2.04	0.85	-2.58	13.76
1975	3.50	3.53	-2.09	5.95
1976	7.55	-2.04	0.38	-3.58
1977	-3.85	2.15	0.47	-3.18
1978	-4.77	4.73	1.40	-2.00
1979	3.76	0.11	-1.19	-5.22
1980	2.90	-1.51	6.83	4.83
1981	-0.73	-0.96	-0.34	2.59
1982	-4.35	4.33	1.33	13.54
1983	4.10	4.43	-2.20	1.05
1984	1.59	-0.80	-1.16	1.20
1985	2.44	0.10	1.32	2.72
1986	-1.35	1.46	-5.77	3.25
1987	9.96	-1.64	3.48	-12.16
1988	1.94	0.12	-1.09	2.75
1989	3.17	3.78	4.20	-2.12
1990	-4.30	0.23	1.73	-0.10
1991	0.61	3.53	3.83	1.20
1992	0.42	3.06	1.83	-1.45
1993	0.26	-0.60	-1.06	2.07
1994	1.67	-0.74	2.46	1.07
1995	2.27	0.93	2.52	0.52
1996	-1.25	-0.29	-4.04	3.42
1997	4.78	1.22	3.41	-0.33
1998	-0.92	1.90	4.67	3.88
1999	1.14	2.54	3.36	-2.23
2000	-0.96	-3.80	2.69	-6.57
2001	2.10	6.71	-1.36	2.66
2002	-1.79	-2.00	-10.94	8.48
2003	2.50	5.35	1.93	4.35
2004	2.51	0.75	-3.46	-0.05
2005	-1.32	-2.93	2.50	-4.12
2006	2.55	1.22	0.51	3.15
2007	1.41	4.33	-3.20	1.48
Avg	0.82 %	1.38 %	0.76 %	0.97 %

30 MONDAY 089 / 276

30 day	Wednesday April 29
60 day	Friday May 29
90 day	Sunday June 28
180 day	Saturday September 26
1 year	Tuesday March 30

31 TUESDAY 090 / 275

30 day	Thursday April 30
60 day	Saturday May 30
90 day	Monday June 29
180 day	Sunday September 27
1 year	Wednesday March 31

1 WEDNESDAY 091 / 274

30 day	Friday May 1
60 day	Sunday May 31
90 day	Tuesday June 30
180 day	Monday September 28
1 year	Thursday April 1

2 THURSDAY 092 / 273

30 day	Saturday May 2
60 day	Monday June 1
90 day	Wednesday July 1
180 day	Tuesday September 29
1 year	Friday April 2

3 FRIDAY 093 / 272

30 day	Sunday May 3
60 day	Tuesday June 2
90 day	Thursday July 2
180 day	Wednesday September 30
1 year	Saturday April 3

WEEK 14

Market Indices & Rates
Weekly Values*

Stock Markets	**2007**	**2008**
Dow	12,496	12,552
S&P500	1,436	1,360
Nasdaq	2,451	2,348
TSX	13,375	13,505
FTSE	6,361	5,862
DAX	7,039	6,708
Nikkei	17,359	13,011
Hang Seng	20,007	23,678

Commodities	**2007**	**2008**
Oil	64.82	103.46
Gold	667.06	902.65

Bond Yields	**2007**	**2008**
USA 5 Yr Treasury	4.58	2.64
USA 10 Yr T	4.68	3.55
USA 20 Yr T	4.94	4.37
Moody's Aaa	5.48	5.53
Moody's Baa	6.42	6.96
CAN 5 Yr T	4.03	3.05
CAN 10 Yr T	4.13	3.54

Money Market	**2007**	**2008**
USA Fed Funds	5.25	2.25
USA 3 Mo T-B	5.05	1.39
CAN tgt overnight rate	4.25	3.50
CAN 3 Mo T-B	4.16	1.98

Foreign Exchange	**2007**	**2008**
USD/EUR	1.34	1.57
USD/GBP	1.97	1.99
CAN/USD	1.15	1.02
JPY/USD	118.65	101.67

APRIL

M	T	W	T	F	S	S
		1	2	3	4	5
6	7	8	9	10	11	12
13	14	15	16	17	18	19
20	21	22	23	24	25	26
27	28	29	30			

MAY

M	T	W	T	F	S	S
				1	2	3
4	5	6	7	8	9	10
11	12	13	14	15	16	17
18	19	20	21	22	23	24
25	26	27	28	29	30	31

JUNE

M	T	W	T	F	S	S
1	2	3	4	5	6	7
8	9	10	11	12	13	14
15	16	17	18	19	20	21
22	23	24	25	26	27	28
29	30					

* Weekly avg closing values - except Fed Funds Rate & CAN overnight tgt rate which are weekly closing values.

APRIL

	MONDAY	TUESDAY	WEDNESDAY
WEEK 14	30	31	1 (29) USA ISM Manufacturing Report on Business (10:00 am ET)
WEEK 15	6 (24)	7 (23)	8 (22)
WEEK 16	13 (17)	14 (16)	15 (15) USA Empire State Manufacturing Survey - Federal Reserve Bank of New York (8:30 am ET) USA Federal Reserve Board's Beige Book
WEEK 17	20 (10)	21 (9)	22 (8)
WEEK 18	27 (3) USA UBS Index of Investor Optimism (8:30 am ET)	28 (2) USA FOMC Meetings USA Consumer Confidence Index 10:00 am ET	29 (1) USA FOMC Meetings

THURSDAY	FRIDAY
2 28	**3** 27
	USA The Employment Situation (8:30 am ET) USA ISM Non-Manufacturing Report on Business (10:00 am ET)
9 21	**10** 20
	USA Market Closed- Good Friday CAN Market Closed- Good Friday
16 14	**17** 13
USA Federal Reserve Bank of Philadelphia: Business Outlook Survey (12:00 pm ET)	
23 7	**24** 6
	USA Strike Report (8:30 am ET)
30	**1**
USA Help-Wanted Advertising Index (10:00 am ET) USA Chicago Purchasing Managers Index (Business Barometer) 9:45am ET USA Employment Cost Index	

MAY

M	T	W	T	F	S	S
				1	2	3
4	5	6	7	8	9	10
11	12	13	14	15	16	17
18	19	20	21	22	23	24
25	26	27	28	29	30	31

JUNE

M	T	W	T	F	S	S
1	2	3	4	5	6	7
8	9	10	11	12	13	14
15	16	17	18	19	20	21
22	23	24	25	26	27	28
29	30					

JULY

M	T	W	T	F	S	S
		1	2	3	4	5
6	7	8	9	10	11	12
13	14	15	16	17	18	19
20	21	22	23	24	25	26
27	28	29	30	31		

AUGUST

M	T	W	T	F	S	S
					1	2
3	4	5	6	7	8	9
10	11	12	13	14	15	16
17	18	19	20	21	22	23
24	25	26	27	28	29	30
31						

APRIL SUMMARY

1.5%
1.0%
0.5%
0.0%
S&P 500 Cumulative Daily Gains for Avg Month 1950 to 2008

STRATEGIES	PAGE
STRATEGIES STARTING	
Oil– Equipment and Services	17
Post-Tax Date Yield Effect– Avoid Bonds	37
18 Day Earnings Month Effect	39
Consumer Switch - Sell Con. Disc. - Buy Con Staples	45
1/2 and 1/2	47
STRATEGIES FINISHING	
Retail– Post Holiday Bargain	9
Beware the Tech Ides of March (Bearish)	31
Pre-Tax Date– Yield Effect	37
18 Day Earnings Month Effect	39
1/2 and 1/2	47
Consumer Switch- Sell Con. Staples. - Buy Con. Disc.	123
Financial Year End Clean Up	147

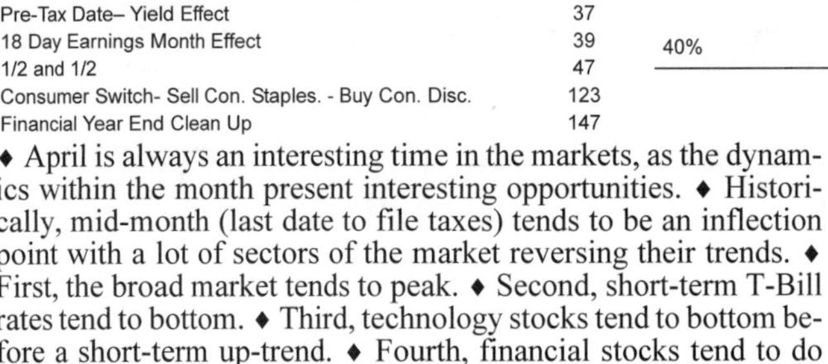

BEST / WORST APRIL BROAD MKTS. 1999-2008

BEST APRIL MARKETS

- Nasdaq (2001) 15.0%
- Russell 3000 Gr (2001) 12.6%
- Dow (1999) 10.2%

WORST APRIL MARKETS

- Nasdaq (2000) -15.6%
- Nasdaq (2002) -8.5%
- Russell 3000 Gr (2002) -7.8%

♦ April is always an interesting time in the markets, as the dynamics within the month present interesting opportunities. ♦ Historically, mid-month (last date to file taxes) tends to be an inflection point with a lot of sectors of the market reversing their trends. ♦ First, the broad market tends to peak. ♦ Second, short-term T-Bill rates tend to bottom. ♦ Third, technology stocks tend to bottom before a short-term up-trend. ♦ Fourth, financial stocks tend to do well in the first half of the month and poorly in the second half (although in 2007/08 this trend reversed itself).

Index Values End of Month

	1999	2000	2001	2002	2003	2004	2005	2006	2007	2008
Dow	10,789	10,734	10,735	9,946	8,480	10,226	10,193	11,367	13,063	12,820
S&P 500	1,335	1,452	1,249	1,077	917	1,107	1,157	1,311	1,482	1,386
Nasdaq	2,543	3,861	2,116	1,688	1,464	1,920	1,922	2,323	2,525	2,413
TSX	7,015	9,348	7,947	7,663	6,586	8,244	9,275	12,204	13,417	13,937
Russell 1000	1,336	1,484	1,266	1,100	934	1,138	1,198	1,373	1,553	1,453
Russell 2000	1,078	1,260	1,206	1,269	991	1,391	1,440	1,900	2,024	1,780
Russell 3000 Growth	2,568	3,263	2,218	1,778	1,495	1,820	1,807	2,090	2,305	2,261
Russell 3000 Value	2,176	2,061	2,174	2,084	1,759	2,188	2,426	2,825	3,241	2,858

Percent Gain for April

	1999	2000	2001	2002	2003	2004	2005	2006	2007	2008
Dow	10.2	-1.7	8.7	-4.4	6.1	-1.3	-3.0	2.3	5.7	4.5
S&P 500	3.8	-3.1	7.7	-6.1	8.1	-1.7	-2.0	1.2	4.3	4.8
Nasdaq	3.3	-15.6	15.0	-8.5	9.2	-3.7	-3.9	-0.7	4.3	5.9
TSX	6.3	-1.2	4.5	-2.4	3.8	-4.0	-3.5	0.8	1.9	4.4
Russell 1000	4.1	-3.4	7.9	-5.8	7.9	-1.9	-2.0	1.1	4.1	5.0
Russell 2000	8.9	-6.1	7.7	0.8	9.4	-5.2	-5.8	-0.1	1.7	4.1
Russell 3000 Growth	0.7	-5.2	12.6	-7.8	7.5	-1.5	-2.3	-0.2	4.5	5.2
Russell 3000 Value	9.2	-1.2	4.7	-3.0	8.6	-2.8	-2.2	2.1	3.3	4.6

April Market Avg. Performance 1999 to 2008 (1)

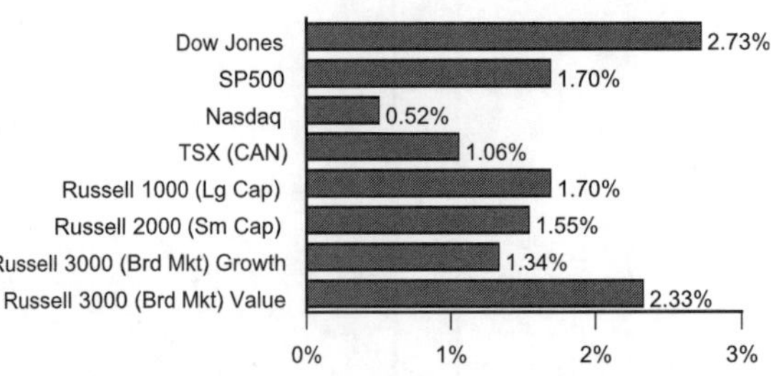

Interest Corner Apr(2)

	Fed Funds % (3)	3 Mo. T-Bill % (4)	10 Yr % (5)	20 Yr % (6)
2008	2.00	1.43	3.77	4.49
2007	5.25	4.91	4.63	4.88
2006	4.75	4.77	5.07	5.31
2005	2.75	2.90	4.21	4.61
2004	1.00	0.98	4.53	5.31

(1) Russell Data provided by Russell (2) Federal Reserve Bank of St. Louis- end of month values (3) Target rate set by FOMC (4)(5)(6) Constant yield maturities.

APRIL SECTOR / SUB-SECTOR PERFORMANCE

THACKRAY SECTOR THERMOMETER

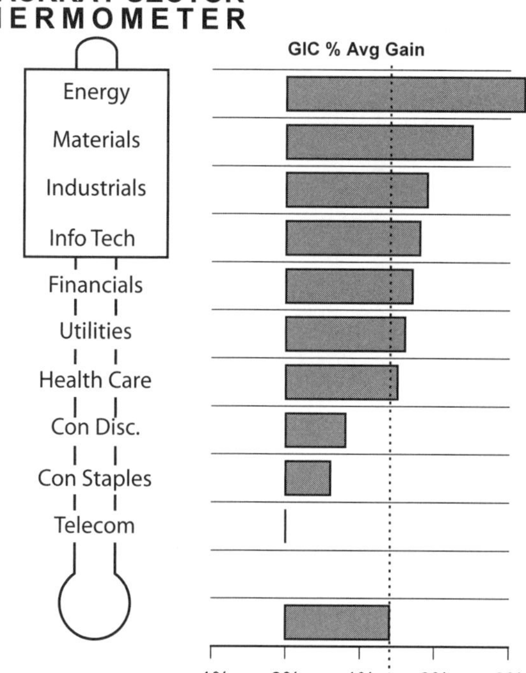

GIC[2] % Avg Gain	Fq % Gain >S&P 500	SP GIC SECTOR 1990-2008[1]
3.2 %	74 %	Energy
2.5	53	Materials
1.9	63	Industrials
1.8	47	Information Technology
1.7	58	Financials
1.6	42	Utilities
1.5	47	Health Care
0.8	47	Consumer Discretionary
0.6	42	Consumer Staples
0.0	32	Telecom
1.4 %	N/A %	S&P 500

GIC % Avg Gain	Fq % Gain >S&P 500	SELECTED SUB-SECTORS 1990-2008[3]
4.1 %	50 %	Semiconductor (SOX) (95-2008)
3.9	47	Autos & Components
3.0	74	Oil Integrated
2.1	53	Pharmaceuticals
2.1	59	Airlines
2.0	53	Transportation
1.9	59	Banks
1.8	47	Metals & Mining
1.6	53	Oil & Gas Exploration & Production
1.2	42	Software & Services
0.8	47	Insurance
-0.5	29	Retailing
-0.5	35	Biotech (92-2008)
-0.7	32	Gold (XAU)

Sector

♦ Energy is still at the top of the thermometer. The difference between the ranking for the favored sectors in April versus March is the order and Consumer Discretionary falling off to below market performance. ♦ Consumer Discretionary ends up neck-and-neck with Consumer Staples ♦ In the strong month of April, Information Technology makes a resurgence. ♦ Telecom is at the bottom of the ranking, producing an average return of 0.0% and beating the S&P 500 32% of the time.

Sub-Sector

♦ The big changes this month are: the SOX index returning to the top of the selected list, Retailing falling from substantial outperformance of the market to substantial underperformance and Pharmaceuticals climbing from the bottom of the list.

(1) Sector data provided by Standard and Poors (2) GIC is short form for Global Industry Classification (3) Sub Sector data provided by Standard and Poors, except where marked by symbol

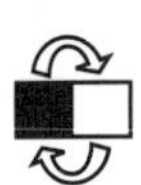

CONSUMER SWITCH SELL CONSUMER DISCRETIONARY BUY CONSUMER STAPLES

Consumer Staples Outperform Apr 23 to Oct 27

The *Consumer Switch* strategy has allowed investors to use a set portion of their account to switch between the two related consumer sectors. The end result has been outperformance compared with buying and holding both consumer sectors, or buying and holding the broad market.

1,194% total aggregate gain compared with 347% in the S&P 500

The basic premise of the strategy is that the consumer discretionary sector tends to outperform during the favorable six months when more money flows into the market, pushing up stock prices. On the other hand, the consumer staples sector tends to outperform when investors are looking for safety and stability of earnings in the six months when the market tends to move into a defensive mode.

In the relative strength chart below, the rising line represents outperformance of the discretionary sector and the decreasing line represents outperformance of the staples sector.

Consumer Staples & Discretionary Switch Strategy*

Investment Period	Buy @ Beginning of Period	% Gain @ End of Period	% Gain Cumulative
90 Apr23 - 90 Oct29	Staples	7.7%	8%
90 Oct29 - 91 Apr23	Discretionary	41.7	53
91 Apr23 - 91 Oct28	Staples	2.1	56
91 Oct28 - 92 Apr23	Discretionary	15.9	81
92 Apr23 - 92 Oct27	Staples	6.3	92
92 Oct27 - 93 Apr23	Discretionary	6.3	104
93 Apr23 - 93 Oct27	Staples	5.8	116
93 Oct27 - 94 Apr25	Discretionary	-3.7	108
94 Apr25 - 94 Oct27	Staples	10.2	129
94 Oct27 - 95 Apr24	Discretionary	4.4	139
95 Apr24 - 95 Oct27	Staples	15.3	176
95 Oct27 - 96 Apr23	Discretionary	17.3	227
96 Apr23 - 96 Oct27	Staples	12.6	265
96 Oct27 - 97 Apr23	Discretionary	5.1	283
97 Apr23 - 97 Oct27	Staples	2.5	293
97 Oct27 - 98 Apr23	Discretionary	35.9	434
98 Apr23 - 98 Oct27	Staples	-0.7	423
98 Oct27 - 99 Apr23	Discretionary	41.8	651
99 Apr23 - 99 Oct27	Staples	-9.7	578
99 Oct27 - 00 Apr24	Discretionary	11.9	659
00 Apr24 - 00 Oct27	Staples	16.5	785
00 Oct27 - 01 Apr23	Discretionary	9.8	872
01 Apr23 - 01 Oct29	Staples	4.0	910
01 Oct29 - 02 Apr23	Discretionary	16.1	1073
02 Apr23 - 02 Oct28	Staples	-13.9	910
02 Oct28 - 03 Apr23	Discretionary	3.0	941
03 Apr23 - 03 Oct27	Staples	8.4	1028
03 Oct27 - 04 Apr23	Discretionary	9.6	1137
04 Apr23 - 04 Oct27	Staples	-7.4	1045
04 Oct27 - 05 Apr25	Discretionary	-2.0	1021
05 Apr25 - 05 Oct27	Staples	-0.5	1016
05 Oct27 - 06 Apr24	Discretionary	9.2	1119
06 Apr24 06 Oct27	Staples	10.6	1249
06 Oct27 07 Apr23	Discretionary	6.3	1334
07 Apr23 07 Oct29	Staples	4.6	1400
07 Oct29 08 Apr23	Discretionary	-13.7	1194

* If buy date lands on weekend or holiday, then date used is next trading date

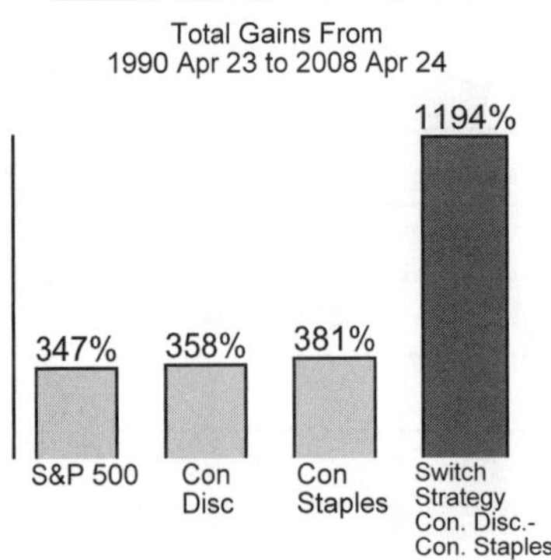

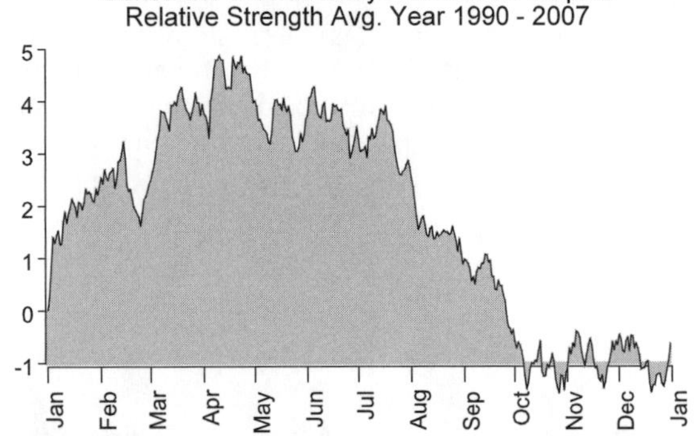

6 MONDAY 096 / 269

30 day	Wednesday May 6
60 day	Friday June 5
90 day	Sunday July 5
180 day	Saturday October 3
1 year	Tuesday April 6

7 TUESDAY 097 / 268

30 day	Thursday May 7
60 day	Saturday June 6
90 day	Monday July 6
180 day	Sunday October 4
1 year	Wednesday April 7

8 WEDNESDAY 098 / 267

30 day	Friday May 8
60 day	Sunday June 7
90 day	Tuesday July 7
180 day	Monday October 5
1 year	Thursday April 8

9 THURSDAY 099 / 266

30 day	Saturday May 9
60 day	Monday June 8
90 day	Wednesday July 8
180 day	Tuesday October 6
1 year	Friday April 9

10 FRIDAY 100 / 265

30 day	Sunday May 10
60 day	Tuesday June 9
90 day	Thursday July 9
180 day	Wednesday October 7
1 year	Saturday April 10

WEEK 15

Market Indices & Rates Weekly Values*

Stock Markets	2007	2008
Dow	12,559	12,525
S&P500	1,447	1,357
Nasdaq	2,476	2,336
TSX	13,479	13,763
FTSE	6,421	5,970
DAX	7,169	6,724
Nikkei	17,597	13,216
Hang Seng	20,380	24,346
Commodities	**2007**	**2008**
Oil	62.58	109.71
Gold	678.65	922.85
Bond Yields	**2007**	**2008**
USA 5 Yr Treasury	4.66	2.66
USA 10 Yr T	4.74	3.54
USA 20 Yr T	5.00	4.33
Moody's Aaa	5.53	5.47
Moody's Baa	6.46	6.91
CAN 5 Yr T	4.12	3.07
CAN 10 Yr T	4.19	3.58
Money Market	**2007**	**2008**
USA Fed Funds	5.25	2.25
USA 3 Mo T-B	5.03	1.33
CAN tgt overnight rate	4.25	3.50
CAN 3 Mo T-B	4.17	2.23
Foreign Exchange	**2007**	**2008**
USD/EUR	1.34	1.58
USD/GBP	1.97	1.97
CAN/USD	1.14	1.02
JPY/USD	119.19	101.96

APRIL

M	T	W	T	F	S	S
		1	2	3	4	5
6	7	8	9	10	11	12
13	14	15	16	17	18	19
20	21	22	23	24	25	26
27	28	29	30			

MAY

M	T	W	T	F	S	S
				1	2	3
4	5	6	7	8	9	10
11	12	13	14	15	16	17
18	19	20	21	22	23	24
25	26	27	28	29	30	31

JUNE

M	T	W	T	F	S	S
1	2	3	4	5	6	7
8	9	10	11	12	13	14
15	16	17	18	19	20	21
22	23	24	25	26	27	28
29	30					

* Weekly avg closing values- except Fed Funds Rate & CAN overnight tgt rate which are weekly closing values.

1/2 and 1/2
First 1/2 of April – Financial Stocks
Second 1/2 of April – Information Technology Stocks

The half and half is a short-term switch combination that takes advantage of the superior performance of the financial stocks in the first part of April and information technology stocks in the second half.

The opportunity exists at this time because technology stocks tend to increase at the same time financial stocks tend to decrease, creating an ideal switch opportunity.

2.6% extra & better than the S&P 500, 14 times out of 19

Why do financial stocks tend to start their decline relative to the broad market at mid-month? Is it a coincidence that the rate on the three month T-Bill tends to bottom out at the same time? The common denominator that affects both of these markets is liquidity. Basically, investors sell-off their money market positions to cover their taxes, decreasing short-term money market rates. See the *Pre-Tax Yield Effect* strategy for more information on decreasing short-term yields in the first half of April.

Decreasing short-term yields are good for financial stocks, particularly banks. Banks tend to make more money with a steeper yield curve. They borrow short-term money (your meagre savings account) and lend out long-term (mortgages). The steeper the curve, the more money banks make. The end result is that financial stocks benefit from this trend in the first half of April.

On the flip side, investors stop selling their money market positions to cover taxes by mid-month. At this time, yields tend to increase and financial stocks decrease.

Fortunately, information technology stocks tend to present a good opportunity at this time. By mid-April, technology stocks tend to become oversold for two reasons. First, technology stocks typically start to correct after a strong December and January (see *Information Technology- Use It or Lose It* strategy). The correction becomes exacerbated by investors selling off their holdings to pay their tax bill in mid-April. Investors typically sell off information technology stocks rather than the staid blue chip companies because technology stocks have usually outperformed the broad market over the last few months and investors want to lock in a profit. They are also more inclined to see the riskier technology stocks as short-term investments and are more willing to liquidate them to pay their debts.

Financial & Info Tech & 1/2 & 1/2 > S&P 500 (shaded)

	April 1st to April 15th		April 16th to April 30		April Compound Growth	
Year	S&P 500	Financials	S&P 500	Info Tech	S&P 500	1/2 & 1/2
1990	1.3 %	1.3 %	-3.9 %	-1.9 %	-2.7 %	-0.7 %
1991	1.6	2.3	-1.5	-3.1	0.0	-0.9
1992	3.1	1.0	-0.3	-1.3	2.8	-0.3
1993	-0.7	3.5	-1.8	-2.2	-2.5	1.3
1994	0.1	4.9	1.1	3.5	1.2	8.6
1995	1.7	2.9	1.1	5.8	2.8	8.8
1996	-0.5	-2.3	1.8	8.2	1.3	5.8
1997	-0.3	0.3	6.2	11.3	5.8	11.6
1998	1.6	5.5	-0.7	4.3	0.9	10.0
1999	2.8	5.0	0.9	1.3	3.8	6.4
2000	-9.5	-7.0	7.1	14.8	-3.1	6.8
2001	2.0	0.2	5.6	8.3	7.7	8.5
2002	-3.9	-1.6	-2.3	-3.5	-6.1	-5.1
2003	5.0	9.3	2.9	5.3	8.1	15.1
2004	0.2	-3.0	-1.9	-5.0	-1.7	-7.8
2005	-3.2	-2.6	1.2	2.3	-2.0	-0.4
2006	-0.4	-0.3	1.7	-1.3	1.2	-1.6
2007	2.3	0.5	2.0	2.7	4.3	3.2
2008	0.9	-0.6	3.8	6.8	4.8	6.2
Avg.	0.2 %	1.0 %	1.2 %	3.0 %	1.4 %	4.0 %

Alternate Strategy—
The first few days in May tend to produce gains. An alternate strategy is to hold the information technology position for the first three trading days in May.

The SP GICS Financial Sector # 40 encompasses a wide range financial based companies.
The SP GICS Information Technology Sector # 45 encompasses a wide range technology based companies.
For more information on the information technology sector, see www.standardandpoors.com

13 MONDAY 103 / 262

30 day	Wednesday May 13
60 day	Friday June 12
90 day	Sunday July 12
180 day	Saturday October 10
1 year	Tuesday April 13

14 TUESDAY 104 / 261

30 day	Thursday May 14
60 day	Saturday June 13
90 day	Monday July 13
180 day	Sunday October 11
1 year	Wednesday April 14

15 WEDNESDAY 105 / 260

30 day	Friday May 15
60 day	Sunday June 14
90 day	Tuesday July 14
180 day	Monday October 12
1 year	Thursday April 15

16 THURSDAY 106 / 259

30 day	Saturday May 16
60 day	Monday June 15
90 day	Wednesday July 15
180 day	Tuesday October 13
1 year	Friday April 16

17 FRIDAY 107 / 258

30 day	Sunday May 17
60 day	Tuesday June 16
90 day	Thursday July 16
180 day	Wednesday October 14
1 year	Saturday April 17

WEEK 16

Market Indices & Rates Weekly Values*

Stock Markets	2007	2008
Dow	12,814	12,551
S&P500	1,473	1,357
Nasdaq	2,516	2,331
TSX	13,654	14,008
FTSE	6,478	5,964
DAX	7,311	6,673
Nikkei	17,530	13,186
Hang Seng	20,638	24,010

Commodities	2007	2008
Oil	63.06	114.33
Gold	687.31	931.20

Bond Yields	2007	2008
USA 5 Yr Treasury	4.60	2.79
USA 10 Yr T	4.69	3.67
USA 20 Yr T	4.93	4.44
Moody's Aaa	5.44	5.60
Moody's Baa	6.37	7.03
CAN 5 Yr T	4.13	3.10
CAN 10 Yr T	4.19	3.64

Money Market	2007	2008
USA Fed Funds	5.25	2.25
USA 3 Mo T-B	5.00	1.18
CAN tgt overnight rate	4.25	3.50
CAN 3 Mo T-B	4.16	2.50

Foreign Exchange	2007	2008
USD/EUR	1.36	1.59
USD/GBP	2.00	1.98
CAN/USD	1.13	1.01
JPY/USD	118.85	102.08

APRIL

M	T	W	T	F	S	S
		1	2	3	4	5
6	7	8	9	10	11	12
13	14	15	16	17	18	19
20	21	22	23	24	25	26
27	28	29	30			

MAY

M	T	W	T	F	S	S
				1	2	3
4	5	6	7	8	9	10
11	12	13	14	15	16	17
18	19	20	21	22	23	24
25	26	27	28	29	30	31

JUNE

M	T	W	T	F	S	S
1	2	3	4	5	6	7
8	9	10	11	12	13	14
15	16	17	18	19	20	21
22	23	24	25	26	27	28
29	30					

* Weekly avg closing values- except Fed Funds Rate & CAN overnight tgt rate which are weekly closing values.

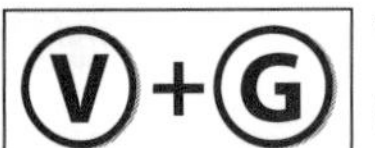

VALUE FOR FIRST 4 MONTHS OF THE YR. GROWTH FOR LAST 3 MONTHS

There are many ways to invest in the markets. Investing in value or growth stocks is an investment style that is becoming more popular with retail investors.

> Value stocks generally have low prices relative to their book values and/or low price to earnings ratios.
>
> Growth stocks generally have high prices relative to their book values and/or high price to earnings ratios.

There have been many studies over time about which style of investing, value or growth, produces better returns with less risk, and in which type of economic environment. The scope of this book is concerned with the annual cycle of outperformance. On an annual basis, growth tends to outperform value during the last three months of the year. Value stocks tend to outperform for the first four months. In the middle of the year, June is an anomaly as growth stocks tend to outperform value.

Compared with value stocks, growth stocks tend to be better known companies with greater earnings stability. As a result, investors are willing to pay a higher premium for growth stocks. In the beginning of the year, almost every analyst on Wall Street calls for a market return between 8% and 12%. In this positive environment value stocks tend to outperform. In the summer months there is not a clear trend between growth and value styles, except for the month of June when growth stocks outperform. In the last three months of the year growth stocks take over. Although the market tends to do well at this time, it is not without its fair share of volatility and questions on how the market will end the year.

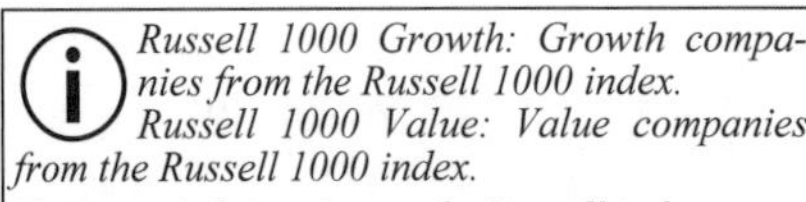

Russell 1000 Growth: Growth companies from the Russell 1000 index.
Russell 1000 Value: Value companies from the Russell 1000 index.
For more information on the Russell indexes, see www.russell.com.

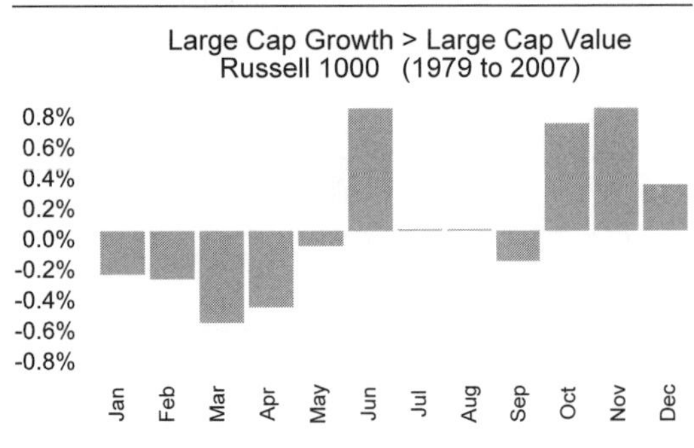

Large Cap Growth (Russell 1000 Growth) vs. Large Cap Value (Russell 1000 Value)

Jan. to Apr. (Value > Growth) — unshaded box

Oct. to Dec. (Growth > Value) — shaded box

	Jan to Apr % Gain			Oct to Dec % Gain		
Year	Value	- Growth	= Diff	Growth	- Value	= Diff
1979	7.9	6.0	1.9	3.7	-4.2	7.9
1980	-2.8	-2.2	-0.7	10.6	4.7	5.9
1981	2.9	-6.6	9.5	8.0	4.1	4.0
1982	-5.1	-7.0	2.0	20.3	14.2	6.1
1983	17.7	15.6	2.1	-3.3	0.1	-3.4
1984	-1.7	-8.2	6.6	0.4	1.1	-0.7
1985	8.8	7.6	1.2	18.4	13.3	5.1
1986	9.6	15.0	-5.4	4.4	2.6	1.8
1987	13.6	20.9	-7.3	-23.9	-22.5	-1.4
1988	10.0	2.5	7.5	2.2	1.1	1.1
1989	10.3	12.6	-2.3	2.1	-1.4	3.4
1990	-7.9	-5.6	-2.3	10.2	6.7	3.4
1991	12.4	16.6	-4.2	12.3	3.4	8.9
1992	4.3	-4.9	9.1	6.4	4.9	1.5
1993	7.2	-5.4	12.6	3.4	-1.1	4.4
1994	-2.7	-4.5	1.8	0.3	-2.6	2.9
1995	11.6	11.4	0.3	4.2	5.8	-1.6
1996	5.1	7.7	-2.6	5.7	9.2	-3.5
1997	6.0	6.8	-0.8	1.3	3.9	-2.6
1998	11.6	16.4	-4.8	26.5	16.0	10.5
1999	10.2	6.2	4.0	25.0	4.9	20.1
2000	-1.4	1.9	-3.2	-21.4	3.1	-24.5
2001	-1.8	-11.0	9.2	14.9	6.8	8.1
2002	-0.1	-10.7	10.6	6.8	8.4	-1.6
2003	2.6	5.9	-3.2	10.1	13.4	-3.4
2004	-0.2	-0.7	0.4	8.9	9.7	0.8
2005	-2.5	-6.2	3.8	2.7	0.6	2.1
2006	7.8	2.6	5.2	5.6	7.3	-1.7
2007	4.2	5.6	5.6	-1.1	-6.5	5.4
Avg.	4.7	3.0	3.0	5.7	3.7	2.0

20 MONDAY 110 / 255

30 day	Wednesday May 20
60 day	Friday June 19
90 day	Sunday July 19
180 day	Saturday October 17
1 year	Tuesday April 20

21 TUESDAY 111 / 254

30 day	Thursday May 21
60 day	Saturday June 20
90 day	Monday July 20
180 day	Sunday October 18
1 year	Wednesday April 21

22 WEDNESDAY 112 / 253

30 day	Friday May 22
60 day	Sunday June 21
90 day	Tuesday July 21
180 day	Monday October 19
1 year	Thursday April 22

23 THURSDAY 113 / 252

30 day	Saturday May 23
60 day	Monday June 22
90 day	Wednesday July 22
180 day	Tuesday October 20
1 year	Friday April 23

24 FRIDAY 114 / 251

30 day	Sunday May 24
60 day	Tuesday June 23
90 day	Thursday July 23
180 day	Wednesday October 21
1 year	Saturday April 24

WEEK 17

Market Indices & Rates Weekly Values*

Stock Markets	2007	2008
Dow	13,038	12,810
S&P500	1,489	1,386
Nasdaq	2,542	2,408
TSX	13,624	14,146
FTSE	6,452	6,063
DAX	7,343	6,806
Nikkei	17,395	13,646
Hang Seng	20,572	25,230

Commodities	2007	2008
Oil	65.26	118.53
Gold	682.32	904.40

Bond Yields	2007	2008
USA 5 Yr Treasury	4.56	3.05
USA 10 Yr T	4.67	3.81
USA 20 Yr T	4.92	4.52
Moody's Aaa	5.43	5.58
Moody's Baa	6.35	6.98
CAN 5 Yr T	4.13	3.17
CAN 10 Yr T	4.18	3.69

Money Market	2007	2008
USA Fed Funds	5.25	2.25
USA 3 Mo T-B	4.97	1.29
CAN tgt overnight rate	4.25	3.00
CAN 3 Mo T-B	4.16	2.53

Foreign Exchange	2007	2008
USD/EUR	1.36	1.58
USD/GBP	2.00	1.98
CAN/USD	1.12	1.01
JPY/USD	118.94	103.60

APRIL

M	T	W	T	F	S	S
		1	2	3	4	5
6	7	8	9	10	11	12
13	14	15	16	17	18	19
20	21	22	23	24	25	26
27	28	29	30			

MAY

M	T	W	T	F	S	S
				1	2	3
4	5	6	7	8	9	10
11	12	13	14	15	16	17
18	19	20	21	22	23	24
25	26	27	28	29	30	31

JUNE

M	T	W	T	F	S	S
1	2	3	4	5	6	7
8	9	10	11	12	13	14
15	16	17	18	19	20	21
22	23	24	25	26	27	28
29	30					

* Weekly avg closing values- except Fed Funds Rate & CAN overnight tgt rate which are weekly closing values.

FIRST 3 MARKET DAYS IN MAY

The 1/2% Difference

A lot of investors have profited by using the *6'N'6 Strategy* (the six favorable months strategy from the beginning of November to the end of April). Although they have done well, they could have increased their profits by making two small adjustments: investing four trading days before the end of October and selling at the end of the first three trading days in May. Investing at the end of October is discussed later in the calendar.

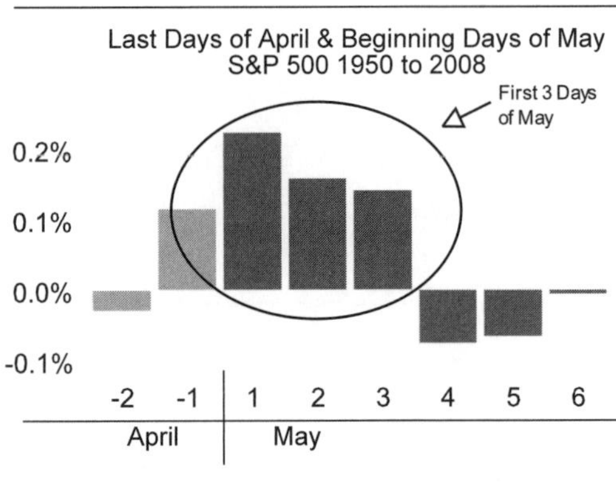

1/2% extra gain & positive 69% of the time

For those investors that use the *6'N'6 Strategy*, selling just three trading days later has increased returns by an average of 1/2% from 1950 to 2008 (S&P 500). Using this strategy has produced positive returns 69% of the time.

The rationale for this is quite simple. The beginning of most months tends to be positive and May is no exception. The the first three trading days tend to be very strong. On average, they have had much better gains than the rest of the days in May, and the average trading day for the entire year. The first three days in May have an average return that is almost five times the average daily gain for the entire year. Given that May tends to peak early, the average daily gain for the rest of the month is negative. The bottom line is that the third trading day is an attractive time to take profits.

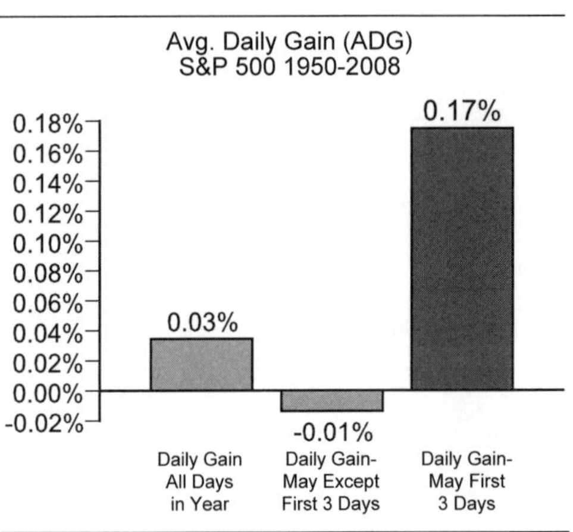

First 3 Days in May % Gain S&P 500 -1950 to 2008 — Positive (shaded)

Year	%	Year	%	Year	%	Year	%	Year	%	Year	%
1950	1.1 %	1960	1.2 %	1970	-3.6 %	1980	0.1 %	1990	1.4 %	2000	-2.6 %
1951	1.7	1961	1.3	1971	-0.2	1981	-1.9	1991	1.5	2001	-0.1
1952	1.2	1962	2.0	1972	-1.6	1982	1.1	1992	0.5	2002	-0.3
1953	1.7	1963	0.3	1973	3.0	1983	-0.7	1993	1.0	2003	1.1
1954	0.1	1964	1.8	1974	1.1	1984	0.7	1994	0.2	2004	1.3
1955	-0.8	1965	0.7	1975	3.2	1985	0.1	1995	1.1	2005	1.6
1956	-0.1	1966	-1.8	1976	-0.7	1986	0.9	1996	-1.9	2006	-0.2
1957	1.3	1967	-0.1	1977	1.5	1987	2.4	1997	3.6	2007	1.4
1958	0.8	1968	1.2	1978	-0.6	1988	-0.4	1998	0.3	2008	1.6
1959	0.3	1969	0.7	1979	0.0	1989	-0.5	1999	0.9		
Average	0.7 %		0.7 %		0.2 %		0.2 %		0.9 %		0.4 %

27 MONDAY 117 / 248

30 day	Wednesday May 27
60 day	Friday June 26
90 day	Sunday July 26
180 day	Saturday October 24
1 year	Tuesday April 27

28 TUESDAY 118 / 247

30 day	Thursday May 28
60 day	Saturday June 27
90 day	Monday July 27
180 day	Sunday October 25
1 year	Wednesday April 28

29 WEDNESDAY 119 / 246

30 day	Friday May 29
60 day	Sunday June 28
90 day	Tuesday July 28
180 day	Monday October 26
1 year	Thursday April 29

30 THURSDAY 120 / 245

30 day	Saturday May 30
60 day	Monday June 29
90 day	Wednesday July 29
180 day	Tuesday October 27
1 year	Friday April 30

1 FRIDAY 121 / 244

30 day	Sunday May 31
60 day	Tuesday June 30
90 day	Thursday July 30
180 day	Wednesday October 28
1 year	Saturday May 1

WEEK 18

Market Indices & Rates Weekly Values*

Stock Markets	2007	2008
Dow	13,183	12,918
S&P500	1,495	1,399
Nasdaq	2,550	2,444
TSX	13,572	14,039
FTSE	6,499	6,114
DAX	7,465	6,951
Nikkei	17,335	13,890
Hang Seng	20,510	25,866

Commodities	2007	2008
Oil	63.82	115.42
Gold	676.62	869.60

Bond Yields	2007	2008
USA 5 Yr Treasury	4.55	3.10
USA 10 Yr T	4.65	3.83
USA 20 Yr T	4.89	4.54
Moody's Aaa	5.40	5.56
Moody's Baa	6.31	6.90
CAN 5 Yr T	4.14	3.11
CAN 10 Yr T	4.18	3.63

Money Market	2007	2008
USA Fed Funds	5.25	2.00
USA 3 Mo T-B	4.90	1.45
CAN tgt overnight rate	4.25	3.00
CAN 3 Mo T-B	4.16	2.66

Foreign Exchange	2007	2008
USD/EUR	1.36	1.55
USD/GBP	1.99	1.98
CAN/USD	1.11	1.01
JPY/USD	119.95	104.32

MAY

M	T	W	T	F	S	S
				1	2	3
4	5	6	7	8	9	10
11	12	13	14	15	16	17
18	19	20	21	22	23	24
25	26	27	28	29	30	31

JUNE

M	T	W	T	F	S	S
1	2	3	4	5	6	7
8	9	10	11	12	13	14
15	16	17	18	19	20	21
22	23	24	25	26	27	28
29	30					

JULY

M	T	W	T	F	S	S
		1	2	3	4	5
6	7	8	9	10	11	12
13	14	15	16	17	18	19
20	21	22	23	24	25	26
27	28	29	30	31		

* Weekly avg closing values- except Fed Funds Rate & CAN overnight tgt rate which are weekly closing values.

MAY

	MONDAY	TUESDAY	WEDNESDAY
WEEK 18	27	28	29
WEEK 19	4 27	5 26 USA ISM Non-Manufacturing Report on Business - Semi-annual (1:00 pm ET)	6 25
WEEK 20	11 20	12 19	13 18
WEEK 21	18 13 CAN Market Closed- Victoria Day	19 12	20 11
WEEK 22	25 6 USA Market Closed- Memorial Day	26 5 USA Consumer Confidence Index 10:00 am ET USA UBS Index of Investor Optimism (8:30 am ET)	27 4

THURSDAY	FRIDAY
30	**1** 30 USA The Employment Situation (8:30 am ET) USA ISM Manufacturing Report on Business (10:00 am ET)
7 24	**8** 23
14 17	**15** 16 USA Empire State Manufacturing Survey - Federal Reserve Bank of New York (8:30 am ET)
21 10 USA Federal Reserve Bank of Philadelphia: Business Outlook Survey (12:00 pm ET)	**22** 9
28 3 USA Help-Wanted Advertising Index (10:00 am ET)	**29** 2 USA Strike Report (8:30 am ET) USA Chicago Purchasing Managers Index (Business Barometer) 9:45am ET

JUNE

M	T	W	T	F	S	S
1	2	3	4	5	6	7
8	9	10	11	12	13	14
15	16	17	18	19	20	21
22	23	24	25	26	27	28
29	30					

JULY

M	T	W	T	F	S	S
		1	2	3	4	5
6	7	8	9	10	11	12
13	14	15	16	17	18	19
20	21	22	23	24	25	26
27	28	29	30	31		

AUGUST

M	T	W	T	F	S	S
					1	2
3	4	5	6	7	8	9
10	11	12	13	14	15	16
17	18	19	20	21	22	23
24	25	26	27	28	29	30
31						

SEPTEMBER

M	T	W	T	F	S	S
	1	2	3	4	5	6
7	8	9	10	11	12	13
14	15	16	17	18	19	20
21	22	23	24	25	26	27
28	29	30				

MAY SUMMARY

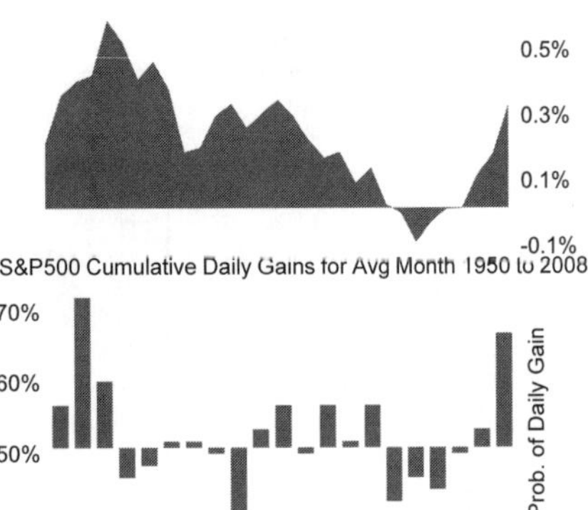

♦ The first three days in May tend to be positive (see *First 3 Market Days in May* strategy). The market typically fades until the last few days. ♦ Value stocks tend to beat growth. From 1999 to 2008 the Russell 3000 Value outperformed the Russell 3000 Growth, 6 out of 10 times with an avg. gain of 1.2% vs. 0.3% respectively. ♦ Memorial Day presents a good opportunity (see *Memorial Day Be Early Stay Late*).

BEST / WORST MAY BROAD MKTS. 1999-2008

BEST MAY MARKETS

- Russell 2000 (2003) 10.6%
- Nasdaq (2003) 9.0%
- Nasdaq (2005) 7.6%

WORST MAY MARKETS

- Nasdaq (2000) -11.9%
- Nasdaq (2006) -6.2%
- Russell 2000 (2000) -5.9%

Index Values End of Month

	1999	2000	2001	2002	2003	2004	2005	2006	2007	2008
Dow	10,560	10,522	10,912	9,925	8,850	10,188	10,467	11,168	13,628	12,638
S&P 500	1,302	1,421	1,256	1,067	964	1,121	1,192	1,270	1,531	1,400
Nasdaq	2,471	3,401	2,110	1,616	1,596	1,987	2,068	2,179	2,605	2,523
TSX	6,842	9,252	8,162	7,656	6,860	8,417	9,607	11,745	14,057	14,715
Russell 1000	1,306	1,444	1,273	1,088	986	1,152	1,239	1,330	1,605	1,477
Russell 2000	1,092	1,185	1,234	1,211	1,096	1,412	1,533	1,792	2,105	1,860
Russell 3000 Growth	2,494	3,089	2,190	1,729	1,574	1,852	1,895	2,009	2,386	2,344
Russell 3000 Value	2,155	2,074	2,219	2,084	1,873	2,206	2,486	2,742	3,348	2,853

Percent Gain for May

	1999	2000	2001	2002	2003	2004	2005	2006	2007	2008
Dow	-2.1	-2.0	1.6	-0.2	4.4	-0.4	2.7	-1.7	4.3	-1.4
S&P 500	-2.5	-2.2	0.5	-0.9	5.1	1.2	3.0	-3.1	3.3	1.1
Nasdaq	-2.8	-11.9	-0.3	-4.3	9.0	3.5	7.6	-6.2	3.1	4.6
TSX	-2.5	-1.0	2.7	-0.1	4.2	2.1	3.6	-3.8	4.8	5.6
Russell 1000	-2.3	-2.7	0.5	-1.0	5.5	1.3	3.4	-3.2	3.4	1.6
Russell 2000	1.4	-5.9	2.3	-4.5	10.6	1.5	6.4	-5.7	4.0	4.5
Russell 3000 Growth	-2.9	-5.3	-1.2	-2.7	5.3	1.8	4.9	-3.9	3.5	3.7
Russell 3000 Value	-1.0	0.6	2.1	0.0	6.4	0.8	2.5	-2.9	3.3	-0.2

May Market Avg. Performance 1999 to 2008 (1)

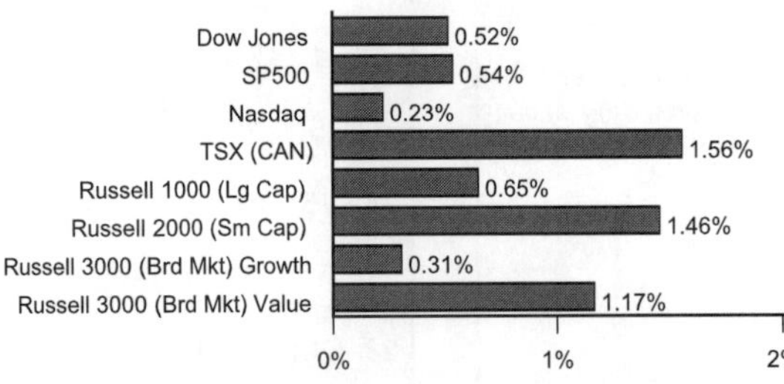

Interest Corner May(2)

	Fed Funds % (3)	3 Mo. T-Bill % (4)	10 Yr % (5)	20 Yr % (6)
2008	2.00	1.89	4.06	4.74
2007	5.25	4.73	4.90	5.10
2006	5.00	4.86	5.12	5.35
2005	3.00	2.99	4.00	4.40
2004	1.00	1.08	4.66	5.39

(1) Russell Data provided by Russell (2) Federal Reserve Bank of St. Louis- end of month values (3) Target rate set by FOMC (4)(5)(6) Constant yield maturities.

MAY SECTOR / SUB-SECTOR PERFORMANCE

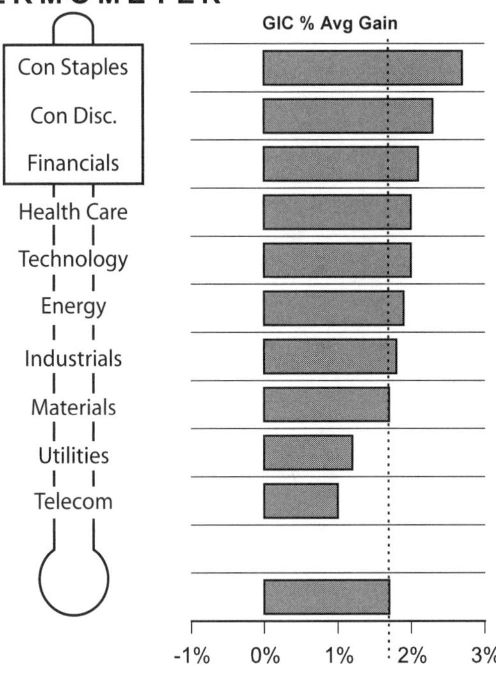

GIC[2] % Avg Gain	Fq % Gain >S&P 500	SP GIC SECTOR 1990-2008[1]
2.7 %	58 %	Consumer Staples
2.3	53	Consumer Discretionary
2.1	47	Financials
2.0	42	Health Care
2.0	63	Information Technology
1.9	37	Energy
1.8	42	Industrials
1.7	37	Materials
1.2	42	Utilities
1.0	47	Telecom
1.7 %	N/A %	S&P 500

		SUB-SECTOR 1990-2008[3]
3.4 %	63 %	Gold (XAU)
3.1	71	Retailing
2.5	53	Banks
2.2	59	Insurance
2.2	42	Oil & Gas Exploration & Production
2.0	53	Metals & Mining
1.8	37	Pharmaceuticals
1.7	37	Oil Integrated
1.4	37	Software & Services
1.2	35	Autos & Components
1.1	35	Transportation
0.4	71	Biotech (92-2008)
-0.2	43	Semiconductor (SOX) (95-2008)
-0.2	29	Airlines

Sector

♦ The Consumer Sector of the market tends to do well. Both the Staples and Discretionary sectors are at the top. ♦ May is often a pivot month in the markets as it slips into a defensive posture. As a result the Consumer Staples sector tends to outperform in this month. ♦ The Financial sector, after typical underperformance for the second half of April, bounces back to do well in May. Although the average return is higher than the S&P 500, its frequency of outperformance is just 47%. ♦ The gains for the Consumer Discretionary sector tend to be made in the first and last few days of the month.

Sub-Sector

♦ The Semiconductor (SOX) index has dropped to second from the bottom of the pack and the Retail sector has moved to second from the top. Both of these changes represent significant changes♦ The performance of the Retail sector is very similar to the Financial sector. On average, after a correction in the second half of April the sector bounces back to do well in May. ♦ Gold stocks also rank high this month, but be careful as they typically peak at the beginning of the month.

(1) Sector data provided by Standard and Poors (2) GIC is short form for Global Industry Classification (3) Sub Sector data provided by Standard and Poors, except where marked by symbol.

6n6 SIX 'N' SIX
Take a Break for Six Months - May 6th to October 27th

Being out of the market feels good when it is going down. And the market has a habit of going down after the beginning of May. Although sometimes a strong market can continue into July and less frequently into autumn, it has historically made sense to reduce your equity exposure in May.

$806,204 gain on $10,000

The accompanying table uses the S&P 500 to compare the returns made from Oct 28th to May 5th, to the returns made during the remainder of the year. From 1950 to 2008, the October to May time period has produced stunning results.

Starting with $10,000 and investing from October 28th to May 5th every year has produced a gain of $806,204. On the flip side, being invested from May 6th to October 27th, has actually lost money. An initial investment of $10,000 has lost $535 over the same time period.

S&P 500 Non-Favorable 6 Month Avg. Gain vs Favorable 6 Month Avg. Gain

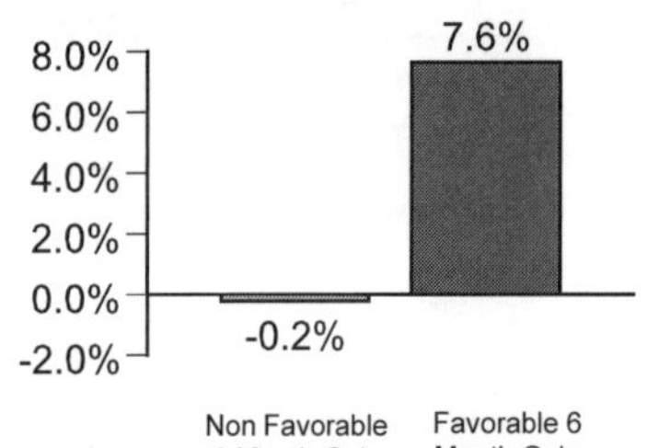

The above growth rates are geometric averages in order to represent the cumulative growth of a dollar investment over time. These figures differ from the arithmetic mean calculations used in the Six 'N' Six Take a Break Strategy, which are used to represent an average year.

In 1999 I co-authored, with Bruce Lindsay, Time In Time Out, Outsmart the Market Using Calendar Investment Strategies. A large part of the book explores the six month seasonal cycle and analyzes the merits of exiting the market from May to October. It also includes an analysis of using the strategy when dividends and interest are figured into the equation. Using these additional variables, the six month seasonal of investing from October 28th to May 5th, outperformed the remainder of the year to an even greater extent.

	S&P 500 % May 6 to Oct 27	$10,000 Start	S&P 500 % Oct 28 to May 5	$10,000 Start
1950/51	8.5%	10,851	14.8%	11,477
1951/52	-1.1	10,736	5.4	12,096
1952/53	1.8	10,931	3.9	12,568
1953/54	-3.1	10,595	16.6	14,655
1954/55	13.2	11,992	18.1	17,310
1955/56	12.0	13,425	14.6	19,832
1956/57	-4.6	12,805	0.2	19,862
1957/58	-12.4	11,216	7.9	21,428
1958/59	15.1	12,914	14.5	24,543
1959/60	-0.6	12,840	-4.5	23,449
1960/61	-2.3	12,550	24.1	29,091
1961/62	2.7	12,894	-3.1	28,197
1962/63	-17.7	10,616	28.4	36,205
1963/64	5.7	11,220	9.3	39,566
1964/65	5.1	11,791	5.5	41,758
1965/66	3.1	12,159	-5.0	39,691
1966/67	-8.8	11,094	17.7	46,720
1967/68	0.6	11,155	3.9	48,541
1968/69	5.6	11,782	0.2	48,620
1969/70	-6.1	11,059	-19.8	39,007
1970/71	5.8	11,695	24.9	48,703
1971/72	-9.6	10,570	13.7	55,370
1972/73	3.7	10,965	0.3	55,560
1973/74	0.3	11,003	-18.0	45,539
1974/75	-23.2	8,451	28.5	58,502
1975/76	-0.4	8,418	12.4	65,771
1976/77	0.9	8,492	-1.6	64,705
1977/78	-7.8	7,833	4.5	67,641
1978/79	-2.0	7,675	6.4	72,003
1979/80	-0.1	7,666	5.8	76,162
1980/81	20.2	9,215	1.9	77,616
1981/82	-8.5	8,435	-1.4	76,562
1982/83	15.0	9,699	21.4	92,967
1983/84	0.3	9,732	-3.5	89,736
1984/85	3.9	10,110	8.9	97,765
1985/86	4.1	10,527	26.8	123,942
1986/87	0.4	10,573	23.7	153,307
1987/88	-21.0	8,348	11.0	170,138
1988/89	7.1	8,945	10.9	188,748
1989/90	8.9	9,743	1.0	190,624
1990/91	-10.0	8,773	25.0	238,225
1991/92	0.9	8,852	8.5	258,463
1992/93	0.4	8,887	6.2	274,540
1993/94	4.5	9,288	-2.8	266,722
1994/95	3.2	9,586	11.6	297,794
1995/96	11.5	10,684	10.7	329,608
1996/97	9.2	11,671	18.5	390,445
1997/98	5.6	12,328	27.2	496,632
1998/99	-4.5	11,773	26.5	628,078
1999/00	-3.8	11,331	10.5	693,913
2000/01	-3.7	10,912	-8.2	637,090
2001/02	-12.8	9,516	-2.8	619,107
2002/03	-16.4	7,958	3.2	639,039
2003/04	11.3	8,856	8.8	695,064
2004/05	0.3	8,887	4.2	724,234
2005/06	0.5	8,934	12.5	814,455
2006/07	3.9	9,282	9.3	890,310
2007/08	2.0	9,465	-8.3	816,204
Total Gain (Loss)		**($-535)**		**$806,204**

4 MONDAY 124 / 241

30 day	Wednesday June 3
60 day	Friday July 3
90 day	Sunday August 2
180 day	Saturday October 31
1 year	Tuesday May 4

5 TUESDAY 125 / 240

30 day	Thursday June 4
60 day	Saturday July 4
90 day	Monday August 3
180 day	Sunday November 1
1 year	Wednesday May 5

6 WEDNESDAY 126 / 239

30 day	Friday June 5
60 day	Sunday July 5
90 day	Tuesday August 4
180 day	Monday November 2
1 year	Thursday May 6

7 THURSDAY 127 / 238

30 day	Saturday June 6
60 day	Monday July 6
90 day	Wednesday August 5
180 day	Tuesday November 3
1 year	Friday May 7

8 FRIDAY 128 / 237

30 day	Sunday June 7
60 day	Tuesday July 7
90 day	Thursday August 6
180 day	Wednesday November 4
1 year	Saturday May 8

WEEK 19

Market Indices & Rates
Weekly Values*

Stock Markets	**2007**	**2008**
Dow	13,305	12,883
S&P500	1,505	1,401
Nasdaq	2,563	2,457
TSX	13,907	14,438
FTSE	6,547	6,238
DAX	7,468	7,044
Nikkei	17,673	13,900
Hang Seng	20,732	25,714

Commodities	**2007**	**2008**
Oil	61.90	123.01
Gold	677.44	875.31

Bond Yields	**2007**	**2008**
USA 5 Yr Treasury	4.56	3.07
USA 10 Yr T	4.65	3.85
USA 20 Yr T	4.89	4.58
Moody's Aaa	5.42	5.57
Moody's Baa	6.31	6.89
CAN 5 Yr T	4.16	3.13
CAN 10 Yr T	4.18	3.64

Money Market	**2007**	**2008**
USA Fed Funds	5.25	2.00
USA 3 Mo T-B	4.88	1.64
CAN tgt overnight rate	4.25	3.00
CAN 3 Mo T-B	4.16	2.60

Foreign Exchange	**2007**	**2008**
USD/EUR	1.35	1.55
USD/GBP	1.99	1.96
CAN/USD	1.11	1.01
JPY/USD	120.04	104.36

MAY

M	T	W	T	F	S	S
				1	2	3
4	5	6	7	8	9	10
11	12	13	14	15	16	17
18	19	20	21	22	23	24
25	26	27	28	29	30	31

JUNE

M	T	W	T	F	S	S
1	2	3	4	5	6	7
8	9	10	11	12	13	14
15	16	17	18	19	20	21
22	23	24	25	26	27	28
29	30					

JULY

M	T	W	T	F	S	S
		1	2	3	4	5
6	7	8	9	10	11	12
13	14	15	16	17	18	19
20	21	22	23	24	25	26
27	28	29	30	31		

* Weekly avg closing values- except Fed Funds Rate & CAN overnight tgt rate which are weekly closing values.

BOND YIELD INDICATOR – JAN TO MAY

007

If, 10 Year Gov. Bond Yield Decreases from Jan 1 to May 5 Then, Safe to Stay in the Market

Bond...James Bond...always gets his man.

Although it does not have quite the track record of James Bond, nevertheless the bond yield indicator has done very well.

> *Bond Yield Indicator:* If the yield on the 10 year U.S. Government Bond decreases from Jan. 1st to May 5th, it is typically safe to stay in the stock market during the non-favorable season (May 5th to October 27th). For example, if the U.S. Government 10 yr. bond yield changes from 6.0% on Jan. 1st to 5.4% on May 5th (a 10% decrease), then it is safe to stay in the market.

Historically, a very good investment strategy has been to exit the market on May 5th and return on October 27th to establish a position for the six favorable months starting October 28th (see *Six 'n' Six* strategy). The *Bond Yield Indicator* from January to May fine tunes this strategy. By using the indicator, the seasonal investor has been able to increase returns compared with always exiting at the beginning of May and re-entering the market in October.

13 out of 15 times successful &
4.0% avg. gain in a flat period for the market

The 10 year government bond yield is an indicator of both economic and inflation expectations. The beginning of the year is the time that expectations are set up for the full year. If the yield on the 10 year government bond falls from the start of the year, it is often a reflection of tempered economic expectations. Similar expectations are reflected in the stock market at the same time. A subsequent rise in the market after the beginning of May typically reflects that the negative expectations set earlier in the year have already been built into the stock prices, and the market now represents a good value proposition.

The results have been very good for the indicator. It has been successful 14 out of 15 times and produced an average gain of 4.0%, all in a time when the stock market is typically flat. This indicator can be classified as a semi-indicator as it does not attempt to forecast the market when the change in the 10 year government bond yield is positive.

May 5th to Oct 27th Avg. Gain
1965 to 2007

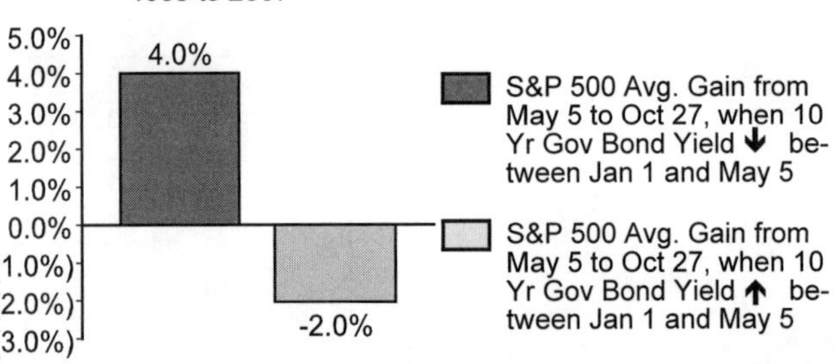

☐ ↓ 10Yr. Gov Bond Yield From Jan 1 to May 5

▨ ↑ SP 500 May 5 to Oct 27 (if 10 Yr Yield ↓ from Jan 1 to May 5)

Year	10 Yr. Bond Yield Gain	S&P 500 Gain
1965	-0.2%	3.4%
1966	3.4	-10.2
1967	2.8	0.7
1968	1.8	5.6
1969	0.5	-5.8
1970	0.5	4.7
1971	-3.7	-9.6
1972	4.8	4.1
1973	5.9	0.3
1974	10.9	-23.2
1975	9.2	0.6
1976	-1.0	0.3
1977	9.7	-7.6
1978	7.2	-1.4
1979	2.6	-0.1
1980	-1.5	21.1
1981	18.2	-8.7
1982	-1.3	15.2
1983	-1.9	0.9
1984	10.6	3.9
1985	-2.9	4.1
1986	-17.2	1.7
1987	16.9	-19.4
1988	1.0	6.5
1989	-1.6	8.9
1990	11.5	-10.0
1991	-0.5	0.9
1992	12.7	0.4
1993	-11.5	4.6
1994	22.0	3.1
1995	-14.7	11.4
1996	23.7	9.2
1997	3.7	7.9
1998	-0.9	-5.1
1999	16.1	-2.6
2000	0.9	-2.1
2001	1.8	-12.8
2002	0.2	-16.4
2003	2.3	10.9
2004	8.0	0.5
2005	-1.2	0.3
2006	16.6	5.0
2007	-1.3	2.0

ⓘ *Yield of the 10 year government bond, source: Federal Reserve St. Louis, website: http://research.stlouisfed.org/fred2/categories/47*

11 MONDAY 131 / 234

30 day	Wednesday June 10
60 day	Friday July 10
90 day	Sunday August 9
180 day	Saturday November 7
1 year	Tuesday May 11

12 TUESDAY 132 / 233

30 day	Thursday June 11
60 day	Saturday July 11
90 day	Monday August 10
180 day	Sunday November 8
1 year	Wednesday May 12

13 WEDNESDAY 133 / 232

30 day	Friday June 12
60 day	Sunday July 12
90 day	Tuesday August 11
180 day	Monday November 9
1 year	Thursday May 13

14 THURSDAY 134 / 231

30 day	Saturday June 13
60 day	Monday July 13
90 day	Wednesday August 12
180 day	Tuesday November 10
1 year	Friday May 14

15 FRIDAY 135 / 230

30 day	Sunday June 14
60 day	Tuesday July 14
90 day	Thursday August 13
180 day	Wednesday November 11
1 year	Saturday May 15

WEEK 20

Market Indices & Rates Weekly Values*

Stock Markets	2007	2008
Dow	13,450	12,917
S&P500	1,511	1,413
Nasdaq	2,543	2,509
TSX	14,014	14,744
FTSE	6,581	6,241
DAX	7,511	7,083
Nikkei	17,524	14,057
Hang Seng	20,937	25,456

Commodities	2007	2008
Oil	63.61	124.96
Gold	663.99	878.65

Bond Yields	2007	2008
USA 5 Yr Treasury	4.66	3.12
USA 10 Yr T	4.74	3.86
USA 20 Yr T	4.97	4.58
Moody's Aaa	5.46	5.56
Moody's Baa	6.38	6.92
CAN 5 Yr T	4.25	3.16
CAN 10 Yr T	4.26	3.58

Money Market	2007	2008
USA Fed Funds	5.25	2.00
USA 3 Mo T-B	4.82	1.82
CAN tgt overnight rate	4.25	3.00
CAN 3 Mo T-B	4.16	2.65

Foreign Exchange	2007	2008
USD/EUR	1.35	1.55
USD/GBP	1.98	1.95
CAN/USD	1.10	1.00
JPY/USD	120.74	104.38

MAY

M	T	W	T	F	S	S
				1	2	3
4	5	6	7	8	9	10
11	12	13	14	15	16	17
18	19	20	21	22	23	24
25	26	27	28	29	30	31

JUNE

M	T	W	T	F	S	S
1	2	3	4	5	6	7
8	9	10	11	12	13	14
15	16	17	18	19	20	21
22	23	24	25	26	27	28
29	30					

JULY

M	T	W	T	F	S	S
		1	2	3	4	5
6	7	8	9	10	11	12
13	14	15	16	17	18	19
20	21	22	23	24	25	26
27	28	29	30	31		

* Weekly avg closing values- except Fed Funds Rate & CAN overnight tgt rate which are weekly closing values.

BONDS ARE ATTRACTIVE
10 Year Treasury Yield Decreases May 10th to Oct 7th

Investors get a double return by investing in bonds during a time period of decreasing yields. First, bonds increase in value. Second, interest payments are received for holding the bonds. Together, these two returns equal an increased total return.

On average bonds have increased in value starting at two different points in time: the beginning of May and early August. These points in time correlate closely to the typical times that the stock market tends to peak (May and July).

57% of time, 10 year government bond yield has decreased May 10th to Oct 7th

Many investors make the timing of their bond investment decision based upon the expected stock market peak. If the expected peak is in May, an allocation is made at that time to bonds. If the expected peak is July, an allocation is made in August to bonds.

Although the August to October time period is generally the sweet spot for bond investments, using the more conservative time of May to rotate from a stock market investment has the added bonus of interest payments. Similarly, a 57% success rate of bond yields decreasing from May 10th to Oct 7th may not seem high, but investors are also compensated with interest payments.

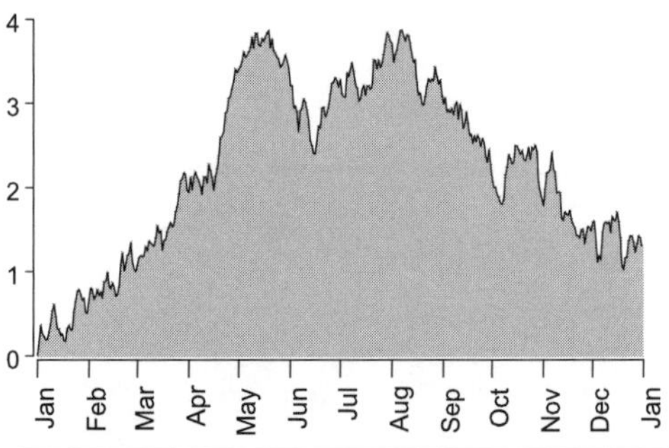

* Figures represent % of change, not actual interest rates.
Source: Federal Reserve- 10 Year Constant Maturity % Yield

CAUTION:
The figures used in this analysis are based upon the % change of the 10 year constant maturity government bond. The % change should not be used a proxy for the actual yield of bonds. Bonds with different durations and credit risk profiles can produce different results.

Source: Federal Reserve Bank of St. Louis
The Federal Reserve has a vast database of free financial information that is updated on a regular basis. The yield for the 10 year government bond: http://research.stlouisfed.org/fred2/categories/47

10 Year Gov Yield % Change May 10 to Oct 7th (1962 to 2007)* — Negative (shaded)

Year	%	Year	%	Year	%	Year	%	Year	%
		1970	-7.07 %	1980	10.97 %	1990	-2.59 %	2000	-10.87 %
		1971	-4.48	1981	5.69	1991	-7.73	2001	-13.08
1962	2.62 %	1972	5.16	1982	-19.07	1992	-12.82	2002	-30.00
1963	3.82	1973	0.88	1983	10.54	1993	-9.97	2003	15.72
1964	-0.24	1974	4.03	1984	-6.21	1994	2.80	2004	-11.06
1965	2.62	1975	3.09	1985	-6.96	1995	-8.32	2005	1.40
1966	5.68	1976	-5.59	1986	-2.67	1996	-4.53	2006	-8.38
1967	10.27	1977	-0.27	1987	15.18	1997	-10.94	2007	-0.43
1968	-4.15	1978	2.88	1988	-3.65	1998	-23.99		
1969	17.34	1979	2.56	1989	-12.24	1999	9.21		

* Source: Federal Reserve- 10 Yr. Bond Constant Maturity Yield

18 MONDAY 138 / 227

30 day	Wednesday June 17
60 day	Friday July 17
90 day	Sunday August 16
180 day	Saturday November 14
1 year	Tuesday May 18

19 TUESDAY 139 / 226

30 day	Thursday June 18
60 day	Saturday July 18
90 day	Monday August 17
180 day	Sunday November 15
1 year	Wednesday May 19

20 WEDNESDAY 140 / 225

30 day	Friday June 19
60 day	Sunday July 19
90 day	Tuesday August 18
180 day	Monday November 16
1 year	Thursday May 20

21 THURSDAY 141 / 224

30 day	Saturday June 20
60 day	Monday July 20
90 day	Wednesday August 19
180 day	Tuesday November 17
1 year	Friday May 21

22 FRIDAY 142 / 223

30 day	Sunday June 21
60 day	Tuesday July 21
90 day	Thursday August 20
180 day	Wednesday November 18
1 year	Saturday May 22

WEEK 21

Market Indices & Rates Weekly Values*

Stock Markets	**2007**	**2008**
Dow	13,511	12,713
S&P500	1,519	1,400
Nasdaq	2,568	2,473
TSX	14,056	14,838
FTSE	6,599	6,207
DAX	7,690	7,080
Nikkei	17,624	14,069
Hang Seng	20,778	25,226
Commodities	**2007**	**2008**
Oil	64.89	130.14
Gold	659.27	918.85
Bond Yields	**2007**	**2008**
USA 5 Yr Treasury	4.77	3.12
USA 10 Yr T	4.84	3.84
USA 20 Yr T	5.07	4.56
Moody's Aaa	5.55	5.53
Moody's Baa	6.47	6.91
CAN 5 Yr T	4.41	3.22
CAN 10 Yr T	4.39	3.60
Money Market	**2007**	**2008**
USA Fed Funds	5.25	2.00
USA 3 Mo T-B	4.90	1.85
CAN tgt overnight rate	4.25	3.00
CAN 3 Mo T-B	4.18	2.64
Foreign Exchange	**2007**	**2008**
USD/EUR	1.35	1.57
USD/GBP	1.98	1.97
CAN/USD	1.08	0.99
JPY/USD	121.55	103.76

MAY

M	T	W	T	F	S	S
				1	2	3
4	5	6	7	8	9	10
11	12	13	14	15	16	17
18	19	20	21	22	23	24
25	26	27	28	29	30	31

JUNE

M	T	W	T	F	S	S
1	2	3	4	5	6	7
8	9	10	11	12	13	14
15	16	17	18	19	20	21
22	23	24	25	26	27	28
29	30					

JULY

M	T	W	T	F	S	S
		1	2	3	4	5
6	7	8	9	10	11	12
13	14	15	16	17	18	19
20	21	22	23	24	25	26
27	28	29	30	31		

* Weekly avg closing values- except Fed Funds Rate & CAN overnight tgt rate which are weekly closing values.

MEMORIAL DAY - BE EARLY & STAY LATE

Positive 2 Market Days Before Memorial Day to 5 Market Days into June

A lot of strategies that focus on investing around holidays concentrate on the market performance a day before and a day after a holiday.

Not all holidays were created equal. The typical Memorial Day trade is to invest the day before and sell the day after. If you invested just for these two days you would be missing out on a lot of gains.

Historically, the best strategy has been to invest two market days before the holiday and hold until five market days into June. Extending the investment into June makes sense. The first few days in June tend to be positive...so why sell early?

1.2% average gain and positive 68% of the time

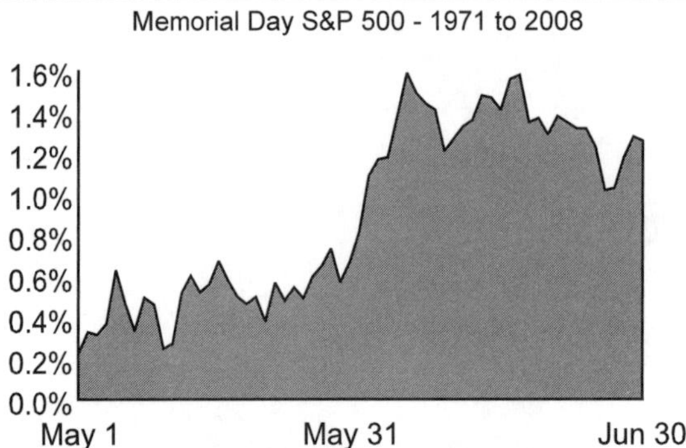

The graph shows the performance of the S&P 500 on a calendar basis for the months of May and June from 1971 to 2008 (see information box for start year details). The increase from the end of May into June represents the opportunity with the "*Memorial Day- Be Early & Stay Late*" trade. The graph clearly shows a spike in the market that occurs at the end of the month and carries on into June. Investors using the typical Memorial Day trade, miss out on the majority of the gain. The *Memorial Day- Be Early & Stay Late* strategy has produced an average gain of 1.2% and has been positive 68% of the time (S&P 500 1971 to 2008). Not a bad gain for being invested an average of ten market days.

The Memorial Day trade can be extended into June primarily because the first days in June tend to be positive. These days are part of the end of the month effect, or the Super Seven (see *Super Seven* strategy).

The Memorial Day opportunity is worthy of consideration by investors who have moved to a defensive position at the beginning of May and are looking for a short-term investment to "juice" their returns.

At the end of the Memorial Day trade, the month of June tends to move sideways. It changes course, once again, at the end of the month to set up for the next short-term opportunity–Independence Day (see *Independence Day* strategy).

2 Market Days Before Memorial Day to 5 Market Days Into June - S&P 500   Positive [shaded]

Year	%	Year	%	Year	%	Year	%
		1980	5.1 %	1990	1.1 %	2000	5.2 %
1971	1.5 %	1981	0.2	1991	0.9	2001	-0.9
1972	-2.4	1982	-2.6	1992	-0.5	2002	-5.4
1973	1.7	1983	-2.1	1993	-1.3	2003	7.0
1974	6.3	1984	1.2	1994	0.4	2004	2.3
1975	3.8	1985	4.3	1995	0.9	2005	0.6
1976	-0.7	1986	4.3	1996	0.0	2006	-0.2
1977	1.0	1987	5.5	1997	2.2	2007	-2.1
1978	3.1	1988	4.5	1998	-0.5	2008	-2.2
1979	1.9	1989	2.4	1999	2.3		
Avg.	1.8 %		2.3 %		0.6 %		0.5 %

History of Memorial Day: Originally called Decoration Day in remembrance of those who died in the nation's service. Memorial day was first observed on May 30th 1868 when flowers were placed on the graves of Union and Confederate soldiers at Arlington National Cemetery. The South acknowledged the day after World War I, when the holiday changed from honoring just those who died fighting in the Civil War to honoring Americans who died fighting in any war. In 1971 Congress passed the National Holiday Act recognizing Memorial Day as the last Monday in May.

25 MONDAY 145 / 220

30 day	Wednesday June 24
60 day	Friday July 24
90 day	Sunday August 23
180 day	Saturday November 21
1 year	Tuesday May 25

26 TUESDAY 146 / 219

30 day	Thursday June 25
60 day	Saturday July 25
90 day	Monday August 24
180 day	Sunday November 22
1 year	Wednesday May 26

27 WEDNESDAY 147 / 218

30 day	Friday June 26
60 day	Sunday July 26
90 day	Tuesday August 25
180 day	Monday November 23
1 year	Thursday May 27

28 THURSDAY 148 / 217

30 day	Saturday June 27
60 day	Monday July 27
90 day	Wednesday August 26
180 day	Tuesday November 24
1 year	Friday May 28

29 FRIDAY 149 / 216

30 day	Sunday June 28
60 day	Tuesday July 28
90 day	Thursday August 27
180 day	Wednesday November 25
1 year	Saturday May 29

WEEK 22

Market Indices & Rates
Weekly Values*

Stock Markets	2007	2008
Dow	13,613	12,607
S&P500	1,529	1,394
Nasdaq	2,596	2,500
TSX	14,059	14,652
FTSE	6,627	6,062
DAX	7,854	7,020
Nikkei	17,737	13,951
Hang Seng	20,506	24,315

Commodities	2007	2008
Oil	64.07	128.47
Gold	659.60	901.10

Bond Yields	2007	2008
USA 5 Yr Treasury	4.86	3.36
USA 10 Yr T	4.90	4.03
USA 20 Yr T	5.11	4.72
Moody's Aaa	5.58	5.67
Moody's Baa	6.51	7.06
CAN 5 Yr T	4.53	3.33
CAN 10 Yr T	4.48	3.68

Money Market	2007	2008
USA Fed Funds	5.25	2.00
USA 3 Mo T-B	4.82	1.89
CAN tgt overnight rate	4.25	3.00
CAN 3 Mo T-B	4.27	2.66

Foreign Exchange	2007	2008
USD/EUR	1.34	1.56
USD/GBP	1.98	1.98
CAN/USD	1.07	0.99
JPY/USD	121.78	104.91

MAY

M	T	W	T	F	S	S
				1	2	3
4	5	6	7	8	9	10
11	12	13	14	15	16	17
18	19	20	21	22	23	24
25	26	27	28	29	30	31

JUNE

M	T	W	T	F	S	S
1	2	3	4	5	6	7
8	9	10	11	12	13	14
15	16	17	18	19	20	21
22	23	24	25	26	27	28
29	30					

JULY

M	T	W	T	F	S	S
		1	2	3	4	5
6	7	8	9	10	11	12
13	14	15	16	17	18	19
20	21	22	23	24	25	26
27	28	29	30	31		

* Weekly avg closing values- except Fed Funds Rate & CAN overnight tgt rate which are weekly closing values.

1ST DAY OF THE MONTH
Best Day of the Month

Not all days are equal. There is one day of the month that has typically been the best– the first day. This day benefits from portfolio managers finishing off their window dressing (making their portfolios look good on the books) and retail investors buying up new positions to start the month on a favorable footing.

0.14% avg. gain & 5 times better than the average market day

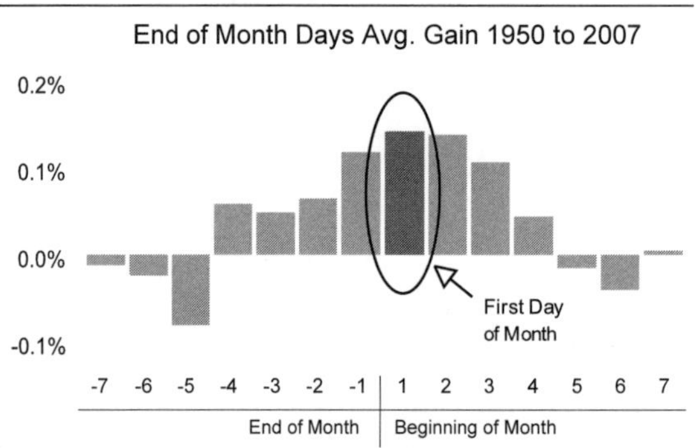

From 1950 to 2007, the first day of the month (FDOM) has produced an average return of 0.14% and has been positive 59% of the time. This compares to the average market day (all trading days of the year) over the same time period, which has produced a return of 0.03% and has been positive 53% of the time. The interesting result is that the average daily gain of first day of the month was almost five times better than the average market day, and yet it had a higher frequency of being positive. What this means is that when the first day is positive, it has a much higher likelihood of producing extraordinarily large gains.

1st Day of Month (FDOM)
Average Monthly Performance 1950 to 2007

	J	F	M	A	M	J	J	A	S	O	N	D
Gain %	0.06	0.09	0.24	0.04	0.20	0.21	0.24	0.01	0.04	0.15	0.35	0.07
Fq > 0 %	47	62	64	60	57	59	71	52	69	50	66	52

Examining the returns on a monthly basis, only the first day of two months has performed below the average market day from 1950 to 2007. It is not surprising that the months are August and September, two of the worst months in which to invest. On the other hand, the best first day of the month has clearly been November: the traditional start of the six month favorable time period to invest and also one of the best months for a stock market gain.

It is interesting to note that a high frequency positive first day of the month does not necessarily mean that the average gain is high. For example, the first day in September has been positive 69% of the time from 1950 to 2007. Yet, although it is still positive, it is one of the worst first days of the month. As a side note, the month of September has also proved unfriendly to the market and has produced an average negative return from 1950 to 2007.

Generally, it is not a wise strategy to invest in the market for only one day. Nevertheless, sophisticated investors can take advantage of the first day of the month trend with strategies that are based on the Super Seven Strategy (see *Super Seven* strategy). One such strategy is to increase an equity position starting on the last day of the month, if the first few days of the Super Seven have been negative.

CAUTION:
Generally, it is not a wise strategy to invest for just one day: the expected rate of return, combined with the risk from volatility do not justify the expected returns.

1 MONDAY 152 / 213

30 day	Wednesday July 1
60 day	Friday July 31
90 day	Sunday August 30
180 day	Saturday November 28
1 year	Tuesday June 1

2 TUESDAY 153 / 212

30 day	Thursday July 2
60 day	Saturday August 1
90 day	Monday August 31
180 day	Sunday November 29
1 year	Wednesday June 2

3 WEDNESDAY 154 / 211

30 day	Friday July 3
60 day	Sunday August 2
90 day	Tuesday September 1
180 day	Monday November 30
1 year	Thursday June 3

4 THURSDAY 155 / 210

30 day	Saturday July 4
60 day	Monday August 3
90 day	Wednesday September 2
180 day	Tuesday December 1
1 year	Friday June 4

5 FRIDAY 156 / 209

30 day	Sunday July 5
60 day	Tuesday August 4
90 day	Thursday September 3
180 day	Wednesday December 2
1 year	Saturday June 5

WEEK 23

Market Indices & Rates Weekly Values*

Stock Markets	2007	2008
Dow	13,486	12,422
S&P500	1,517	1,381
Nasdaq	2,586	2,500
TSX	13,946	14,837
FTSE	6,566	5,988
DAX	7,767	6,948
Nikkei	17,980	14,383
Hang Seng	20,740	24,398

Commodities	2007	2008
Oil	65.90	128.16
Gold	667.26	884.05

Bond Yields	2007	2008
USA 5 Yr Treasury	4.98	3.26
USA 10 Yr T	5.02	3.98
USA 20 Yr T	5.21	4.70
Moody's Aaa	5.67	5.63
Moody's Baa	6.62	7.01
CAN 5 Yr T	4.62	3.22
CAN 10 Yr T	4.55	3.65

Money Market	2007	2008
USA Fed Funds	5.25	2.00
USA 3 Mo T-B	4.80	1.85
CAN tgt overnight rate	4.25	3.00
CAN 3 Mo T-B	4.30	2.53

Foreign Exchange	2007	2008
USD/EUR	1.35	1.55
USD/GBP	1.98	1.96
CAN/USD	1.06	1.01
JPY/USD	121.45	105.20

JUNE

M	T	W	T	F	S	S
1	2	3	4	5	6	7
8	9	10	11	12	13	14
15	16	17	18	19	20	21
22	23	24	25	26	27	28
29	30					

JULY

M	T	W	T	F	S	S
		1	2	3	4	5
6	7	8	9	10	11	12
13	14	15	16	17	18	19
20	21	22	23	24	25	26
27	28	29	30	31		

AUGUST

M	T	W	T	F	S	S
					1	2
3	4	5	6	7	8	9
10	11	12	13	14	15	16
17	18	19	20	21	22	23
24	25	26	27	28	29	30
31						

* Weekly avg closing values- except Fed Funds Rate & CAN overnight tgt rate which are weekly closing values.

JUNE

	MONDAY	TUESDAY	WEDNESDAY
WEEK 23	**1** 29 USA ISM Manufacturing Report on Business (10:00 am ET)	**2** 28	**3** 27 USA Federal Reserve Board's Beige Book USA ISM Non-Manufacturing Report on Business (10:00 am ET)
WEEK 24	**8** 22	**9** 21	**10** 20 USA Federal Reserve Board's Beige Book
WEEK 25	**15** 15 USA Empire State Manufacturing Survey - Federal Reserve Bank of New York (8:30 am ET)	**16** 14	**17** 13
WEEK 26	**22** 8 USA UBS Index of Investor Optimism (8:30 am ET)	**23** 7 USA FOMC Meetings	**24** 6 USA FOMC Meetings
WEEK 27	**29** 1 	**30** USA Chicago Purchasing Managers Index (Business Barometer) 9:45 am ET USA Consumer Confidence Index 10:00 am ET	**1**

THURSDAY	FRIDAY
4 26	**5** 25 USA The Employment Situation (8:30 am ET)
11 19	**12** 18
18 12 USA Federal Reserve Bank of Philadelphia: Business Outlook Survey (12:00 pm ET)	**19** 11
25 5 USA Help-Wanted Advertising Index (10:00 am ET)	**26** 4 USA Strike Report (8:30 am ET)
2	**3**

JULY

M	T	W	T	F	S	S
		1	2	3	4	5
6	7	8	9	10	11	12
13	14	15	16	17	18	19
20	21	22	23	24	25	26
27	28	29	30	31		

AUGUST

M	T	W	T	F	S	S
					1	2
3	4	5	6	7	8	9
10	11	12	13	14	15	16
17	18	19	20	21	22	23
24	25	26	27	28	29	30
31						

SEPTEMBER

M	T	W	T	F	S	S
	1	2	3	4	5	6
7	8	9	10	11	12	13
14	15	16	17	18	19	20
21	22	23	24	25	26	27
28	29	30				

OCTOBER

M	T	W	T	F	S	S
			1	2	3	4
5	6	7	8	9	10	11
12	13	14	15	16	17	18
19	20	21	22	23	24	25
26	27	28	29	30	31	

JUNE
SUMMARY

STRATEGIES	PAGE
STRATEGIES STARTING	
Biotech Summer Solstice	73
Independence Day– Full Trade Profit	75
STRATEGIES FINISHING	
Memorial Day– Be Early and Stay Late	63

S&P500 Cumulative Daily Gains for Avg Month 1950 to 2008

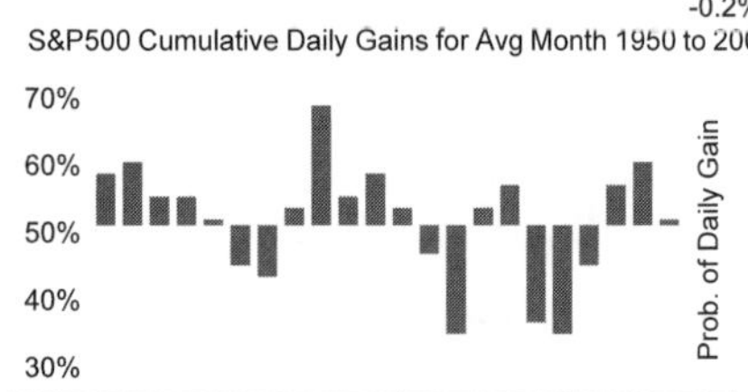

♦ June, on average, is a "see-saw" month. The first half of the month does well and then fades. ♦ The Biotechnology sector usually starts to pick up at the end of the month (see *Biotech Summer Solstice* strategy). ♦ The Nasdaq usually outperforms the S&P 500. ♦ Large Cap Growth (large companies with a growth profile- Russell 1000 Growth) tend to perform well in June (see *Value for First Four Months and Growth for Last Three Months* strategy).

BEST / WORST JUNE BROAD MKTS. 1999-2008

BEST JUNE MARKETS

- Nasdaq (2000) 16.6%
- TSX (2000) 10.2%
- Nasdaq (1999) 8.7%

WORST JUNE MARKETS

- Dow (2008) -10.2%
- Russell 3000 Val (2008) -9.8%
- Nasdaq (2002) -9.4%

Index Values End of Month

	1999	2000	2001	2002	2003	2004	2005	2006	2007	2008
Dow	10,971	10,448	10,502	9,243	8,985	10,435	10,275	11,150	13,409	11,350
S&P 500	1,373	1,455	1,224	990	975	1,141	1,191	1,270	1,503	1,280
Nasdaq	2,686	3,966	2,161	1,463	1,623	2,048	2,057	2,172	2,603	2,293
TSX	7,010	10,196	7,736	7,146	6,983	8,546	9,903	11,613	13,907	14,467
Russell 1000	1,371	1,479	1,244	1,007	998	1,171	1,242	1,330	1,573	1,352
Russell 2000	1,140	1,286	1,275	1,150	1,114	1,470	1,590	1,801	2,072	1,714
Russell 3000 Growth	2,663	3,333	2,148	1,569	1,595	1,876	1,892	2,000	2,350	2,175
Russell 3000 Value	2,216	1,987	2,177	1,967	1,894	2,258	2,515	2,757	3,265	2,574

Percent Gain for June

	1999	2000	2001	2002	2003	2004	2005	2006	2007	2008
Dow	3.9	-0.7	-3.8	-6.9	1.5	2.4	-1.8	-0.2	-1.6	-10.2
S&P 500	5.4	2.4	-2.5	-7.2	1.1	1.8	0.0	0.0	-1.8	-8.6
Nasdaq	8.7	16.6	2.4	-9.4	1.7	3.1	-0.5	-0.3	0.0	-9.1
TSX	2.5	10.2	-5.2	-6.7	1.8	1.5	3.1	-1.1	-1.1	-1.7
Russell 1000	5.0	2.5	-2.3	-7.5	1.2	1.7	0.3	0.0	-2.0	-8.5
Russell 2000	4.4	8.6	3.3	-5.1	1.7	4.1	3.7	0.5	-1.6	-7.8
Russell 3000 Growth	6.8	7.9	-1.9	-9.3	1.3	1.3	-0.1	-0.5	-1.5	-7.2
Russell 3000 Value	2.8	-4.2	-1.9	-5.6	1.1	2.4	1.2	0.5	-2.5	-9.8

June Market Avg. Performance 1999 to 2008 (1)

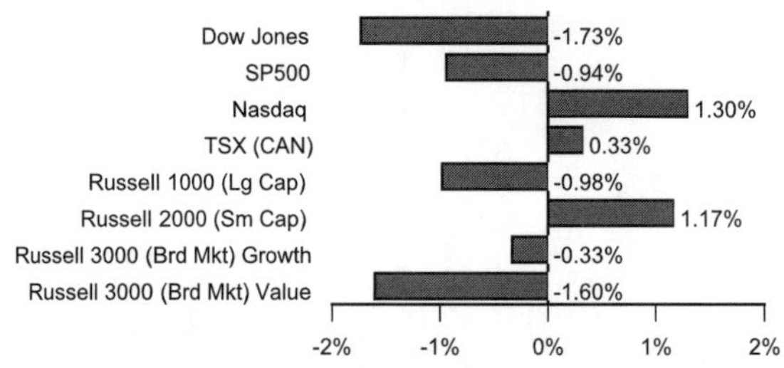

Interest Corner Jun(2)

	Fed Funds % (3)	3 Mo. T-Bill % (4)	10 Yr % (5)	20 Yr % (6)
2008	2.00	1.90	3.99	4.59
2007	5.25	4.82	5.03	5.21
2006	5.25	5.01	5.15	5.31
2005	3.25	3.13	3.94	4.28
2004	1.25	1.33	4.62	5.33

(1) Russell Data provided by Russell (2) Federal Reserve Bank of St. Louis- end of month values (3) Target rate set by FOMC (4)(5)(6) Constant yield maturities

JUNE SECTOR / SUB-SECTOR PERFORMANCE

THACKRAY SECTOR THERMOMETER

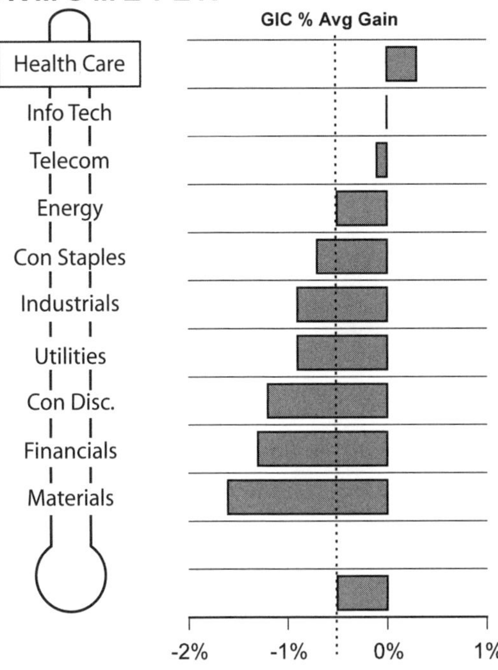

GIC[2] % Avg Gain	Fq % Gain >S&P 500	SP GIC SECTOR 1990-2008[1]
0.3 %	53 %	Health Care
0.0	42	Information Technology
-0.1	58	Telecom
-0.5	42	Energy
-0.7	32	Consumer Staples
-0.9	42	Industrials
-0.9	42	Utilities
-1.2	42	Consumer Discretionary
-1.3	42	Financials
-1.6	32	Materials
-0.5 %	N/A %	S&P 500

		SUB-SECTOR 1990-2008[3]
3.0 %	79 %	Software & Services
0.3	58	Pharmaceuticals
0.0	43	Semiconductor (SOX) (95-2008)
-0.3	65	Retailing
-0.4	42	Oil Integrated
-0.5	58	Metals & Mining
-0.6	53	Insurance
-0.6	41	Airlines
-0.7	47	Gold (XAU)
-1.2	47	Autos & Components
-1.5	29	Transportation
-1.5	35	Biotech (92-2008)
-1.5	42	Oil & Gas Exploration & Production
-2.6	29	Banks

Sector

♦ At the sector level, the market has not had a lot of leadership. There is only one positive sector for the month: Health Care ♦ The Information Technology sector, next on the list, has only outperformed the S&P 500 42% of the time, not making it an attractive investment. ♦ Stay alert with the bottom sector, Materials, as it moves up the list next month.

Sub-Sector

♦ Of the sub-sectors listed, only two have a positive performance. Software and Services dominates with an average 3.0% return and a 79% positive return rate. ♦ Although the software industry tends to push its workforce to close deals for the half year, boosting the price of stocks, the numbers should be taken with a "grain of salt." With the rapid development of the web in the 90s, the sector had a number of years with stellar performance, skewing the results upwards.

(1) Sector data provided by Standard and Poors (2) GIC is short form for Global Industry Classification (3) Sub Sector data provided by Standard and Poors, except where marked by symbol

8 MONDAY 159 / 206

30 day	Wednesday July 8
60 day	Friday August 7
90 day	Sunday September 6
180 day	Saturday December 5
1 year	Tuesday June 8

9 TUESDAY 160 / 205

30 day	Thursday July 9
60 day	Saturday August 8
90 day	Monday September 7
180 day	Sunday December 6
1 year	Wednesday June 9

10 WEDNESDAY 161 / 204

30 day	Friday July 10
60 day	Sunday August 9
90 day	Tuesday September 8
180 day	Monday December 7
1 year	Thursday June 10

11 THURSDAY 162 / 203

30 day	Saturday July 11
60 day	Monday August 10
90 day	Wednesday September 9
180 day	Tuesday December 8
1 year	Friday June 11

12 FRIDAY 163 / 202

30 day	Sunday July 12
60 day	Tuesday August 11
90 day	Thursday September 10
180 day	Wednesday December 9
1 year	Saturday June 12

* Weekly avg closing values- except Fed Funds Rate & CAN overnight tgt rate which are weekly closing values.

WEEK 24

Market Indices & Rates Weekly Values*

Stock Markets	**2007**	**2008**
Dow	13,479	12,221
S&P500	1,515	1,351
Nasdaq	2,586	2,432
TSX	13,911	14,759
FTSE	6,606	5,804
DAX	7,789	6,743
Nikkei	17,828	14,050
Hang Seng	20,743	23,080
Commodities	**2007**	**2008**
Oil	66.62	134.80
Gold	650.31	875.75
Bond Yields	**2007**	**2008**
USA 5 Yr Treasury	5.13	3.57
USA 10 Yr T	5.20	4.15
USA 20 Yr T	5.37	4.78
Moody's Aaa	5.89	5.68
Moody's Baa	6.79	7.08
CAN 5 Yr T	4.70	3.52
CAN 10 Yr T	4.67	3.82
Money Market	**2007**	**2008**
USA Fed Funds	5.25	2.00
USA 3 Mo T-B	4.66	1.97
CAN tgt overnight rate	4.25	3.00
CAN 3 Mo T-B	4.35	2.71
Foreign Exchange	**2007**	**2008**
USD/EUR	1.33	1.55
USD/GBP	1.97	1.96
CAN/USD	1.07	1.02
JPY/USD	122.49	107.18

JUNE

M	T	W	T	F	S	S
1	2	3	4	5	6	7
8	9	10	11	12	13	14
15	16	17	18	19	20	21
22	23	24	25	26	27	28
29	30					

JULY

M	T	W	T	F	S	S
		1	2	3	4	5
6	7	8	9	10	11	12
13	14	15	16	17	18	19
20	21	22	23	24	25	26
27	28	29	30	31		

AUGUST

M	T	W	T	F	S	S
					1	2
3	4	5	6	7	8	9
10	11	12	13	14	15	16
17	18	19	20	21	22	23
24	25	26	27	28	29	30
31						

BIOTECH SUMMER SOLSTICE

June 23rd to Sep 13th

The *Biotech Summer Solstice* trade starts on June 23rd and lasts until September 13th. The trade is aptly named as its outperformance starts approximately on the day of the summer solstice – the longest day of the year. There are two main drivers of the trade: biotech is a good substitute for technology stocks in the summer, and investors taking a position in the sector before the autumn conferences.

13% extra & 14 out of 16 times better than the S&P 500

First, the biotechnology sector is often considered the cousin of the technology sector, a good place for speculative investments. The sectors are similar as both include concept companies (companies without a product but have good potential). Despite their similarity, investors view the sectors differently. The technology sector is viewed as being largely dependent on the economy. The biotech sector is viewed as being much less dependent on the economy. The end product of biotechnology companies is mainly medicine, which is not economically sensitive. As a result, in the softer summer months, investors are more willing to commit speculative money into the biotech sector, compared with the technology sector.

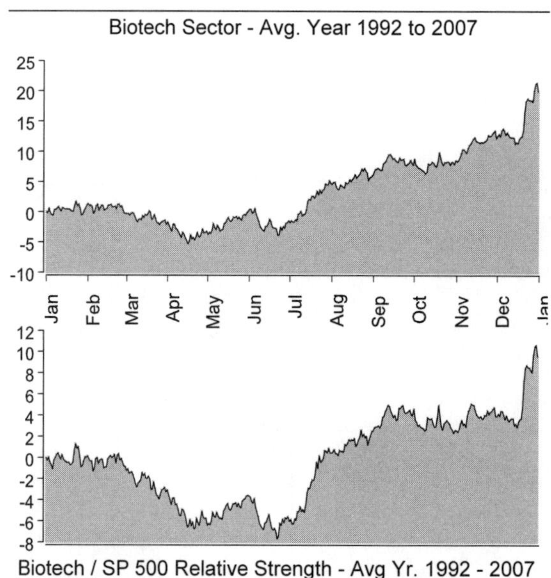

Biotech / SP 500 Relative Strength - Avg Yr. 1992 - 2007

Second, the biotech sector is one of the few sectors that starts its outperformance in June. This is in part because of the biotech conferences that occur in autumn. With positive announcements, biotech companies can increase dramatically. As a result, investors try to lock in positions early.

Biotech vs. S&P 500 1992 to 2007

Performance > S&P 500 (shaded)

Jun 23 to Sep 13	Biotech	S&P 500	Diff
1992	17.9 %	4.0 %	13.8 %
1993	3.6	3.6	0.0
1994	24.2	3.2	21.0
1995	31.5	5.0	26.5
1996	7.0	2.1	4.9
1997	-18.9	2.8	-21.7
1998	20.6	-8.5	29.1
1999	64.3	0.6	63.7
2000	7.6	2.3	5.4
2001	-3.6	-10.8	7.2
2002	8.1	-10.0	18.2
2003	6.4	2.3	4.1
2004	8.9	-0.8	9.6
2005	26.0	1.4	24.5
2006	7.4	5.8	1.6
2007	6.0	-1.2	7.2
Avg	13.5 %	0.1 %	13.4 %

It is interesting to note that the biotech sector's outperformance picks up dramatically in mid-December. This has been attributed to the influential Morgan Stanley Pharmaceutical CEO's Unplugged Conference that takes place at the beginning of January each year.

The outperformance of the biotech sector versus the S&P 500 in the summer is quite remarkable. This performance is noteworthy because it has occurred during the summer doldrums when the S&P 500 has been slightly negative.

Biotech SP GIC Sector # 352010: Companies primarily engaged in the research, development, manufacturing and/or marketing of products based on genetic analysis and genetic engineering. This includes companies specializing in protein-based therapeutics to treat human diseases.

15 MONDAY 166 / 199

30 day	Wednesday July 15
60 day	Friday August 14
90 day	Sunday September 13
180 day	Saturday December 12
1 year	Tuesday June 15

16 TUESDAY 167 / 198

30 day	Thursday July 16
60 day	Saturday August 15
90 day	Monday September 14
180 day	Sunday December 13
1 year	Wednesday June 16

17 WEDNESDAY 168 / 197

30 day	Friday July 17
60 day	Sunday August 16
90 day	Tuesday September 15
180 day	Monday December 14
1 year	Thursday June 17

18 THURSDAY 169 / 196

30 day	Saturday July 18
60 day	Monday August 17
90 day	Wednesday September 16
180 day	Tuesday December 15
1 year	Friday June 18

19 FRIDAY 170 / 195

30 day	Sunday July 19
60 day	Tuesday August 18
90 day	Thursday September 17
180 day	Wednesday December 16
1 year	Saturday June 19

* Weekly avg closing values- except Fed Funds Rate & CAN overnight tgt rate which are weekly closing values.

WEEK 25

Market Indices & Rates Weekly Values*

Stock Markets	**2007**	**2008**
Dow	13,529	12,073
S&P500	1,520	1,342
Nasdaq	2,612	2,446
TSX	14,071	14,891
FTSE	6,633	5,749
DAX	8,015	6,711
Nikkei	18,191	14,246
Hang Seng	21,761	22,991
Commodities	**2007**	**2008**
Oil	68.78	134.34
Gold	654.67	893.55
Bond Yields	**2007**	**2008**
USA 5 Yr Treasury	5.04	3.64
USA 10 Yr T	5.14	4.20
USA 20 Yr T	5.33	4.81
Moody's Aaa	5.85	5.74
Moody's Baa	6.73	7.14
CAN 5 Yr T	4.66	3.54
CAN 10 Yr T	4.65	3.85
Money Market	**2007**	**2008**
USA Fed Funds	5.25	2.00
USA 3 Mo T-B	4.69	1.95
CAN tgt overnight rate	4.25	3.00
CAN 3 Mo T-B	4.36	2.64
Foreign Exchange	**2007**	**2008**
USD/EUR	1.34	1.55
USD/GBP	1.99	1.96
CAN/USD	1.07	1.02
JPY/USD	123.69	107.93

JUNE

M	T	W	T	F	S	S
1	2	3	4	5	6	7
8	9	10	11	12	13	14
15	16	17	18	19	20	21
22	23	24	25	26	27	28
29	30					

JULY

M	T	W	T	F	S	S
		1	2	3	4	5
6	7	8	9	10	11	12
13	14	15	16	17	18	19
20	21	22	23	24	25	26
27	28	29	30	31		

AUGUST

M	T	W	T	F	S	S
					1	2
3	4	5	6	7	8	9
10	11	12	13	14	15	16
17	18	19	20	21	22	23
24	25	26	27	28	29	30
31						

INDEPENDENCE DAY – THE FULL TRADE PROFIT BEFORE & AFTER FIREWORKS

Two Market Days Before June Month End To 5 Market Days After Independence Day

The beginning of July is a time for celebration and the markets tend to agree.

Based on previous market data, the best way to take advantage of this trend is to be invested for the two market days previous to the June month end and hold until five market days after Independence Day. This time period has produced above average returns on a fairly consistent basis.

1% avg. gain & 71% of the time positive

The typical Independence Day trade put forward by quite a few pundits has been to invest one or two days before the holiday and take profits one or two days after the holiday. Although this strategy has produced profits, it has left a lot of money on the table. This strategy misses out on the positive days at the end of June and on the full slate of positive days after Independence Day.

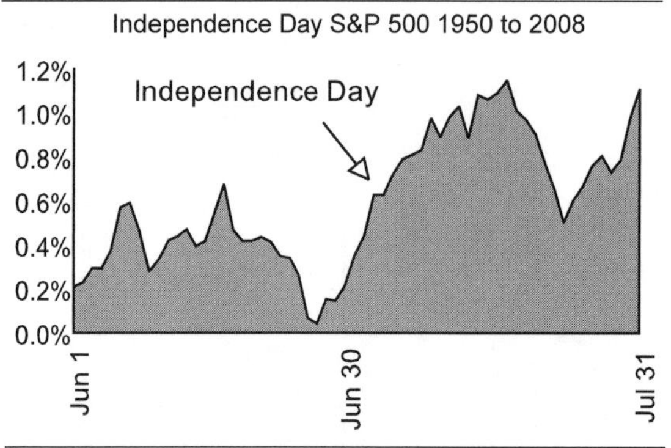

The beginning part of the Independence Day positive trend is driven by two combining factors. First, portfolio managers "window dress" (buying stocks that have a favorable perception in the market); thereby pushing stock prices up at the end of the month. Second, investors becoming "wise" to the Independence Day Trade and try to jump in before everyone else.

The days after Independence Day have benefited from the tendency of July to have a strong first half. This has been the result of the momentum established before the holiday combined with the tendency of the first month of each quarter to have superior performance in the first eighteen calendar days (see *18 Day Earnings Month Effect* strategy).

> *History of Independence Day: Independence Day is celebrated on July 4th because that is the day when the Continental Congress adopted the final draft of the Declaration of Independence in 1776. Independence Day was made an official holiday at the end of the War of Independence in 1783. In 1941 Congress declared the 4th of July a federal holiday.*

S&P 500, 2 Market Days Before June Month End To 5 Market Days after Independence Day % Gain 1950 to 2008

Positive (shaded)

Year	%	Year	%	Year	%	Year	%	Year	%	Year	%
1950	-4.4 %	1960	-0.1 %	1970	1.5 %	1980	1.4 %	1990	1.7 %	2000	1.8 %
1951	1.5	1961	1.7	1971	3.2	1981	-2.4	1991	1.4	2001	-2.6
1952	0.9	1962	9.8	1972	0.3	1982	-0.6	1992	2.8	2002	-4.7
1953	0.8	1963	0.5	1973	2.1	1983	1.5	1993	-0.6	2003	1.2
1954	2.9	1964	2.3	1974	-8.8	1984	-0.7	1994	0.4	2004	-1.7
1955	4.9	1965	5.0	1975	-0.2	1985	1.5	1995	1.8	2005	1.5
1956	3.4	1966	2.1	1976	2.4	1986	-2.6	1996	-2.8	2006	2.1
1957	3.8	1967	1.3	1977	-0.6	1987	0.4	1997	3.7	2007	0.8
1958	2.0	1968	2.3	1978	0.6	1988	-0.6	1998	2.7	2008	-3.4
1959	3.3	1969	-1.5	1979	1.3	1989	0.9	1999	5.1		
Average	1.9 %		2.3 %		0.2 %		-0.1 %		1.8 %		-0.5 %

22 MONDAY 173 / 192

30 day	Wednesday July 22
60 day	Friday August 21
90 day	Sunday September 20
180 day	Saturday December 19
1 year	Tuesday June 22

23 TUESDAY 174 / 191

30 day	Thursday July 23
60 day	Saturday August 22
90 day	Monday September 21
180 day	Sunday December 20
1 year	Wednesday June 23

24 WEDNESDAY 175 / 190

30 day	Friday July 24
60 day	Sunday August 23
90 day	Tuesday September 22
180 day	Monday December 21
1 year	Thursday June 24

25 THURSDAY 176 / 189

30 day	Saturday July 25
60 day	Monday August 24
90 day	Wednesday September 23
180 day	Tuesday December 22
1 year	Friday June 25

26 FRIDAY 177 / 188

30 day	Sunday July 26
60 day	Tuesday August 25
90 day	Thursday September 24
180 day	Wednesday December 23
1 year	Saturday June 26

* Weekly avg closing values- except Fed Funds Rate & CAN overnight tgt rate which are weekly closing values.

WEEK 26

Market Indices & Rates Weekly Values*

Stock Markets	2007	2008
Dow	13,390	11,652
S&P500	1,501	1,303
Nasdaq	2,594	2,358
TSX	13,774	14,438
FTSE	6,571	5,603
DAX	7,904	6,525
Nikkei	18,015	13,781
Hang Seng	21,808	22,461

Commodities	2007	2008
Oil	69.13	137.00
Gold	647.52	896.45

Bond Yields	2007	2008
USA 5 Yr Treasury	4.97	3.50
USA 10 Yr T	5.09	4.09
USA 20 Yr T	5.28	4.69
Moody's Aaa	5.80	5.67
Moody's Baa	6.68	7.08
CAN 5 Yr T	4.61	3.43
CAN 10 Yr T	4.61	3.72

Money Market	2007	2008
USA Fed Funds	5.25	2.00
USA 3 Mo T-B	4.80	1.79
CAN tgt overnight rate	4.25	3.00
CAN 3 Mo T-B	4.41	2.57

Foreign Exchange	2007	2008
USD/EUR	1.35	1.56
USD/GBP	2.00	1.98
CAN/USD	1.07	1.01
JPY/USD	123.25	107.50

JUNE

M	T	W	T	F	S	S
1	2	3	4	5	6	7
8	9	10	11	12	13	14
15	16	17	18	19	20	21
22	23	24	25	26	27	28
29	30					

JULY

M	T	W	T	F	S	S
		1	2	3	4	5
6	7	8	9	10	11	12
13	14	15	16	17	18	19
20	21	22	23	24	25	26
27	28	29	30	31		

AUGUST

M	T	W	T	F	S	S
					1	2
3	4	5	6	7	8	9
10	11	12	13	14	15	16
17	18	19	20	21	22	23
24	25	26	27	28	29	30
31						

1st Half of Year Strategy Review

Month	Strategy	Security	Quantity	Buy Date	Buy Price	Sell Date	Sell Price	Profit

Comments

Month	Strategy	Security	Quantity	Buy Date	Buy Price	Sell Date	Sell Price	Profit

Month	Strategy	Security	Quantity	Buy Date	Buy Price	Sell Date	Sell Price	Profit

Month	Strategy	Security	Quantity	Buy Date	Buy Price	Sell Date	Sell Price	Profit

Month	Strategy	Security	Quantity	Buy Date	Buy Price	Sell Date	Sell Price	Profit

Month	Strategy	Security	Quantity	Buy Date	Buy Price	Sell Date	Sell Price	Profit

Month	Strategy	Security	Quantity	Buy Date	Buy Price	Sell Date	Sell Price	Profit

Month	Strategy	Security	Quantity	Buy Date	Buy Price	Sell Date	Sell Price	Profit

29 MONDAY 180 / 185

30 day	Wednesday July 29
60 day	Friday August 28
90 day	Sunday September 27
180 day	Saturday December 26
1 year	Tuesday June 29

30 TUESDAY 181 / 184

30 day	Thursday July 30
60 day	Saturday August 29
90 day	Monday September 28
180 day	Sunday December 27
1 year	Wednesday June 30

1 WEDNESDAY 182 / 183

30 day	Friday July 31
60 day	Sunday August 30
90 day	Tuesday September 29
180 day	Monday December 28
1 year	Thursday July 1

2 THURSDAY 183 / 182

30 day	Saturday August 1
60 day	Monday August 31
90 day	Wednesday September 30
180 day	Tuesday December 29
1 year	Friday July 2

3 FRIDAY 184 / 181

30 day	Sunday August 2
60 day	Tuesday September 1
90 day	Thursday October 1
180 day	Wednesday December 30
1 year	Saturday July 3

* Weekly avg closing values- except Fed Funds Rate & CAN overnight tgt rate which are weekly closing values.

WEEK 27

Market Indices & Rates Weekly Values*

Stock Markets	2006	2007
Dow	11,174	13,573
S&P 500	1,273	1,525
Nasdaq	2,157	2,650
TSX	11,648	14,081
FTSE	5,875	6,646
DAX	5,689	8,024
Nikkei	15,473	18,165
Hang Seng	16,373	22,289

Commodities	2006	2007
Oil (WTI)	74.65	71.78
Gold (London PM)	625.09	652.58

Bond Yields	2006	2007
USA 5 Yr Treasury	5.14	5.00
USA 10 Yr Treasury	5.18	5.10
USA 20 Yr Treasury	5.34	5.27
Moody's Aaa Corporate	5.94	5.80
Moody's Baa Corporate	6.85	6.69
CAN 5 Yr Treasury	4.47	4.63
CAN 10 Yr Treasury	4.57	4.62

Money Market	2006	2007
USA Fed Funds	5.25	5.25
USA 3 Mo T-Bill	5.03	4.95
CAN tgt overnight rate	4.25	4.25
CAN 3 Mo T-Bill	4.29	4.43

Foreign Exchange	2006	2007
USD / EUR	1.28	1.36
USD / GBP	1.84	2.01
CAN / USD	1.11	1.05
JPY / USD	114.93	122.70

JULY

M	T	W	T	F	S	S
		1	2	3	4	5
6	7	8	9	10	11	12
13	14	15	16	17	18	19
20	21	22	23	24	25	26
27	28	29	30	31		

AUGUST

M	T	W	T	F	S	S
					1	2
3	4	5	6	7	8	9
10	11	12	13	14	15	16
17	18	19	20	21	22	23
24	25	26	27	28	29	30
31						

SEPTEMBER

M	T	W	T	F	S	S
	1	2	3	4	5	6
7	8	9	10	11	12	13
14	15	16	17	18	19	20
21	22	23	24	25	26	27
28	29	30				

JULY

	MONDAY	TUESDAY	WEDNESDAY
WEEK 27	29	30	1 (30) CAN Market Closed-Canada Day
WEEK 28	6 (25) USA Employment Cost Index USA The Employment Situation (8:30 am ET)	7 (24)	8 (23)
WEEK 29	13 (18)	14 (17)	15 (16) USA Empire State Manufacturing Survey - Federal Reserve Bank of New York (8:30 am ET)
WEEK 30	20 (11)	21 (10)	22 (9)
WEEK 31	27 (4) USA UBS Index of Investor Optimism (8:30 am ET)	28 (3) USA Consumer Confidence Index 10:00 am ET	29 (2) USA Federal Reserve Board's Beige Book

THURSDAY	FRIDAY
2 29	**3** 28
USA Early Market Close Independence Day)	USA Market Closed - Independence Day)
USA ISM Manufacturing Report on Business (10:00 am ET)	
9 22	**10** 21
16 15	**17** 14
USA Federal Reserve Bank of Philadelphia: Business Outlook Survey (12:00 pm ET) USA Empire State Manufacturing Survey - Federal Reserve Bank of New York (8:30 am ET)	
23 8	**24** 7
30 1	**31**
USA Employment Cost Index (8:30 am ET) USA Help-Wanted Advertising Index (10:00 am ET)	USA Strike Report (8:30 am ET) USA Chicago Purchasing Managers Index (Business Barometer) 9:45 am ET

AUGUST

M	T	W	T	F	S	S
					1	2
3	4	5	6	7	8	9
10	11	12	13	14	15	16
17	18	19	20	21	22	23
24	25	26	27	28	29	30
31						

SEPTEMBER

M	T	W	T	F	S	S
	1	2	3	4	5	6
7	8	9	10	11	12	13
14	15	16	17	18	19	20
21	22	23	24	25	26	27
28	29	30				

OCTOBER

M	T	W	T	F	S	S
			1	2	3	4
5	6	7	8	9	10	11
12	13	14	15	16	17	18
19	20	21	22	23	24	25
26	27	28	29	30	31	

NOVEMBER

M	T	W	T	F	S	S
						1
2	3	4	5	6	7	8
9	10	11	12	13	14	15
16	17	18	19	20	21	22
23	24	25	26	27	28	29
30						

JULY SUMMARY

STRATEGIES	PAGE
STRATEGIES STARTING	
18 Day Earnings Month Effect	39
Utilities – Summer Bounce	83
Gold (Metal) Shines	85
Golden Times	87
Oil – Summer/Autumn Strategy II of II	89
Mid-Summer Triple Combo	91
STRATEGIES FINISHING	
18 Day Earnings Month Effect	39
Independence Day – Full Trade Profit	75

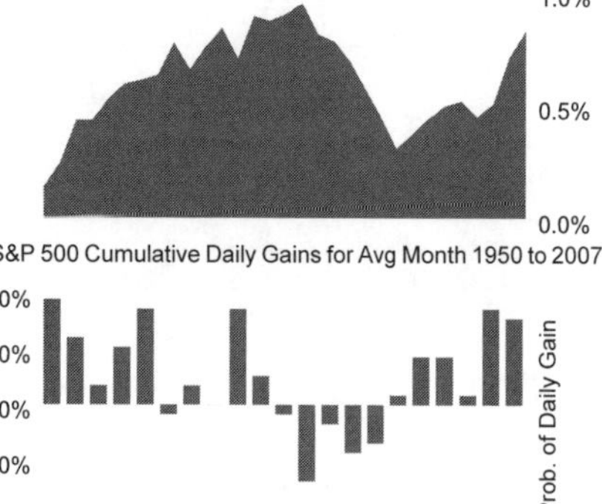

♦ When a summer rally does occur, the bulk of the gains are made in July. ♦ July gets a positive start with Independence Day (see *Independence Day Profit Before and After Fireworks* strategy). ♦ The broad market tends to do well in the first half of the month (see *18 Days Earnings Effect* strategy). ♦ The market tends to rotate a lot of sectors as it becomes more defensive. ♦ In the last half of the month the energy, gold and utility stocks start their seasonal rallies (see strategies in this month).

BEST / WORST JULY BROAD MKTS. 1998-2007

BEST JULY MARKETS

- Nasdaq (2003) 6.9%
- Russell 2000 (2005) 6.3%
- Nasdaq (2005) 6.2%

WORST JULY MARKETS

- Russell 2000 (2002) -15.2%
- Russell 3000 Val (2002) -9.9%
- Nasdaq (2002) -9.2%

Index Values End of Month

	1998	1999	2000	2001	2002	2003	2004	2005	2006	2007
Dow	8,883	10,655	10,522	10,523	8,737	9,234	10,140	10,641	11,186	13,212
S&P 500	1,121	1,329	1,431	1,211	912	990	1,102	1,234	1,277	1,455
Nasdaq	1,872	2,638	3,767	2,027	1,328	1,735	1,887	2,185	2,091	2,546
TSX	6,931	7,081	10,406	7,690	6,605	7,258	8,458	10,423	11,831	13,869
Russell 1000	1,125	1,328	1,454	1,225	931	1,016	1,129	1,288	1,331	1,523
Russell 2000	1,046	1,108	1,244	1,205	975	1,183	1,370	1,689	1,741	1,929
Russell 3000 Growth	2,107	2,577	3,183	2,084	1,471	1,639	1,764	1,988	1,955	2,305
Russell 3000 Value	1,929	2,149	2,012	2,166	1,773	1,922	2,216	2,589	2,809	3,099

Percent Gain for July

	1998	1999	2000	2001	2002	2003	2004	2005	2006	2007
Dow	-0.8	-2.9	0.7	0.2	-5.5	2.8	-2.8	3.6	0.3	-1.5
S&P 500	-1.2	-3.2	-1.6	-1.1	-7.9	1.6	-3.4	3.6	0.5	-3.2
Nasdaq	-1.2	-1.8	-5.0	-6.2	-9.2	6.9	-7.8	6.2	-3.7	-2.2
TSX	-5.9	1.0	2.1	-0.6	-7.6	3.9	-1.0	5.3	1.9	-0.3
Russell 1000	-1.3	-3.1	-1.7	-1.5	-7.5	1.8	-3.6	3.8	0.1	-3.2
Russell 2000	-8.2	-2.8	-3.3	-5.5	-15.2	6.2	-6.8	6.3	-3.3	-6.9
Russell 3000 Growth	-1.4	-3.2	-4.5	-3.0	-6.2	2.8	-6.0	5.0	-2.2	-1.9
Russell 3000 Value	-2.5	-3.0	1.3	-0.5	-9.9	1.5	-1.9	2.9	1.9	-5.1

July Market Avg. Performance 1998 to 2007 (1)

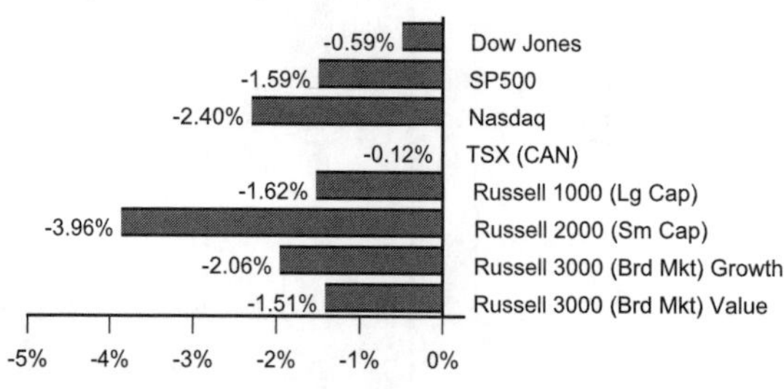

Interest Corner Jul(2)

	Fed Funds % (3)	3 Mo. T-Bill % (4)	10 Yr % (5)	20 Yr % (6)
2007	5.25	4.96	4.78	5.00
2006	5.25	5.10	4.99	5.17
2005	3.25	3.42	4.28	4.56
2004	1.25	1.45	4.50	5.24
2003	1.00	0.96	4.49	5.43

(1) Russell Data provided by Russell (2) Federal Reserve Bank of St. Louis - end of month values (3) Target rate set by FOMC (4)(5)(6) Constant yield maturities.

JULY SECTOR / SUB-SECTOR PERFORMANCE

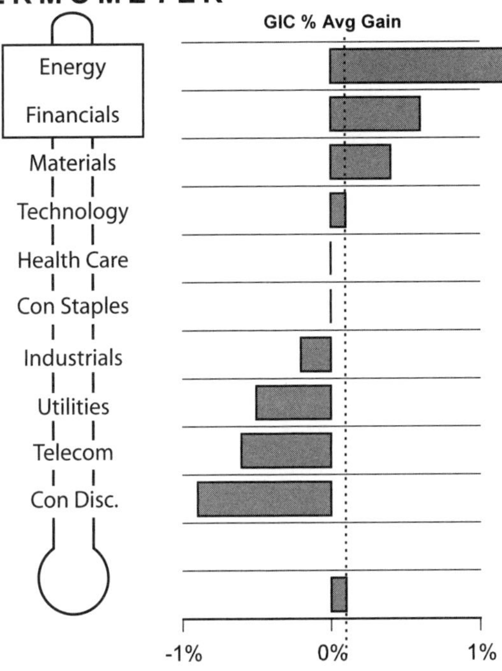

GIC[2] % Avg Gain	Fq % Gain >S&P 500	
SP GIC SECTOR 1990-2007[1]		
1.2	67	Energy
0.6	50	Financials
0.4	67	Materials
0.1	44	Information Technology
0.0	44	Health Care
0.0	61	Consumer Staples
-0.2	44	Industrials
-0.5	44	Utilities
-0.6	50	Telecom
-0.9	39	Consumer Discretionary
0.6 %	N/A %	S&P 500

GIC % Avg Gain	Fq % Gain >S&P 500	
SUB-SECTOR 1990-2007[3]		
6.0 %	81 %	Biotech (92-2007)
1.4	61	Oil Integrated
0.6	63	Insurance
0.6	69	Banks
0.6	56	Metals & Mining
0.3	44	Transportation
0.3	56	Oil & Gas Exploration & Production
-0.3	56	Retailing
-0.3	50	Autos & Components
-0.4	50	Pharmaceuticals
-0.7	31	Airlines
-0.9	44	Gold (XAU)
-3.0	22	Software & Services
-4.6	46	Semiconductor (SOX) (95-2007)

Sector

♦ On a percentage gain basis, Energy jumps to the top of the pack followed by Financials and Materials.♦ Although the Financial sector has a slightly higher return than the Materials sector, its frequency of beating the S&P 500 is lower. ♦ July's performance is really the tale of two half months. In the first half of the month, the broad market tends to do very well (see *18 Day Earnings Month Effect*). In the second half the performance tends to wither away. This is the time that the Energy sector tends to do well relative to the broad market. ♦ Energy carries its outperformance through to the beginning of October.

Sub-Sector

♦ Biotechnology stocks dominate with an average 6.0% gain and beating the S&P 500 81% of the time (see *Biotech Summer Solstice Strategy*). ♦ The Oil Integrated sub-sector benefits from the outperformance of Energy which tends to start in the second half of the month.

(1) Sector data provided by Standard and Poors (2) GIC is short form for Global Industry Classification (3) Sub Sector data provided by Standard and Poors, except where marked by symbol.

UTILITIES – SUMMER BOUNCE

July 17th to Oct 3rd

Utility stocks are a long forgotten part of the market. Very seldom do you hear pundits sponsoring their virtues. They lost out to the hype of tech stocks in the 90's and are still shunned by a large number of investors because of the fear of rising interest rates. Despite the environment of neglect, utility stocks have managed to outperform the S&P 500 on a fairly consistent basis from July 17th to October 3rd.

3.8% better and positive at a time when the S&P 500 has been negative

Utilities' outperformance from the end of July to the end of September fits in very well with the theme of investors taking a defensive position during this time of year. At this time the broad market tends to produce a negative return and investors are looking for a safe place to invest. Utilities fit the bill.

S&P Utilities Sector vs. S&P 500 1990 to 2007

Jul 17 to Oct 3	Utilities	SP500	Diff (Positive shaded)
1990	-3.4 %	-15.6 %	12.2 %
1991	9.2	0.8	8.5
1992	-0.9	-1.7	0.8
1993	3.6	3.5	0.1
1994	-1.6	1.7	-3.3
1995	6.6	4.0	2.5
1996	-0.9	10.3	-11.2
1997	2.6	3.0	-0.4
1998	6.8	-15.3	22.1
1999	-5.5	-9.6	4.1
2000	23.0	-5.5	28.5
2001	-13.6	-10.8	-2.8
2002	-12.0	-9.1	-2.9
2003	7.2	3.6	3.6
2004	5.1	2.7	2.4
2005	6.0	-0.1	6.1
2006	5.3	7.9	-2.6
2007	0.6	-0.6	1.2
Avg.	2.1 %	-1.7 %	3.8 %

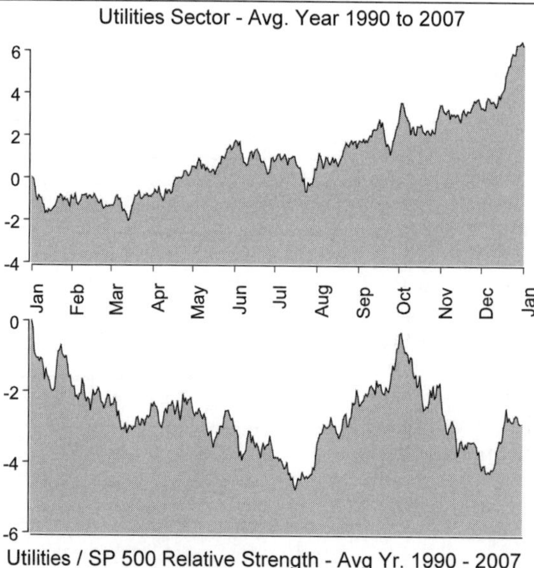

From July 17th to October 3rd, during the years 1990 to 2007, the utilities sector has produced an average return of 2.1%, while the S&P 500 reached into the negative territory with a -1.7% return. Utilities have produced 3.8% more when the S&P 500 has typically been negative. Also, during this time period the utilities sector beat the S&P 500, 12 out of 18 times. Not bad for a defensive sector. The utilities sector is considered defensive because it is a slow growth mature industry that has stable income from long term contracts. When the market gets "spooked," investors typically switch their money into companies with stable earnings.

There is an added bonus of investing in utilities – dividends. Because the sector is mature with stable earnings they tend to pay out a higher dividend yield.

In the last two decades there have been two periods of two back-to-back years of negative performance. In 1996 and 1997 the utilities sector underperformed as the stock market was in a strong bull run. At this time dividends and defensive positions did not matter much and utilities fell by the wayside. In 2001 and 2002 the utilities sector underperformed as a few scandal ridden utilities companies hit the newspaper headlines. The most notorious being Enron.

It appears the utilities trade is once again back on track as the companies have "cleaned house" and moved back to their core business: providing utilities services.

Utilities SP GIC Sector 55:
An index designed to represent a cross section of utility companies.

For more information on the utilities sector, see www.standardandpoors.com.

6 MONDAY 187 / 178

30 day	Wednesday August 5
60 day	Friday September 4
90 day	Sunday October 4
180 day	Saturday January 2
1 year	Tuesday July 6

7 TUESDAY 188 / 177

30 day	Thursday August 6
60 day	Saturday September 5
90 day	Monday October 5
180 day	Sunday January 3
1 year	Wednesday July 7

8 WEDNESDAY 189 / 176

30 day	Friday August 7
60 day	Sunday September 6
90 day	Tuesday October 6
180 day	Monday January 4
1 year	Thursday July 8

9 THURSDAY 190 / 175

30 day	Saturday August 8
60 day	Monday September 7
90 day	Wednesday October 7
180 day	Tuesday January 5
1 year	Friday July 9

10 FRIDAY 191 / 174

30 day	Sunday August 9
60 day	Tuesday September 8
90 day	Thursday October 8
180 day	Wednesday January 6
1 year	Saturday July 10

* Weekly avg closing values- except Fed Funds Rate & CAN overnight tgt rate which are weekly closing values.

WEEK 28

Market Indices & Rates Weekly Values*

Stock Markets	**2006**	**2007**
Dow	10,967	13,700
S&P 500	1,255	1,532
Nasdaq	2,085	2,674
TSX	11,690	14,266
FTSE	5,817	6,675
DAX	5,582	8,017
Nikkei	15,244	18,157
Hang Seng	16,411	22,844
Commodities	**2006**	**2007**
Oil (WTI)	75.21	72.79
Gold (London PM)	643.90	663.94
Bond Yields	**2006**	**2007**
USA 5 Yr Treasury	5.06	5.00
USA 10 Yr Treasury	5.10	5.10
USA 20 Yr Treasury	5.25	5.27
Moody's Aaa Corporate	5.85	5.81
Moody's Baa Corporate	6.76	6.69
CAN 5 Yr Treasury	4.32	4.64
CAN 10 Yr Treasury	4.45	4.63
Money Market	**2006**	**2007**
USA Fed Funds	5.25	5.25
USA 3 Mo T-Bill	5.06	4.96
CAN tgt overnight rate	4.25	4.50
CAN 3 Mo T-Bill	4.19	4.50
Foreign Exchange	**2006**	**2007**
USD / EUR	1.27	1.37
USD / GBP	1.84	2.03
CAN / USD	1.13	1.05
JPY / USD	115.06	122.43

JULY

M	T	W	T	F	S	S
		1	2	3	4	5
6	7	8	9	10	11	12
13	14	15	16	17	18	19
20	21	22	23	24	25	26
27	28	29	30	31		

AUGUST

M	T	W	T	F	S	S
					1	2
3	4	5	6	7	8	9
10	11	12	13	14	15	16
17	18	19	20	21	22	23
24	25	26	27	28	29	30
31						

SEPTEMBER

M	T	W	T	F	S	S
	1	2	3	4	5	6
7	8	9	10	11	12	13
14	15	16	17	18	19	20
21	22	23	24	25	26	27
28	29	30				

(Metal)

GOLD SHINES

Gold (Metal) Outperforms – July 12th to October 9th

"Foul cankering rust the hidden treasure frets, but gold that's put to use more gold begets."

(William Shakespeare, *Venus and Adonis*)

For many years gold was thought to be a dead investment. It was only the "gold bugs" that espoused the virtues of investing in the precious metal. Investors were mezmorized with technology stocks. Central bankers, confident of their currencies, were selling gold, "left, right and center."

3.6% when the S&P 500 has been negative & 58% of the time positive

Times have changed, as they always do, and investors have taken a shine to the metal. In the last few years gold has substantially outperformed the stock market. On a seasonal basis, on average from 1984 to 2007, gold has done well relative to the stock market from July 12th to October 9th. The reasons for gold's seasonal changes in price movements, jewellery production and central bank selling cycles, have been put forward in the *Golden Times* strategy page. The movement of gold stock prices, represented by the index (XAU) on the Philadelphia Exchange, coincides closely with the price of gold (metal). Although there is a strong correlation between gold and gold stocks, there are other factors, such as company operations and hedging policies which determine each company's price in the market.

Gold (Metal) London PM vs S&P 500
1984 to 2007

Jul 12 to Oct 9th	Gold	S&P 500	Diff (Positive shaded)
1984	0.5 %	7.4 %	-6.9 %
1985	4.1	-5.4	9.5
1986	25.2	-2.6	27.8
1987	3.9	0.9	3.0
1988	-7.5	2.8	-10.3
1989	-4.2	9.4	-13.6
1990	12.1	-15.5	27.6
1991	-2.9	0.0	-2.8
1992	0.4	-2.9	3.3
1993	-8.8	2.7	-11.5
1994	1.6	1.6	0.0
1995	-0.1	4.3	-4.3
1996	-0.4	7.9	-8.3
1997	4.4	5.9	-1.5
1998	2.8	-15.5	18.2
1999	25.6	-4.8	30.4
2000	-4.5	-5.3	0.8
2001	8.4	-10.5	18.8
2002	1.7	-16.2	17.9
2003	7.8	4.1	3.8
2004	3.8	0.8	2.9
2005	11.4	-1.9	13.4
2006	-8.8	6.1	-14.9
2007	11.0	3.1	8.0
Avg.	3.6 %	-1.0 %	4.6 %

Gold (metal) has typically started its seasonal strong period a few weeks earlier than gold stocks and finished just after they have turned down.

Gold (metal), during its seasonal strength has been positive 67% of the time and has been positive the last eight years in a row. From 1984, it has produced a gain of 3.7% and beaten the S&P 500 by an average 4.7%.

One of the major benefits of using the gold (metal) seasonal strategy is that it provides a place to invest during a time when the stock market has typically been negative.

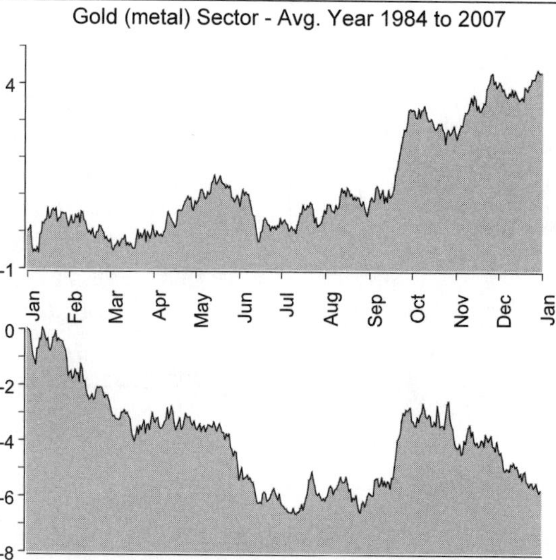

Cliff Warning -- Similar to the XAU pattern, the price of gold tends to correct severely in October.

Source: Bank of England London PM is recognized as the world benchmark for gold prices. London PM represents the close value of gold in afternoon trading in London.

13 MONDAY 194 / 171

30 day	Wednesday August 12
60 day	Friday September 11
90 day	Sunday October 11
180 day	Saturday January 9
1 year	Tuesday July 13

14 TUESDAY 195 / 170

30 day	Thursday August 13
60 day	Saturday September 12
90 day	Monday October 12
180 day	Sunday January 10
1 year	Wednesday July 14

15 WEDNESDAY 196 / 169

30 day	Friday August 14
60 day	Sunday September 13
90 day	Tuesday October 13
180 day	Monday January 11
1 year	Thursday July 15

16 THURSDAY 197 / 168

30 day	Saturday August 15
60 day	Monday September 14
90 day	Wednesday October 14
180 day	Tuesday January 12
1 year	Friday July 16

17 FRIDAY 198 / 167

30 day	Sunday August 16
60 day	Tuesday September 15
90 day	Thursday October 15
180 day	Wednesday January 13
1 year	Saturday July 17

* Weekly avg closing values- except Fed Funds Rate & CAN overnight tgt rate which are weekly closing values.

WEEK 29

Market Indices & Rates Weekly Values*

Stock Markets	**2006**	**2007**
Dow	10,871	13,938
S&P 500	1,244	1,546
Nasdaq	2,044	2,703
TSX	11,491	14,503
FTSE	5,730	6,630
DAX	5,470	7,981
Nikkei	14,676	18,127
Hang Seng	16,229	23,032

Commodities	**2006**	**2007**
Oil (WTI)	73.98	74.92
Gold (London PM)	643.14	671.07

Bond Yields	**2006**	**2007**
USA 5 Yr Treasury	5.03	4.93
USA 10 Yr Treasury	5.07	5.03
USA 20 Yr Treasury	5.23	5.19
Moody's Aaa Corporate	5.82	5.74
Moody's Baa Corporate	6.75	6.62
CAN 5 Yr Treasury	4.30	4.62
CAN 10 Yr Treasury	4.43	4.60

Money Market	**2006**	**2007**
USA Fed Funds	5.25	5.25
USA 3 Mo T-Bill	5.11	4.97
CAN tgt overnight rate	4.25	4.50
CAN 3 Mo T-Bill	4.15	4.49

Foreign Exchange	**2006**	**2007**
USD / EUR	1.26	1.38
USD / GBP	1.84	2.04
CAN / USD	1.13	1.04
JPY / USD	115.06	122.03

JULY

M	T	W	T	F	S	S
		1	2	3	4	5
6	7	8	9	10	11	12
13	14	15	16	17	18	19
20	21	22	23	24	25	26
27	28	29	30	31		

AUGUST

M	T	W	T	F	S	S
					1	2
3	4	5	6	7	8	9
10	11	12	13	14	15	16
17	18	19	20	21	22	23
24	25	26	27	28	29	30
31						

SEPTEMBER

M	T	W	T	F	S	S
	1	2	3	4	5	6
7	8	9	10	11	12	13
14	15	16	17	18	19	20
21	22	23	24	25	26	27
28	29	30				

(Stocks)

GOLDEN TIMES

Gold Stocks Outperform – July 27th to September 25th

Gold stocks were shunned for many years. It is only recently that interest has sparked again. What few investors know is that even during the twenty year bear market in gold that started in 1981, it was possible to make money in gold stocks.

7.9% when the S&P 500 has been negative

From 1984 (start of the XAU index) to 2007, gold stocks as represented by the XAU index, have outperformed the S&P 500 from July 27th to September 25th. One factor that has led to a rise in the price of gold stocks in August and September is the Indian festival and wedding season that starts in October and finishes in November during Diwali. The Asian culture places a great emphasis on gold as a store of value and a lot of it is "consumed" as jewellery during the festival and wedding season. The price of gold tends to increase in the months preceding this season as the jewellery fabricators purchase gold to make their final product.

XAU (Gold Stocks) vs S&P 500
1984 to 2007

Jul 27 to Sep 25	XAU	S&P 500	Diff (Positive shaded)
1984	20.8 %	10.4 %	10.4 %
1985	-5.5	-6.1	0.6
1986	36.9	-3.5	40.4
1987	23.0	3.5	19.5
1988	-11.9	1.7	-13.7
1989	10.5	1.8	8.7
1990	3.8	-13.4	17.2
1991	-11.9	1.6	-13.5
1992	-3.8	0.7	-4.5
1993	-7.3	1.9	-9.2
1994	18.2	1.4	16.8
1995	-1.0	3.6	-4.6
1996	-1.0	7.9	-8.9
1997	8.7	-0.1	8.8
1998	12.0	-8.4	20.5
1999	16.9	-5.2	22.1
2000	-2.8	-0.9	-1.9
2001	3.2	-15.8	19.0
2002	29.8	-1.5	31.4
2003	11.0	0.5	10.5
2004	16.5	2.4	14.1
2005	20.5	-1.3	21.8
2006	-11.9	4.6	-16.8
2007	14.0	2.3	11.7
Avg.	7.9 %	-0.5 %	8.4 %

Gold stocks (XAU) Sector - Avg. Year 1984 to 2007

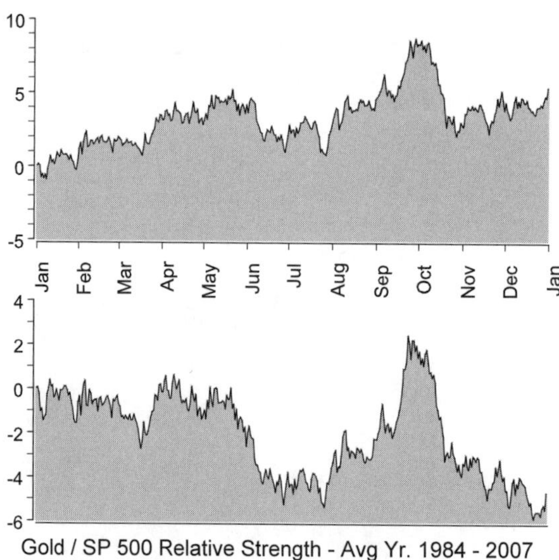

Gold / SP 500 Relative Strength - Avg Yr. 1984 - 2007

The August-September increase in gold stocks coincides with the time that a lot of investors are pulling their money out of the broad market and are looking for a place to invest. If you believe in the merits of gold stocks, this is definitely a great time to consider.

Be careful. Just as the gold stocks tend to go up in August-September, they also tend to go down in October. The fall can be rather abrupt so getting out a little early might be prudent.

Two main factors affecting the decrease in gold stock prices are the decreased demand for gold by jewellery fabricators and the increased selling of European Central Banks' gold reserves.

Every year, at the end of September, the European Central Banks agree on an allotment of their gold reserves that they are allowed to sell. In past years this created a lot of selling pressure at the end of September and October. In more recent years the Central Banks have lost their appetite for selling their gold, reducing the downward pressure on price at this time of year.

XAU is an index traded on the Philadelphia exchange. It consists of 12 precious metal mining companies.

20 MONDAY 201 / 164

30 day	Wednesday August 19
60 day	Friday September 18
90 day	Sunday October 18
180 day	Saturday January 16
1 year	Tuesday July 20

21 TUESDAY 202 / 163

30 day	Thursday August 20
60 day	Saturday September 19
90 day	Monday October 19
180 day	Sunday January 17
1 year	Wednesday July 21

22 WEDNESDAY 203 / 162

30 day	Friday August 21
60 day	Sunday September 20
90 day	Tuesday October 20
180 day	Monday January 18
1 year	Thursday July 22

23 THURSDAY 204 / 161

30 day	Saturday August 22
60 day	Monday September 21
90 day	Wednesday October 21
180 day	Tuesday January 19
1 year	Friday July 23

24 FRIDAY 205 / 160

30 day	Sunday August 23
60 day	Tuesday September 22
90 day	Thursday October 22
180 day	Wednesday January 20
1 year	Saturday July 24

* Weekly avg closing values- except Fed Funds Rate & CAN overnight tgt rate which are weekly closing values.

WEEK 30

Market Indices & Rates Weekly Values*

Stock Markets	2006	2007
Dow	11,115	13,637
S&P 500	1,268	1,502
Nasdaq	2,071	2,628
TSX	11,768	14,047
FTSE	5,893	6,409
DAX	5,618	7,681
Nikkei	15,041	17,762
Hang Seng	16,711	23,197

Commodities	2006	2007
Oil (WTI)	73.87	75.15
Gold (London PM)	622.97	674.31

Bond Yields	2006	2007
USA 5 Yr Treasury	4.98	4.74
USA 10 Yr Treasury	5.05	4.88
USA 20 Yr Treasury	5.21	5.09
Moody's Aaa Corporate	5.82	5.64
Moody's Baa Corporate	6.72	6.61
CAN 5 Yr Treasury	4.24	4.59
CAN 10 Yr Treasury	4.37	4.54

Money Market	2006	2007
USA Fed Funds	5.25	5.25
USA 3 Mo T-Bill	5.10	4.96
CAN tgt overnight rate	4.25	4.50
CAN 3 Mo T-Bill	4.15	4.55

Foreign Exchange	2006	2007
USD / EUR	1.27	1.37
USD / GBP	1.85	2.05
CAN / USD	1.14	1.05
JPY / USD	116.22	119.98

JULY

M	T	W	T	F	S	S
		1	2	3	4	5
6	7	8	9	10	11	12
13	14	15	16	17	18	19
20	21	22	23	24	25	26
27	28	29	30	31		

AUGUST

M	T	W	T	F	S	S
					1	2
3	4	5	6	7	8	9
10	11	12	13	14	15	16
17	18	19	20	21	22	23
24	25	26	27	28	29	30
31						

SEPTEMBER

M	T	W	T	F	S	S
	1	2	3	4	5	6
7	8	9	10	11	12	13
14	15	16	17	18	19	20
21	22	23	24	25	26	27
28	29	30				

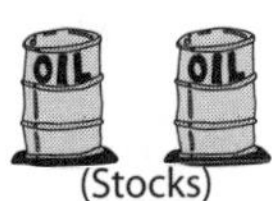

OIL – SUMMER/AUTUMN STRATEGY

IInd of II Oil Stock Strategies for the Year
July 24th to October 3rd

Oil stocks tend to outperform the market once again (see *Oil - Winter/Spring Strategy* for first wave of outperformance from late February to early May, and for details on the XOI oil index). Although the first wave has had an incredible record of outperformance, the second wave is still noteworthy. While the first wave has more to do with inventories during the switch from producing heating oil to gasoline, the second wave has more to do with the conversion of production from gasoline to heating oil and the effects of hurricane season.

Extra 2.9 % &
63% of the time better than S&P 500

First, there is a large difference between how heating oil and gasoline is stored and consumed. For the average individual and business, gasoline is consumed in a fairly immediate fashion. It is stored by the local distributor and the supplies are drawn upon as needed. Heating oil, on the other hand is largely inventoried by individuals, farms and business operations in rural areas in large amounts. The inventory process starts well before the cold weather arrives. Further down the line the production facilities have to start switching from gasoline to heating oil, dropping their inventory levels and boosting prices.

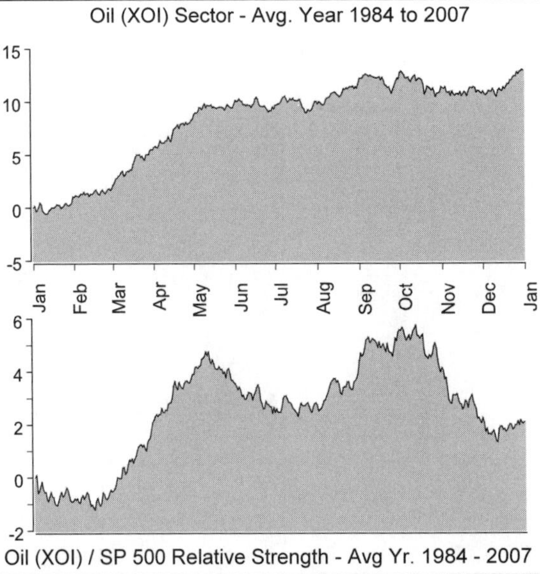

XOI vs. S&P 500
1984 to 2007

Jul 24 to Oct 3	XOI	S&P 500	Diff (Positive shaded)
1984	9.0	9.1	-0.1
1985	6.7	-4.3	11.0
1986	15.7	-2.1	17.7
1987	-1.2	6.6	-7.8
1988	-3.6	3.0	-6.6
1989	5.7	5.6	0.1
1990	-0.5	-12.4	11.8
1991	0.7	1.3	-0.7
1992	2.9	-0.4	3.3
1993	7.8	3.2	4.6
1994	-3.6	1.9	-5.5
1995	-2.2	5.2	-7.4
1996	7.7	10.5	-2.8
1997	8.9	3.0	5.9
1998	1.4	-12.0	13.5
1999	-2.1	-5.5	3.3
2000	12.2	-3.6	15.8
2001	-5.1	-10.0	4.8
2002	7.3	2.7	4.6
2003	5.5	4.2	1.4
2004	10.9	4.2	6.7
2005	14.3	-0.6	14.9
2006	-8.5	7.6	-16.9
2007	-4.2	-0.1	-4.1
Avg	3.6 %	0.7 %	2.9 %

Second, hurricane season can play havoc with the production of oil and drive up prices substantially. Every year hurricane season arrives in the Gulf of Mexico. The official duration of the season is from June 1st to November 30th, but most major hurricanes occur in September and early October. The threat of a strong hurricane can shut down the oil platforms temporarily, interrupting production. If a strong hurricane strikes the oil platforms it can do significant damage and put the platform out of commission for an extended period of time.

The hurricane season is unpredictable. Overall, the trend has been for more and stronger hurricanes each year. A lot of experts believe that global warming is the main cause for increased hurricane activity. If they are correct, we can only expect the impact of hurricane season to increase.

27 MONDAY 208 / 157

30 day	Wednesday August 26
60 day	Friday September 25
90 day	Sunday October 25
180 day	Saturday January 23
1 year	Tuesday July 27

28 TUESDAY 209 / 156

30 day	Thursday August 27
60 day	Saturday September 26
90 day	Monday October 26
180 day	Sunday January 24
1 year	Wednesday July 28

29 WEDNESDAY 210 / 155

30 day	Friday August 28
60 day	Sunday September 27
90 day	Tuesday October 27
180 day	Monday January 25
1 year	Thursday July 29

30 THURSDAY 211 / 154

30 day	Saturday August 29
60 day	Monday September 28
90 day	Wednesday October 28
180 day	Tuesday January 26
1 year	Friday July 30

31 FRIDAY 212 / 153

30 day	Sunday August 30
60 day	Tuesday September 29
90 day	Thursday October 29
180 day	Wednesday January 27
1 year	Saturday July 31

* Weekly avg closing values- except Fed Funds Rate & CAN overnight tgt rate which are weekly closing values.

WEEK 31

Market Indices & Rates Weekly Values*

Stock Markets	2006	2007
Dow	11,199	13,316
S&P 500	1,277	1,460
Nasdaq	2,082	2,554
TSX	11,916	13,753
FTSE	5,894	6,268
DAX	5,665	7,497
Nikkei	15,466	17,075
Hang Seng	16,970	22,672

Commodities	2006	2007
Oil (WTI)	75.20	76.75
Gold (London PM)	644.16	665.90

Bond Yields	2006	2007
USA 5 Yr Treasury	4.89	4.60
USA 10 Yr Treasury	4.96	4.77
USA 20 Yr Treasury	5.14	5.00
Moody's Aaa Corporate	5.76	5.63
Moody's Baa Corporate	6.65	6.62
CAN 5 Yr Treasury	4.19	4.56
CAN 10 Yr Treasury	4.31	4.51

Money Market	2006	2007
USA Fed Funds	5.25	5.25
USA 3 Mo T-Bill	5.10	4.91
CAN tgt overnight rate	4.25	4.50
CAN 3 Mo T-Bill	4.15	4.55

Foreign Exchange	2006	2007
USD / EUR	1.28	1.37
USD / GBP	1.88	2.03
CAN / USD	1.13	1.06
JPY / USD	114.68	118.81

JULY

M	T	W	T	F	S	S
		1	2	3	4	5
6	7	8	9	10	11	12
13	14	15	16	17	18	19
20	21	22	23	24	25	26
27	28	29	30	31		

AUGUST

M	T	W	T	F	S	S
					1	2
3	4	5	6	7	8	9
10	11	12	13	14	15	16
17	18	19	20	21	22	23
24	25	26	27	28	29	30
31						

SEPTEMBER

M	T	W	T	F	S	S
	1	2	3	4	5	6
7	8	9	10	11	12	13
14	15	16	17	18	19	20
21	22	23	24	25	26	27
28	29	30				

MID-SUMMER TRIPLE COMBO

Oil Stocks, Gold Stocks and Utility Stocks Prosper from July 27th to September 25th

Would you like some utilities with your oil and gold stocks? Why not! Unlike fast food this combination has been good for you. The full meal deal (gold, oil and utility stocks) is a good order for the summer time as all three sectors have typically increased at the same time of year (July 27th to September 25th).

3.0% average return & 67% of the time better than the S&P 500

Part of the value of this combination is that the sectors have not always increased together in the same year. For example, in 2000 during the seasonal combo time period, gold stocks lost ground as the gold market failed to gain traction in its new bull market. Gold stocks returned -2.8%. During the same time period, oil stocks were up 8.9% and utility stocks were up 17.3%, producing an overall blended combination return of 7.8%. This was 8.7% better than the S&P 500. In 2001 and 2002 the tables turned with gold stocks making up for the performance of the oil and utility stocks. The end result in both cases was the *Mid-Summer Triple Combo* outperforming the S&P 500.

From 1990 to 2007 the gold, oil and utility stock combo has produced a positive return of 3.0%, which is 4.1% better than the S&P 500 over the same time period. What makes this combo so attractive is that it occurs during the summer months when the market typically has a negative return.

Although the gold stocks are clearly the outperforming winner, they have typically been more volatile. Adding oil stocks and utilities to the order, despite lowering the return, has added to the frequency of outperforming the S&P 500. Gold stocks have outperformed the S&P 500 61% of the time, oil stocks 61% and utility stocks 61%. The combination of all three has produced an outperformance 67% of the time.

For convenience we have made the triple combo 1/3 gold, 1/3 oil and 1/3 utilities. An investor's mix depends on risk tolerance and expectations. At the time of this writing, using the S&P GIC sector weights, the energy (oil) sector represented 11% of the market, utilities 4%, and gold under 2% of the S&P 500. If you are managing your portfolio relative to these benchmarks, oil stocks should generally be favored as it is the largest sector.

Combo Gold Stocks & Oil Stocks & Utility Stocks vs S&P 500 Jul 27 to Sep 25, 1990 to 2007

Performance > S&P 500 (shaded)

Year	XAU	XOI	Utilities	Avg Combo	SP500
1990	3.8%	2.1%	-4.3%	0.5%	-13.4 %
1991	-11.9	0.5	4.8	-2.2	1.6
1992	-3.8	3.5	0.0	-0.1	0.7
1993	-7.3	1.5	2.3	-1.2	1.9
1994	18.2	-3.8	-2.8	3.9	1.4
1995	-1.0	-2.0	2.2	-0.3	3.6
1996	-1.0	6.7	1.5	2.4	7.9
1997	8.7	6.8	3.3	6.3	-0.1
1998	12.0	2.4	4.6	6.4	-8.4
1999	16.9	-2.1	-7.5	2.4	-5.2
2000	-2.8	8.9	17.3	7.8	-0.9
2001	3.2	-14.3	-13.0	-8.0	-15.8
2002	29.8	-1.8	-3.5	8.2	-1.5
2003	11.0	2.9	2.7	5.5	0.5
2004	16.5	9.0	6.0	10.5	2.4
2005	20.5	13.1	2.6	12.1	-1.3
2006	-11.9	-12.8	-0.1	-8.3	4.6
2007	14.0	4.1	5.6	7.9	2.3
Avg.	6.4%	1.4%	1.2%	3.0%	-1.1 %

When you are finished your seasonal triple combo, make sure that you do not come back for seconds at the end of September - it is not good for you. All three sectors have typically started their underperformance relative to the S&P 500 at this time.

For a detailed analysis of each sector in the combo, please see the proceeding strategy pages in the month of July.

3 MONDAY 215 / 150

30 day	Wednesday September 2
60 day	Friday October 2
90 day	Sunday November 1
180 day	Saturday January 30
1 year	Tuesday August 3

4 TUESDAY 216 / 149

30 day	Thursday September 3
60 day	Saturday October 3
90 day	Monday November 2
180 day	Sunday January 31
1 year	Wednesday August 4

5 WEDNESDAY 217 / 148

30 day	Friday September 4
60 day	Sunday October 4
90 day	Tuesday November 3
180 day	Monday February 1
1 year	Thursday August 5

6 THURSDAY 218 / 147

30 day	Saturday September 5
60 day	Monday October 5
90 day	Wednesday November 4
180 day	Tuesday February 2
1 year	Friday August 6

7 FRIDAY 219 / 146

30 day	Sunday September 6
60 day	Tuesday October 6
90 day	Thursday November 5
180 day	Wednesday February 3
1 year	Saturday August 7

* Weekly avg closing values- except Fed Funds Rate & CAN overnight tgt rate which are weekly closing values.

WEEK 32

Market Indices & Rates Weekly Values*

Stock Markets	2006	2007
Dow	11,136	13,428
S&P 500	1,270	1,470
Nasdaq	2,065	2,565
TSX	11,978	13,566
FTSE	5,830	6,240
DAX	5,648	7,472
Nikkei	15,494	16,960
Hang Seng	17,164	22,123

Commodities	2006	2007
Oil (WTI)	75.63	71.92
Gold (London PM)	646.80	669.22

Bond Yields	2006	2007
USA 5 Yr Treasury	4.87	4.60
USA 10 Yr Treasury	4.94	4.79
USA 20 Yr Treasury	5.13	5.06
Moody's Aaa Corporate	5.76	5.78
Moody's Baa Corporate	6.65	6.66
CAN 5 Yr Treasury	4.19	4.55
CAN 10 Yr Treasury	4.32	4.52

Money Market	2006	2007
USA Fed Funds	5.25	5.25
USA 3 Mo T-Bill	5.08	4.83
CAN tgt overnight rate	4.25	4.50
CAN 3 Mo T-Bill	4.15	4.56

Foreign Exchange	2006	2007
USD / EUR	1.28	1.37
USD / GBP	1.90	2.03
CAN / USD	1.12	1.05
JPY / USD	115.35	118.59

AUGUST

M	T	W	T	F	S	S
					1	2
3	4	5	6	7	8	9
10	11	12	13	14	15	16
17	18	19	20	21	22	23
24	25	26	27	28	29	30
31						

SEPTEMBER

M	T	W	T	F	S	S
	1	2	3	4	5	6
7	8	9	10	11	12	13
14	15	16	17	18	19	20
21	22	23	24	25	26	27
28	29	30				

OCTOBER

M	T	W	T	F	S	S
			1	2	3	4
5	6	7	8	9	10	11
12	13	14	15	16	17	18
19	20	21	22	23	24	25
26	27	28	29	30	31	

AUGUST

	MONDAY	TUESDAY	WEDNESDAY
WEEK 32	**3** 28 CAN Market Closed- Civic Day USA ISM Manufacturing Report on Business (10:00 am ET)	**4** 27	**5** 26 USA ISM Non-Manufacturing Report on Business (10:00 am ET)
WEEK 33	**10** 21	**11** 20 USA FOMC Meetings	**12** 19
WEEK 34	**17** 14 USA Empire State Manufacturing Survey - Federal Reserve Bank of New York (8:30 am ET)	**18** 13	**19** 12
WEEK 35	**24** 7 USA UBS Index of Investor Optimism (8:30 am ET)	**25** 6 USA Consumer Confidence Index 10:00 am ET	**26** 5
WEEK 36	**31** USA Chicago Purchasing Managers Index (Business Barometer) 9:45 am ET	1	2

THURSDAY		FRIDAY	
6	25	**7**	24
		USA The Employment Situation (8:30 am ET)	
13	18	**14**	17
20	11	**21**	10
USA Federal Reserve Bank of Philadelphia: Business Outlook Survey (12:00 pm ET)			
27	4	**28**	3
USA Help-Wanted Advertising Index (10:00 am ET)		USA Strike Report (8:30 am ET)	
3		**4**	

SEPTEMBER

M	T	W	T	F	S	S
	1	2	3	4	5	6
7	8	9	10	11	12	13
14	15	16	17	18	19	20
21	22	23	24	25	26	27
28	29	30				

OCTOBER

M	T	W	T	F	S	S
			1	2	3	4
5	6	7	8	9	10	11
12	13	14	15	16	17	18
19	20	21	22	23	24	25
26	27	28	29	30	31	

NOVEMBER

M	T	W	T	F	S	S
						1
2	3	4	5	6	7	8
9	10	11	12	13	14	15
16	17	18	19	20	21	22
23	24	25	26	27	28	29
30						

DECEMBER

M	T	W	T	F	S	S
	1	2	3	4	5	6
7	8	9	10	11	12	13
14	15	16	17	18	19	20
21	22	23	24	25	26	27
28	29	30	31			

AUGUST SUMMARY

STRATEGIES	PAGE
STRATEGIES STARTING	
Agriculture Moooves	97
Gas For 5 Months	99
Health Care August Prescription Renewal	103
STRATEGIES FINISHING	
None	

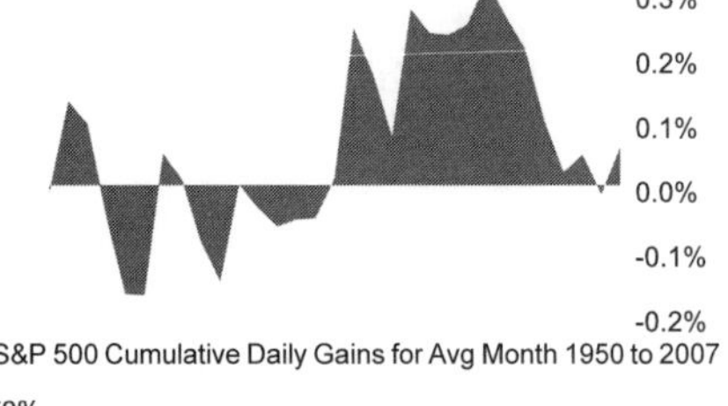

S&P 500 Cumulative Daily Gains for Avg Month 1950 to 2007

August has been a poor month across all major markets. ♦ The averages in the table below are influenced by very poor returns in 1998 when the Asian Financial Crisis rippled through the stock market. ♦ If there is a summer rally, it is often in jeopardy in August. Over the last ten years the S&P 500 has only been positive 60% of the time. ♦ Ironically, the best August over the last ten years occurred in 2000 (Nasdaq 11.7%; Russell 3000, 9.1%, and the TSX (Canada) 8.1%.

BEST / WORST AUGUST BROAD MKTS. 1998-2007

BEST AUGUST MARKETS

- Nasdaq (2000) 11.7%
- Russell 3000 Gr (2000) 9.1%
- TSX (2000) 8.1%

WORST AUGUST MARKETS

- TSX (1998) -20.2%
- Nasdaq (1998) -19.9%
- Russell 2000 (1998) -19.5%

Index Values End of Month

	1998	1999	2000	2001	2002	2003	2004	2005	2006	2007
Dow	7,539	10,829	11,215	9,950	8,664	9,416	10,174	10,482	11,381	13,358
S&P 500	957	1,320	1,518	1,134	916	1,008	1,104	1,220	1,304	1,474
Nasdaq	1,499	2,739	4,206	1,805	1,315	1,810	1,838	2,152	2,184	2,596
TSX	5,531	6,971	11,248	7,399	6,612	7,517	8,377	10,669	12,074	13,660
Russell 1000	956	1,314	1,559	1,149	934	1,035	1,132	1,275	1,360	1,540
Russell 2000	842	1,066	1,337	1,165	972	1,236	1,362	1,656	1,791	1,970
Russell 3000 Growth	1,776	2,608	3,473	1,915	1,474	1,682	1,751	1,959	2,013	2,341
Russell 3000 Value	1,637	2,065	2,118	2,080	1,780	1,951	2,242	2,567	2,851	3,127

Percent Gain for August

	1998	1999	2000	2001	2002	2003	2004	2005	2006	2007
Dow	-15.1	1.6	6.6	-5.4	-0.8	2.0	0.3	-1.5	1.7	1.1
S&P 500	-14.6	-0.6	6.1	-6.4	0.5	1.8	0.2	-1.1	2.1	1.3
Nasdaq	-19.9	3.8	11.7	-10.9	-1.0	4.3	-2.6	-1.5	4.4	2.0
TSX	-20.2	-1.6	8.1	-3.8	0.1	3.6	-1.0	2.4	2.1	-1.5
Russell 1000	-15.1	-1.1	7.3	-6.2	0.4	1.9	0.3	-1.1	2.2	1.1
Russell 2000	-19.5	-3.8	7.5	-3.3	-0.4	4.5	-0.6	-1.9	2.8	2.2
Russell 3000 Growth	-15.7	1.2	9.1	-8.1	0.2	2.6	-0.8	-1.4	3.0	1.5
Russell 3000 Value	-15.1	-3.9	5.3	-4.0	0.4	1.5	1.2	-0.9	1.5	0.9

August Market Avg. Performance 1998 to 2007 (1)

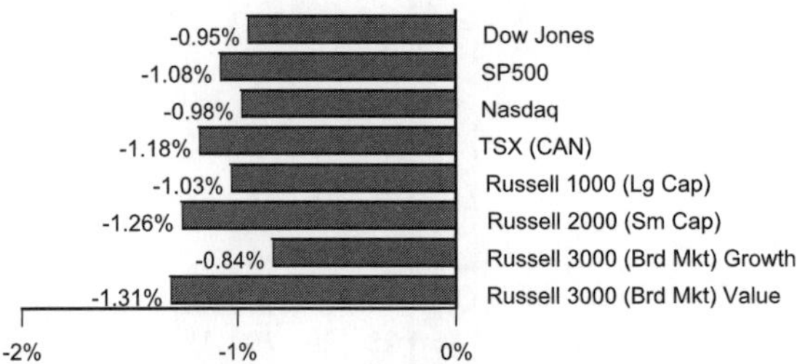

Interest Corner Aug(2)

	Fed Funds % (3)	3 Mo. T-Bill % (4)	10 Yr % (5)	20 Yr % (6)
2007	5.25	4.01	4.54	4.87
2006	5.25	5.05	4.74	4.95
2005	3.50	3.52	4.02	4.30
2004	1.50	1.59	4.13	4.93
2003	1.00	0.98	4.45	5.33

(1) Russell Data provided by Russell (2) Federal Reserve Bank of St. Louis- end of month values (3) Target rate set by FOMC (4)(5)(6) Constant yield maturities.

THACKRAY SECTOR THERMOMETER

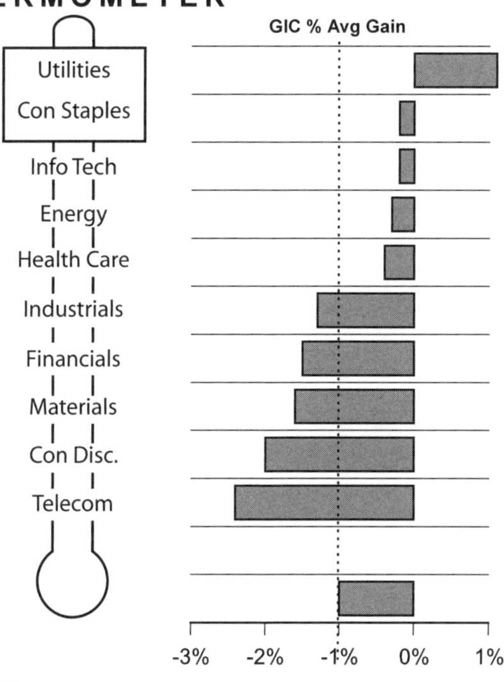

GIC[2] % Avg Gain	Fq % Gain >S&P 500	SP GIC SECTOR 1990-2007[1]
1.1 %	72 %	Utilities
-0.2	67	Consumer Staples
-0.2	56	Information Technology
-0.3	50	Energy
-0.4	72	Health Care
-1.3	28	Industrials
-1.5	39	Financials
-1.6	44	Materials
-2.0	28	Consumer Discretionary
-2.4	39	Telecom
-1.0 %	N/A %	S&P 500

GIC % Avg Gain	Fq % Gain >S&P 500	SUB-SECTOR 1990-2007[3]
1.7 %	61 %	Oil & Gas Exploration & Production
1.4	56	Biotech (92-2007)
0.9	61	Gold (XAU)
-0.4	44	Oil Integrated
-0.4	46	Semiconductor (SOX) (95-2007)
-0.7	67	Pharmaceuticals
-0.8	56	Software & Services
-0.9	44	Banks
-1.4	50	Metals & Mining
-1.6	50	Retailing
-2.1	31	Insurance
-3.4	31	Autos & Components
-3.4	25	Transportation
-5.7	25	Airlines

Sector

♦ There has only been one positive sector in the month of August – Utilities. Investors use this sector as a safe haven. Not knowing where to put their money in the summer months, investors are attracted to the stability and safety of the high dividend yielding utilities sector. ♦ The Energy sector is relatively flat and is still on the list as its performance tends to pick up once again in September.

Sub-Sector

♦ Choosing the right sub-sectors in this month is important. In several cases the parent sector has flat or negative performance but the related child sub-sector has a respectable positive performance. ♦ The Oil and Gas Exploration and Production (E&P) sub-sector has an average return of 1.7% and has beaten the S&P 500 61% of the time. ♦ The E&P sub-sector tends to be more speculative than the Oil Integrated sector and often leads the sector into a period of outperformance. The Energy sector ramps up its outperformance towards the end of the month. ♦ Gold stocks, unlike its parent sector, Materials, outperform the S&P 500 (see *Golden Times Strategy*).

(1) Sector data provided by Standard and Poors (2) GIC is short form for Global Industry Classification (3) Sub Sector data provided by Standard and Poors, except where marked by symbol.

AGRICULTURE MOOOVES LAST 5 MONTHS OF THE YEAR – Aug to Dec

Agriculture, one of the hot sectors in recent years, has typically been hot during the last five months of the year (August to December). This is the result of the major summer growing season in the northern hemisphere producing cash for the growers and subsequently increasing sales for the farming suppliers (fertilizer, farming machinery - see note at bottom of page for description of sector).

Agriculture vs. S&P 500 1994 to 2007

Aug 1 to Dec 31	Agri	S&P 500	Diff (Positive shaded)
1994 %	8.0 %	0.2 %	7.8 %
1995	31.7	9.6	22.1
1996	30.2	15.7	14.5
1997	14.6	1.7	13.0
1998	-3.4	9.7	-13.1
1999	-2.6	10.6	-13.2
2000	68.0	-7.7	75.7
2001	12.5	-5.2	17.7
2002	6.0	-3.5	9.5
2003	15.8	12.3	3.5
2004	44.6	10.0	34.6
2005	7.5	1.1	6.4
2006	-27.4	11.1	-38.5
2007	38.2	0.9	37.3
Avg.	17.4 %	4.7 %	12.7 %

79% of the time better than the S&P 500

Although this sector can represent a good opportunity, investors should be wary of the wide performance swings. Out of the fourteen cycles from August to December, there have been six years with absolute returns +/- 25%, and nine years +/- 10%

Agriculture Sector - Avg. Year 1994 to 2007

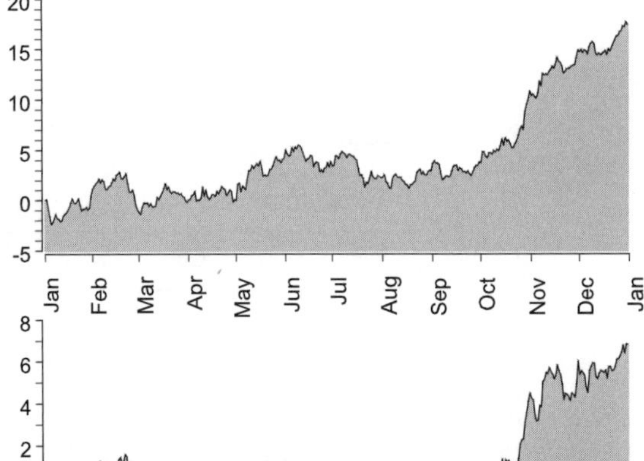

Agriculture / SP 500 Relative Strength - Avg Yr. 1994 - 2007

In 2007 and the first half of 2008, the agriculture sector rocketed upwards due to the increase in prices of agricultural products, which in turn were a result of worldwide food shortages. The major driver of this trend has been the increasing wealth in the Asian countries, creating a diet change of greater meat consumption. As it requires nine times the amount of grain to produce a pound of meat, than a pound of grain itself, grain shortages have ensued.

The results of major trend changes such as the above are often overestimated in the short-term and underestimated in the long-term. On a go forward basis, seasonal investing should help "skim the cream off the top" of the agriculture sector.

On a year by year basis, the year 2000 produced the biggest return at 68%, the same year the technology bubble burst. The agriculture sector benefited from the market correction because investors were looking for a safe haven to invest in – people need to eat, regardless of the performance of worldwide stock markets. The negative performance of 2006 was a correction from the rapid rise of the sector in the first half of the year. This time period was the start of investors having an epiphany that the world might be running out of food and as the market marched upwards, it produced some big swings.

The SP GICS Agriculture Sector # 30202010

For more information on the agriculture sector, see www.standardandpoors.com

10 MONDAY 222 / 143

30 day	Wednesday September 9
60 day	Friday October 9
90 day	Sunday November 8
180 day	Saturday February 6
1 year	Tuesday August 10

11 TUESDAY 223 / 142

30 day	Thursday September 10
60 day	Saturday October 10
90 day	Monday November 9
180 day	Sunday February 7
1 year	Wednesday August 11

12 WEDNESDAY 224 / 141

30 day	Friday September 11
60 day	Sunday October 11
90 day	Tuesday November 10
180 day	Monday February 8
1 year	Thursday August 12

13 THURSDAY 225 / 140

30 day	Saturday September 12
60 day	Monday October 12
90 day	Wednesday November 11
180 day	Tuesday February 9
1 year	Friday August 13

14 FRIDAY 226 / 139

30 day	Sunday September 13
60 day	Tuesday October 13
90 day	Thursday November 12
180 day	Wednesday February 10
1 year	Saturday August 14

WEEK 33

Market Indices & Rates
Weekly Values*

Stock Markets	2006	2007
Dow	11,274	13,010
S&P 500	1,290	1,429
Nasdaq	2,131	2,491
TSX	11,992	13,123
FTSE	5,894	6,079
DAX	5,786	7,399
Nikkei	15,974	16,308
Hang Seng	17,344	21,267

Commodities	2006	2007
Oil (WTI)	71.79	72.05
Gold (London PM)	629.97	664.82

Bond Yields	2006	2007
USA 5 Yr Treasury	4.85	4.42
USA 10 Yr Treasury	4.90	4.70
USA 20 Yr Treasury	5.11	5.05
Moody's Aaa Corporate	5.70	5.85
Moody's Baa Corporate	6.61	6.70
CAN 5 Yr Treasury	4.16	4.36
CAN 10 Yr Treasury	4.29	4.43

Money Market	2006	2007
USA Fed Funds	5.25	5.25
USA 3 Mo T-Bill	5.10	4.23
CAN tgt overnight rate	4.25	4.50
CAN 3 Mo T-Bill	4.11	4.33

Foreign Exchange	2006	2007
USD / EUR	1.28	1.35
USD / GBP	1.89	1.99
CAN / USD	1.12	1.07
JPY / USD	115.89	116.34

AUGUST

M	T	W	T	F	S	S
					1	2
3	4	5	6	7	8	9
10	11	12	13	14	15	16
17	18	19	20	21	22	23
24	25	26	27	28	29	30
31						

SEPTEMBER

M	T	W	T	F	S	S
	1	2	3	4	5	6
7	8	9	10	11	12	13
14	15	16	17	18	19	20
21	22	23	24	25	26	27
28	29	30				

OCTOBER

M	T	W	T	F	S	S
			1	2	3	4
5	6	7	8	9	10	11
12	13	14	15	16	17	18
19	20	21	22	23	24	25
26	27	28	29	30	31	

* Weekly avg closing values- except Fed Funds Rate & CAN overnight tgt rate which are weekly closing values.

GAS FOR 5 MONTHS

Natural Gas (Commodity) – Outperforms last 5 months Cash price increases from Aug 1st to Dec 21st

The *Gas For 5 Months* strategy is based on work by Don Vialoux. Don runs a highly regarded investment website, www.timingthemarket.ca, where he has highlighted the natural gas trade in his writings.

We may not use natural gas ourselves, but most of us depend on it in one way or another. It is used for furnaces and hot water tanks and is usually responsible for producing some portion of the electrical power that we consume. As a result, there are two high consumption times for natural gas: winter and summer. The colder it gets in winter, the more natural gas is consumed to keep the furnaces going. The warmer it gets in the summer, the more natural gas is used to produce power for air conditioners.

On the supply side, weather also plays a large factor in determining price. During the hurricane season in the Gulf of Mexico, the price of natural gas is effected by the forecast for the number, severity and impact of hurricanes. The tail end of the hurricane season occurs in late autumn and early winter, at the same time distributors are accumulating natural gas inventories for the winter heating season. The result is that the price of natural gas tends to rise in the last five months of the year. As the price is very dependent on the weather, it is also extremely volatile. Large percentage moves are not uncommon.

There are two noteworthy anomalies in natural gas prices during the year. First, March has a high frequency of positive occurrences as this is the month that distributors start to accumulate inventory for summertime cooling. Second, as a result of hurricane season being over and the slowdown by distributors in accumulating natural gas inventories for winter heating, the price of natural gas frequently decreases during the last part of December. The *Seasonal Gains* table illustrates high frequency of declines from December 22nd to the end of the year.

Natural Gas (Cash) Henry Hub LA
Seasonal Gains 1995 to 2007

	Negative	Positive	Negative
	Jan 1 to Jul 31	Aug 1 to Dec 21	Dec 22 to Dec 31
1995		144.6 %	-11.9 %
1996	-16.0 %	90.0	-7.7
1997	-45.2	6.8	-4.6
1998	-18.1	10.8	-4.0
1999	32.1	1.2	-12.9
2000	62.6	180.7	5.4
2001	-68.2	-19.3	5.8
2002	11.0	67.2	-9.1
2003	0.9	49.5	-16.8
2004	4.7	13.3	-15.7
2005	28.9	74.7	-31.0
2006	-15.5	-24.3	-14.5
2007	18.7	7.7	-1.1
Avg.	-0.3 %	46.4 %	-9.1 %

Natural Gas (Cash) Henry Hub LA
Avg. Year 1996 to 2007

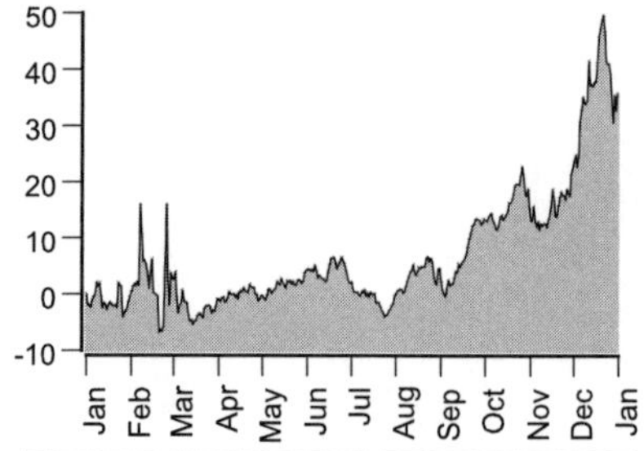

Caution:
The cash price for natural gas is extremely volatile and extreme caution should be used. Futures and options are used to invest in natural gas utilize leverage. Care must be taken to ensure that investments are within risk tolerances.

Source: New York Mercantile Exchange. NYMX is an exchange provider of futures and options.

Natural Gas (Cash Price) Henry Hub Louisiana % Month Gain

	Jan	Feb	Mar	Apr	May	Jun	Jul	Aug	Sep	Oct	Nov	Dec	Year
1996	27	-16	-3	-22	6	13	-13	-26	8	47	39	6	47
1997	-28	-39	6	13	6	-6	3	22	16	3	-25	-6	-44
1998	-6	3	5	-5	-4	12	-22	-14	38	-19	-9	18	-15
1999	-6	-8	19	13	0	4	10	13	-20	21	-22	6	19
2000	17	0	7	8	45	-4	-14	27	8	-15	46	64	353
2001	-44	-11	3	-12	-21	-21	12	-34	-17	68	-40	47	-74
2002	-21	16	28	15	-14	2	-6	3	31	7	-5	10	69
2003	22	94	-54	5	14	-11	-13	5	-4	-15	22	19	25
2004	1	-9	7	3	11	-7	0	-16	26	1	6	-11	5
2005	2	8	13	-11	-5	11	11	64	17	-18	-4	-19	58
2006	-8	-23	4	-5	-10	-2	38	-28	-37	81	25	-34	-42
2007	41	-7	4	3	1	-18	2	-16	12	18	0	-2	29
Avg	0%	1%	3%	0%	3%	-2%	1%	0%	7%	15%	3%	8%	36%

17 MONDAY 229 / 136

30 day	Wednesday September 16
60 day	Friday October 16
90 day	Sunday November 15
180 day	Saturday February 13
1 year	Tuesday August 17

18 TUESDAY 230 / 135

30 day	Thursday September 17
60 day	Saturday October 17
90 day	Monday November 16
180 day	Sunday February 14
1 year	Wednesday August 18

19 WEDNESDAY 231 / 134

30 day	Friday September 18
60 day	Sunday October 18
90 day	Tuesday November 17
180 day	Monday February 15
1 year	Thursday August 19

20 THURSDAY 232 / 133

30 day	Saturday September 19
60 day	Monday October 19
90 day	Wednesday November 18
180 day	Tuesday February 16
1 year	Friday August 20

21 FRIDAY 233 / 132

30 day	Sunday September 20
60 day	Tuesday October 20
90 day	Thursday November 19
180 day	Wednesday February 17
1 year	Saturday August 21

* Weekly avg closing values- except Fed Funds Rate & CAN overnight tgt rate which are weekly closing values.

WEEK 34

Market Indices & Rates Weekly Values*

Stock Markets	2006	2007
Dow	11,314	13,213
S&P 500	1,296	1,460
Nasdaq	2,142	2,540
TSX	12,157	13,357
FTSE	5,885	6,156
DAX	5,803	7,470
Nikkei	16,043	16,020
Hang Seng	17,017	22,312

Commodities	2006	2007
Oil (WTI)	72.12	70.19
Gold (London PM)	624.17	659.62

Bond Yields	2006	2007
USA 5 Yr Treasury	4.77	4.34
USA 10 Yr Treasury	4.81	4.62
USA 20 Yr Treasury	5.03	5.00
Moody's Aaa Corporate	5.62	5.85
Moody's Baa Corporate	6.53	6.68
CAN 5 Yr Treasury	4.09	4.28
CAN 10 Yr Treasury	4.20	4.39

Money Market	2006	2007
USA Fed Funds	5.25	5.25
USA 3 Mo T-Bill	5.10	3.70
CAN tgt overnight rate	4.25	4.50
CAN 3 Mo T-Bill	4.12	3.95

Foreign Exchange	2006	2007
USD / EUR	1.28	1.35
USD / GBP	1.89	1.99
CAN / USD	1.11	1.06
JPY / USD	116.52	115.16

AUGUST

M	T	W	T	F	S	S
					1	2
3	4	5	6	7	8	9
10	11	12	13	14	15	16
17	18	19	20	21	22	23
24	25	26	27	28	29	30
31						

SEPTEMBER

M	T	W	T	F	S	S
	1	2	3	4	5	6
7	8	9	10	11	12	13
14	15	16	17	18	19	20
21	22	23	24	25	26	27
28	29	30				

OCTOBER

M	T	W	T	F	S	S
			1	2	3	4
5	6	7	8	9	10	11
12	13	14	15	16	17	18
19	20	21	22	23	24	25
26	27	28	29	30	31	

8n4 SMALL CAP VALUE – FIRST 8 MONTHS SMALL CAP GROWTH – LAST 4 MONTHS

Over the long-term, small companies have produced better returns than large companies. Most pundits agree that this outcome is a result of investors being rewarded for taking on greater risks. From 1979 to 2007, if an investor had invested in small value companies for the first eight months of the year and then switched to small growth companies for the last four months, they would have increased their returns even more.

For definitions of value and growth, information on the Russell small cap indices, and the trend of value outperforming growth at the beginning of the year and growth outperforming at the end, see *Value For First Four Months of Year - Growth For Last 3 Months* strategy.

It is important to note that the performance for this strategy has been very volatile. Sometimes value or growth small caps can outperform significantly in their seasonal time and other times not. Even within the year there can be a large difference in performance. On a yearly basis from 1979 the switch strategy outperformed the S&P 500, 62% of the time. Other than the four years, 1995 to 1999, when "big company" mania was occurring, the worst string of underperformance was two years in a row.

Small Cap Value & Small Cap Growth Switch Strategy*

Val>Gr ▭ Gr>Val ▭ 8n4> S&P 500 ▭

	Jan to Aug		Sep to Dec		Yr. % Gain	
Year	Sm Cap Gr	Sm Cap Val	Sm Cap Val	Sm Cap Gr	S&P 500	Sm Cap 8n4
1979	36.2%	35.7%	-5.0%	8.1%	12.3%	46.7%
1980	27.4	15.6	2.9	17.3	25.8	35.6
1981	-8.9	9.4	1.0	-1.8	-9.7	7.5
1982	-12.4	-1.6	24.4	35.2	14.8	33.1
1983	28.2	31.8	1.7	-7.3	17.3	22.2
1984	-9.3	-1.2	-0.1	-8.5	1.4	-9.6
1985	19.4	17.2	8.0	8.2	26.3	26.8
1986	10.9	10.4	-5.0	-7.4	14.6	2.2
1987	31.2	28.2	-29.1	-32.5	2.0	-13.5
1988	17.0	24.7	1.0	1.5	12.4	26.6
1989	22.4	18.8	-7.7	-2.8	27.3	15.5
1990	-16.1	-18.0	-7.7	-2.8	-6.6	-20.3
1991	36.6	34.6	2.5	9.6	26.3	47.4
1992	-10.9	10.3	14.5	19.8	4.5	32.2
1993	6.4	16.4	4.4	5.8	7.1	23.1
1994	-2.6	1.2	-4.8	-0.6	-1.5	0.6
1995	25.9	18.5	3.6	3.3	34.1	22.4
1996	5.1	5.7	12.1	5.3	20.3	11.2
1997	13.6	19.7	7.6	-1.0	31.0	18.5
1998	-25.9	-19.9	14.2	36.0	26.7	8.9
1999	5.0	-2.6	-1.4	35.8	19.5	32.3
2000	2.1	12.3	6.5	-24.2	-10.1	-14.9
2001	-14.4	8.2	3.0	5.7	-13.0	14.3
2002	-30.3	-10.2	-3.4	-0.6	-23.4	-10.7
2003	34.6	25.3	14.3	9.6	26.4	37.4
2004	-6.1	2.8	16.8	21.3	9.0	24.6
2005	1.4	3.0	-0.2	2.2	3.0	5.3
2006	3.2	10.9	9.3	9.3	13.6	21.2
2007	5.9	-4.3	-7.6	0.5	3.5	-3.7
Avg.	6.7%	10.4%	2.6%	5.0%	10.9%	15.3%
Fq >		59%		62%		62%

* Small Cap Growth (Russell 2000 Growth)
Small Cap Value (Russell 2000 Value)

CAUTION: The small cap sector can be very volatile. There can also be large performance differences between the two different styles of management, value and growth. Like all strategies in this book, proper care should be taken so that risk tolerances are not exceeded.

Total Gains From 1979 to 2007

	S&P 500	Switch Strategy Sm. Cap Val Sm. Cap Gr
Total Gain	1428%	4111%

Russell 2000 Growth less Russell 2000 Value 1979-2007

24 MONDAY 236 / 129

30 day	Wednesday September 23
60 day	Friday October 23
90 day	Sunday November 22
180 day	Saturday February 20
1 year	Tuesday August 24

25 TUESDAY 237 / 128

30 day	Thursday September 24
60 day	Saturday October 24
90 day	Monday November 23
180 day	Sunday February 21
1 year	Wednesday August 25

26 WEDNESDAY 238 / 127

30 day	Friday September 25
60 day	Sunday October 25
90 day	Tuesday November 24
180 day	Monday February 22
1 year	Thursday August 26

27 THURSDAY 239 / 126

30 day	Saturday September 26
60 day	Monday October 26
90 day	Wednesday November 25
180 day	Tuesday February 23
1 year	Friday August 27

28 FRIDAY 240 / 125

30 day	Sunday September 27
60 day	Tuesday October 27
90 day	Thursday November 26
180 day	Wednesday February 24
1 year	Saturday August 28

* Weekly avg closing values- except Fed Funds Rate & CAN overnight tgt rate which are weekly closing values.

WEEK 35

Market Indices & Rates Weekly Values*

Stock Markets	2006	2007
Dow	11,390	13,250
S&P 500	1,305	1,459
Nasdaq	2,179	2,557
TSX	12,103	13,470
FTSE	5,923	6,187
DAX	5,861	7,503
Nikkei	15,960	16,265
Hang Seng	17,221	23,486

Commodities	2006	2007
Oil (WTI)	69.89	72.93
Gold (London PM)	618.93	667.06

Bond Yields	2006	2007
USA 5 Yr Treasury	4.73	4.28
USA 10 Yr Treasury	4.76	4.55
USA 20 Yr Treasury	4.98	4.90
Moody's Aaa Corporate	5.57	5.77
Moody's Baa Corporate	6.50	6.60
CAN 5 Yr Treasury	4.03	4.28
CAN 10 Yr Treasury	4.13	4.36

Money Market	2006	2007
USA Fed Funds	5.25	5.25
USA 3 Mo T-Bill	5.06	4.17
CAN tgt overnight rate	4.25	4.50
CAN 3 Mo T-Bill	4.13	3.89

Foreign Exchange	2006	2007
USD / EUR	1.28	1.36
USD / GBP	1.90	2.01
CAN / USD	1.11	1.06
JPY / USD	117.14	115.58

AUGUST

M	T	W	T	F	S	S
					1	2
3	4	5	6	7	8	9
10	11	12	13	14	15	16
17	18	19	20	21	22	23
24	25	26	27	28	29	30
31						

SEPTEMBER

M	T	W	T	F	S	S
	1	2	3	4	5	6
7	8	9	10	11	12	13
14	15	16	17	18	19	20
21	22	23	24	25	26	27
28	29	30				

OCTOBER

M	T	W	T	F	S	S
			1	2	3	4
5	6	7	8	9	10	11
12	13	14	15	16	17	18
19	20	21	22	23	24	25
26	27	28	29	30	31	

HEALTH CARE AUGUST PRESCRIPTION RENEWAL

August 15th to October 18th

Health care stocks have traditionally been classified as defensive stocks because of the stability of their earnings. Pharmaceutical and other health care companies typically still do well in an economic downturn. Even in tough times, people still need to take their medication. As a result, investors have typically found comfort in this sector starting in the late summer doldrums and riding the momentum into early December.

3.2% more & 13 out of 18 times better than the S&P 500

From August 15th to October 18th (1990 to 2007), health care stocks have had a tendency to outperform the S&P 500 on a yearly basis. During this time period, the broad market (S&P 500) has produced an average return of 0.0%, compared with the health care stocks that produced 3.2%. Despite competing with a runaway market in 2003 and legal problems which required drugs to be withdrawn from the market in 2004, the sector has beaten the S&P 500 thirteen out of eighteen times from 1990 to 2007.

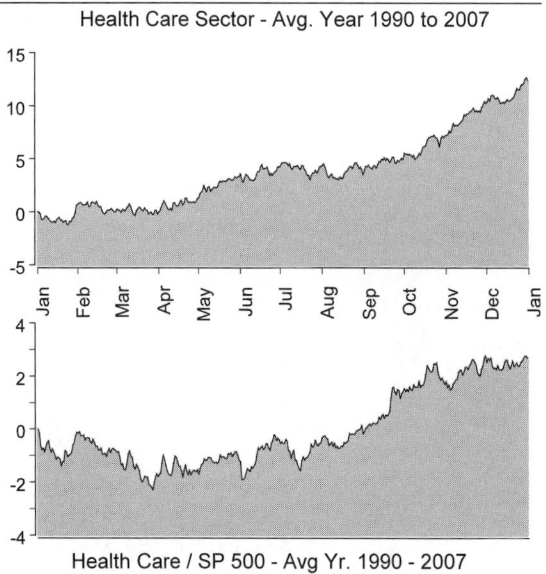

Health Care / SP 500 - Avg Yr. 1990 - 2007

The real benefit of investing in this sector has been the positive returns that have been generated when the market has typically been negative. August and September have been the worst two month combination for gains in the broad stock market. A lot of investors are uncomfortable investing in the market in the summertime, but do not want to go to cash. For these investors, finding a sector of the market that tends to do well in the summertime is golden. Health care stocks are attractive at this time because of their defensive nature.

Health Care vs. S&P 500
Performance 1990 to 2007

Aug 15 to Oct 18	Health Care	S&P 500	Diff (Positive shaded)
1990	-1.3 %	-9.9 %	8.6 %
1991	1.3	0.7	0.6
1992	-9.0	-1.9	-7.1
1993	13.5	4.1	9.5
1994	7.2	1.2	6.0
1995	11.7	4.9	6.7
1996	9.4	7.4	2.1
1997	5.8	2.1	3.7
1998	3.0	-0.6	3.6
1999	-0.5	-5.5	5.0
2000	6.9	-10.0	16.9
2001	-0.4	-10.0	9.6
2002	2.4	-3.8	6.2
2003	-0.5	4.9	-5.4
2004	-0.8	4.6	-5.4
2005	-3.1	-4.2	1.2
2006	6.4	7.7	-1.3
2007	6.0	8.0	-2.0
Avg	3.2 %	0.0 %	3.2 %

The late summer rally in health care stocks is also supported by investors increasing their positions ahead of the health care conferences that take place in September.

Alternate Strategy—As the health care sector has had a tendency to perform at par with the broad market from late October to early December, an alternative strategy is to continue holding the health care sector during this time period if the fundamentals or technicals are favorable.

Health Care SP GIC Sector# 35: An index designed to represent a cross section of utility companies. For more information on the materials sector, see www.standardandpoors.com.

31 MONDAY 243 / 122

30 day	Wednesday September 30
60 day	Friday October 30
90 day	Sunday November 29
180 day	Saturday February 27
1 year	Tuesday August 31

1 TUESDAY 244 / 121

30 day	Thursday October 1
60 day	Saturday October 31
90 day	Monday November 30
180 day	Sunday February 28
1 year	Wednesday September 1

2 WEDNESDAY 245 / 120

30 day	Friday October 2
60 day	Sunday November 1
90 day	Tuesday December 1
180 day	Monday March 1
1 year	Thursday September 2

3 THURSDAY 246 / 119

30 day	Saturday October 3
60 day	Monday November 2
90 day	Wednesday December 2
180 day	Tuesday March 2
1 year	Friday September 3

4 FRIDAY 247 / 118

30 day	Sunday October 4
60 day	Tuesday November 3
90 day	Thursday December 3
180 day	Wednesday March 3
1 year	Saturday September 4

* Weekly avg closing values- except Fed Funds Rate & CAN overnight tgt rate which are weekly closing values.

WEEK 36

Market Indices & Rates
Weekly Values*

Stock Markets	**2006**	**2007**
Dow	11,400	13,308
S&P 500	1,302	1,473
Nasdaq	2,174	2,604
TSX	11,991	13,721
FTSE	5,927	6,293
DAX	5,835	7,603
Nikkei	16,224	16,297
Hang Seng	17,291	23,978
Commodities	**2006**	**2007**
Oil (WTI)	67.14	75.96
Gold (London PM)	626.28	684.03
Bond Yields	**2006**	**2007**
USA 5 Yr Treasury	4.73	4.16
USA 10 Yr Treasury	4.79	4.48
USA 20 Yr Treasury	5.01	4.82
Moody's Aaa Corporate	5.59	5.73
Moody's Baa Corporate	6.52	6.55
CAN 5 Yr Treasury	4.02	4.28
CAN 10 Yr Treasury	4.13	4.34
Money Market	**2006**	**2007**
USA Fed Funds	5.25	5.25
USA 3 Mo T-Bill	4.97	4.30
CAN tgt overnight rate	4.25	4.50
CAN 3 Mo T-Bill	4.14	4.04
Foreign Exchange	**2006**	**2007**
USD / EUR	1.28	1.37
USD / GBP	1.88	2.02
CAN / USD	1.11	1.05
JPY / USD	116.49	115.22

SEPTEMBER

M	T	W	T	F	S	S
	1	2	3	4	5	6
7	8	9	10	11	12	13
14	15	16	17	18	19	20
21	22	23	24	25	26	27
28	29	30				

OCTOBER

M	T	W	T	F	S	S
			1	2	3	4
5	6	7	8	9	10	11
12	13	14	15	16	17	18
19	20	21	22	23	24	25
26	27	28	29	30	31	

NOVEMBER

M	T	W	T	F	S	S
						1
2	3	4	5	6	7	8
9	10	11	12	13	14	15
16	17	18	19	20	21	22
23	24	25	26	27	28	29
30						

SEPTEMBER

	MONDAY	TUESDAY	WEDNESDAY
WEEK 36	31	1 (29) USA ISM Manufacturing Report on Business (10:00 am ET)	2 (28)
WEEK 37	7 (23) USA Market Closed- Labour Day CAN Market Closed- Labour Day	8 (22)	9 (21) USA Federal Reserve Board's Beige Book
WEEK 38	14 (16)	15 (15) USA Empire State Manufacturing Survey - Federal Reserve Bank of New York (8:30 am ET)	16 (14)
WEEK 39	21 (9)	22 (8) USA FOMC Meetings	23 (7)
WEEK 40	28 (2) USA UBS Index of Investor Optimism (8:30 am ET)	29 (1) USA Consumer Confidence Index 10:00 am ET	30 USA Chicago Purchasing Managers Index (Business Barometer) 9:45 am ET

THURSDAY	FRIDAY
3 27	**4** 26
USA ISM Non-Manufacturing Report on Business (10:00 am ET)	USA The Employment Situation (8:30 am ET)
10 20	**11** 19
17 13	**18** 12
USA Federal Reserve Bank of Philadelphia: Business Outlook Survey (12:00 pm ET) USA Empire State Manufacturing Survey - Federal Reserve Bank of New York (8:30 am ET)	
24 6	**25** 5
USA Help-Wanted Advertising Index (10:00 am ET))	USA Strike Report (8:30 am ET)
1	**2**

OCTOBER

M	T	W	T	F	S	S
			1	2	3	4
5	6	7	8	9	10	11
12	13	14	15	16	17	18
19	20	21	22	23	24	25
26	27	28	29	30	31	

NOVEMBER

M	T	W	T	F	S	S
						1
2	3	4	5	6	7	8
9	10	11	12	13	14	15
16	17	18	19	20	21	22
23	24	25	26	27	28	29
30						

DECEMBER

M	T	W	T	F	S	S
	1	2	3	4	5	6
7	8	9	10	11	12	13
14	15	16	17	18	19	20
21	22	23	24	25	26	27
28	29	30	31			

JANUARY

M	T	W	T	F	S	S
				1	2	3
4	5	6	7	8	9	10
11	12	13	14	15	16	17
18	19	20	21	22	23	24
25	26	27	28	29	30	31

SEPTEMBER SUMMARY

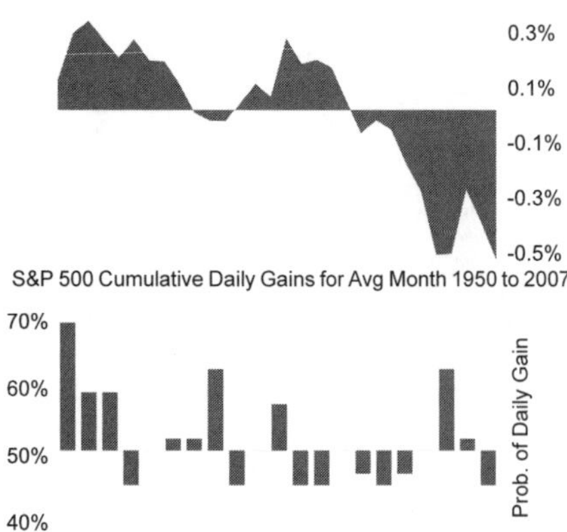

♦ September earns the sad face award (see *September Not A Favorable Month*). ♦ Although it is not always negative, overall it has not fared well. September often tests the resolve of investors, particularly in the last half of the month. ♦ Small companies, although still negative, have fared better than the large companies. ♦ Gold is golden until month end when it tends to lose its shine (see *Golden Times* strategy).

BEST / WORST SEPTEMBER BROAD MKTS. 1998-2007

BEST SEPTEMBER MARKETS

- Nasdaq (1998) 13.0%
- Russell 3000 Gr (1998) 7.7%
- Russell 2000 (1998) 7.7%

WORST SEPTEMBER MARKETS

- Nasdaq (2001) -17.0%
- Russell 2000 (2001) -13.6%
- Nasdaq (2000) -12.7%

Index Values End of Month

	1998	1999	2000	2001	2002	2003	2004	2005	2006	2007
Dow	7,843	10,337	10,651	8,848	7,592	9,275	10,080	10,569	11,679	13,896
S&P 500	1,017	1,283	1,437	1,041	815	996	1,115	1,229	1,336	1,527
Nasdaq	1,694	2,746	3,673	1,499	1,172	1,787	1,897	2,152	2,258	2,702
TSX	5,614	6,958	10,378	6,839	6,180	7,421	8,668	11,012	11,761	14,099
Russell 1000	1,018	1,276	1,486	1,050	833	1,023	1,145	1,285	1,391	1,597
Russell 2000	906	1,064	1,296	1,006	900	1,212	1,424	1,660	1,803	2,002
Russell 3000 Growth	1,913	2,558	3,154	1,714	1,322	1,660	1,772	1,967	2,063	2,434
Russell 3000 Value	1,727	1,992	2,132	1,925	1,584	1,928	2,277	2,595	2,901	3,220

Percent Gain for September

	1998	1999	2000	2001	2002	2003	2004	2005	2006	2007
Dow	4.0	-4.5	-5.0	-11.1	-12.4	-1.5	-0.9	0.8	2.6	4.0
S&P 500	6.2	-2.9	-5.3	-8.2	-11.0	-1.2	0.9	0.7	2.5	3.6
Nasdaq	13.0	0.2	-12.7	-17.0	-10.9	-1.3	3.2	0.0	3.4	4.0
TSX	1.5	-0.2	-7.7	-7.6	-6.5	-1.3	3.5	3.2	-2.6	3.2
Russell 1000	6.6	-2.9	-4.7	-8.6	-10.9	-1.2	1.1	0.8	2.3	3.7
Russell 2000	7.7	-0.1	-3.1	-13.6	-7.3	-2.0	4.6	0.2	0.7	1.6
Russell 3000 Growth	7.7	-1.9	-9.2	-10.5	-10.3	-1.3	1.2	0.4	2.5	4.0
Russell 3000 Value	5.5	-3.6	0.7	-7.5	-11.0	-1.2	1.5	1.1	1.7	3.0

September Market Avg. Performance 1998 to 2007

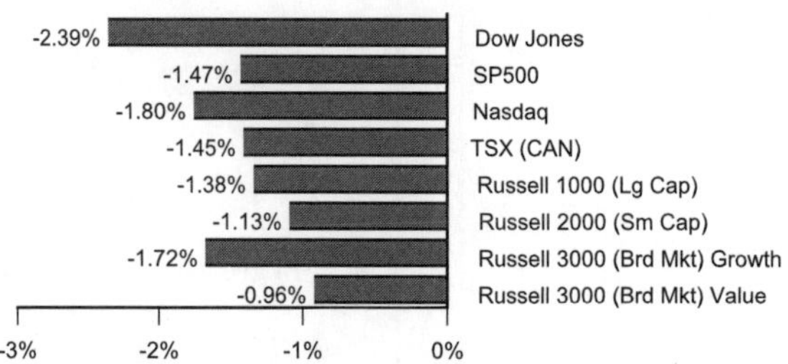

Interest Corner Sep(2)

	Fed Funds % (3)	3 Mo. T-Bill % (4)	10 Yr % (5)	20 Yr % (6)
2007	4.75	3.82	4.59	4.89
2006	5.25	4.89	4.64	4.84
2005	3.75	3.55	4.34	4.62
2004	1.75	1.71	4.14	4.89
2003	1.00	0.95	3.96	4.91

(1) Russell Data provided by Russell (2) Federal Reserve Bank of St. Louis - end of month values (3) Target rate set by FOMC (4)(5)(6) Constant yield maturities

SEPTEMBER SECTOR / SUB-SECTOR PERFORMANCE

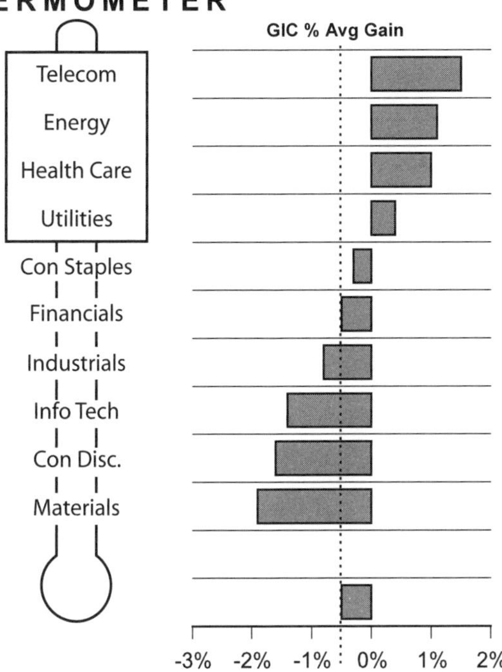

GIC[2] % Avg Gain	Fq % Gain >S&P 500	SP GIC SECTOR 1990-2007[1]
1.5 %	72 %	Telecom
1.1	61	Energy
1.0	61	Health Care
0.4	39	Utilities
-0.3	61	Consumer Staples
-0.5	61	Financials
-0.8	44	Industrials
-1.4	67	Information Technology
-1.6	39	Consumer Discretionary
-1.9	17	Materials
-0.5 %	N/A %	S&P 500

		SUB-SECTOR 1990-2007[3]
6.3 %	78 %	Gold (XAU)
1.7	50	Oil & Gas Exploration & Production
1.6	63	Biotech (92-2007)
1.3	61	Oil Integrated
1.0	67	Pharmaceuticals
0.5	61	Software & Services
0.3	56	Insurance
-0.8	39	Metals & Mining
-0.8	50	Transportation
-1.3	56	Banks
-1.3	38	Retailing
-3.1	19	Autos & Components
-3.6	38	Airlines
-6.0	23	Semiconductor (SOX) (95-2007)

Sector

♦ Defensive sectors rule this month. As investors look for a safe place to park their money, they turn to the defensive sectors. The performance of the Consumer Staples sector has been in the grey area. Although it has outperformed the S&P 500, 61% of the time, it has produced a return of -0.3%. ♦ The worst performer by far has been the Materials sector, with a -1.9% return; it has only beaten the market a dismal 17% of the time. ♦ If the Gold sub-sector were factored out of the Materials sector, the performance would be a travesty.

Sub-Sector

♦ Gold stocks are the "solid" winner with an average 6.3% gain and 78% frequency of outperformance. ♦ Caution should be used because the sector tends to peak before the end of the month (see Golden Times strategy). ♦ As the Energy sector gets closer to its seasonal finish in the beginning of October (see Oil - Summer/Autumn strategy), the more conservative Oil Integrated sub-sector moves up the ranks. ♦ The Automotive, Airlines and Semiconductor sectors make the "Bottom of the Barrel" ranking for the month with an average gain of - 3.1%, 3.6% and -6.0% respectively.

(1) Sector data provided by Standard and Poors (2) GIC is short form for Global Industry Classification (3) Sub Sector data provided by Standard and Poors, except where marked by symbol.

SEPTEMBER NOT A FAVORABLE MONTH

Wake Me Up When September Ends...
Green Day (2005)

A lot of investors feel the same way as the rock group Green Day. September has not been the best month for the markets: in fact it has been the worst.

-0.5% return & positive 43% of the time

You have to ask yourself why you would want to be invested up to your risk tolerance during the month of September. It has been positive less than half the time from 1950 to 2007 and has produced an average negative return (43% of the time positive and a return of -0.5%).

Over the years, numerous explanations have been suggested as to why September is a poor performer. The most commonly accepted reason is that in the month of September investors return from their summer vacations and get serious about their portfolios. They sell off securities that they had previously intended to sell, and generally "clean house." The result has been an underperforming September.

Another reason that the markets tend to underperform in September is that mutual fund companies clean their books of their "bad" stocks in September in order to purchase "good" stocks in October. This makes their year end holdings on their annual statements look good at the end of October.

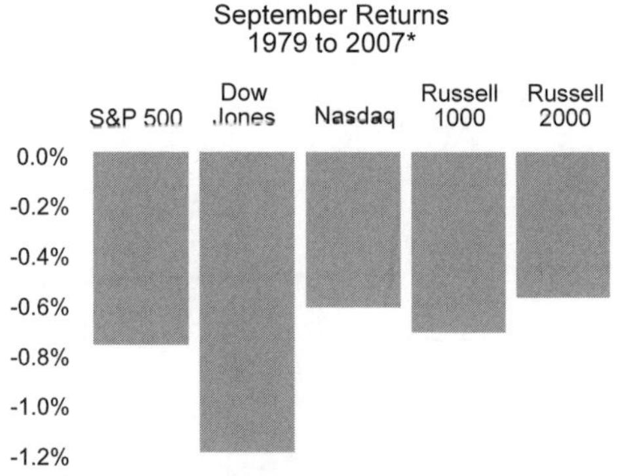

* 1979 inception year for Russell indices

The good news is that there are parts of the market in which you can hide. The basic defensive sectors: telecom, energy, health care and utilities have all produced an average positive return from 1990 to 2007 (see *September Sector/Sub-Sector Performance* page).

September's negative performance has been fairly well spread out over the decades. There have only been two decades with an average positive performance: the 1950s and the 1990s. September's performance in the 1950s was barely positive and in the 1990s it was influenced by an extremely strong bull market.

It is interesting to note that out of the broad markets, it is the Dow Jones Industrial Average that has fared the worst during the month. Although there is no known research into this phenomenon, it is possible that investors are more anxious to sell their large cap losers at this time of year and sell their small cap losers at the end of the year.

S&P 500 September Monthly % Gain 1950 to 2007 — Negative (shaded)

Year	%	Year	%	Year	%	Year	%	Year	%	Year	%
1950	5.6 %	1960	-6.0 %	1970	3.4 %	1980	2.5 %	1990	-5.1 %	2000	-5.3 %
1951	-0.1	1961	-2.0	1971	-0.7	1981	-5.4	1991	-1.9	2001	-8.2
1952	-2.0	1962	-4.8	1972	-0.5	1982	0.8	1992	0.9	2002	-11.0
1953	0.1	1963	-1.1	1973	4.0	1983	1.0	1993	-1.0	2003	-1.2
1954	8.3	1964	2.9	1974	-11.9	1984	-0.3	1994	-2.7	2004	0.9
1955	1.1	1965	3.2	1975	-3.5	1985	-3.5	1995	4.0	2005	0.7
1956	-4.5	1966	-0.7	1976	2.3	1986	-8.5	1996	5.4	2006	2.5
1957	-6.2	1967	3.3	1977	-0.2	1987	-2.4	1997	5.3	2007	3.6
1958	4.8	1968	3.9	1978	-0.7	1988	4.0	1998	6.2		
1959	-4.6	1969	-2.5	1979	0.0	1989	-0.7	1999	-2.9		
Average	0.3 %		-0.4 %		-0.8 %		-1.3 %		0.8 %		-2.3 %

7 MONDAY 250 / 115

30 day	Wednesday October 7
60 day	Friday November 6
90 day	Sunday December 6
180 day	Saturday March 6
1 year	Tuesday September 7

8 TUESDAY 251 / 114

30 day	Thursday October 8
60 day	Saturday November 7
90 day	Monday December 7
180 day	Sunday March 7
1 year	Wednesday September 8

9 WEDNESDAY 252 / 113

30 day	Friday October 9
60 day	Sunday November 8
90 day	Tuesday December 8
180 day	Monday March 8
1 year	Thursday September 9

10 THURSDAY 253 / 112

30 day	Saturday October 10
60 day	Monday November 9
90 day	Wednesday December 9
180 day	Tuesday March 9
1 year	Friday September 10

11 FRIDAY 254 / 111

30 day	Sunday October 11
60 day	Tuesday November 10
90 day	Thursday December 10
180 day	Wednesday March 10
1 year	Saturday September 11

* Weekly avg closing values- except Fed Funds Rate & CAN overnight tgt rate which are weekly closing values.

WEEK 37

Market Indices & Rates Weekly Values*

Stock Markets	2006	2007
Dow	11,505	13,319
S&P 500	1,313	1,473
Nasdaq	2,216	2,590
TSX	11,683	13,755
FTSE	5,879	6,275
DAX	5,885	7,468
Nikkei	15,815	15,878
Hang Seng	17,131	24,339
Commodities	**2006**	**2007**
Oil (WTI)	63.98	78.95
Gold (London PM)	585.14	706.90
Bond Yields	**2006**	**2007**
USA 5 Yr Treasury	4.73	4.12
USA 10 Yr Treasury	4.79	4.42
USA 20 Yr Treasury	4.99	4.73
Moody's Aaa Corporate	5.58	5.66
Moody's Baa Corporate	6.49	6.54
CAN 5 Yr Treasury	4.02	4.25
CAN 10 Yr Treasury	4.12	4.32
Money Market	**2006**	**2007**
USA Fed Funds	5.25	5.25
USA 3 Mo T-Bill	4.93	4.04
CAN tgt overnight rate	4.25	4.50
CAN 3 Mo T-Bill	4.15	3.93
Foreign Exchange	**2006**	**2007**
USD / EUR	1.27	1.39
USD / GBP	1.88	2.03
CAN / USD	1.12	1.04
JPY / USD	117.61	114.46

SEPTEMBER

M	T	W	T	F	S	S
	1	2	3	4	5	6
7	8	9	10	11	12	13
14	15	16	17	18	19	20
21	22	23	24	25	26	27
28	29	30				

OCTOBER

M	T	W	T	F	S	S
			1	2	3	4
5	6	7	8	9	10	11
12	13	14	15	16	17	18
19	20	21	22	23	24	25
26	27	28	29	30	31	

NOVEMBER

M	T	W	T	F	S	S
						1
2	3	4	5	6	7	8
9	10	11	12	13	14	15
16	17	18	19	20	21	22
23	24	25	26	27	28	29
30						

TELECOM – RINGS UP PROFITS

September 9th to October 9th

At one time the telecommunications sector was considered a defensive stable sector as it was mainly made up of land-line based telephone companies. With the advent of the wireless phone and the internet, the sector has changed into a modern, highly competitive industry. With high hopes for the "New World", massive over investment took place and the sector experienced the boom-bust scenario of the late 1990s and 2000.

2.9% extra & 11 out of 18 times better than the S&P 500

Although the sector has changed forever, a lot of the excesses in the industry have been worked out. Through it all, the industry has demonstrated seasonal tendencies that favor the transitional period of the market, starting at the beginning of September and ending at the beginning of October: the time when the market tends to perform strongly.

Telecom Sector vs. S&P 500
Sep. 9th to Oct 9th 1990 to 2007

Sep 9 to Oct 9	Telecom	SP 500	Diff (Positive shaded)
1990	6.1 %	-5.7 %	11.7 %
1991	-3.7	-3.2	-0.6
1992	-1.4	-2.8	1.5
1993	-2.7	0.8	-3.5
1994	-3.6	-3.8	0.2
1995	6.7	1.0	5.7
1996	5.1	6.3	-1.2
1997	9.7	4.2	5.5
1998	5.0	-3.8	8.8
1999	8.5	-0.6	9.1
2000	-1.2	-6.2	5.0
2001	9.1	-2.7	11.8
2002	-8.3	-13.1	4.8
2003	-5.2	0.7	-5.9
2004	2.3	0.5	1.8
2005	-5.0	-2.9	-2.1
2006	3.5	4.0	-0.5
2007	7.2	7.7	-0.5
Avg.	1.8 %	-1.1 %	2.9 %

Telecom Sector - Avg. Year 1990 to 2007

Jan Feb Mar Apr May Jun Jul Aug Sep Oct Nov Dec Jan

Telecom / SP 500 Relative Strength - Avg Yr. 1990 - 2007

The performance of the telecom sector relative to the S&P 500, from the beginning of the year to September is like a dying cell phone battery: it just keeps fading. It is only at the beginning of September that the fortunes of the sector turn around.

On a yearly basis the telecom sector has outperformed quite consistently. From 1990 to 2007, the biggest loss for the sector during its period of seasonal strength took place in 2003. In the last three years (2005-2007) telecom has marginally underperformed the market.

In the past, traditional telephone companies were known as widows and orphans stocks because they did not change much in price, and paid out high dividends. In times of uncertainty and a poor market, investors were attracted to sectors that have high dividends and a more stable earning base. With the advent of deregulation, competition entered the market. Regardless of economic conditions, households would keep their phone lines. Today's telecom market is totally different. Earnings have been built on the rapid growth of wireless telephone usage, ancillary products and services, and other entertainment communications.

As a lot of the revenue for the industry is based on more discretionary expenditures, it is possible that in a future major slump in the stock market, the telecom sector may not provide the refuge it has in the past.

14 MONDAY 257 / 108

30 day	Wednesday October 14
60 day	Friday November 13
90 day	Sunday December 13
180 day	Saturday March 13
1 year	Tuesday September 14

15 TUESDAY 258 / 107

30 day	Thursday October 15
60 day	Saturday November 14
90 day	Monday December 14
180 day	Sunday March 14
1 year	Wednesday September 15

16 WEDNESDAY 259 / 106

30 day	Friday October 16
60 day	Sunday November 15
90 day	Tuesday December 15
180 day	Monday March 15
1 year	Thursday September 16

17 THURSDAY 260 / 105

30 day	Saturday October 17
60 day	Monday November 16
90 day	Wednesday December 16
180 day	Tuesday March 16
1 year	Friday September 17

18 FRIDAY 261 / 104

30 day	Sunday October 18
60 day	Tuesday November 17
90 day	Thursday December 17
180 day	Wednesday March 17
1 year	Saturday September 18

* Weekly avg closing values- except Fed Funds Rate & CAN overnight tgt rate which are weekly closing values.

WEEK 38

Market Indices & Rates Weekly Values*

Stock Markets	2006	2007
Dow	11,550	13,709
S&P 500	1,319	1,514
Nasdaq	2,234	2,645
TSX	11,662	13,907
FTSE	5,861	6,362
DAX	5,920	7,667
Nikkei	15,786	16,227
Hang Seng	17,493	25,255
Commodities	**2006**	**2007**
Oil (WTI)	61.40	82.26
Gold (London PM)	582.40	726.08
Bond Yields	**2006**	**2007**
USA 5 Yr Treasury	4.66	4.25
USA 10 Yr Treasury	4.71	4.57
USA 20 Yr Treasury	4.91	4.87
Moody's Aaa Corporate	5.49	5.77
Moody's Baa Corporate	6.40	6.65
CAN 5 Yr Treasury	3.96	4.29
CAN 10 Yr Treasury	4.06	4.38
Money Market	**2006**	**2007**
USA Fed Funds	5.25	4.75
USA 3 Mo T-Bill	4.93	3.92
CAN tgt overnight rate	4.25	4.50
CAN 3 Mo T-Bill	4.16	4.04
Foreign Exchange	**2006**	**2007**
USD / EUR	1.27	1.40
USD / GBP	1.89	2.00
CAN / USD	1.12	1.01
JPY / USD	117.22	115.33

SEPTEMBER

M	T	W	T	F	S	S
	1	2	3	4	5	6
7	8	9	10	11	12	13
14	15	16	17	18	19	20
21	22	23	24	25	26	27
28	29	30				

OCTOBER

M	T	W	T	F	S	S
			1	2	3	4
5	6	7	8	9	10	11
12	13	14	15	16	17	18
19	20	21	22	23	24	25
26	27	28	29	30	31	

NOVEMBER

M	T	W	T	F	S	S
						1
2	3	4	5	6	7	8
9	10	11	12	13	14	15
16	17	18	19	20	21	22
23	24	25	26	27	28	29
30						

TRANSPORTATION – ON A ROLL

September 24th to November 13th

Many investors believe that transportation stocks measure the health of the economy. When the economy is expanding there is a greater need for companies to move goods and people, and transportation stocks respond accordingly. In fact, the Dow Theory, one of the oldest market timing models is built on the relationship between rail stocks (transportation) and industrial stocks. One of the basic premises of the theory is that direction of the transportation and industrial indexes lead the overall direction of the market.

3.4% extra compared with the S&P 500
In a short period of time

From a seasonal perspective the transportation sector tends to do well starting in late September, ahead of the broad market. This trend appears in both the absolute graph (top graph) and the relative performance graph (bottom graph). Investors should be attentive to the trade, as on average, the transportation sector puts in a definitive bottom at the end of September, and then puts in a solid performance for a short period of time.

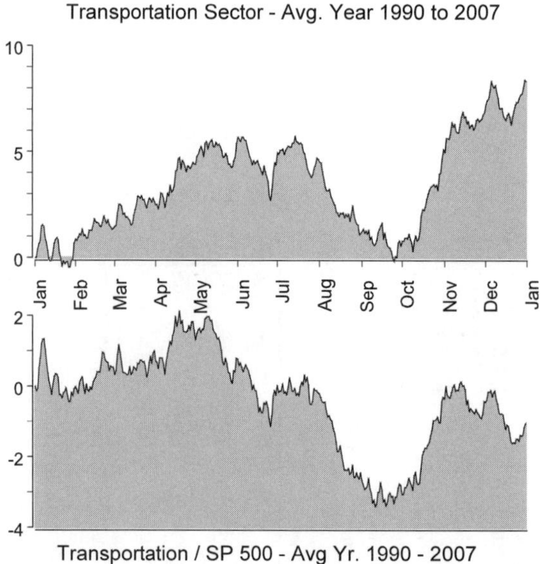

The transportation sector is "driven" by two factors: increased movement of goods in autumn and declining fuel prices. In autumn, the rail and truck sectors are busy moving harvest crops, and retail goods for the Christmas holiday season. This increased activity leads to greater projections of future earnings. In addition, one of the biggest cost components of the transportation sector is fuel. In the "shoulder season" between summer driving season and the heating season, there is often a reprieve in fuel prices. As a result, transportation stocks benefit.

The airline industry which is just coming off its busiest time of year, does very well, benefiting from lower fuel prices. It moves from dramatically underperforming the markets in September to dramatically outperforming in October.

Although the airlines over the long-term have been poor performers, constantly going bankrupt, if there were one time of the year to consider investing in the sector, this would be it. For a more diversified and less risky proposition, consider the transportation sector.

Transportation vs. S&P 500
Sep. 27th to Nov. 6th 1990-2007

Sep 27 to Nov 6	Trans	S&P 500	Diff (Positive shaded)
1990	0.3 %	2.0 %	-1.8 %
1991	10.6	3.0	7.7
1992	9.3	1.2	8.2
1993	6.4	1.7	4.7
1994	-1.9	0.6	-2.5
1995	2.1	1.8	0.3
1996	4.5	6.5	-2.0
1997	-5.4	-3.7	-1.7
1998	-0.8	5.6	-6.4
1999	8.5	9.0	-0.5
2000	15.4	-6.7	22.1
2001	21.3	17.9	3.3
2002	1.9	5.9	-4.0
2003	9.9	2.9	7.1
2004	15.8	6.8	9.0
2005	10.9	1.6	9.3
2006	10.2	5.3	5.0
2007	0.1	-2.9	3.1
Avg	6.6 %	3.2 %	3.4 %

Transportation Sector
GIC # 2030
An index designed to represent a cross section of widely held corporations involved in various phases of the transportation industry.

21 MONDAY 264 / 101

30 day	Wednesday October 21
60 day	Friday November 20
90 day	Sunday December 20
180 day	Saturday March 20
1 year	Tuesday September 21

22 TUESDAY 265 / 100

30 day	Thursday October 22
60 day	Saturday November 21
90 day	Monday December 21
180 day	Sunday March 21
1 year	Wednesday September 22

23 WEDNESDAY 266 / 099

30 day	Friday October 23
60 day	Sunday November 22
90 day	Tuesday December 22
180 day	Monday March 22
1 year	Thursday September 23

24 THURSDAY 267 / 098

30 day	Saturday October 24
60 day	Monday November 23
90 day	Wednesday December 23
180 day	Tuesday March 23
1 year	Friday September 24

25 FRIDAY 268 / 097

30 day	Sunday October 25
60 day	Tuesday November 24
90 day	Thursday December 24
180 day	Wednesday March 24
1 year	Saturday September 25

* Weekly avg closing values- except Fed Funds Rate & CAN overnight tgt rate which are weekly closing values.

WEEK 39

Market Indices & Rates Weekly Values*

Stock Markets	2006	2007
Dow	11,666	13,845
S&P 500	1,335	1,524
Nasdaq	2,260	2,692
TSX	11,711	14,044
FTSE	5,907	6,450
DAX	5,969	7,815
Nikkei	15,858	16,614
Hang Seng	17,490	26,724

Commodities	2006	2007
Oil (WTI)	61.94	81.70
Gold (London PM)	594.35	733.60

Bond Yields	2006	2007
USA 5 Yr Treasury	4.56	4.26
USA 10 Yr Treasury	4.60	4.61
USA 20 Yr Treasury	4.81	4.92
Moody's Aaa Corporate	5.39	5.79
Moody's Baa Corporate	6.32	6.63
CAN 5 Yr Treasury	3.87	4.26
CAN 10 Yr Treasury	3.97	4.38

Money Market	2006	2007
USA Fed Funds	5.25	4.75
USA 3 Mo T-Bill	4.88	3.78
CAN tgt overnight rate	4.25	4.50
CAN 3 Mo T-Bill	4.15	3.97

Foreign Exchange	2006	2007
USD / EUR	1.27	1.41
USD / GBP	1.89	2.02
CAN / USD	1.11	1.00
JPY / USD	117.39	115.16

SEPTEMBER

M	T	W	T	F	S	S
	1	2	3	4	5	6
7	8	9	10	11	12	13
14	15	16	17	18	19	20
21	22	23	24	25	26	27
28	29	30				

OCTOBER

M	T	W	T	F	S	S
			1	2	3	4
5	6	7	8	9	10	11
12	13	14	15	16	17	18
19	20	21	22	23	24	25
26	27	28	29	30	31	

NOVEMBER

M	T	W	T	F	S	S
						1
2	3	4	5	6	7	8
9	10	11	12	13	14	15
16	17	18	19	20	21	22
23	24	25	26	27	28	29
30						

ODD COUPLE CONSUMER STAPLES & INFO TECH

Live Together for the Month of October

Consumer staples and information technology make an odd couple for the month of October.

Usually stocks of a similar type move together. For example, the growth sectors of the market tend to rise and fall together. The defensive sectors tend to rise and fall together. Although this relationship is not always true, it is true more often than not.

1.5% extra and 67% of the time better than the S&P 500

October is considered a transition month, where the market tends to bottom and new sectors tend to rotate into positions of outperformance. It also tends to be the most volatile month of the year. In this month two unlikely sectors tend to outperform the market: consumer staples and information technology.

Why does this odd couple outperform? It is a combination of two factors. First, investors seek the stability of earnings from the consumer staples sector during volatile times. Second, investors desire to establish a position in information technology before the best three months of the market in a row- November, December and January (see *Three Stars* strategy).

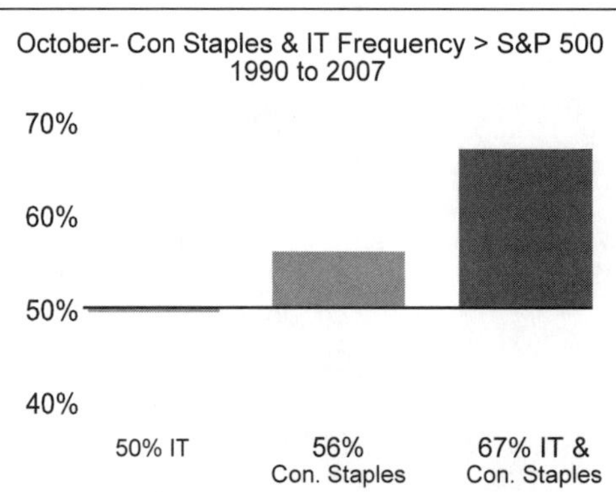

Consumer Staples & Information Technology
October Performance vs S&P 500- 1990-2007

% Gain > S&P 500 (shaded)

	Consumer Staples	Info Tech	Consumer Staples & Info Tech	S&P 500
1990	5.1 %	-4.2 %	0.5 %	-0.7 %
1991	-0.1	-0.1	-0.1	1.2
1992	-0.1	-0.4	-0.3	0.2
1993	6.8	2.6	4.7	1.9
1994	3.1	8.9	6.0	2.1
1995	2.5	3.8	3.2	-0.5
1996	1.5	1.1	1.3	2.6
1997	-2.1	-9.2	-5.6	-3.4
1998	14.9	6.7	10.8	8.0
1999	7.1	1.8	4.5	6.3
2000	11.6	-5.8	2.9	-0.5
2001	-0.6	17.4	8.4	1.8
2002	3.4	22.3	12.9	8.6
2003	4.8	8.1	6.5	5.5
2004	0.6	5.2	2.9	1.4
2005	-0.4	-2.2	-1.3	-1.8
2006	1.8	4.1	3.0	3.2
2007	1.7	7.1	4.4	1.5
Avg	3.4 %	3.7 %	3.6 %	2.1 %

Another month of transition is May. The market tends to peak at the beginning of the month and take on a defensive posture. It is no surprise that the consumer staples sector tends to do well during this month. The "Odd Couple" (consumer staples and information technology) does not work in this month of transition because the market is starting to get defensive and looks for an opportunity to sell off some of the growth sectors. As a result, the information technology sector underperforms in May.

In the transition month of October the *Odd Couple* sectors, consumer staples and information technology have the same approximate gain in October, 3.4% and 3.7% respectively. The real value of the odd couple comes in its combined performance of how often it outperforms the S&P 500.

Alone, consumer staples has outperformed the S&P 500 in the month of October from 1990 to 2007, 56% of the time and information technology 50% of the time. Together this odd couple, has outperformed the S&P 500, 67% of the time.

Odd Couple Strategy is similar to a Barbell Strategy- The term barbell strategy is usually reserved for fixed income managers who overweight both short-term and long-term bonds. The odd couple strategy is similar in that it combines sectors that usually do not perform well together.

28 MONDAY 271 / 094

30 day	Wednesday October 28
60 day	Friday November 27
90 day	Sunday December 27
180 day	Saturday March 27
1 year	Tuesday September 28

29 TUESDAY 272 / 093

30 day	Thursday October 29
60 day	Saturday November 28
90 day	Monday December 28
180 day	Sunday March 28
1 year	Wednesday September 29

30 WEDNESDAY 273 / 092

30 day	Friday October 30
60 day	Sunday November 29
90 day	Tuesday December 29
180 day	Monday March 29
1 year	Thursday September 30

1 THURSDAY 274 / 091

30 day	Saturday October 31
60 day	Monday November 30
90 day	Wednesday December 30
180 day	Tuesday March 30
1 year	Friday October 1

2 FRIDAY 275 / 090

30 day	Sunday November 1
60 day	Tuesday December 1
90 day	Thursday December 31
180 day	Wednesday March 31
1 year	Saturday October 2

* Weekly avg closing values- except Fed Funds Rate & CAN overnight tgt rate which are weekly closing values.

WEEK 40

Market Indices & Rates Weekly Values*

Stock Markets	**2006**	**2007**
Dow	11,793	14,029
S&P 500	1,344	1,547
Nasdaq	2,276	2,746
TSX	11,675	14,147
FTSE	5,973	6,537
DAX	6,040	7,954
Nikkei	16,293	17,050
Hang Seng	17,718	27,526
Commodities	**2006**	**2007**
Oil (WTI)	59.77	80.59
Gold (London PM)	578.10	733.25
Bond Yields	**2006**	**2007**
USA 5 Yr Treasury	4.56	4.25
USA 10 Yr Treasury	4.62	4.57
USA 20 Yr Treasury	4.84	4.86
Moody's Aaa Corporate	5.42	5.72
Moody's Baa Corporate	6.36	6.55
CAN 5 Yr Treasury	3.91	4.23
CAN 10 Yr Treasury	4.00	4.35
Money Market	**2006**	**2007**
USA Fed Funds	5.25	4.75
USA 3 Mo T-Bill	4.92	3.96
CAN tgt overnight rate	4.25	4.50
CAN 3 Mo T-Bill	4.16	3.97
Foreign Exchange	**2006**	**2007**
USD / EUR	1.27	1.42
USD / GBP	1.88	2.04
CAN / USD	1.12	0.99
JPY / USD	118.02	116.38

OCTOBER

M	T	W	T	F	S	S
			1	2	3	4
5	6	7	8	9	10	11
12	13	14	15	16	17	18
19	20	21	22	23	24	25
26	27	28	29	30	31	

NOVEMBER

M	T	W	T	F	S	S
						1
2	3	4	5	6	7	8
9	10	11	12	13	14	15
16	17	18	19	20	21	22
23	24	25	26	27	28	29
30						

DECEMBER

M	T	W	T	F	S	S
	1	2	3	4	5	6
7	8	9	10	11	12	13
14	15	16	17	18	19	20
21	22	23	24	25	26	27
28	29	30	31			

OCTOBER

	MONDAY	TUESDAY	WEDNESDAY
WEEK 40	28	29	30
WEEK 41	5 26 USA ISM Non-Manufacturing Report on Business (10:00 am ET)	6 25	7 24
WEEK 42	12 19 USA Bond Market Closed-Columbus Day CAN Market Closed-Thanksgiving Day	13 18	14 17
WEEK 43	19 12	20 11	21 10 USA Federal Reserve Board's Beige Book
WEEK 44	26 5 USA UBS Index of Investor Optimism (8:30 am ET)	27 4 USA Consumer Confidence Index 10:00 am ET	28 3

OCTOBER

THURSDAY	FRIDAY
1 30	**2** 29
USA ISM Manufacturing Report on Business (10:00 am ET)	USA The Employment Situation (8:30 am ET)
8 23	**9** 22
15 16	**16** 15
USA Federal Reserve Bank of Philadelphia: Business Outlook Survey (12:00 pm ET) USA Empire State Manufacturing Survey - Federal Reserve Bank of New York (8:30 am ET)	
22 9	**23** 8
29 2	**30** 1
USA Help-Wanted Advertising Index (10:00 am ET)	USA Strike Report (8:30 am ET) USA Chicago Purchasing Managers Index (Business Barometer) 9:45am ET

NOVEMBER

M	T	W	T	F	S	S
						1
2	3	4	5	6	7	8
9	10	11	12	13	14	15
16	17	18	19	20	21	22
23	24	25	26	27	28	29
30						

DECEMBER

M	T	W	T	F	S	S
	1	2	3	4	5	6
7	8	9	10	11	12	13
14	15	16	17	18	19	20
21	22	23	24	25	26	27
28	29	30	31			

JANUARY

M	T	W	T	F	S	S
				1	2	3
4	5	6	7	8	9	10
11	12	13	14	15	16	17
18	19	20	21	22	23	24
25	26	27	28	29	30	31

FEBRUARY

M	T	W	T	F	S	S
1	2	3	4	5	6	7
8	9	10	11	12	13	14
15	16	17	18	19	20	21
22	23	24	25	26	27	28

OCTOBER
SUMMARY

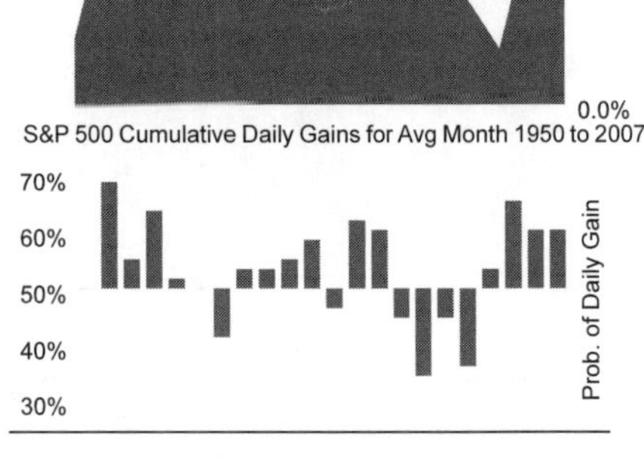

♦ Memories of the Black Mondays in 1929 and 1987 still haunt investors. Despite its bad reputation, October has a positive average return. ♦ The market tends to bottom on approximately October 9th and October 27th (see *Information Technology - Use It or Lose It and Six 'n' Six* strategies).

BEST / WORST OCTOBER BROAD MKTS. 1998-2007

BEST OCTOBER MARKETS

- Nasdaq (2002) 13.5%
- Nasdaq (2001) 12.8%
- Dow (2002) 10.6%

WORST OCTOBER MARKETS

- Nasdaq (2000) -8.3%
- TSX (2000) -7.1%
- TSX (2005) -5.7%

Index Values End of Month

	1998	1999	2000	2001	2002	2003	2004	2005	2006	2007
Dow	8,592	10,730	10,971	9,075	8,397	9,801	10,027	10,440	12,081	13,930
S&P 500	1,099	1,363	1,429	1,060	886	1,051	1,130	1,207	1,378	1,549
Nasdaq	1,771	2,966	3,370	1,690	1,330	1,932	1,975	2,120	2,367	2,859
TSX	6,208	7,256	9,640	6,886	6,249	7,773	8,871	10,383	12,345	14,625
Russell 1000	1,098	1,361	1,467	1,071	900	1,081	1,162	1,261	1,437	1,623
Russell 2000	942	1,068	1,237	1,064	928	1,313	1,451	1,607	1,906	2,058
Russell 3000 Growth	2,062	2,742	2,997	1,808	1,439	1,756	1,800	1,942	2,140	2,518
Russell 3000 Value	1,851	2,092	2,178	1,910	1,691	2,045	2,310	2,526	2,996	3,219

Percent Gain for October

	1998	1999	2000	2001	2002	2003	2004	2005	2006	2007
Dow	9.6	3.8	3.0	2.6	10.6	5.7	-0.5	-1.2	3.4	0.2
S&P 500	8.0	6.3	-0.5	1.8	8.6	5.5	1.4	-1.8	3.2	1.5
Nasdaq	4.6	8.0	-8.3	12.8	13.5	8.1	4.1	-1.5	4.8	5.8
TSX	10.6	4.3	-7.1	0.7	1.1	4.7	2.3	-5.7	5.0	3.7
Russell 1000	7.8	6.6	-1.3	2.0	8.1	5.7	1.5	-1.9	3.3	1.6
Russell 2000	4.0	0.3	-4.6	5.8	3.1	8.3	1.9	-3.2	5.7	2.8
Russell 3000 Growth	7.8	7.2	-5.0	5.5	8.8	5.8	1.6	-1.3	3.7	3.4
Russell 3000 Value	7.2	5.0	2.1	-0.8	6.7	6.1	1.5	-2.7	3.3	-0.1

October Market Avg. Performance 1998 to 2007 (1)

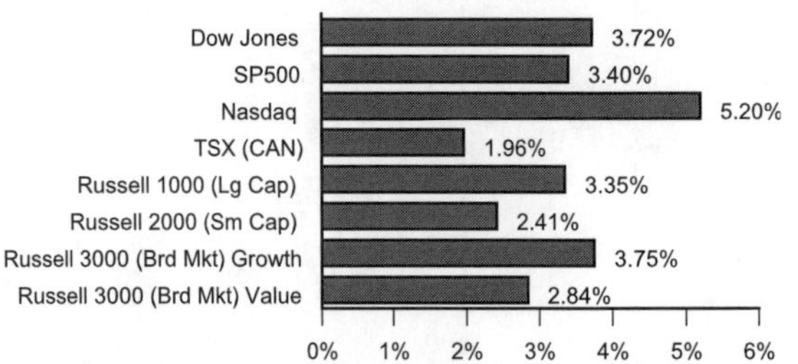

Interest Corner Oct(2)

	Fed Funds % (3)	3 Mo. T-Bill % (4)	10 Yr % (5)	20 Yr % (6)
2007	4.50	3.94	4.48	4.79
2006	5.25	5.08	4.61	4.81
2005	3.75	3.98	4.57	4.84
2004	1.75	1.91	4.05	4.79
2003	1.00	0.96	4.33	5.20

(1) Russell Data provided by Russell (2) Federal Reserve Bank of St. Louis- end of month values (3) Target rate set by FOMC (4)(5)(6) Constant yield maturities

OCTOBER SECTOR / SUB-SECTOR PERFORMANCE

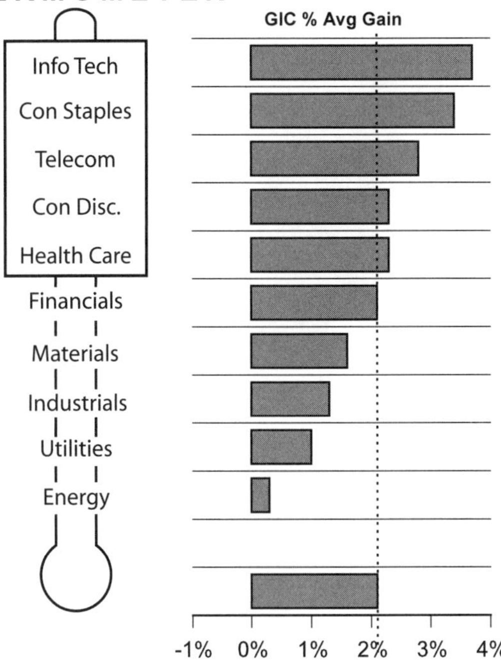

GIC[2] % Avg Gain	Fq % Gain >S&P 500	SP GIC SECTOR 1990-2007[1]
3.7 %	50 %	Information Technology
3.4	56	Consumer Staples
2.8	44	Telecom
2.3	50	Consumer Discretionary
2.3	50	Health Care
2.1	44	Financials
1.6	50	Materials
1.3	33	Industrials
1.0	39	Utilities
0.3	39	Energy
2.1 %	N/A %	S&P 500

GIC % Avg Gain	Fq % Gain >S&P 500	SUB-SECTOR 1990-2007[3]
5.7 %	81 %	Airlines
5.5	72	Software & Services
4.9	46	Semiconductor (SOX) (95-2007)
4.6	69	Transportation
2.9	56	Pharmaceuticals
2.4	56	Retailing
2.4	50	Insurance
2.0	50	Biotech (92-2007)
1.0	50	Banks
0.9	33	Metals & Mining
0.7	31	Autos & Components
0.2	33	Oil Integrated
-0.4	39	Oil & Gas Exploration & Production
-3.4	33	Gold (XAU)

Sector

♦ Consumer Staples and Information Technology live together at the top of the rankings for this month (see *Odd Couple* strategy). ♦ Information Technology, although it has a better average return than the S&P 500, outperforms the market less than half of the time during the month. The sector's outperformance has typically started after September's spell has worn off (see *Information Technology Use It Or Lose It* strategy). ♦ Energy and Utilities fall from the top part of the thermometer to the bottom.

Sub-Sector

♦ "Fasten your seat belt." Airlines take-off for an incredible average gain of 5.7% and an outperformance of the market 81% of the time. ♦ Both the Software & Services and Semiconductor sectors have a strong outperformance record, as they benefit from the outperformance of the Information Technology sector described above. ♦ Out of the sectors listed, the five members of the "Bottom of the Barrel" ranking, (Oil Integrated, Metals & Mining, Autos & Components, Oil E&P, Gold), are also members of the dismal 1/3 club (sectors that outperform the broad market less than approximately 1/3 of the time).

(1) Sector data provided by Standard and Poors (2) GIC is short form for Global Industry Classification (3) Sub Sector data provided by Standard and Poors, except where marked by symbol.

INFORMATION TECHNOLOGY USE IT OR LOSE IT

October 9th to January 17th

Information technology....the sector that investors love to love and love to hate. In recent times most investors have made and lost money in this sector. When the sector is good, it can be really good. When it is bad, it can be really bad. Through it all there is a seasonally strong period for technology: October 9th to January 17th.

6.1% extra compared with the S&P 500

Technology stocks get bid up at the end of the year for three reasons:

First, a lot of companies operate with year end budgets and if they do not spend the money in their budget, they lose it. In the last few months of the year, whatever money they have they spend. Hence, the saying "use it or lose it." The number one purchase item for this budget flush is technology equipment. An upgrade in technology equipment is something in which a large number of employees in the company can benefit. Technology is an easy purchase to justify and it flushes out the budget fast.

Second, consumers indirectly help push up technology stocks by purchasing electronic items during the holiday season. Retail sales ramp up significantly on Black Friday, the Friday after Thanksgiving. Investors anticipate the upswing in sales and increase money flows into technology stocks.

Third, the "Conference Effect" helps maintain the momentum in January. This phenomenon is the result of investors increasing positions ahead of major conferences in order to benefit from positive announcements. In the case of Information Technology, investors increase their holdings ahead of the Las Vegas Consumer Electronics Conference in the second week of January. At this time, technology companies often announce new devices that are going to drive the market.

Results for both the information technology sector and Nasdaq, in comparison to the S&P 500, have been included in the table on this page.

Info Tech & Nasdaq vs S&P 500
Oct 9 to Jan 17, 1990-2008

Positive (shaded)

	Info Tech	Nasdaq	S&P 500	Diff IT to S&P	Diff Nas to S&P
1990	-6.9 %	-9.3 %	-6.0 %	-1.0 %	-3.3 %
1991	13.4	8.0	4.6	8.8	3.3
1992	16.4	21.2	10.0	6.4	11.2
1993	11.2	21.5	7.2	4.0	14.3
1994	12.5	3.7	2.8	9.7	0.8
1995	16.0	3.0	3.3	12.7	-0.3
1996	-8.9	-1.4	4.1	-13.0	-5.5
1997	21.2	8.8	10.8	10.4	-2.0
1998	-14.2	-10.3	-1.3	-12.9	-9.0
1999	71.8	65.5	29.6	42.2	35.9
2000	29.2	40.8	9.7	19.5	31.1
2001	-21.7	-20.2	-5.6	-16.1	-14.5
2002	26.8	23.7	7.2	19.6	16.5
2003	30.0	21.9	12.9	17.0	8.9
2004	14.2	13.0	10.3	4.0	2.8
2005	6.8	8.7	5.6	1.2	3.2
2006	9.7	10.2	7.3	2.4	2.9
2007	7.1	7.8	6.0	1.1	1.8
2008	-14.9	-15.8	-14.1	-0.7	-1.7
Avg	11.6 %	10.6 %	5.5 %	6.1 %	5.1 %

Technology Sector - Avg. Year 1990 to 2007

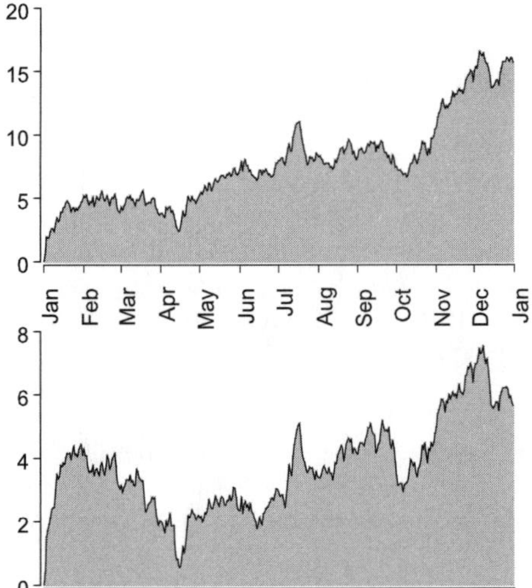

Technology / SP 500 - Avg Yr. 1990 - 2007

Information Technology SP GIC Sector 45: An index designed to represent a cross section of information technology companies.

For more information on the information technology sector, see www.standardandpoors.com.

5 MONDAY 278 / 087

30 day	Wednesday November 4
60 day	Friday December 4
90 day	Sunday January 3
180 day	Saturday April 3
1 year	Tuesday October 5

6 TUESDAY 279 / 086

30 day	Thursday November 5
60 day	Saturday December 5
90 day	Monday January 4
180 day	Sunday April 4
1 year	Wednesday October 6

7 WEDNESDAY 280 / 085

30 day	Friday November 6
60 day	Sunday December 6
90 day	Tuesday January 5
180 day	Monday April 5
1 year	Thursday October 7

8 THURSDAY 281 / 084

30 day	Saturday November 7
60 day	Monday December 7
90 day	Wednesday January 6
180 day	Tuesday April 6
1 year	Friday October 8

9 FRIDAY 282 / 083

30 day	Sunday November 8
60 day	Tuesday December 8
90 day	Thursday January 7
180 day	Wednesday April 7
1 year	Saturday October 9

* Weekly avg closing values- except Fed Funds Rate & CAN overnight tgt rate which are weekly closing values.

WEEK 41

Market Indices & Rates
Weekly Values*

Stock Markets	**2006**	**2007**
Dow	11,897	14,079
S&P 500	1,356	1,559
Nasdaq	2,328	2,796
TSX	11,749	14,266
FTSE	6,091	6,649
DAX	6,131	8,003
Nikkei	16,446	17,282
Hang Seng	17,845	28,508
Commodities	**2006**	**2007**
Oil (WTI)	58.58	81.46
Gold (London PM)	575.97	741.90
Bond Yields	**2006**	**2007**
USA 5 Yr Treasury	4.74	4.38
USA 10 Yr Treasury	4.78	4.67
USA 20 Yr Treasury	4.99	4.95
Moody's Aaa Corporate	5.56	5.78
Moody's Baa Corporate	6.50	6.57
CAN 5 Yr Treasury	4.05	4.40
CAN 10 Yr Treasury	4.14	4.46
Money Market	**2006**	**2007**
USA Fed Funds	5.25	4.75
USA 3 Mo T-Bill	5.03	4.11
CAN tgt overnight rate	4.25	4.50
CAN 3 Mo T-Bill	4.16	3.96
Foreign Exchange	**2006**	**2007**
USD / EUR	1.25	1.42
USD / GBP	1.86	2.04
CAN / USD	1.13	0.98
JPY / USD	119.63	117.24

OCTOBER

M	T	W	T	F	S	S
			1	2	3	4
5	6	7	8	9	10	11
12	13	14	15	16	17	18
19	20	21	22	23	24	25
26	27	28	29	30	31	

NOVEMBER

M	T	W	T	F	S	S
						1
2	3	4	5	6	7	8
9	10	11	12	13	14	15
16	17	18	19	20	21	22
23	24	25	26	27	28	29
30						

DECEMBER

M	T	W	T	F	S	S
	1	2	3	4	5	6
7	8	9	10	11	12	13
14	15	16	17	18	19	20
21	22	23	24	25	26	27
28	29	30	31			

CONSUMER SWITCH
SELL CONSUMER STAPLES
BUY CONSUMER DISCRETIONARY

Con. Discretionary Outperforms From Oct 28 to Apr 22

Time to sell the sector of "need" and buy the sector of "want."

Companies that are classified as consumer staples sell products to the consumer that they need for their everyday life. Consumers will generally still buy products from a consumer staples company, such as a drugstore, even if the economy turns down.

On the other hand, consumer discretionary companies sell products that consumers do not necessarily need, such as furniture.

Why is this important? Consumer discretionary companies tend to outperform in the six favorable months of the market. The discretionary sector benefits from the positive market forces and positive market forecasts that tend to take place in this period.

The consumer staples and discretionary sectors average year graphs illustrate the individual trends of the sectors. The discretionary sector tends to outperform strongly from the end of December to April. Although the staples sector in the summer months has a slightly average negative performance, it still outperforms the discretionary sector. At the end of the year, both sectors do well, but the discretionary sector outperforms the staples sector.

The *Consumer Switch* strategy is an ideal strategy for portfolio managers who must maintain a certain amount in the consumer sector. The two sectors have approximately the same weight in the S&P 500 and provide the opportunity for switching back and forth from one sector to another for six months of the year.

Consumer Discretionary Avg. Year 1990 to 2007

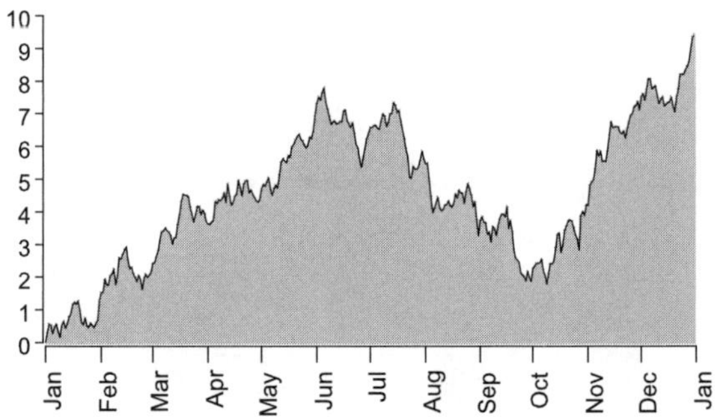

Consumer Staples Avg. Year 1990 to 2007

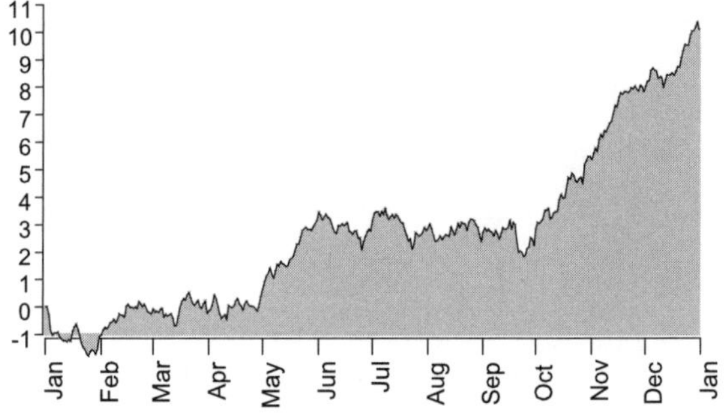

Con. Discretionary / Staples - Relative Strength
Avg. Year 1990 to 2007

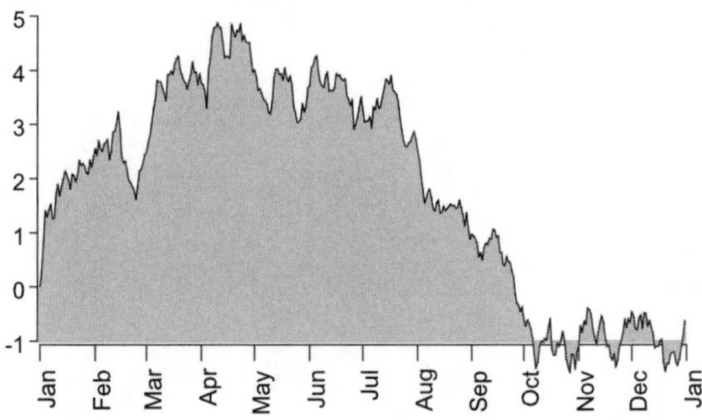

Alternate Strategy — The consumer discretionary stocks have dramatically outperformed the consumer staples stocks from December 27th to April 22nd. With both the discretionary and staples sectors performing well in November and December, depending on market conditions, investors can delay some or all of their allocation to the discretionary sector until the end of December.

12 MONDAY 285 / 080

30 day	Wednesday November 11
60 day	Friday December 11
90 day	Sunday January 10
180 day	Saturday April 10
1 year	Tuesday October 12

13 TUESDAY 286 / 079

30 day	Thursday November 12
60 day	Saturday December 12
90 day	Monday January 11
180 day	Sunday April 11
1 year	Wednesday October 13

14 WEDNESDAY 287 / 078

30 day	Friday November 13
60 day	Sunday December 13
90 day	Tuesday January 12
180 day	Monday April 12
1 year	Thursday October 14

15 THURSDAY 288 / 077

30 day	Saturday November 14
60 day	Monday December 14
90 day	Wednesday January 13
180 day	Tuesday April 13
1 year	Friday October 15

16 FRIDAY 289 / 076

30 day	Sunday November 15
60 day	Tuesday December 15
90 day	Thursday January 14
180 day	Wednesday April 14
1 year	Saturday October 16

* Weekly avg closing values- except Fed Funds Rate & CAN overnight tgt rate which are weekly closing values.

WEEK 42

Market Indices & Rates Weekly Values*

Stock Markets	**2006**	**2007**
Dow	11,987	13,840
S&P 500	1,367	1,534
Nasdaq	2,346	2,772
TSX	12,024	14,188
FTSE	6,149	6,615
DAX	6,173	7,945
Nikkei	16,632	17,074
Hang Seng	18,035	29,345

Commodities	**2006**	**2007**
Oil (WTI)	58.48	87.80
Gold (London PM)	594.59	761.05

Bond Yields	**2006**	**2007**
USA 5 Yr Treasury	4.75	4.23
USA 10 Yr Treasury	4.78	4.57
USA 20 Yr Treasury	4.99	4.88
Moody's Aaa Corporate	5.56	5.68
Moody's Baa Corporate	6.49	6.49
CAN 5 Yr Treasury	4.06	4.33
CAN 10 Yr Treasury	4.17	4.41

Money Market	**2006**	**2007**
USA Fed Funds	5.25	4.75
USA 3 Mo T-Bill	5.09	4.04
CAN tgt overnight rate	4.25	4.50
CAN 3 Mo T-Bill	4.16	3.90

Foreign Exchange	**2006**	**2007**
USD / EUR	1.26	1.42
USD / GBP	1.87	2.04
CAN / USD	1.13	0.97
JPY / USD	118.81	116.28

OCTOBER

M	T	W	T	F	S	S
			1	2	3	4
5	6	7	8	9	10	11
12	13	14	15	16	17	18
19	20	21	22	23	24	25
26	27	28	29	30	31	

NOVEMBER

M	T	W	T	F	S	S
						1
2	3	4	5	6	7	8
9	10	11	12	13	14	15
16	17	18	19	20	21	22
23	24	25	26	27	28	29
30						

DECEMBER

M	T	W	T	F	S	S
	1	2	3	4	5	6
7	8	9	10	11	12	13
14	15	16	17	18	19	20
21	22	23	24	25	26	27
28	29	30	31			

RETAIL - SHOP EARLY

IInd of **II** Retail Strategies for the Year
Oct 28th to Nov 29th

Although the *Retail – Shop Early* strategy is the second retail sector strategy of the year, it occurs before the biggest shopping season of the year– the Christmas holiday season.

> ***3.0% extra & 14 of 18 times better than S&P 500***

The time to go shopping for retail stocks is at the end of October, which is about one month before Thanksgiving. It is the time when two favorable influences happen at the same time.

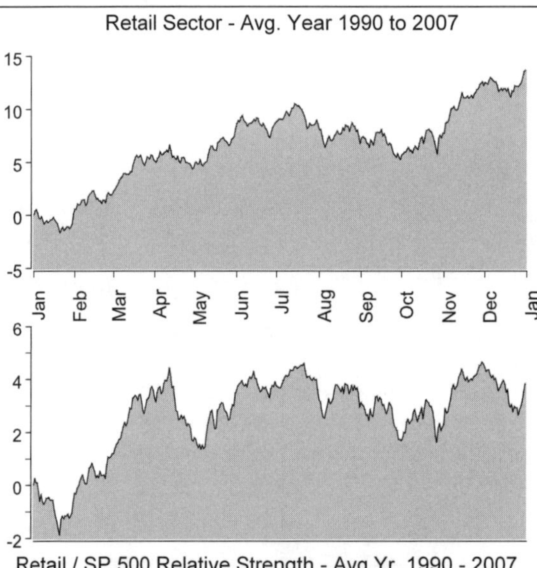

Retail / SP 500 Relative Strength - Avg Yr. 1990 - 2007

The three best months in a row for the market have been November, December and January (see *Three Stars* strategy). The end of October usually represents an excellent buying opportunity, not only for the next three months, but the next six (see *Six 'n' Six- The Better Half* strategy).

Second, investors tend to buy retail stocks in anticipation of a strong holiday sales season. At the same time that the market tends to increase, investors are attracted back into the retail sector. Retail sales tend to be lower in the summer and a lot of investors view investing in retail stocks at this time as dead money. They prefer to invest in another sector of the market until the retail sector comes back into favor. The end of October presents that opportunity.

The trick to investing is not to be too early, but early. If an investor gets into a sector too early they can suffer from the frustration of having dead money (having an investment that goes nowhere, while the rest of the market increases). If you move into a sector too late there is very little upside potential. In fact, this can be a dangerous strategy because if the sales or earnings numbers disappoint the analysts, the sector can severely correct.

Generally speaking, the time to get into the sector is one to three months before the event that acts as a catalyst in pushing the sector higher. One to three months is a broad range, but it depends on the sector, market expectations and general market conditions that exist at that time of year.

Generally the time to exit a sector is when everyone else is buying in. This is typically at the time when the catalyst event is occurring, or shortly after.

Retail Sector vs. S&P 500 1990 to 2007

Oct 28 to Nov 29	Retail	S&P500	Diff (Positive shaded)
1990	9.9 %	3.8 %	6.0 %
1991	2.7	-2.3	5.0
1992	5.5	2.8	2.8
1993	6.3	-0.6	6.9
1994	0.4	-2.3	2.7
1995	9.5	4.8	4.7
1996	0.4	8.0	-7.6
1997	16.9	8.9	7.9
1998	20.4	11.9	8.4
1999	14.1	8.6	5.5
2000	9.9	-2.7	12.6
2001	7.9	3.2	4.7
2002	-1.7	4.3	-6.0
2003	2.5	2.6	0.1
2004	7.0	4.7	2.3
2005	9.9	6.7	3.2
2006	0.2	1.6	-1.4
2007	-7.5	-4.3	-3.2
Avg.	6.3 %	3.3 %	3.0 %

19 MONDAY 292 / 073

30 day	Wednesday November 18
60 day	Friday December 18
90 day	Sunday January 17
180 day	Saturday April 17
1 year	Tuesday October 19

20 TUESDAY 293 / 072

30 day	Thursday November 19
60 day	Saturday December 19
90 day	Monday January 18
180 day	Sunday April 18
1 year	Wednesday October 20

21 WEDNESDAY 294 / 071

30 day	Friday November 20
60 day	Sunday December 20
90 day	Tuesday January 19
180 day	Monday April 19
1 year	Thursday October 21

22 THURSDAY 295 / 070

30 day	Saturday November 21
60 day	Monday December 21
90 day	Wednesday January 20
180 day	Tuesday April 20
1 year	Friday October 22

23 FRIDAY 296 / 069

30 day	Sunday November 22
60 day	Tuesday December 22
90 day	Thursday January 21
180 day	Wednesday April 21
1 year	Saturday October 23

* Weekly avg closing values- except Fed Funds Rate & CAN overnight tgt rate which are weekly closing values.

WEEK 43

Market Indices & Rates Weekly Values*

Stock Markets	**2006**	**2007**
Dow	12,127	13,679
S&P 500	1,381	1,518
Nasdaq	2,357	2,777
TSX	12,252	14,100
FTSE	6,182	6,539
DAX	6,260	7,870
Nikkei	16,750	16,407
Hang Seng	18,210	29,469
Commodities	**2006**	**2007**
Oil (WTI)	58.88	89.23
Gold (London PM)	586.32	762.73
Bond Yields	**2006**	**2007**
USA 5 Yr Treasury	4.74	4.04
USA 10 Yr Treasury	4.77	4.39
USA 20 Yr Treasury	4.97	4.72
Moody's Aaa Corporate	5.55	5.54
Moody's Baa Corporate	6.42	6.37
CAN 5 Yr Treasury	4.06	4.21
CAN 10 Yr Treasury	4.15	4.30
Money Market	**2006**	**2007**
USA Fed Funds	5.25	4.75
USA 3 Mo T-Bill	5.12	3.95
CAN tgt overnight rate	4.25	4.50
CAN 3 Mo T-Bill	4.17	3.88
Foreign Exchange	**2006**	**2007**
USD / EUR	1.26	1.43
USD / GBP	1.88	2.05
CAN / USD	1.12	0.97
JPY / USD	118.79	114.15

OCTOBER

M	T	W	T	F	S	S
			1	2	3	4
5	6	7	8	9	10	11
12	13	14	15	16	17	18
19	20	21	22	23	24	25
26	27	28	29	30	31	

NOVEMBER

M	T	W	T	F	S	S
						1
2	3	4	5	6	7	8
9	10	11	12	13	14	15
16	17	18	19	20	21	22
23	24	25	26	27	28	29
30						

DECEMBER

M	T	W	T	F	S	S
	1	2	3	4	5	6
7	8	9	10	11	12	13
14	15	16	17	18	19	20
21	22	23	24	25	26	27
28	29	30	31			

LAST 4 MARKET DAYS IN OCTOBER

The 1% Difference

The adage "buy at the beginning of November and sell at the end of April" has been around a long time. A lot of prudent investors believe in the merits of this strategy and have profited handsomely. Nevertheless, if they entered the market four market days earlier they would have received, on average, an extra 0.9% per year (almost 1%) from 1950 to 2007.

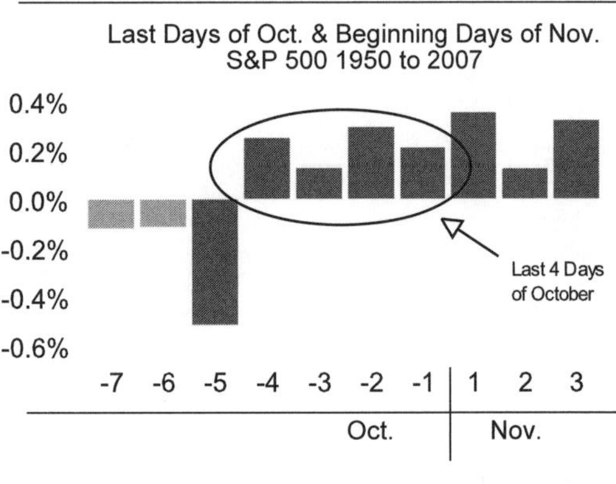

Average Return of 1% & Positive 59% of the time

It is not just the four days gain that is attractive, the seasonal safety net that follows has been very solid. The last four days is followed by one of the best months: November. This month is also the first month of the best three months in a row (see *Three Stars* strategy) and the first month of the six favorable months (see *Six 'n' Six- The Better Half* strategy).

Although October has a reputation for being a "tough month," its average return has been positive from 1950 to 2007. It is October's volatility that shakes investors up. The interesting fact is that almost all of the gains for October can be attributed to the last four market days. The average daily gain for all days in October, except the last four, is 0.01%. This pales in comparison to the average daily gain for the last four days of the market, 0.22%.

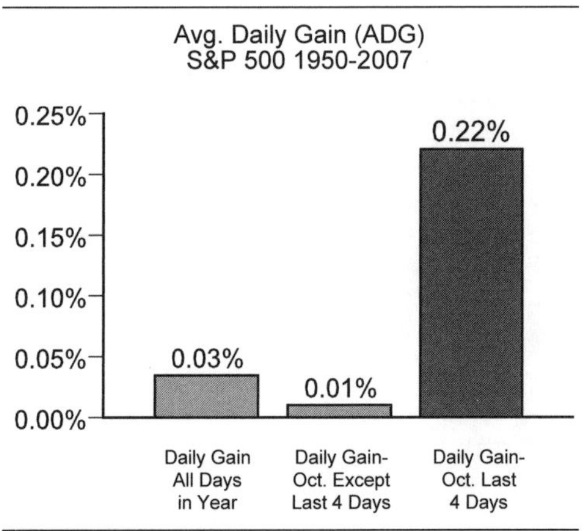

Last 4 Market Days in October % Gain 1950 to 2007 (shaded = Positive)

Year	%	Year	%	Year	%	Year	%	Year	%	Year	%
1950	-0.4 %	1960	2.3 %	1970	-0.1 %	1980	-0.3 %	1990	-2.0 %	2000	4.7 %
1951	0.6	1961	0.4	1971	-0.9	1981	3.2	1991	2.1	2001	-3.7
1952	1.8	1962	3.3	1972	0.8	1982	0.3	1992	0.1	2002	-1.3
1953	0.9	1963	0.0	1973	-2.0	1983	-1.8	1993	0.8	2003	1.9
1954	-0.9	1964	-0.2	1974	5.4	1984	-0.1	1994	2.3	2004	3.2
1955	-0.7	1965	0.8	1975	-0.8	1985	1.2	1995	-0.2	2005	0.9
1956	-0.6	1966	1.6	1976	2.8	1986	2.2	1996	0.6	2006	-0.3
1957	1.2	1967	-1.3	1977	1.5	1987	10.6	1997	4.3	2007	2.3
1958	1.8	1968	-0.4	1978	-4.3	1988	-1.2	1998	2.5		
1959	1.0	1969	-0.9	1979	1.8	1989	-0.6	1999	5.4		
Average	0.5 %		0.6 %		0.4 %		1.3 %		1.6 %		1.0 %

26 MONDAY 299 / 066

30 day	Wednesday November 25
60 day	Friday December 25
90 day	Sunday January 24
180 day	Saturday April 24
1 year	Tuesday October 26

27 TUESDAY 300 / 065

30 day	Thursday November 26
60 day	Saturday December 26
90 day	Monday January 25
180 day	Sunday April 25
1 year	Wednesday October 27

28 WEDNESDAY 301 / 064

30 day	Friday November 27
60 day	Sunday December 27
90 day	Tuesday January 26
180 day	Monday April 26
1 year	Thursday October 28

29 THURSDAY 302 / 063

30 day	Saturday November 28
60 day	Monday December 28
90 day	Wednesday January 27
180 day	Tuesday April 27
1 year	Friday October 29

30 FRIDAY 303 / 062

30 day	Sunday November 29
60 day	Tuesday December 29
90 day	Thursday January 28
180 day	Wednesday April 28
1 year	Saturday October 30

* Weekly avg closing values- except Fed Funds Rate & CAN overnight tgt rate which are weekly closing values.

WEEK 44

Market Indices & Rates Weekly Values*

Stock Markets	2006	2007
Dow	12,041	13,751
S&P 500	1,371	1,528
Nasdaq	2,346	2,820
TSX	12,208	14,420
FTSE	6,141	6,641
DAX	6,257	7,947
Nikkei	16,369	16,695
Hang Seng	18,508	31,308
Commodities	**2006**	**2007**
Oil (WTI)	58.55	93.46
Gold (London PM)	613.97	789.60
Bond Yields	**2006**	**2007**
USA 5 Yr Treasury	4.60	4.04
USA 10 Yr Treasury	4.64	4.39
USA 20 Yr Treasury	4.83	4.71
Moody's Aaa Corporate	5.41	5.54
Moody's Baa Corporate	6.27	6.39
CAN 5 Yr Treasury	3.95	4.19
CAN 10 Yr Treasury	4.04	4.28
Money Market	**2006**	**2007**
USA Fed Funds	5.25	4.50
USA 3 Mo T-Bill	5.08	3.87
CAN tgt overnight rate	4.25	4.50
CAN 3 Mo T-Bill	4.17	3.95
Foreign Exchange	**2006**	**2007**
USD / EUR	1.27	1.44
USD / GBP	1.91	2.07
CAN / USD	1.13	0.95
JPY / USD	117.28	114.86

OCTOBER

M	T	W	T	F	S	S
			1	2	3	4
5	6	7	8	9	10	11
12	13	14	15	16	17	18
19	20	21	22	23	24	25
26	27	28	29	30	31	

NOVEMBER

M	T	W	T	F	S	S
						1
2	3	4	5	6	7	8
9	10	11	12	13	14	15
16	17	18	19	20	21	22
23	24	25	26	27	28	29
30						

DECEMBER

M	T	W	T	F	S	S
	1	2	3	4	5	6
7	8	9	10	11	12	13
14	15	16	17	18	19	20
21	22	23	24	25	26	27
28	29	30	31			

6n6 SIX 'N' SIX – THE BETTER HALF
Oct 28th to May 5th

The favorable six month period starts at the end of October (October 28th). This period has typically been the "better half" of the year for investing. The results using investable money have been staggering.

Earlier in the calendar the, "Six 'n' Six" strategy illustrated the difference between investing during the favorable six months and investing during the other six months. From 1950 to 2008, starting with $10,000 and investing during the favorable six months produced a cumulative profit of $806,204 and starting with the same $10,000 and investing in the other six months produced a loss of $535.

8.5% average gain & 79% of the time positive

Anyway you look at it, the period from October 28th to May 5th is the "better half" of the year. During this time period the S&P 500 has produced an average gain of 8.8% and has been positive 81% of the time.

The table below shows the year by year performance. Out of the fifty-eight years, there were only two times that a loss of greater than 10% occurred (1969/70 and 1973/74). Interestingly, in the 2000/01/02 bear market, during the favorable six months, the S&P 500 produced returns of -8.2%, -2.8% and 3.2%. Investing in only the "better half" of the year allowed investors to avoid most of the carnage of the bear market.

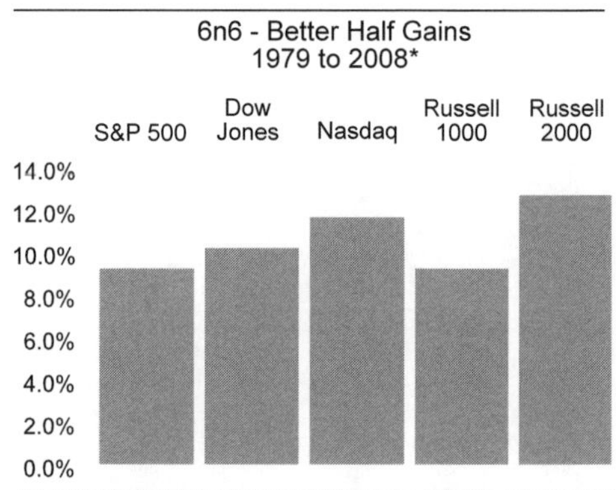

* 1979 inception year for Russell indices

Major Market Performance (Oct 28 to May 5) 79/80 to 07/08

	S&P 500	Dow Jones	Nasdaq	Russell 1000	Russell 2000
Avg. Gain	9.2%	10.2%	11.6%	9.2%	12.7%
Fq Positive	79%	93%	72%	76%	83%

The graph above has been included to illustrate the returns during the favorable six months of the major markets since 1979 (1979 is the inception year for the Russell indices). All of the markets have done well in the "better half" of the year. The Dow Jones Industrial Average has the greatest frequency of being positive and the Russell 2000 (small cap index) has the largest average gain.

The major markets have been included to show the strength of the "better half." The superior gains for each market are largely accounted for at different times within the six month period. Please refer to other calendar strategies in the calendar to identify the best times for each market.

S&P 500 Favorable Six Month % Gain 1950/51 to 2007/08 — Positive (shaded)

1950/51	14.8 %	1960/61	24.1 %	1970/71	24.9 %	1980/81	1.9 %	1990/91	25.0 %	2000/01	-8.2 %
1951/52	5.4	1961/62	-3.1	1971/72	13.7	1981/82	-1.4	1991/92	8.5	2001/02	-2.8
1952/53	3.9	1962/63	28.4	1972/73	0.3	1982/83	21.4	1992/93	6.2	2002/03	3.2
1953/54	16.6	1963/64	9.3	1973/74	-18.0	1983/84	-3.5	1993/94	-2.8	2003/04	8.8
1954/55	18.1	1964/65	5.5	1974/75	28.5	1984/85	8.9	1994/95	11.6	2004/05	4.2
1955/56	14.6	1965/66	-5.0	1975/76	12.4	1985/86	26.8	1995/96	10.7	2005/06	12.5
1956/57	0.2	1966/67	17.7	1976/77	-1.6	1986/87	23.7	1996/97	18.5	2006/07	9.3
1957/58	7.9	1967/68	3.9	1977/78	4.5	1987/88	11.0	1997/98	27.2	2007/08	-8.3
1958/59	14.5	1968/69	0.2	1978/79	6.4	1988/89	10.9	1998/99	26.5		
1959/60	-4.5	1969/70	-19.8	1979/80	5.8	1989/90	1.0	1999/00	10.5		
Average	9.1 %		6.1 %		7.7 %		10.1 %		14.2 %		2.3 %

2 MONDAY 306 / 059

30 day	Wednesday December 2
60 day	Friday January 1
90 day	Sunday January 31
180 day	Saturday May 1
1 year	Tuesday November 2

3 TUESDAY 307 / 058

30 day	Thursday December 3
60 day	Saturday January 2
90 day	Monday February 1
180 day	Sunday May 2
1 year	Wednesday November 3

4 WEDNESDAY 308 / 057

30 day	Friday December 4
60 day	Sunday January 3
90 day	Tuesday February 2
180 day	Monday May 3
1 year	Thursday November 4

5 THURSDAY 309 / 056

30 day	Saturday December 5
60 day	Monday January 4
90 day	Wednesday February 3
180 day	Tuesday May 4
1 year	Friday November 5

6 FRIDAY 310 / 055

30 day	Sunday December 6
60 day	Tuesday January 5
90 day	Thursday February 4
180 day	Wednesday May 5
1 year	Saturday November 6

* Weekly avg closing values- except Fed Funds Rate & CAN overnight tgt rate which are weekly closing values.

WEEK 45

Market Indices & Rates
Weekly Values*

Stock Markets	**2006**	**2007**
Dow	12,130	13,363
S&P 500	1,382	1,485
Nasdaq	2,379	2,739
TSX	12,354	14,152
FTSE	6,229	6,402
DAX	6,352	7,813
Nikkei	16,257	15,994
Hang Seng	18,906	29,127
Commodities	**2006**	**2007**
Oil (WTI)	59.96	95.81
Gold (London PM)	625.92	826.87
Bond Yields	**2006**	**2007**
USA 5 Yr Treasury	4.62	3.89
USA 10 Yr Treasury	4.64	4.32
USA 20 Yr Treasury	4.83	4.68
Moody's Aaa Corporate	5.39	5.53
Moody's Baa Corporate	6.25	6.41
CAN 5 Yr Treasury	3.95	4.14
CAN 10 Yr Treasury	4.04	4.26
Money Market	**2006**	**2007**
USA Fed Funds	5.25	4.50
USA 3 Mo T-Bill	5.09	3.52
CAN tgt overnight rate	4.25	4.50
CAN 3 Mo T-Bill	4.18	3.96
Foreign Exchange	**2006**	**2007**
USD / EUR	1.28	1.46
USD / GBP	1.91	2.09
CAN / USD	1.13	0.93
JPY / USD	117.79	113.18

NOVEMBER

M	T	W	T	F	S	S
						1
2	3	4	5	6	7	8
9	10	11	12	13	14	15
16	17	18	19	20	21	22
23	24	25	26	27	28	29
30						

DECEMBER

M	T	W	T	F	S	S
	1	2	3	4	5	6
7	8	9	10	11	12	13
14	15	16	17	18	19	20
21	22	23	24	25	26	27
28	29	30	31			

JANUARY

M	T	W	T	F	S	S
				1	2	3
4	5	6	7	8	9	10
11	12	13	14	15	16	17
18	19	20	21	22	23	24
25	26	27	28	29	30	31

NOVEMBER

	MONDAY	TUESDAY	WEDNESDAY
WEEK 45	**2** 28 USA ISM Manufacturing Report on Business (10:00 am ET)	**3** 27 USA FOMC Meetings	**4** 26 USA FOMC Meetings USA ISM Non-Manufacturing Report on Business (10:00 am ET)
WEEK 46	**9** 21	**10** 20	**11** 19 Veterans' Day
WEEK 47	**16** 14 USA Empire State Manufacturing Survey - Federal Reserve Bank of New York (8:30 am ET)	**17** 13	**18** 12
WEEK 48	**23** 7 USA UBS Index of Investor Optimism (8:30 am ET)	**24** 6 USA Consumer Confidence Index 10:00 am ET	**25** 5
WEEK 49	**30** USA Chicago Purchasing Managers Index (Business Barometer) 9:45am ET	1	2

THURSDAY	FRIDAY
5 25	**6** 24 USA The Employment Situation (8:30 am ET)
12 18	**13** 17
19 11 USA Federal Reserve Bank of Philadelphia: Business Outlook Survey (12:00 pm ET)	**20** 10
26 4 USA Market Closed-Thanksgiving Day	**27** 3 USA Early Market Close Thanksgiving USA Strike Report (8:30 am ET) USA Employment Cost Index USA Help-Wanted Advertising Index (10:00 am ET)
3	**4**

DECEMBER

M	T	W	T	F	S	S
	1	2	3	4	5	6
7	8	9	10	11	12	13
14	15	16	17	18	19	20
21	22	23	24	25	26	27
28	29	30	31			

JANUARY

M	T	W	T	F	S	S
				1	2	3
4	5	6	7	8	9	10
11	12	13	14	15	16	17
18	19	20	21	22	23	24
25	26	27	28	29	30	31

FEBRUARY

M	T	W	T	F	S	S
1	2	3	4	5	6	7
8	9	10	11	12	13	14
15	16	17	18	19	20	21
22	23	24	25	26	27	28

MARCH

M	T	W	T	F	S	S
1	2	3	4	5	6	7
8	9	10	11	12	13	14
15	16	17	18	19	20	21
22	23	24	25	26	27	28
29	30	31				

NOVEMBER
SUMMARY

STRATEGIES	PAGE
STRATEGIES STARTING	
Metals & Mining - Don't Melt In Your Portfolio	135
Three Stars	137
Thanksgiving - Give Thanks and Take Returns	141
STRATEGIES FINISHING	
Transportation on a Roll	113
Retail – II of II Strategies for the Year	125
Thanksgiving - Give Thanks and Take Returns	141

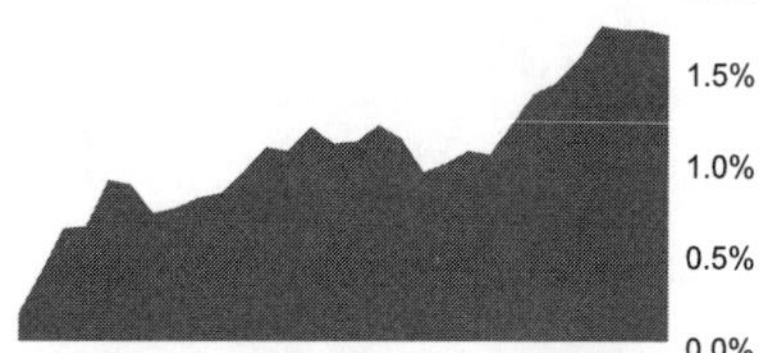

S&P 500 Cumulative Daily Gains for Avg Month 1950 to 2007

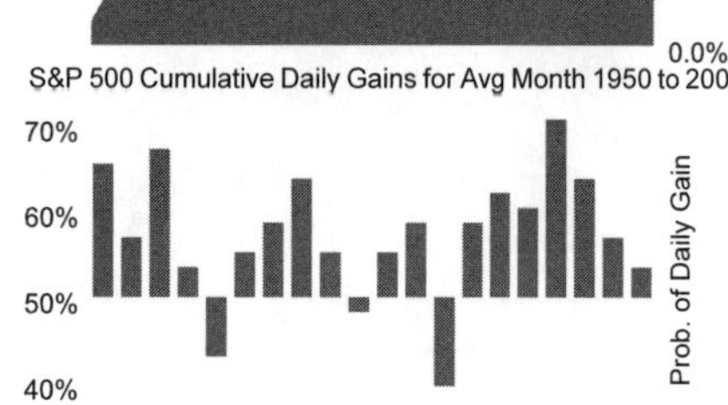

♦ November is one of the best months of the year. It is the first star month of three in a row (see *Three Stars* strategy). The exceptions to November's strong performance in the last decade have been 2000 and 2007 ♦ The strong parts of the month tend to be the first few days and the last few days. ♦ The day before and the day after Thanksgiving tend to be very good (see *Thanksgiving - Give Thanks and Take Returns* strategy). ♦ Information Technology stocks typically continue to do well and rank as one of the top sectors.

BEST / WORST NOVEMBER BROAD MKTS. 1998-2007

BEST NOVEMBER MARKETS

- Nasdaq (2001) 14.2%
- Nasdaq (1999) 12.5%
- Nasdaq (2002) 11.2%

WORST NOVEMBER MARKETS

- Nasdaq (2000) -22.9%
- Russell 3000 Gr (2000) -15.0%
- Russell 2000 (2000) -10.4%

Index Values End of Month

	1998	1999	2000	2001	2002	2003	2004	2005	2006	2007
Dow	9,117	10,878	10,415	9,852	8,896	9,782	10,428	10,806	12,222	13,372
S&P 500	1,164	1,389	1,315	1,139	936	1,058	1,174	1,249	1,401	1,481
Nasdaq	1,950	3,336	2,598	1,931	1,479	1,960	2,097	2,233	2,432	2,661
TSX	6,344	7,520	8,820	7,426	6,570	7,859	9,030	10,824	12,752	13,689
Russell 1000	1,164	1,394	1,331	1,152	952	1,093	1,210	1,306	1,464	1,550
Russell 2000	991	1,130	1,108	1,145	1,010	1,358	1,575	1,683	1,954	1,908
Russell 3000 Growth	2,218	2,898	2,547	1,979	1,520	1,776	1,868	2,026	2,180	2,415
Russell 3000 Value	1,931	2,073	2,095	2,018	1,795	2,072	2,429	2,601	3,057	3,046

Percent Gain for November

	1998	1999	2000	2001	2002	2003	2004	2005	2006	2007
Dow	6.1	1.4	-5.1	8.6	5.9	-0.2	4.0	3.5	1.2	-4.0
S&P 500	5.9	1.9	-8.0	7.5	5.7	0.7	3.9	3.5	1.6	-4.4
Nasdaq	10.1	12.5	-22.9	14.2	11.2	1.5	6.2	5.3	2.7	-6.9
TSX	2.2	3.6	-8.5	7.8	5.1	1.1	1.8	4.2	3.3	-6.4
Russell 1000	6.0	2.4	-9.3	7.5	5.7	1.0	4.1	3.5	1.9	-4.5
Russell 2000	5.1	5.8	-10.4	7.6	8.8	3.5	8.6	4.7	2.5	-7.3
Russell 3000 Growth	7.5	5.7	-15.0	9.5	5.6	1.1	3.7	4.3	1.9	-4.1
Russell 3000 Value	4.3	-0.9	-3.8	5.7	6.1	1.3	5.1	3.0	2.0	-5.4

November Market Avg. Performance 1998 to 2007 (1)

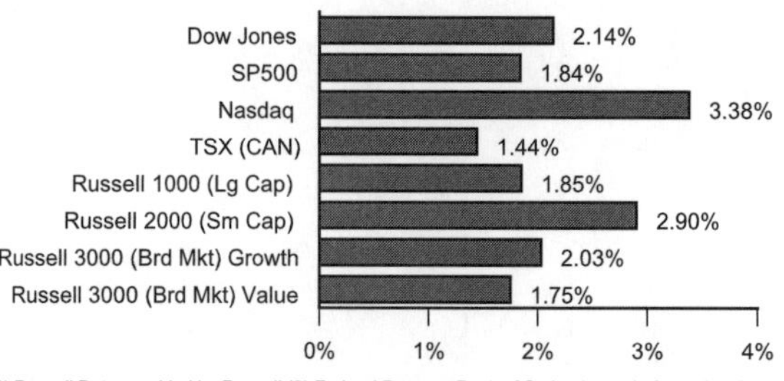

Interest Corner Nov(2)

	Fed Funds % (3)	3 Mo. T-Bill %(4)	10 Yr %(5)	20 Yr %(6)
2007	4.50	3.15	3.97	4.44
2006	5.25	5.03	4.46	4.66
2005	4.00	3.95	4.49	4.81
2004	2.00	2.23	4.36	5.03
2003	1.00	0.93	4.34	5.20

(1) Russell Data provided by Russell (2) Federal Reserve Bank of St. Louis- end of month values (3) Target rate set by FOMC (4)(5)(6) Constant yield maturities

NOVEMBER SECTOR / SUB-SECTOR PERFORMANCE

THACKRAY SECTOR THERMOMETER

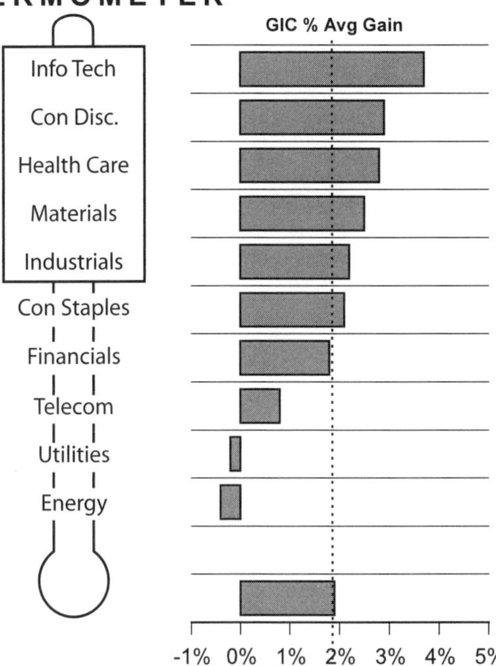

GIC[2] % Avg Gain	Fq % Gain >S&P 500	SP GIC SECTOR 1990-2007[1]
3.7 %	72 %	Information Technology
2.9	67	Consumer Discretionary
2.8	56	Health Care
2.5	56	Materials
2.2	67	Industrials
2.1	44	Consumer Staples
1.8	39	Financials
0.8	33	Telecom
-0.2	33	Utilities
-0.4	22	Energy
1.9 %	N/A %	S&P 500

		SUB-SECTOR 1990-2007[3]
6.8 %	62 %	Semiconductor (SOX) (95-2007)
4.1	81	Retailing
3.4	72	Software & Services
3.3	50	Biotech (92-2007)
3.2	38	Airlines
2.6	56	Insurance
2.5	56	Pharmaceuticals
2.0	50	Metals & Mining
2.0	38	Transportation
1.3	50	Banks
0.5	44	Autos & Components
-0.1	22	Oil Integrated
-1.1	33	Gold (XAU)
-3.3	28	Oil & Gas Exploration & Production

Sector

♦ The top two sectors of this month, Information Technology and Consumer Discretionary have produced average gains of 3.7% and 2.9% respectively. ♦ Telecom moves down the thermometer to join its peers, Utilities and Energy. The top half of the thermometer is dominated by the non-defensive sectors, and the bottom half by the defensives.

Sub-Sector

♦ The top two sub-sectors from the list get their boost from investors jumping in early to benefit from the upcoming holiday sales (for Retailing see *Retail- Shop Early* strategy). ♦ The Gold and Oil sectors have on average ended up at the bottom of the list. ♦ The Oil Integrated, Gold and Oil E&P are members of the 1/3 Club, beating the S&P 500 less than one-third of the time for the month. ♦ Although the Airline sector has a better average return than the market, it has only outperformed the market 38% of the time. On average the gains for this sector have been made in the first and last few days of the month.

(1) Sector data provided by Standard and Poors (2) GIC is short form for Global Industry Classification (3) Sub Sector data provided by Standard and Poors, except where marked by symbol

METALS AND MINING
(M&Ms Don't Melt In Your Portfolio)
November 19th to Dec 31st OR May 5th

At the macro level, the metals and mining (M&M) sector is driven by future growth expectations of the economy. When worldwide growth expectations are increasing, there is a greater need for raw materials, when they are decreasing, the need is less.

Within the macro trend, the M&M sector has traditionally followed the overall market cycle of performing well in autumn until spring. This is the time of year that investors have a positive outlook on the economy and as a result the cyclical part of the market tends to outperform; for example, the consumer discretionary sector outperforms the consumer staples sector.

The real "sweet spot" for this sector is from November 19th until the end of the year.

From Nov 19 to Dec 31, an extra 3.1% and better than S&P 500 72% of the time

The M&M sector continues to do well on both an absolute and relative basis until May 5th. At this time the sector tends to fall away. Although this time period has both a greater absolute and relative gain to the market, the frequency of outperformance to the S&P 500 is less. From a portfolio perspective, investors should consider partially reducing exposure at the end of the year and then further reducing exposure at the beginning of May.

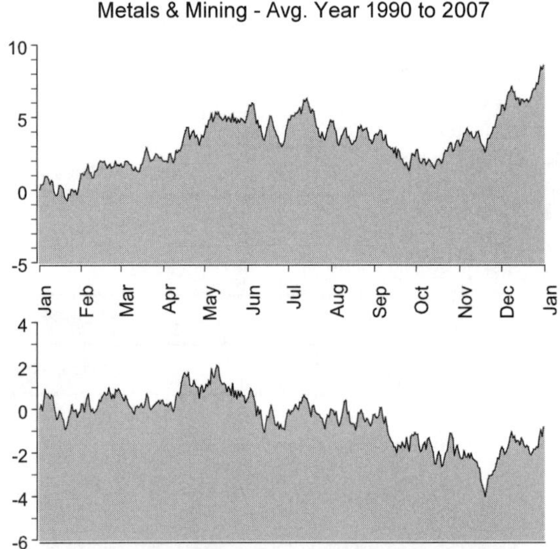

Metals & Mining / SP 500 - Avg Yr. 1990 - 2007

S&P Metals & Mining Sector vs. S&P 500 1990 to 2007

Nov 19 to Dec 31	M&M	SP500	Diff
1990	11.0 %	4.1 %	6.8 %
1991	1.5	8.3	-6.8
1992	10.9	3.0	7.8
1993	5.6	0.6	5.0
1994	1.9	-0.5	2.3
1995	4.0	2.6	1.3
1996	-2.9	0.5	-3.4
1997	-4.9	3.4	-8.4
1998	-10.6	7.4	-18.0
1999	18.8	3.1	15.7
2000	19.0	-3.5	22.5
2001	1.6	0.8	0.8
2002	5.1	-2.3	7.4
2003	15.1	7.5	7.6
2004	-3.2	2.4	-5.6
2005	11.8	0.0	11.8
2006	6.8	1.2	5.6
2007	4.2	0.7	3.6
Avg.	5.3 %	2.2 %	3.1 %

Positive: shaded

S&P Metals & Mining Sector vs. S&P 500 1990/01 to 2007/08

Nov 19 to May 5	M&M	SP500	Diff
1990 / 01	15.0 %	20.1 %	-5.1 %
1991 / 02	4.8	8.2	-3.4
1992 / 03	16.9	5.1	11.8
1993 / 04	-1.7	-2.6	1.0
1994 / 05	-1.1	12.7	-13.8
1995 / 06	15.3	6.9	8.4
1996 / 07	-2.7	12.7	-15.4
1997 / 08	8.4	18.9	-10.5
1998 / 09	20.3	17.7	2.6
1999 / 00	-2.4	0.5	-3.0
2000 / 01	41.9	-7.4	49.3
2001 / 02	13.2	-5.7	18.9
2002 / 03	5.4	2.9	2.5
2003 / 04	-4.6	8.4	-13.0
2004 / 05	-11.0	-0.9	-10.1
2005 / 06	45.1	6.2	38.8
2006 / 07	25.2	7.5	17.7
2007 / 08	13.7	-3.5	17.2
Avg.	11.2 %	6.0 %	5.2 %

Positive: shaded

Metals & Mining
SP GIC Sector #151040
An index designed to represent a cross section of metals and mining companies.

For more information on the metals and mining sector, see www.standardandpoors.com.

9 MONDAY 313 / 052

30 day	Wednesday December 9
60 day	Friday January 8
90 day	Sunday February 7
180 day	Saturday May 8
1 year	Tuesday November 9

10 TUESDAY 314 / 051

30 day	Thursday December 10
60 day	Saturday January 9
90 day	Monday February 8
180 day	Sunday May 9
1 year	Wednesday November 10

11 WEDNESDAY 315 / 050

30 day	Friday December 11
60 day	Sunday January 10
90 day	Tuesday February 9
180 day	Monday May 10
1 year	Thursday November 11

12 THURSDAY 316 / 049

30 day	Saturday December 12
60 day	Monday January 11
90 day	Wednesday February 10
180 day	Tuesday May 11
1 year	Friday November 12

13 FRIDAY 317 / 048

30 day	Sunday December 13
60 day	Tuesday January 12
90 day	Thursday February 11
180 day	Wednesday May 12
1 year	Saturday November 13

* Weekly avg closing values- except Fed Funds Rate & CAN overnight tgt rate which are weekly closing values.

WEEK 46

Market Indices & Rates Weekly Values*

Stock Markets	2006	2007
Dow	12,250	13,162
S&P 500	1,395	1,460
Nasdaq	2,435	2,632
TSX	12,351	13,628
FTSE	6,212	6,357
DAX	6,413	7,729
Nikkei	16,162	15,275
Hang Seng	19,035	28,200

Commodities	2006	2007
Oil (WTI)	57.56	93.56
Gold (London PM)	622.70	801.00

Bond Yields	2006	2007
USA 5 Yr Treasury	4.61	3.77
USA 10 Yr Treasury	4.61	4.22
USA 20 Yr Treasury	4.80	4.61
Moody's Aaa Corporate	5.34	5.49
Moody's Baa Corporate	6.21	6.42
CAN 5 Yr Treasury	3.92	4.04
CAN 10 Yr Treasury	4.01	4.17

Money Market	2006	2007
USA Fed Funds	5.25	4.50
USA 3 Mo T-Bill	5.09	3.40
CAN tgt overnight rate	4.25	4.50
CAN 3 Mo T-Bill	4.19	3.98

Foreign Exchange	2006	2007
USD / EUR	1.28	1.46
USD / GBP	1.89	2.06
CAN / USD	1.14	0.97
JPY / USD	117.95	110.88

NOVEMBER

M	T	W	T	F	S	S
						1
2	3	4	5	6	7	8
9	10	11	12	13	14	15
16	17	18	19	20	21	22
23	24	25	26	27	28	29
30						

DECEMBER

M	T	W	T	F	S	S
	1	2	3	4	5	6
7	8	9	10	11	12	13
14	15	16	17	18	19	20
21	22	23	24	25	26	27
28	29	30	31			

JANUARY

M	T	W	T	F	S	S
				1	2	3
4	5	6	7	8	9	10
11	12	13	14	15	16	17
18	19	20	21	22	23	24
25	26	27	28	29	30	31

THREE STARS

Having one "star" month is good. Having three "star" months is very good. Having three "star" months in a row—who could ask for anything more!

4.6% average gain from November to December & positive 74% of the time

November is the start of the traditional six month favorable time period. It performs well by itself, but so do the two following months: December and January. Put them all together and you have a powerhouse. From 1950 to 2007 this combination has produced a return of 4.6% and has been positive 74% of the time.

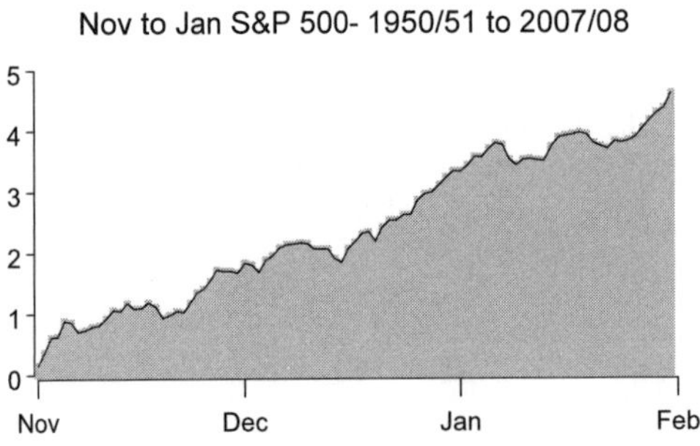

November by itself is typically an excellent month. It has an average return of 1.7% and has been positive 67% of the time.

Over the last fifty-six years, there have been only three years when November and December have both been negative (1969, 1974 and 2007). In the same fifty-six year period, only twice have all three months (Nov, Dec and Jan) been negative. The 1969/70 bear market produced a return of -12.5% and the bear market of 2007/08 produced a return of -11.0%

Also, very impressive is the ratio of compounded positive returns greater than 10% to returns of negative 10% or less. Over the last fifty-six years, there have been only three cases of returns of -10% or less (1969/70, 1973/74 and 2007/08). This compares to thirteen times when the return has been 10% or greater.

S&P 500 % Gain 1950-2007/08 — Positive (shaded)

	Nov	Dec	Jan	Compound Growth
50 / 51	-0.1 %	4.6 %	6.1 %	10.9 %
51 / 52	-0.3	3.9	1.6	5.2
52 / 53	4.6	3.5	-0.7	7.6
53 / 54	0.9	0.2	5.1	6.3
54 / 55	8.1	5.1	1.8	15.6
55 / 56	7.5	-0.1	-3.6	3.5
56 / 57	-1.1	3.5	-4.2	-1.9
57 / 58	1.6	-4.1	4.3	1.6
58 / 59	2.2	5.2	0.4	8.0
59 / 60	1.3	2.8	-7.1	-3.3
60 / 61	4.0	4.6	6.3	15.7
61 / 62	3.9	0.3	-3.8	0.3
62 / 63	10.2	1.3	4.9	17.1
63 / 64	-1.1	2.4	2.7	4.1
64 / 65	-0.5	0.4	3.3	3.2
65 / 66	-0.9	0.9	0.5	0.5
66 / 67	0.3	-0.1	7.8	8.0
67 / 68	0.8	2.6	-4.4	-1.1
68 / 69	4.8	-4.2	-0.8	-0.4
69 / 70	-3.4	-1.9	-7.6	-12.5
70 / 71	4.7	5.7	4.0	15.2
71 / 72	-0.3	8.6	1.8	10.3
72 / 73	4.6	1.2	-1.7	4.0
73 / 74	-11.4	1.7	-1.0	-10.8
74 / 75	-5.3	-2.0	12.3	4.2
75 / 76	2.5	-1.2	11.8	13.3
76 / 77	-0.8	5.2	-5.1	-0.8
77 / 78	2.7	0.3	-6.2	-3.3
78 / 79	1.7	1.5	4.0	7.3
79 / 80	4.3	1.7	5.8	12.1
80 / 81	10.2	-3.4	-4.6	1.6
81 / 82	3.7	-3.0	-1.8	-1.2
82 / 83	3.6	1.5	3.3	8.7
83 / 84	1.7	-0.9	-0.9	-0.1
84 / 85	-1.5	2.2	7.4	8.2
85 / 86	6.5	4.5	0.2	11.6
86 / 87	2.1	-2.8	13.2	12.3
87 / 88	-8.5	7.3	4.0	2.1
88 / 89	-1.9	1.5	7.1	6.6
89 / 90	1.7	2.1	-6.9	-3.3
90 / 91	6.0	2.5	4.2	13.1
91 / 92	-4.4	11.2	-2.0	4.2
92 / 93	3.0	1.0	0.7	4.8
93 / 94	-1.3	1.0	3.3	2.9
94 / 95	-4.0	1.2	2.4	-0.4
95 / 96	4.1	1.7	3.3	9.4
96 / 97	7.3	-2.2	6.1	11.5
97 / 98	4.5	1.6	1.0	7.2
98 / 99	5.9	5.6	4.1	16.5
99 / 00	1.9	5.8	-5.1	2.3
00 / 01	-8.0	0.4	3.5	-4.4
01 / 02	7.5	0.8	-1.6	6.6
02 / 03	5.7	-6.0	-2.7	-3.4
03 / 04	0.7	5.1	1.7	7.7
04 / 05	3.9	3.2	-2.5	4.5
05 / 06	3.5	-0.1	2.5	6.1
06 / 07	1.6	1.3	1.4	4.4
07 / 08	-4.4	-0.9	-6.1	-11.0
Avg	1.7 %	1.7 %	1.3 %	4.6 %
Fq > 0	67 %	74 %	62 %	74 %

16 MONDAY 320 / 045

30 day	Wednesday December 16
60 day	Friday January 15
90 day	Sunday February 14
180 day	Saturday May 15
1 year	Tuesday November 16

17 TUESDAY 321 / 044

30 day	Thursday December 17
60 day	Saturday January 16
90 day	Monday February 15
180 day	Sunday May 16
1 year	Wednesday November 17

18 WEDNESDAY 322 / 043

30 day	Friday December 18
60 day	Sunday January 17
90 day	Tuesday February 16
180 day	Monday May 17
1 year	Thursday November 18

19 THURSDAY 323 / 042

30 day	Saturday December 19
60 day	Monday January 18
90 day	Wednesday February 17
180 day	Tuesday May 18
1 year	Friday November 19

20 FRIDAY 324 / 041

30 day	Sunday December 20
60 day	Tuesday January 19
90 day	Thursday February 18
180 day	Wednesday May 19
1 year	Saturday November 20

* Weekly avg closing values- except Fed Funds Rate & CAN overnight tgt rate which are weekly closing values.

WEEK 47

Market Indices & Rates Weekly Values*

Stock Markets	2006	2007
Dow	12,311	12,937
S&P 500	1,403	1,433
Nasdaq	2,458	2,587
TSX	12,570	13,369
FTSE	6,166	6,167
DAX	6,455	7,566
Nikkei	15,777	14,995
Hang Seng	19,148	26,879

Commodities	2006	2007
Oil (WTI)	57.24	97.93
Gold (London PM)	630.31	798.17

Bond Yields	2006	2007
USA 5 Yr Treasury	4.58	3.52
USA 10 Yr Treasury	4.58	4.06
USA 20 Yr Treasury	4.76	4.50
Moody's Aaa Corporate	5.30	5.40
Moody's Baa Corporate	6.18	6.39
CAN 5 Yr Treasury	3.90	3.80
CAN 10 Yr Treasury	3.98	4.01

Money Market	2006	2007
USA Fed Funds	5.25	4.50
USA 3 Mo T-Bill	5.06	3.24
CAN tgt overnight rate	4.25	4.50
CAN 3 Mo T-Bill	4.17	3.93

Foreign Exchange	2006	2007
USD / EUR	1.29	1.48
USD / GBP	1.91	2.06
CAN / USD	1.14	0.99
JPY / USD	117.29	109.07

NOVEMBER

M	T	W	T	F	S	S
						1
2	3	4	5	6	7	8
9	10	11	12	13	14	15
16	17	18	19	20	21	22
23	24	25	26	27	28	29
30						

DECEMBER

M	T	W	T	F	S	S
	1	2	3	4	5	6
7	8	9	10	11	12	13
14	15	16	17	18	19	20
21	22	23	24	25	26	27
28	29	30	31			

JANUARY

M	T	W	T	F	S	S
				1	2	3
4	5	6	7	8	9	10
11	12	13	14	15	16	17
18	19	20	21	22	23	24
25	26	27	28	29	30	31

U.S. DOLLAR WEAK DECEMBER – STRONG JANUARY

After the bubble burst in 2000, investors started looking for opportunities other than stocks. One type of investment that has become popular is FX, or foreign exchange. Although investing in the currency market is not for everyone, stock investors can also use foreign exchange strategies in helping determine their foreign asset allocation.

0.8% gain & 67% of the time better than Trade Weighted Major World Currencies in Jan.

From 1973 to 2008 the U.S. dollar (USD) has had a seasonal trend of decreasing in December and increasing in January.

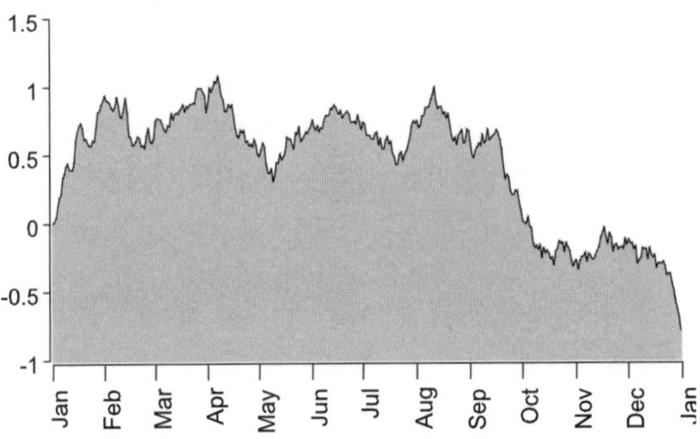

This "v" shape trend provides an opportunity for a nimble trader to sell the USD at the beginning of December and buy it back at the end of the month, in the expectation of making a profit. The second half of the opportunity is in January when the dollar tends to reverse its downward trend. An investor would have reaped a double benefit from 1982 to 2008 with the combined strategy of going "short" the dollar in December and "long" in January. The focus of this analysis is on profiting from the rising dollar in January.

Why does the dollar, on average, produce this "v" shape pattern?

Typically, firms in other countries tend to settle their foreign exchange books at end of year in their domestic currency. The conversion to non-USD currencies tends to push the USD down.

The good news is that the reverse process takes place in January. Foreign firms increase their net dollar holdings to pay for purchases that require USD. This upward bounce has taken place on a fairly consistent basis with the dollar rising 67% of the time.

The dollar has risen in January in both up and down years for the currency. The worst streak that the trade has had since 1973 is two years of negative performance in a row and the best streak of positive performance is five years in a row.

January U.S. Dollar vs. Trade Weighted Major World Currencies- Month of January Gain   Positive

		1980	-0.2 %	1990	0.2 %	2000	2.5 %
		1981	3.0	1991	-1.6	2001	1.0
		1982	2.7	1992	2.8	2002	2.1
1973	-0.5 %	1983	2.4	1993	0.2	2003	-1.9
1974	2.7	1984	1.8	1994	-1.3	2004	0.9
1975	-1.0	1985	0.9	1995	-0.3	2005	2.7
1976	-0.3	1986	-1.3	1996	2.5	2006	-2.2
1977	0.5	1987	-3.2	1997	3.6	2007	1.3
1978	0.4	1988	3.9	1998	0.6	2008	-1.2
1979	2.5	1989	3.0	1999	0.9		
Avg.	0.6 %		1.3 %		0.8 %		0.6 %

Source: Federal Reserve

CAUTION: Most currency traders use leverage to make a profit. The use of leverage can be risky and it is important to make sure that all investments are done within risk tolerance.

The U.S. dollar is measured against the Trade Weighted Major World Currencies. The Euro is becoming a substantial benchmark, but at the current time there is not enough data to establish long-term trends.

23 MONDAY 327 / 038

30 day	Wednesday December 23
60 day	Friday January 22
90 day	Sunday February 21
180 day	Saturday May 22
1 year	Tuesday November 23

24 TUESDAY 328 / 037

30 day	Thursday December 24
60 day	Saturday January 23
90 day	Monday February 22
180 day	Sunday May 23
1 year	Wednesday November 24

25 WEDNESDAY 329 / 036

30 day	Friday December 25
60 day	Sunday January 24
90 day	Tuesday February 23
180 day	Monday May 24
1 year	Thursday November 25

26 THURSDAY 330 / 035

30 day	Saturday December 26
60 day	Monday January 25
90 day	Wednesday February 24
180 day	Tuesday May 25
1 year	Friday November 26

27 FRIDAY 331 / 034

30 day	Sunday December 27
60 day	Tuesday January 26
90 day	Thursday February 25
180 day	Wednesday May 26
1 year	Saturday November 27

* Weekly avg closing values- except Fed Funds Rate & CAN overnight tgt rate which are weekly closing values.

WEEK 48

Market Indices & Rates
Weekly Values*

Stock Markets	**2006**	**2007**
Dow	12,180	13,135
S&P 500	1,393	1,451
Nasdaq	2,419	2,623
TSX	12,650	13,535
FTSE	6,046	6,282
DAX	6,299	7,692
Nikkei	16,083	15,341
Hang Seng	18,855	27,867
Commodities	**2006**	**2007**
Oil (WTI)	62.02	92.47
Gold (London PM)	641.74	804.10
Bond Yields	**2006**	**2007**
USA 5 Yr Treasury	4.48	3.39
USA 10 Yr Treasury	4.49	3.94
USA 20 Yr Treasury	4.69	4.40
Moody's Aaa Corporate	5.23	5.29
Moody's Baa Corporate	6.12	6.37
CAN 5 Yr Treasury	3.82	3.80
CAN 10 Yr Treasury	3.91	3.99
Money Market	**2006**	**2007**
USA Fed Funds	5.25	4.50
USA 3 Mo T-Bill	5.04	3.10
CAN tgt overnight rate	4.25	4.50
CAN 3 Mo T-Bill	4.17	3.90
Foreign Exchange	**2006**	**2007**
USD / EUR	1.32	1.48
USD / GBP	1.96	2.06
CAN / USD	1.14	0.99
JPY / USD	115.89	109.63

NOVEMBER

M	T	W	T	F	S	S
						1
2	3	4	5	6	7	8
9	10	11	12	13	14	15
16	17	18	19	20	21	22
23	24	25	26	27	28	29
30						

DECEMBER

M	T	W	T	F	S	S
	1	2	3	4	5	6
7	8	9	10	11	12	13
14	15	16	17	18	19	20
21	22	23	24	25	26	27
28	29	30	31			

JANUARY

M	T	W	T	F	S	S
				1	2	3
4	5	6	7	8	9	10
11	12	13	14	15	16	17
18	19	20	21	22	23	24
25	26	27	28	29	30	31

THANKSGIVING
GIVE THANKS & TAKE RETURNS
Day Before and After – Two of the Best Days

We have a lot to be thankful for on Thanksgiving Day. As a bonus, the day before and the day after Thanksgiving have been two of the best days of the year in the stock market. Each day by itself has produced spectacular results. From 1950 to 2007, the S&P 500 has had an average gain of 0.3% on the day before Thanksgiving and 0.4% on the day after.

The day before Thanksgiving and the day after have had an average cumulative return of 0.7% and have each been positive 78% of the time

To put the performance of these two days in perspective, the average daily return of the market over the same time period is 0.034%. The Thanksgiving days are almost ten times better. Also, the frequency of positive Thanksgiving days is a very high 78%.

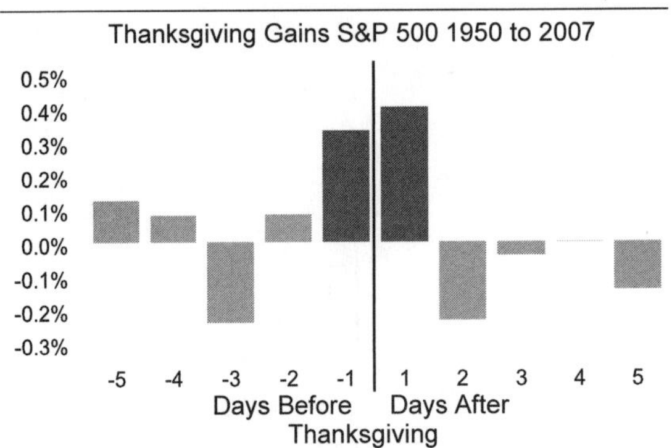

The Thanksgiving bonus is that the two superior days are in a row. Together they have a cumulative return of 0.7% and an incredible 86% frequency of being positive.

Alternate Strategy — Although the focus has been on the performance of two specific days, the day before and the day after Thanksgiving, the holiday occurs at the end of November which tends to be a strong month. December, the next month is also strong. Investors have the good option of expanding their trade out to include the "Santa Arrives Early & Stays Late" Strategy.

History of Thanksgiving:
It was originally a "thanksgiving feast" by the pilgrims for surviving their first winter. Initially it was celebrated sporadically and the holiday, when it was granted, had its date changed several times. It was not until 1941 that it was proclaimed to be the 4th Thursday in November.

(Shaded = Positive)

S&P500	Day Before	THANKSGIVING DAY	Day After
1950	1.4		0.8
1951	-0.2		-1.1
1952	0.6		0.5
1953	0.1		0.6
1954	0.6		1.0
1955	0.1		-0.1
1956	-0.5		1.1
1957	2.9		1.1
1958	1.7		1.1
1959	0.2		0.5
1960	0.1		0.6
1961	-0.1		0.2
1962	0.6		1.2
1963	-0.2		1.4
1964	-0.3		-0.3
1965	0.2		0.1
1966	0.7		0.8
1967	0.6		0.3
1968	0.5		0.6
1969	0.4		0.6
1970	0.4		1.0
1971	0.2		1.8
1972	0.6		0.3
1973	1.1		-0.3
1974	0.7		0.0
1975	0.3		0.3
1976	0.4		0.7
1977	0.4		0.2
1978	0.5		0.3
1979	0.2		0.8
1980	0.6		0.2
1981	0.4		0.8
1982	0.7		0.7
1983	0.1		0.1
1984	0.2		1.5
1985	0.9		-0.2
1986	0.2		0.2
1987	-0.9		-1.5
1988	0.7		-0.7
1989	0.7		0.6
1990	0.2		-0.3
1991	-0.4		-0.4
1992	0.4		0.2
1993	0.3		0.2
1994	0.0		0.5
1995	-0.3		0.3
1996	-0.1		0.3
1997	0.1		0.4
1998	0.3		0.5
1999	0.9		0.0
2000	-1.9		1.5
2001	-0.5		1.2
2002	2.8		-0.3
2003	0.4		0.0
2004	0.4		0.1
2005	0.3		0.2
2006	0.2		-0.4
2007	-1.6		1.7
Total Avg %	0.3%		0.4%
Fq > 0 %	78 %		78 %

30 MONDAY 334 / 031

30 day	Wednesday December 30
60 day	Friday January 29
90 day	Sunday February 28
180 day	Saturday May 29
1 year	Tuesday November 30

1 TUESDAY 335 / 030

30 day	Thursday December 31
60 day	Saturday January 30
90 day	Monday March 1
180 day	Sunday May 30
1 year	Wednesday December 1

2 WEDNESDAY 336 / 029

30 day	Friday January 1
60 day	Sunday January 31
90 day	Tuesday March 2
180 day	Monday May 31
1 year	Thursday December 2

3 THURSDAY 337 / 028

30 day	Saturday January 2
60 day	Monday February 1
90 day	Wednesday March 3
180 day	Tuesday June 1
1 year	Friday December 3

4 FRIDAY 338 / 027

30 day	Sunday January 3
60 day	Tuesday February 2
90 day	Thursday March 4
180 day	Wednesday June 2
1 year	Saturday December 4

WEEK 49

Market Indices & Rates
Weekly Values*

Stock Markets	2006	2007
Dow	12,302	13,451
S&P 500	1,411	1,486
Nasdaq	2,442	2,668
TSX	12,890	13,737
FTSE	6,102	6,447
DAX	6,376	7,905
Nikkei	16,366	15,710
Hang Seng	18,851	29,057

Commodities	2006	2007
Oil (WTI)	62.32	88.71
Gold (London PM)	638.61	793.75

Bond Yields	2006	2007
USA 5 Yr Treasury	4.44	3.35
USA 10 Yr Treasury	4.48	3.97
USA 20 Yr Treasury	4.69	4.46
Moody's Aaa Corporate	5.24	5.37
Moody's Baa Corporate	6.13	6.53
CAN 5 Yr Treasury	3.79	3.73
CAN 10 Yr Treasury	3.89	3.94

Money Market	2006	2007
USA Fed Funds	5.25	4.50
USA 3 Mo T-Bill	4.99	3.08
CAN tgt overnight rate	4.25	4.25
CAN 3 Mo T-Bill	4.16	3.84

Foreign Exchange	2006	2007
USD / EUR	1.33	1.47
USD / GBP	1.97	2.04
CAN / USD	1.15	1.01
JPY / USD	115.36	110.75

DECEMBER

M	T	W	T	F	S	S
	1	2	3	4	5	6
7	8	9	10	11	12	13
14	15	16	17	18	19	20
21	22	23	24	25	26	27
28	29	30	31			

JANUARY

M	T	W	T	F	S	S
				1	2	3
4	5	6	7	8	9	10
11	12	13	14	15	16	17
18	19	20	21	22	23	24
25	26	27	28	29	30	31

FEBRUARY

M	T	W	T	F	S	S
1	2	3	4	5	6	7
8	9	10	11	12	13	14
15	16	17	18	19	20	21
22	23	24	25	26	27	28

* Weekly avg closing values- except Fed Funds Rate & CAN overnight tgt rate which are weekly closing values.

DECEMBER

	MONDAY	TUESDAY	WEDNESDAY
WEEK 49	30	1 (30) USA ISM Manufacturing Report on Business (10:00 am ET)	2 (29) USA Federal Reserve Board's Beige Book
WEEK 50	7 (24)	8 (23)	9 (22)
WEEK 51	14 (17)	15 (16) USA FOMC Meetings USA Empire State Manufacturing Survey - Federal Reserve Bank of New York (8:30 am ET)	16 (15)
WEEK 52	21 (10) USA	22 (9)	23 (8)
WEEK 1	28 (3) CAN Market Closed-Boxing Day USA UBS Index of Investor Optimism (8:30 am ET)	29 (2) USA Consumer Confidence Index 10:00 am ET USA The Strike Report	30 (1)

THURSDAY		FRIDAY	
3	28	**4**	27
USA ISM Non-Manufacturing Report on Business (10:00 am ET)		USA The Employment Situation (8:30 am ET)	
10	21	**11**	20
17	14	**18**	13
USA Federal Reserve Bank of Philadelphia: Business Outlook Survey (12:00 pm ET)			
24	7	**25**	6
USA Early Market Close Christmas Day		USA Market Closed-Christmas Day CAN Market Closed-Christmas Day	
31			
USA Chicago Purchasing Managers Index (Business Barometer) 9:45 am ET USA Help-Wanted Advertising Index (10:00 am ET)			

JANUARY

M	T	W	T	F	S	S
				1	2	3
4	5	6	7	8	9	10
11	12	13	14	15	16	17
18	19	20	21	22	23	24
25	26	27	28	29	30	31

FEBRUARY

M	T	W	T	F	S	S
1	2	3	4	5	6	7
8	9	10	11	12	13	14
15	16	17	18	19	20	21
22	23	24	25	26	27	28

MARCH

M	T	W	T	F	S	S
1	2	3	4	5	6	7
8	9	10	11	12	13	14
15	16	17	18	19	20	21
22	23	24	25	26	27	28
29	30	31				

APRIL

M	T	W	T	F	S	S
			1	2	3	4
5	6	7	8	9	10	11
12	13	14	15	16	17	18
19	20	21	22	23	24	25
26	27	28	29	30		

DECEMBER SUMMARY

STRATEGIES	PAGE
STRATEGIES STARTING	
Small Cap (Small Company) Effect	5
Agriculture Moooves	97
Financials Year End Clean Up	147
Do The "Naz" With Santa	149
Santa Arrives Early and Stays Late	151
STRATEGIES FINISHING	
Gas For 5 Months	99
Metals & Mining - Don't Melt In Your Portfolio	135

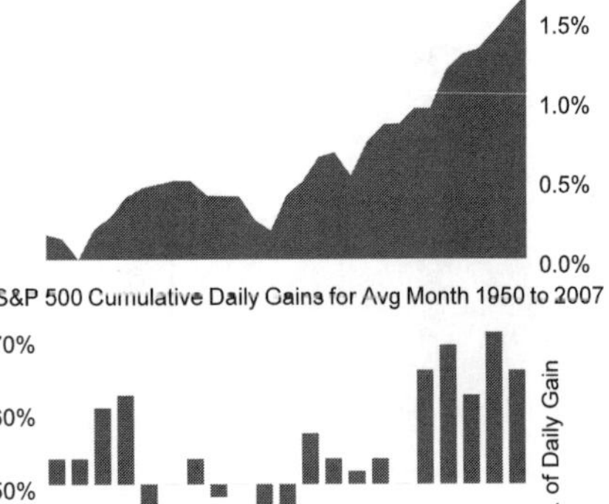

♦ December is one of the best months of the year. Make sure your Christmas shopping includes stocks. ♦ The best method of participating in the Christmas rally has been to enter the stock market on December 15th (see *Santa Arrives Early & Stays Late* strategy). ♦ The Nasdaq tends to outperform the S&P 500 from December 15th to January 23rd. ♦ The US dollar has a habit of weakening in December for a rally in January. ♦ Financial stocks typically start their outperformance at mid-month (see *Financials Year End Clean Up* strategy).

BEST / WORST DECEMBER BROAD MKTS. 1998-2007

BEST DECEMBER MARKETS

- Nasdaq (1999) 22.0%
- Nasdaq (1998) 12.5%
- TSX (1999) 11.9%

WORST DECEMBER MARKETS

- Nasdaq (2002) -9.7%
- Russell 3000 Gr (2002) -7.0%
- Dow (2002) -6.2%

Index Values End of Month

	1998	1999	2000	2001	2002	2003	2004	2005	2006	2007
Dow	9,181	11,497	10,788	10,022	8,342	10,454	10,783	10,718	12,463	13,265
S&P 500	1,229	1,469	1,320	1,148	880	1,112	1,212	1,248	1,418	1,498
Nasdaq	2,193	4,069	2,471	1,950	1,336	2,003	2,175	2,205	2,415	2,652
TSX	6,486	8,414	8,934	7,688	6,615	8,221	9,247	11,272	12,908	13,833
Russell 1000	1,237	1,477	1,346	1,163	896	1,143	1,251	1,306	1,480	1,538
Russell 2000	1,050	1,256	1,202	1,214	952	1,384	1,619	1,673	1,958	1,904
Russell 3000 Growth	2,416	3,211	2,481	1,982	1,413	1,831	1,939	2,018	2,184	2,406
Russell 3000 Value	1,993	2,083	2,204	2,068	1,713	2,191	2,502	2,610	3,116	3,009

Percent Gain for December

	1998	1999	2000	2001	2002	2003	2004	2005	2006	2007
Dow	0.7	5.7	3.6	1.7	-6.2	6.9	3.4	-0.8	2.0	-0.8
S&P 500	5.6	5.8	0.4	0.8	-6.0	5.1	3.2	-0.1	1.3	1.1
Nasdaq	12.5	22.0	-4.9	1.0	-9.7	2.2	3.7	-1.2	-0.7	-0.3
TSX	2.2	11.9	1.3	3.5	0.7	4.6	2.4	4.1	1.2	1.1
Russell 1000	6.2	5.9	1.1	0.9	-5.8	4.6	3.5	0.0	1.1	-0.8
Russell 2000	6.0	11.2	8.4	6.0	-5.7	1.9	2.8	-0.6	0.2	-0.2
Russell 3000 Growth	8.9	10.8	-2.6	0.1	-7.0	3.1	3.8	-0.4	0.2	-0.4
Russell 3000 Value	3.2	0.5	5.2	2.4	-4.5	5.7	3.0	0.3	1.9	-1.2

December Market Avg. Performance 1998 to 2007 (1)

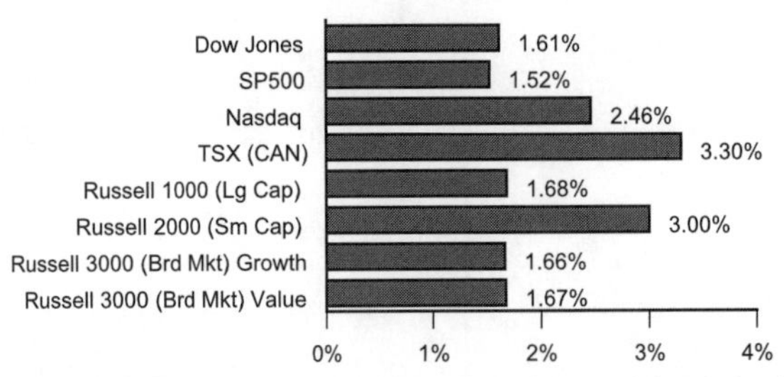

Interest Corner Dec(2)

	Fed Funds % (3)	3 Mo. T-Bill % (4)	10 Yr % (5)	20 Yr % (6)
2007	4.25	3.36	4.04	4.50
2006	5.25	5.02	4.71	4.91
2005	4.25	4.08	4.39	4.61
2004	2.25	2.22	4.24	4.85
2003	1.00	0.95	4.27	5.10

(1) Russell Data provided by Russell (2) Federal Reserve Bank of St. Louis- end of month values (3) Target rate set by FOMC (4)(5)(6) Constant yield maturities

DECEMBER SECTOR / SUB-SECTOR PERFORMANCE

THACKRAY SECTOR THERMOMETER

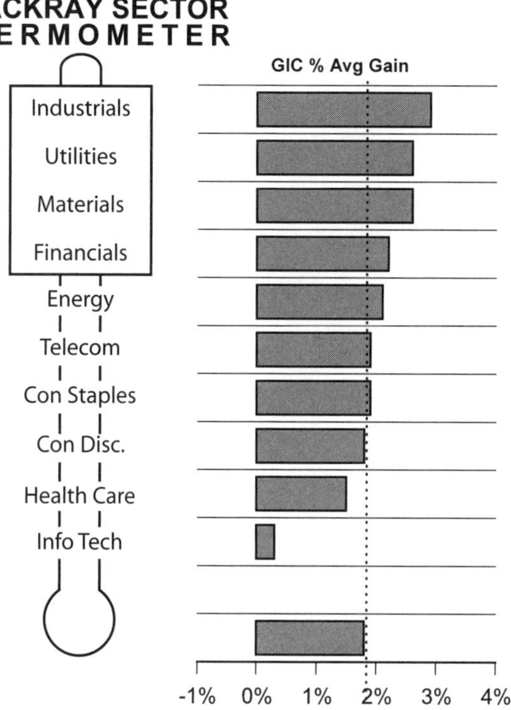

GIC(2) % Avg Gain	Fq % Gain >S&P 500	SP GIC SECTOR 1990-2007(1)
2.9 %	67 %	Industrials
2.6	56	Utilities
2.6	50	Materials
2.2	61	Financials
2.1	44	Energy
1.9	50	Telecom
1.9	50	Consumer Staples
1.8	50	Consumer Discretionary
1.5	50	Health Care
0.3	33	Information Technology
1.9 %	N/A %	S&P 500

		SUB SECTOR 1990-2007(3)
4.8 %	56 %	Biotech (92-2007)
3.6	56	Gold (XAU)
3.0	56	Metals & Mining
2.4	50	Insurance
1.9	44	Oil Integrated
1.8	56	Banks
1.5	39	Software & Services
1.4	44	Autos & Components
1.3	44	Transportation
1.0	44	Oil & Gas Exploration & Production
1.0	44	Pharmaceuticals
0.8	31	Retailing
-0.6	38	Semiconductor (SOX) (95-2007)
-0.9	38	Airlines

Sector

♦ The average December poor performance of Technology stocks surprises a lot of investors. After a strong November and a few days into December, Information Technology stocks tend to underperform the broad market. This can be explained somewhat by investors selling off their more volatile holdings and generating tax losses at the end of the year (see *Small Company Effect* strategy). ♦ Santa needs a sleigh and sleigh production helps the Industrial sector. This is a sector that usually tracks the market closely. In January it is different, as the Industrial sector makes the top of the thermometer with an average gain of 2.9% and a 67% frequency of outperforming the market.

Sub-Sector

♦ Biotechnology and Gold are the two winning sub-sectors from the list. ♦ The Biotechnology sector's outperformance has been attributed to the Morgan Stanley's Pharmaceutical CEO's Unplugged conference at the beginning of January. Investors move into the sector at year end to benefit from any positive announcements forthcoming at the beginning of the year. ♦ Gold stocks rise rapidly on the thermometer with an average performance of 3.6% and a slightly better than 50% frequency of beating the market.

(1) Sector data provided by Standard and Poors (2) GIC is short form for Global Industry Classification (3) Sub Sector data provided by Standard and Poors, except where marked by symbol

FINANCIALS YEAR END CLEAN UP

Outperform December 14th to April 13th

Financials, companies in the business of managing money or investments, have outperformed the broad market since 1990. In the 1990s and early 2000s, financial stocks have had the tailwind of falling interest rates. During this period, with a few exceptions, this sector has participated in both the rallies and the declines. The real sweet spot on average each year, from 1989/90 to 2007/08, has been from mid-December to mid-April.

Extra 2.3% &
14 out of 19 times better than the S&P 500

As financial companies come under greater scrutiny compared with the average company, they tend to "clean up" their books before their financial year end. With most banks, a major part of the financial sector, having their financial year end at the calendar year end, the bad news is laid bare before the start of the calendar year. This sets up the financial stocks for a healthy rally from December 14th to April 13th.

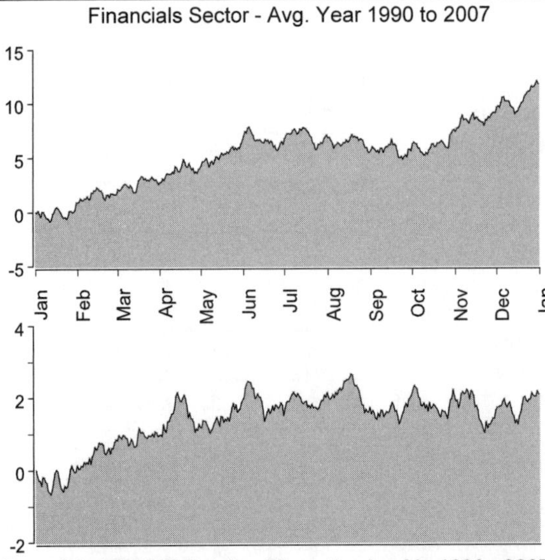

Financials / SP 500 Relative Strength - Avg Yr. 1990 - 2007

Mid-December tends to be a very good time for the markets as they typically accelerate into the New Year. Financial stocks not only do well at this time of year, but they typically outperform the broad market. As the market moves into spring, financial stocks continue to perform well. From the beginning of April until mid-month, financial stocks once again accelerate their performance.

Financial Sector vs. S&P 500
1989/90 to 2007/08

Dec 14 to Apr 13	Financials	S&P 500	Diff (Positive shaded)
1989/90	-10.5 %	-2.4 %	-8.1 %
1990/91	27.4	15.5	11.9
1991/92	9.2	5.6	3.5
1992/93	18.0	3.6	14.4
1993/94	-1.1	-4.2	3.1
1994/95	15.7	13.1	2.6
1995/96	4.1	2.4	1.7
1996/97	4.7	1.2	3.4
1997/98	19.7	16.4	3.3
1998/99	22.1	15.7	6.4
1999/00	2.0	1.8	0.2
2000/01	-6.9	-13.0	6.0
2001/02	5.9	-0.7	6.7
2002/03	-1.8	-2.4	0.6
2003/04	6.6	5.1	1.5
2004/05	-5.9	-2.1	-3.8
2005/06	1.5	1.7	-0.2
2006/07	-1.4	2.8	-4.2
2007/08	-15.7	-10.5	-5.2
Avg.	4.9 %	2.6 %	2.3 %

This part of the financial sector's outperformance coincides with the run-up to the last day to file taxes and is also interlinked with the 3 month TBill yield decrease (see *Pre-Tax Yield Effect* strategy). Basically, as taxpayers sell off their money market holdings to pay their tax liabilities, liquidity in the market is increased, which in turn pushes the yield down on short-term rates. Financial stocks, particularly banks, tend to benefit from falling rates. The situation is reversed when the liquidity is sucked out of the market after the tax deadline.

Financial stocks have outperformed in their seasonal strong time in both up markets and down markets. More recently, they have had a string of four underperforming years in a row, 2004/05 to 2007/08.

Financial SP GIC Sector # 40:
An index that contains companies involved in activities such as banking, mortgage finance, consumer finance, specialized finance, investment banking and brokerage, asset management and custody, corporate lending, insurance, financial investment, and real estate, including REITs.

7 MONDAY 341 / 024

30 day	Wednesday January 6
60 day	Friday February 5
90 day	Sunday March 7
180 day	Saturday June 5
1 year	Tuesday December 7

8 TUESDAY 342 / 023

30 day	Thursday January 7
60 day	Saturday February 6
90 day	Monday March 8
180 day	Sunday June 6
1 year	Wednesday December 8

9 WEDNESDAY 343 / 022

30 day	Friday January 8
60 day	Sunday February 7
90 day	Tuesday March 9
180 day	Monday June 7
1 year	Thursday December 9

10 THURSDAY 344 / 021

30 day	Saturday January 9
60 day	Monday February 8
90 day	Wednesday March 10
180 day	Tuesday June 8
1 year	Friday December 10

11 FRIDAY 345 / 020

30 day	Sunday January 10
60 day	Tuesday February 9
90 day	Thursday March 11
180 day	Wednesday June 9
1 year	Saturday December 11

WEEK 50

Market Indices & Rates Weekly Values*

Stock Markets	2006	2007
Dow	12,365	13,498
S&P 500	1,418	1,487
Nasdaq	2,444	2,669
TSX	12,907	13,779
FTSE	6,199	6,485
DAX	6,522	7,999
Nikkei	16,720	15,790
Hang Seng	18,916	28,311

Commodities	2006	2007
Oil (WTI)	61.91	91.18
Gold (London PM)	625.98	804.49

Bond Yields	2006	2007
USA 5 Yr Treasury	4.53	3.49
USA 10 Yr Treasury	4.56	4.12
USA 20 Yr Treasury	4.77	4.61
Moody's Aaa Corporate	5.31	5.55
Moody's Baa Corporate	6.21	6.72
CAN 5 Yr Treasury	3.85	3.91
CAN 10 Yr Treasury	3.95	4.06

Money Market	2006	2007
USA Fed Funds	5.25	4.25
USA 3 Mo T-Bill	4.93	2.92
CAN tgt overnight rate	4.25	4.25
CAN 3 Mo T-Bill	4.17	3.86

Foreign Exchange	2006	2007
USD / EUR	1.32	1.46
USD / GBP	1.96	2.04
CAN / USD	1.15	1.01
JPY / USD	117.41	112.27

DECEMBER

M	T	W	T	F	S	S
	1	2	3	4	5	6
7	8	9	10	11	12	13
14	15	16	17	18	19	20
21	22	23	24	25	26	27
28	29	30	31			

JANUARY

M	T	W	T	F	S	S
				1	2	3
4	5	6	7	8	9	10
11	12	13	14	15	16	17
18	19	20	21	22	23	24
25	26	27	28	29	30	31

FEBRUARY

M	T	W	T	F	S	S
1	2	3	4	5	6	7
8	9	10	11	12	13	14
15	16	17	18	19	20	21
22	23	24	25	26	27	28

* Weekly avg closing values- except Fed Funds Rate & CAN overnight tgt rate which are weekly closing values.

DO THE "NAZ" WITH SANTA

Nasdaq gives more at Christmas – Dec 15th to Jan 23rd

One of the best times to invest in the major markets is Christmas time. What few investors know is that this seasonally strong time favors the Nasdaq market. From December 15th to January 23rd, starting in 1972 and ending in 2008, the Nasdaq has outperformed the S&P 500 by an average 2.4% per year. This rate of return is considered to be very high given that the length of favorable time is just over one month. Even more amazing is the 84% frequency that the Nasdaq has outperformed during this time period.

2.4% extra &
84% of time better than the S&P 500

Looking for reasons that the Nasdaq outperforms? Interestingly, the Nasdaq starts to outperform at the same time as small companies in December (see *Small Company Effect* strategy). As investors move into the market to scoop up bargains that have been sold for tax losses, smaller companies and stocks with greater volatility tend to outperform. Compared with the S&P 500 and Dow Jones, the Nasdaq market, given its composition, tends to be a much greater recipient of the upward move created by investors picking up cheap stocks at this time of the year.

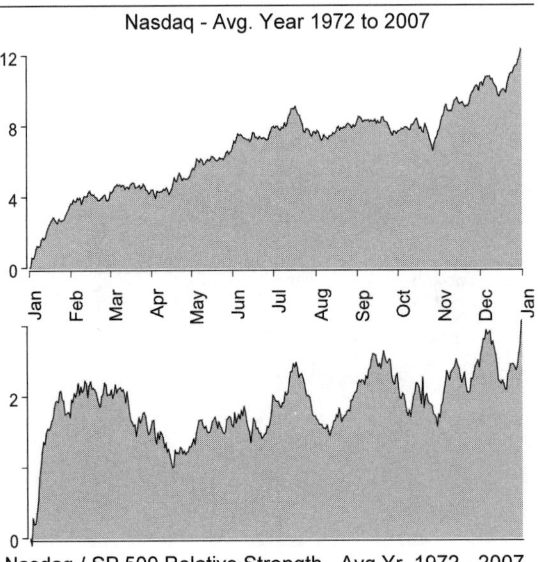

Nasdaq vs. S&P 500 Dec 15th to Jan 23rd 1971/72 To 2007/08

(Positive shaded)

Dec 15 to Jan 23	Nasdaq	S&P 500	Diff
1971/72	7.5 %	6.1 %	1.3 %
1972/73	-0.7	0.0	-0.7
1973/74	6.8	4.1	2.8
1974/75	8.9	7.5	1.4
1975/76	13.8	13.0	0.9
1976/77	2.8	-1.7	4.5
1977/78	-3.5	-5.1	1.6
1978/79	6.2	4.7	1.4
1979/80	5.6	4.1	1.5
1980/81	3.3	0.8	2.5
1981/82	-5.0	-6.0	1.0
1982/83	5.5	4.7	0.8
1983/84	1.4	0.9	0.4
1984/85	13.3	9.0	4.3
1985/86	0.8	-2.7	3.5
1986/87	10.2	9.2	1.0
1987/88	9.1	1.8	7.3
1988/89	4.6	3.3	1.3
1989/90	-3.8	-5.5	1.7
1990/91	4.1	1.0	3.1
1991/92	15.2	7.9	7.2
1992/93	7.2	0.8	6.4
1993/94	5.7	2.5	3.2
1994/95	4.7	2.4	2.3
1995/96	-1.0	-0.7	-0.3
1996/97	7.3	6.7	0.6
1997/98	2.6	0.4	2.1
1998/99	18.9	7.4	11.6
1999/00	18.6	2.7	15.9
2000/01	4.1	1.5	2.6
2001/02	-1.6	0.5	-2.0
2002/03	1.9	-0.2	2.1
2003/04	9.0	6.3	2.7
2004/05	-5.8	-3.0	-2.9
2005/06	-0.6	-0.7	0.1
2006/07	-0.9	0.2	-1.1
2007/08	-12.1	-8.8	-3.3
Avg	4.4 %	2.0 %	2.4 %

Alternate Strategy — For those investors who favor the Nasdaq, an alternative strategy is to invest in the Nasdaq at an earlier date: October 28th. Historically, on average the Nasdaq has started its out performance at this time. The "Do the Naz with Santa" strategy focuses on the sweet spot of the Nasdaq's out performance.

Nasdaq is a market with a number of sectors. It is more focused on technology and is typically more volatile than the S&P 500.

14 MONDAY 348 / 017

30 day	Wednesday January 13
60 day	Friday February 12
90 day	Sunday March 14
180 day	Saturday June 12
1 year	Tuesday December 14

15 TUESDAY 349 / 016

30 day	Thursday January 14
60 day	Saturday February 13
90 day	Monday March 15
180 day	Sunday June 13
1 year	Wednesday December 15

16 WEDNESDAY 350 / 015

30 day	Friday January 15
60 day	Sunday February 14
90 day	Tuesday March 16
180 day	Monday June 14
1 year	Thursday December 16

17 THURSDAY 351 / 014

30 day	Saturday January 16
60 day	Monday February 15
90 day	Wednesday March 17
180 day	Tuesday June 15
1 year	Friday December 17

18 FRIDAY 352 / 013

30 day	Sunday January 17
60 day	Tuesday February 16
90 day	Thursday March 18
180 day	Wednesday June 16
1 year	Saturday December 18

WEEK 51

Market Indices & Rates Weekly Values*

Stock Markets	2006	2007
Dow	12,428	13,261
S&P 500	1,420	1,460
Nasdaq	2,422	2,621
TSX	12,761	13,428
FTSE	6,208	6,324
DAX	6,563	7,877
Nikkei	16,981	15,155
Hang Seng	19,188	27,001

Commodities	2006	2007
Oil (WTI)	62.40	91.16
Gold (London PM)	618.56	800.10

Bond Yields	2006	2007
USA 5 Yr Treasury	4.56	3.52
USA 10 Yr Treasury	4.60	4.12
USA 20 Yr Treasury	4.82	4.58
Moody's Aaa Corporate	5.36	5.51
Moody's Baa Corporate	6.26	6.65
CAN 5 Yr Treasury	3.91	3.90
CAN 10 Yr Treasury	4.01	4.03

Money Market	2006	2007
USA Fed Funds	5.25	4.25
USA 3 Mo T-Bill	4.97	2.99
CAN tgt overnight rate	4.25	4.25
CAN 3 Mo T-Bill	4.16	3.83

Foreign Exchange	2006	2007
USD / EUR	1.32	1.44
USD / GBP	1.96	2.00
CAN / USD	1.15	1.00
JPY / USD	118.32	113.35

DECEMBER

M	T	W	T	F	S	S
	1	2	3	4	5	6
7	8	9	10	11	12	13
14	15	16	17	18	19	20
21	22	23	24	25	26	27
28	29	30	31			

JANUARY

M	T	W	T	F	S	S
				1	2	3
4	5	6	7	8	9	10
11	12	13	14	15	16	17
18	19	20	21	22	23	24
25	26	27	28	29	30	31

FEBRUARY

M	T	W	T	F	S	S
1	2	3	4	5	6	7
8	9	10	11	12	13	14
15	16	17	18	19	20	21
22	23	24	25	26	27	28

* Weekly avg closing values- except Fed Funds Rate & CAN overnight tgt rate which are weekly closing values.

SANTA ARRIVES EARLY & STAYS LATE

Dec 15th to Jan 6th

Every year investors wait for Santa Claus to come to town. They often get rewarded, but many leave with small returns because they focus on one or two days of outperformance. The best way to get the gift of Christmas is to get in early and stay late. The market typically makes a move up about halfway through December and continues through to the first week in January.

The first part of this move can be attributed to investors taking advantage of the "*January Effect*," buying stocks that have been beaten down because of tax loss selling (see *Small Company Effect* strategy). The second part of the move, the start of January, benefits from the beginning of the month effect (see *Super Seven* strategy). The first few days in January are also boosted by money managers locking in their selections for the New Year.

Dec 15th to Jan 6th Avg. Gain vs.
15 Market Day - Avg. Gain

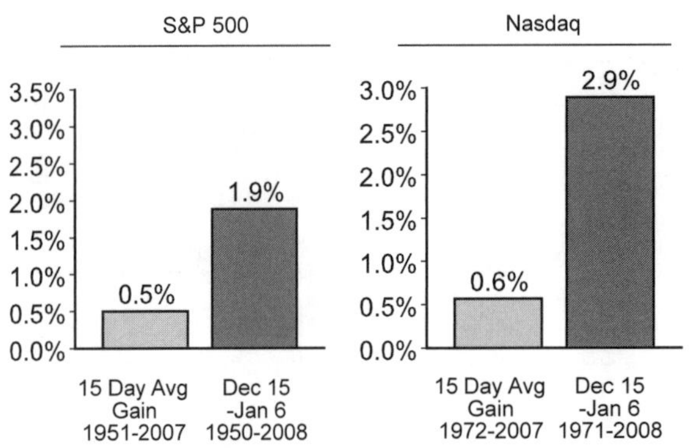

The *Santa Arrives Early & Stays Late* strategy starts on December 15th and ends January 6th. Using this Christmas strategy with the S&P 500 from 1950 to 2008 has on average lasted fifteen days and produced a return of 1.9%. This compares to the 0.5% return for the average fifteen day period from 1951 to 2007 (year adjustment is used to more closely align strategy with benchmark years). The net result is that this Christmas strategy has been four times better than the average fifteen day period.

The Nasdaq has produced similar results. Its gain with the *Santa Arrives Early & Stays Late* strategy has produced an average 2.9% gain, which is five times better than the average fifteen day gain for the Nasdaq from 1972 to 2008.

> *Alternate Strategy—The Extended Santa Rally:*
> *The focus of the "Santa Arrives Early Stays Late" is around the Christmas days, but on average, after the 6th, the market tends to tread water for only a few days before rallying until the beginning of February (February 3rd).*

% Change Dec 15th to Jan 6th

Date	S&P 500 Change	Nasdaq Change
50 / 51	7.5 %	N/A %
51 / 52	2.4	"
52 / 53	1.7	"
53 / 54	1.8	"
54 / 55	2.0	"
55 / 56	0.2	"
56 / 57	0.3	"
57 / 58	-0.1	"
58 / 59	4.5	"
59 / 60	1.8	"
60 / 61	2.7	"
61 / 62	-3.2	"
62 / 63	2.5	"
63 / 64	2.2	"
64 / 65	1.7	"
65 / 66	1.3	"
66 / 67	-0.6	"
67 / 68	0.5	"
68 / 69	-4.7	"
69 / 70	2.2	"
70 / 71	2.8	"
71 / 72	6.0	6.1
72 / 73	1.4	1.9
73 / 74	6.0	5.0
74 / 75	6.0	4.3
75 / 76	6.5	7.2
76 / 77	0.0	2.8
77 / 78	-2.6	-2.2
78 / 79	3.2	3.3
79 / 80	-2.2	-1.3
80 / 81	6.9	6.7
81 / 82	-2.9	-2.3
82 / 83	5.7	2.3
83 / 84	3.6	4.2
84 / 85	0.6	3.0
85 / 86	0.3	0.6
86 / 87	2.2	2.8
87 / 88	6.9	12.1
88 / 89	1.9	3.2
89 / 90	0.4	2.4
90 / 91	-1.8	-0.4
91 / 92	8.7	10.5
92 / 93	0.4	4.1
93 / 94	0.9	3.9
94 / 95	1.3	3.3
95 / 96	0.0	-0.5
96 / 97	2.6	2.5
97 / 98	1.4	2.8
98 / 99	11.5	18.0
99 / 00	0.0	4.4
00 / 01	-3.2	-11.8
01 / 02	4.4	5.4
02 / 03	4.4	4.3
03 / 04	4.6	5.6
04 / 05	-1.3	-3.2
05 / 06	1.0	1.9
06 / 07	-1.1	-0.8
07 / 08	-3.8	-5.0
AVG.	1.9 %	2.9 %

21 MONDAY 355 / 010

30 day	Wednesday January 20
60 day	Friday February 19
90 day	Sunday March 21
180 day	Saturday June 19
1 year	Tuesday December 21

22 TUESDAY 356 / 009

30 day	Thursday January 21
60 day	Saturday February 20
90 day	Monday March 22
180 day	Sunday June 20
1 year	Wednesday December 22

23 WEDNESDAY 357 / 008

30 day	Friday January 22
60 day	Sunday February 21
90 day	Tuesday March 23
180 day	Monday June 21
1 year	Thursday December 23

24 THURSDAY 358 / 007

30 day	Saturday January 23
60 day	Monday February 22
90 day	Wednesday March 24
180 day	Tuesday June 22
1 year	Friday December 24

25 FRIDAY 359 / 006

30 day	Sunday January 24
60 day	Tuesday February 23
90 day	Thursday March 25
180 day	Wednesday June 23
1 year	Saturday December 25

* Weekly avg closing values- except Fed Funds Rate & CAN overnight tgt rate which are weekly closing values.

WEEK 52

Market Indices & Rates Weekly Values*

Stock Markets	2006	2007
Dow	12,471	13,457
S&P500	1,422	1,487
Nasdaq	2,421	2,697
TSX	12,890	13,731
FTSE	6,224	6,485
DAX	6,606	8,053
Nikkei	17,192	15,520
Hang Seng	19,897	27,781
Commodities	**2006**	**2007**
Oil	60.66	95.64
Gold	630.25	831.38
Bond Yields	**2006**	**2007**
USA 5 Yr Treasury	4.65	3.63
USA 10 Yr T	4.67	4.21
USA 20 Yr T	4.88	4.66
Moody's Aaa	5.43	5.57
Moody's Baa	6.32	6.72
CAN 5 Yr T	3.98	3.94
CAN 10 Yr T	4.07	4.07
Money Market	**2006**	**2007**
USA Fed Funds	5.25	4.25
USA 3 Mo T-B	5.00	3.25
CAN tgt overnight rate	4.25	4.25
CAN 3 Mo T-B	4.16	3.85
Foreign Exchange	**2006**	**2007**
USD / EUR	1.32	1.46
USD / GBP	1.96	1.99
CAN / USD	1.16	0.98
JPY / USD	118.92	113.87

DECEMBER

M	T	W	T	F	S	S
	1	2	3	4	5	6
7	8	9	10	11	12	13
14	15	16	17	18	19	20
21	22	23	24	25	26	27
28	29	30	31			

JANUARY

M	T	W	T	F	S	S
				1	2	3
4	5	6	7	8	9	10
11	12	13	14	15	16	17
18	19	20	21	22	23	24
25	26	27	28	29	30	31

FEBRUARY

M	T	W	T	F	S	S
1	2	3	4	5	6	7
8	9	10	11	12	13	14
15	16	17	18	19	20	21
22	23	24	25	26	27	28

2nd Half of Year Strategy Review

Month	Strategy	Security	Quantity	Buy Date	Buy Price	Sell Date	Sell Price	Profit

Comments

Month	Strategy	Security	Quantity	Buy Date	Buy Price	Sell Date	Sell Price	Profit

Month	Strategy	Security	Quantity	Buy Date	Buy Price	Sell Date	Sell Price	Profit

Month	Strategy	Security	Quantity	Buy Date	Buy Price	Sell Date	Sell Price	Profit

Month	Strategy	Security	Quantity	Buy Date	Buy Price	Sell Date	Sell Price	Profit

Month	Strategy	Security	Quantity	Buy Date	Buy Price	Sell Date	Sell Price	Profit

Month	Strategy	Security	Quantity	Buy Date	Buy Price	Sell Date	Sell Price	Profit

Month	Strategy	Security	Quantity	Buy Date	Buy Price	Sell Date	Sell Price	Profit

28 MONDAY 362 / 003

30 day	Wednesday January 27
60 day	Friday February 26
90 day	Sunday March 28
180 day	Saturday June 26
1 year	Tuesday December 28

29 TUESDAY 363 / 002

30 day	Thursday January 28
60 day	Saturday February 27
90 day	Monday March 29
180 day	Sunday June 27
1 year	Wednesday December 29

30 WEDNESDAY 364 / 001

30 day	Friday January 29
60 day	Sunday February 28
90 day	Tuesday March 30
180 day	Monday June 28
1 year	Thursday December 30

31 THURSDAY 365 / 000

30 day	Saturday January 30
60 day	Monday March 1
90 day	Wednesday March 31
180 day	Tuesday June 29
1 year	Friday December 31

1 FRIDAY

30 day	Sunday January 31
60 day	Tuesday March 2
90 day	Thursday April 1
180 day	Wednesday June 30
1 year	Saturday January 1

WEEK 1

Market Indices & Rates
Weekly Values*

Stock Markets	**2007**	**2008**
Dow	12,451	13,041
S&P500	1,415	1,444
Nasdaq	2,437	2,592
TSX	12,664	13,879
FTSE	6,284	6,425
DAX	6,660	7,889
Nikkei	17,223	14,691
Hang Seng	20,240	27,445
Commodities	**2007**	**2008**
Oil	57.76	98.17
Gold	630.14	853.53
Bond Yields	**2007**	**2008**
USA 5 Yr Treasury	4.65	3.29
USA 10 Yr T	4.66	3.94
USA 20 Yr T	4.84	4.43
Moody's Aaa	5.31	5.35
Moody's Baa	6.27	6.49
CAN 5 Yr T	3.93	3.77
CAN 10 Yr T	4.03	3.93
Money Market	**2007**	**2008**
USA Fed Funds	5.25	4.25
USA 3 Mo T-B	5.05	3.27
CAN tgt overnight rate	4.25	4.25
CAN 3 Mo T-B	4.15	3.78
Foreign Exchange	**2007**	**2008**
USD/EUR	1.31	1.47
USD/GBP	1.95	1.98
CAN/USD	1.17	0.99
JPY/USD	119.12	109.84

DECEMBER

M	T	W	T	F	S	S
	1	2	3	4	5	6
7	8	9	10	11	12	13
14	15	16	17	18	19	20
21	22	23	24	25	26	27
28	29	30	31			

JANUARY

M	T	W	T	F	S	S
				1	2	3
4	5	6	7	8	9	10
11	12	13	14	15	16	17
18	19	20	21	22	23	24
25	26	27	28	29	30	31

FEBRUARY

M	T	W	T	F	S	S
1	2	3	4	5	6	7
8	9	10	11	12	13	14
15	16	17	18	19	20	21
22	23	24	25	26	27	28

* Weekly avg closing values- except Fed Funds Rate & CAN overnight tgt rate which are weekly closing values.

APPENDIX

STOCK MARKET RETURNS

STOCK MKT

S&P 500 PERCENT CHANGES

	JAN	FEB	MAR	APR	MAY	JUN
1950	1.7 %	1.0 %	0.4 %	4.5 %	3.9 %	-5.8 %
1951	6.1	0.6	-1.8	4.8	-4.1	-2.6
1952	1.6	-3.6	4.8	-4.3	2.3	4.6
1953	-0.7	-1.8	-2.4	-2.6	-0.3	-1.6
1954	5.1	0.3	3.0	4.9	3.3	0.1
1955	1.8	0.4	-0.5	3.8	-0.1	8.2
1956	-3.6	3.5	6.9	-0.2	-6.6	3.9
1957	-4.2	-3.3	2.0	3.7	3.7	-0.1
1958	4.3	2.1	3.1	3.2	1.5	2.6
1959	0.4	-0.1	0.1	3.9	1.9	-0.4
1960	-7.1	0.9	-1.4	-1.8	2.7	2.0
1961	6.3	2.7	2.6	0.4	1.9	-2.9
1962	-3.8	1.6	-0.6	-6.2	-8.6	-8.2
1963	4.9	-2.9	3.5	4.9	1.4	-2.0
1964	2.7	1.0	1.5	0.6	1.1	1.6
1965	3.3	-0.1	-1.5	3.4	-0.8	-4.9
1966	0.5	-1.8	-2.2	2.1	-5.4	-1.6
1967	7.8	0.2	3.9	4.2	-5.2	1.8
1968	-4.4	-3.1	0.9	8.0	1.3	0.9
1969	-0.8	-4.7	3.4	2.1	-0.2	-5.6
1970	-7.6	5.3	0.1	-9.0	-6.1	-5.0
1971	4.0	0.9	3.7	3.6	-4.2	-0.9
1972	1.8	2.5	0.6	0.4	1.7	-2.2
1973	-1.7	-3.7	-0.1	-4.1	-1.9	-0.7
1974	-1.0	-0.4	-2.3	-3.9	-3.4	-1.5
1975	12.3	6.0	2.2	4.7	4.4	4.4
1976	11.8	-1.1	3.1	-1.1	-1.4	4.1
1977	-5.1	-2.2	-1.4	0.0	-2.4	4.5
1978	-6.2	-2.5	2.5	8.5	0.4	-1.8
1979	4.0	-3.7	5.5	0.2	-2.6	3.9
1980	5.8	-0.4	-10.2	4.1	4.7	2.7
1981	-4.6	1.3	3.6	-2.3	-0.2	-1.0
1982	-1.8	-6.1	-1.0	4.0	-3.9	-2.0
1983	3.3	1.9	3.3	7.5	-1.2	3.2
1984	-0.9	-3.9	1.3	0.5	-5.9	1.7
1985	7.4	0.9	-0.3	-0.5	5.4	1.2
1986	0.2	7.1	5.3	-1.4	5.0	1.4
1987	13.2	3.7	2.6	-1.1	0.6	4.8
1988	4.0	4.2	-3.3	0.9	0.3	4.3
1989	7.1	-2.9	2.1	5.0	3.5	-0.8
1990	-6.9	0.9	2.4	-2.7	9.2	-0.9
1991	4.2	6.7	2.2	0.0	3.9	-4.8
1992	-2.0	1.0	-2.2	2.8	0.1	-1.7
1993	0.7	1.0	1.9	-2.5	2.3	0.1
1994	3.3	-3.0	-4.6	1.2	1.2	-2.7
1995	2.4	3.6	2.7	2.8	3.6	2.1
1996	3.3	0.7	0.8	1.3	2.3	0.2
1997	6.1	0.6	-4.3	5.8	5.9	4.3
1998	1.0	7.0	5.0	0.9	-1.9	3.9
1999	4.1	-3.2	3.9	3.8	-2.5	5.4
2000	-5.1	-2.0	9.7	-3.1	-2.2	2.4
2001	3.5	-9.2	-6.4	7.7	0.5	-2.5
2002	-1.6	-2.1	3.7	-6.1	-0.9	-7.2
2003	-2.7	-1.7	0.8	8.1	5.1	1.1
2004	1.7	1.2	-1.6	-1.7	1.2	1.8
2005	-2.5	1.9	-1.9	-2.0	3.0	0.0
2006	2.5	0.0	1.1	1.2	-3.1	0.0
2007	1.4	-2.2	1.0	4.3	3.3	-1.8
2008	-6.1	-3.5	-0.6	4.8	1.1	-8.6
FQ POS*	37 / 59	31 / 59	38 / 59	40 / 59	34 / 59	30 / 59
% FQ POS*	63 %	53 %	64 %	68 %	58 %	51 %
AVG GAIN*	1.3 %	-0.1 %	1.0 %	1.4 %	0.3 %	0.0 %
RANK GAIN*	4	11	5	3	8	10

S&P 500 PERCENT CHANGES

STOCK MKT

*JUL	*AUG	*SEP	*OCT	*NOV	*DEC		*YEAR
0.8 %	3.3 %	5.6 %	0.4 %	— 0.1 %	4.6 %	**1950**	21.8 %
6.9	3.9	— 0.1	— 1.4	— 0.3	3.9	**1951**	16.5
1.8	— 1.5	— 2.0	— 0.1	4.6	3.5	**1952**	11.8
2.5	— 5.8	0.1	5.1	0.9	0.2	**1953**	— 6.6
5.7	— 3.4	8.3	— 1.9	8.1	5.1	**1954**	45.0
6.1	— 0.8	1.1	— 3.0	7.5	— 0.1	**1955**	26.4
5.2	— 3.8	— 4.5	0.5	— 1.1	3.5	**1956**	2.6
1.1	— 5.6	— 6.2	— 3.2	1.6	— 4.1	**1957**	— 14.3
4.3	1.2	4.8	2.5	2.2	5.2	**1958**	38.1
3.5	— 1.5	— 4.6	1.1	1.3	2.8	**1959**	8.5
— 2.5	2.6	— 6.0	— 0.2	4.0	4.6	**1960**	— 3.0
3.3	2.0	— 2.0	2.8	3.9	0.3	**1961**	23.1
6.4	1.5	— 4.8	0.4	10.2	1.3	**1962**	— 11.8
— 0.3	4.9	— 1.1	3.2	— 1.1	2.4	**1963**	18.9
1.8	— 1.6	2.9	0.8	— 0.5	0.4	**1964**	13.0
1.3	2.3	3.2	2.7	— 0.9	0.9	**1965**	9.1
— 1.3	— 7.8	— 0.7	4.8	0.3	— 0.1	**1966**	— 13.1
4.5	— 1.2	3.3	— 3.5	0.8	2.6	**1967**	20.1
— 1.8	1.1	3.9	0.7	4.8	— 4.2	**1968**	7.7
— 6.0	4.0	— 2.5	4.3	— 3.4	— 1.9	**1969**	— 11.4
7.3	4.4	3.4	— 1.2	4.7	5.7	**1970**	0.1
— 3.2	3.6	— 0.7	— 4.2	— 0.3	8.6	**1971**	10.8
0.2	3.4	— 0.5	0.9	4.6	1.2	**1972**	15.6
3.8	— 3.7	4.0	— 0.1	— 11.4	1.7	**1973**	— 17.4
— 7.8	— 9.0	— 11.9	16.3	— 5.3	— 2.0	**1974**	— 29.7
— 6.8	— 2.1	— 3.5	6.2	2.5	— 1.2	**1975**	31.5
— 0.8	— 0.5	2.3	— 2.2	— 0.8	5.2	**1976**	19.1
— 1.6	— 2.1	— 0.2	— 4.3	2.7	0.3	**1977**	— 11.5
5.4	2.6	— 0.7	— 9.2	1.7	1.5	**1978**	1.1
0.9	5.3	0.0	— 6.9	4.3	1.7	**1979**	12.3
6.5	0.6	2.5	1.6	10.2	— 3.4	**1980**	25.8
— 0.2	— 6.2	— 5.4	4.9	3.7	— 3.0	**1981**	— 9.7
— 2.3	11.6	0.8	11.0	3.6	1.5	**1982**	14.8
— 3.0	1.1	1.0	— 1.5	1.7	— 0.9	**1983**	17.3
— 1.6	10.6	— 0.3	0.0	— 1.5	2.2	**1984**	1.4
— 0.5	— 1.2	— 3.5	4.3	6.5	4.5	**1985**	26.3
— 5.9	7.1	— 8.5	5.5	2.1	— 2.8	**1986**	14.6
4.8	3.5	— 2.4	— 21.8	— 8.5	7.3	**1987**	2.0
— 0.5	— 3.9	4.0	2.6	— 1.9	1.5	**1988**	12.4
8.8	1.6	— 0.7	— 2.5	1.7	2.1	**1989**	27.3
— 0.5	— 9.4	— 5.1	— 0.7	6.0	2.5	**1990**	— 6.6
4.5	2.0	— 1.9	1.2	— 4.4	11.2	**1991**	26.3
3.9	— 2.4	0.9	0.2	3.0	1.0	**1992**	4.5
— 0.5	3.4	— 1.0	1.9	— 1.3	1.0	**1993**	7.1
3.1	3.8	— 2.7	2.1	— 4.0	1.2	**1994**	— 1.5
3.2	0.0	4.0	— 0.5	4.1	1.7	**1995**	34.1
— 4.6	1.9	5.4	2.6	7.3	— 2.2	**1996**	20.3
7.8	— 5.7	5.3	— 3.4	4.5	1.6	**1997**	31.0
— 1.2	— 14.6	6.2	8.0	5.9	5.6	**1998**	26.7
— 3.2	— 0.6	— 2.9	6.3	1.9	5.8	**1999**	19.5
— 1.6	6.1	— 5.3	— 0.5	— 8.0	0.4	**2000**	— 10.1
— 1.1	— 6.4	— 8.2	1.8	7.5	0.8	**2001**	— 13.0
— 7.9	0.5	— 11.0	8.6	5.7	— 6.0	**2002**	— 23.4
1.6	1.8	— 1.2	5.5	0.7	5.1	**2003**	26.4
-3.4	0.2	0.9	1.4	3.9	3.2	**2004**	9.0
3.6	— 1.1	0.7	— 1.8	3.5	— 0.1	**2005**	3.0
0.5	2.1	2.5	3.2	1.6	1.3	**2006**	13.6
— 3.2	1.3	3.6	1.5	— 4.4	1.1	**2007**	3.5
31 / 58	32 / 58	25 / 58	35 / 58	39 / 58	44 / 58		43 / 58
53 %	55 %	43 %	60 %	67 %	76 %		74 %
0.8 %	0.1 %	— 0.5 %	0.9 %	1.7 %	1.7 %		9.3 %
7	9	12	6	2	1		

* 2008 Not Included in Calculations

STOCK MKT

S&P 500 MONTH CLOSING VALUES

	JAN	FEB	MAR	APR	MAY	JUN
1950	17	17	17	18	19	18
1951	22	22	21	22	22	21
1952	24	23	24	23	24	25
1953	26	26	25	25	25	24
1954	26	26	27	28	29	29
1955	37	37	37	38	38	41
1956	44	45	48	48	45	47
1957	45	43	44	46	47	47
1958	42	41	42	43	44	45
1959	55	55	55	58	59	58
1960	56	56	55	54	56	57
1961	62	63	65	65	67	65
1962	69	70	70	65	60	55
1963	66	64	67	70	71	69
1964	77	78	79	79	80	82
1965	88	87	86	89	88	84
1966	93	91	89	91	86	85
1967	87	87	90	94	89	91
1968	92	89	90	97	99	100
1969	103	98	102	104	103	98
1970	85	90	90	82	77	73
1971	96	97	100	104	100	99
1972	104	107	107	108	110	107
1973	116	112	112	107	105	104
1974	97	96	94	90	87	86
1975	77	82	83	87	91	95
1976	101	100	103	102	100	104
1977	102	100	98	98	96	100
1978	89	87	89	97	97	96
1979	100	96	102	102	99	103
1980	114	114	102	106	111	114
1981	130	131	136	133	133	131
1982	120	113	112	116	112	110
1983	145	148	153	164	162	168
1984	163	157	159	160	151	153
1985	180	181	181	180	190	192
1986	212	227	239	236	247	251
1987	274	284	292	288	290	304
1988	257	268	259	261	262	274
1989	297	289	295	310	321	318
1990	329	332	340	331	361	358
1991	344	367	375	375	390	371
1992	409	413	404	415	415	408
1993	439	443	452	440	450	451
1994	482	467	446	451	457	444
1995	470	487	501	515	533	545
1996	636	640	646	654	669	671
1997	786	791	757	801	848	885
1998	980	1049	1102	1112	1091	1134
1999	1280	1238	1286	1335	1302	1373
2000	1394	1366	1499	1452	1421	1455
2001	1366	1240	1160	1249	1256	1224
2002	1130	1107	1147	1077	1067	990
2003	856	841	848	917	964	975
2004	1131	1145	1126	1107	1121	1141
2005	1181	1204	1181	1157	1192	1191
2006	1280	1281	1295	1311	1270	1270
2007	1438	1407	1421	1482	1531	1503
2008	1379	1331	1323	1386	1400	1280

S&P 500 MONTH CLOSING VALUES

JUL	AUG	SEP	OCT	NOV	DEC	
18	18	19	20	20	20	**1950**
22	23	23	23	23	24	**1951**
25	25	25	25	26	27	**1952**
25	23	23	25	25	25	**1953**
31	30	32	32	34	36	**1954**
44	43	44	42	46	45	**1955**
49	48	45	46	45	47	**1956**
48	45	42	41	42	40	**1957**
47	48	50	51	52	55	**1958**
61	60	57	58	58	60	**1959**
56	57	54	53	56	58	**1960**
67	68	67	69	71	72	**1961**
58	59	56	57	62	63	**1962**
69	73	72	74	73	75	**1963**
83	82	84	85	84	85	**1964**
85	87	90	92	92	92	**1965**
84	77	77	80	80	80	**1966**
95	94	97	93	94	96	**1967**
98	99	103	103	108	104	**1968**
92	96	93	97	94	92	**1969**
78	82	84	83	87	92	**1970**
96	99	98	94	94	102	**1971**
107	111	111	112	117	118	**1972**
108	104	108	108	96	98	**1973**
79	72	64	74	70	69	**1974**
89	87	84	89	91	90	**1975**
103	103	105	103	102	107	**1976**
99	97	97	92	95	95	**1977**
101	103	103	93	95	96	**1978**
104	109	109	102	106	108	**1979**
122	122	125	127	141	136	**1980**
131	123	116	122	126	123	**1981**
107	120	120	134	139	141	**1982**
163	164	166	164	166	165	**1983**
151	167	166	166	164	167	**1984**
191	189	182	190	202	211	**1985**
236	253	231	244	249	242	**1986**
319	330	322	252	230	247	**1987**
272	262	272	279	274	278	**1988**
346	351	349	340	346	353	**1989**
356	323	306	304	322	330	**1990**
388	395	388	392	375	417	**1991**
424	414	418	419	431	436	**1992**
448	464	459	468	462	466	**1993**
458	475	463	472	454	459	**1994**
562	562	584	582	605	616	**1995**
640	652	687	705	757	741	**1996**
954	899	947	915	955	970	**1997**
1121	957	1017	1099	1164	1229	**1998**
1329	1320	1283	1363	1389	1469	**1999**
1431	1518	1437	1429	1315	1320	**2000**
1211	1134	1041	1060	1139	1148	**2001**
912	916	815	886	936	880	**2002**
990	1008	996	1051	1058	1112	**2003**
1102	1104	1115	1130	1174	1212	**2004**
1234	1220	1229	1207	1249	1248	**2005**
1277	1304	1336	1378	1401	1418	**2006**
1455	1474	1527	1549	1481	1468	**2007**

STOCK MKT

DOW JONES PERCENT MONTH CHANGES

	JAN	FEB	MAR	APR	MAY	JUN
1950	0.8 %	0.8 %	1.3 %	4.0 %	4.2 %	— 6.4 %
1951	5.7	1.3	— 1.7	4.5	— 3.6	— 2.8
1952	0.6	— 3.9	3.6	— 4.4	2.1	4.3
1953	— 0.7	— 2.0	— 1.5	— 1.8	— 0.9	— 1.5
1954	4.1	0.7	3.1	5.2	2.6	1.8
1955	1.1	0.8	— 0.5	3.9	— 0.2	6.2
1956	— 3.6	2.8	5.8	0.8	— 7.4	3.1
1957	— 4.1	— 3.0	2.2	4.1	2.1	— 0.3
1958	3.3	— 2.2	1.6	2.0	1.5	3.3
1959	1.8	1.6	— 0.3	3.7	3.2	0.0
1960	— 8.4	1.2	— 2.1	— 2.4	4.0	2.4
1961	5.2	2.1	2.2	0.3	2.7	— 1.8
1962	— 4.3	1.2	— 0.2	— 5.9	— 7.8	— 8.5
1963	4.7	— 2.9	3.0	5.2	1.3	— 2.8
1964	2.9	1.9	1.6	— 0.3	1.2	1.3
1965	3.3	0.1	— 1.6	3.7	— 0.5	— 5.4
1966	1.5	— 3.2	— 2.8	1.0	— 5.3	— 1.6
1967	8.2	— 1.2	3.2	3.6	— 5.0	0.9
1968	— 5.5	— 1.8	0.0	8.5	— 1.4	— 0.1
1969	0.2	— 4.3	3.3	1.6	— 1.3	— 6.9
1970	— 7.0	4.5	1.0	— 6.3	— 4.8	— 2.4
1971	3.5	1.2	2.9	4.1	— 3.6	— 1.8
1972	1.3	2.9	1.4	1.4	0.7	— 3.3
1973	— 2.1	— 4.4	— 0.4	— 3.1	— 2.2	— 1.1
1974	0.6	0.6	— 1.6	— 1.2	— 4.1	0.0
1975	14.2	5.0	3.9	6.9	1.3	5.6
1976	14.4	— 0.3	2.8	— 0.3	— 2.2	2.8
1977	— 5.0	— 1.9	— 1.8	0.8	— 3.0	2.0
1978	— 7.4	— 3.6	2.1	10.5	0.4	— 2.6
1979	4.2	— 3.6	6.6	— 0.8	— 3.8	2.4
1980	4.4	— 1.5	— 9.0	4.0	4.1	2.0
1981	— 1.7	2.9	3.0	— 0.6	— 0.6	— 1.5
1982	— 0.4	— 5.4	— 0.2	3.1	— 3.4	— 0.9
1983	2.8	3.4	1.6	8.5	— 2.1	1.8
1984	— 3.0	— 5.4	0.9	0.5	— 5.6	2.5
1985	6.2	— 0.2	— 1.3	— 0.7	4.6	1.5
1986	1.6	8.8	6.4	— 1.9	5.2	0.9
1987	13.8	3.1	3.6	— 0.8	0.2	5.5
1988	1.0	5.8	— 4.0	2.2	— 0.1	5.4
1989	8.0	— 3.6	1.6	5.5	2.5	— 1.6
1990	— 5.9	1.4	3.0	— 1.9	8.3	0.1
1991	3.9	5.3	1.1	— 0.9	4.8	— 4.0
1992	1.7	1.4	— 1.0	3.8	1.1	— 2.3
1993	0.3	1.8	1.9	— 0.2	2.9	— 0.3
1994	6.0	— 3.7	— 5.1	1.3	2.1	— 3.5
1995	0.2	4.3	3.7	3.9	3.3	2.0
1996	5.4	1.7	1.9	— 0.3	1.3	0.2
1997	5.7	0.9	— 4.3	6.5	4.6	4.7
1998	0.0	8.1	3.0	3.0	— 1.8	0.6
1999	1.9	— 0.6	5.2	10.2	— 2.1	3.9
2000	— 4.5	— 7.4	7.8	— 1.7	— 2.0	— 0.7
2001	0.9	— 3.6	— 5.9	8.7	1.6	— 3.8
2002	— 1.0	1.9	2.9	— 4.4	— 0.2	— 6.9
2003	— 3.5	— 2.0	1.3	6.1	4.4	1.5
2004	0.3	0.9	— 2.1	— 1.3	— 0.4	2.4
2005	— 2.7	2.6	— 2.4	— 3.0	2.7	— 1.8
2006	1.4	1.2	1.1	2.3	— 1.7	— 0.2
2007	1.3	— 2.8	0.7	5.7	4.3	— 1.6
2008	— 4.6	— 3.0	0.0	4.5	— 1.4	— 10.2
FQ POS	39 / 59	33 / 59	37 / 59	37 / 59	30 / 59	28 / 59
% FQ POS	66 %	56 %	63 %	63 %	51 %	47 %
AVG GAIN	1.2 %	0.1 %	0.9 %	1.9 %	0.1 %	— 0.3 %
RANK GAIN	4	9	6	1	8	11

DOW JONES PERCENT MONTH CHANGES

STOCK MKT

*JUL	*AUG	*SEP	*OCT	*NOV	*DEC		*YEAR
0.1 %	3.6 %	4.4 %	— 0.6 %	1.2 %	3.4 %	**1950**	17.6 %
6.3	4.8	0.3	— 3.2	— 0.4	3.0	**1951**	14.4
1.9	— 1.6	— 1.6	— 0.5	5.4	2.9	**1952**	8.4
2.6	— 5.2	1.1	4.5	2.0	— 0.2	**1953**	— 3.8
4.3	— 3.5	7.4	— 2.3	9.9	4.6	**1954**	44.0
3.2	0.5	— 0.3	— 2.5	6.2	1.1	**1955**	20.8
5.1	— 3.1	— 5.3	1.0	— 1.5	5.6	**1956**	2.3
1.0	— 4.7	— 5.8	— 3.4	2.0	— 3.2	**1957**	— 12.8
5.2	1.1	4.6	2.1	2.6	4.7	**1958**	34.0
4.9	— 1.6	— 4.9	2.4	1.9	3.1	**1959**	16.4
— 3.7	1.5	— 7.3	0.1	2.9	3.1	**1960**	— 9.3
3.1	2.1	— 2.6	0.4	2.5	1.3	**1961**	18.7
6.5	1.9	— 5.0	1.9	10.1	0.4	**1962**	— 10.8
— 1.6	4.9	0.5	3.1	— 0.6	1.7	**1963**	17.0
1.2	— 0.3	4.4	— 0.3	0.3	— 0.1	**1964**	14.6
1.6	1.3	4.2	3.2	— 1.5	2.4	**1965**	10.9
— 2.6	— 7.0	— 1.8	4.2	— 1.9	— 0.7	**1966**	— 18.9
5.1	— 0.3	2.8	— 5.1	— 0.4	3.3	**1967**	15.2
— 1.6	1.5	4.4	1.8	3.4	— 4.2	**1968**	4.3
— 6.6	2.6	— 2.8	5.3	— 5.1	— 1.5	**1969**	— 15.2
7.4	4.2	— 0.5	— 0.7	5.1	5.6	**1970**	4.8
— 3.7	4.6	— 1.2	— 5.4	— 0.9	7.1	**1971**	6.1
— 0.5	4.2	— 1.1	0.2	6.6	0.2	**1972**	14.6
3.9	— 4.2	6.7	1.0	— 14.0	3.5	**1973**	— 16.6
— 5.6	— 10.4	— 10.4	9.5	— 7.0	— 0.4	**1974**	— 27.6
— 5.4	0.5	— 5.0	5.3	3.0	— 1.0	**1975**	38.3
— 1.8	— 1.1	1.7	— 2.6	— 1.8	6.1	**1976**	17.9
— 2.9	— 3.2	— 1.7	— 3.4	1.4	0.2	**1977**	— 17.3
5.3	1.7	— 1.3	— 8.5	0.8	0.8	**1978**	— 3.2
0.5	4.9	— 1.0	— 7.2	0.8	2.0	**1979**	4.2
7.8	— 0.3	0.0	— 0.8	7.4	— 2.9	**1980**	14.9
— 2.5	— 7.4	— 3.6	0.3	4.3	— 1.6	**1981**	— 9.2
— 0.4	11.5	— 0.6	10.6	4.8	0.7	**1982**	19.6
— 1.9	1.4	1.4	— 0.6	4.1	— 1.4	**1983**	20.3
— 1.5	9.8	— 1.4	0.1	— 1.5	1.9	**1984**	— 3.7
0.9	— 1.0	— 0.4	3.4	7.1	5.1	**1985**	27.7
— 6.2	6.9	— 6.9	6.2	1.9	— 1.0	**1986**	22.6
6.4	3.5	— 2.5	— 23.2	— 8.0	5.7	**1987**	2.3
— 0.6	— 4.6	4.0	1.7	— 1.6	2.6	**1988**	11.9
9.0	2.9	— 1.6	— 1.8	2.3	1.7	**1989**	27.0
0.9	— 10.0	— 6.2	— 0.4	4.8	2.9	**1990**	— 4.3
4.1	0.6	— 0.9	1.7	— 5.7	9.5	**1991**	20.3
2.3	— 4.0	0.4	— 1.4	2.4	— 0.1	**1992**	4.2
0.7	3.2	— 2.6	3.5	0.1	1.9	**1993**	13.7
3.8	4.0	— 1.8	1.7	— 4.3	2.5	**1994**	2.1
3.3	— 2.1	3.9	— 0.7	6.7	0.8	**1995**	33.5
— 2.2	1.6	4.7	2.5	8.2	— 1.1	**1996**	26.0
7.2	— 7.3	4.2	— 6.3	5.1	1.1	**1997**	22.6
— 0.8	— 15.1	4.0	9.6	6.1	0.7	**1998**	16.1
— 2.9	1.6	— 4.5	3.8	1.4	5.3	**1999**	24.7
0.7	6.6	— 5.0	3.0	— 5.1	3.6	**2000**	— 5.8
0.2	— 5.4	— 11.1	2.6	8.6	1.7	**2001**	— 7.1
— 5.5	— 0.8	— 12.4	10.6	5.9	— 6.2	**2002**	— 16.8
2.8	2.0	— 1.5	5.7	— 0.2	6.9	**2003**	25.3
— 2.8	0.3	— 0.9	— 0.5	4.0	3.4	**2004**	3.1
3.6	— 1.5	0.8	— 1.2	3.5	— 0.8	**2005**	— 0.6
0.3	1.7	2.6	3.4	1.2	2.0	**2006**	16.3
— 1.5	1.1	4.0	0.2	— 4.0	— 0.8	**2007**	6.4
35 / 58	33 / 58	22 / 58	34 / 58	39 / 58	41 / 58		41 / 58
60 %	57 %	38 %	59 %	67 %	71 %		71 %
1.0 %	0.0 %	— 0.9 %	0.6 %	1.6 %	1.7 %		8.7 %
5	10	12	7	3	2		

* 2008 Not Included in Calculations

STOCK MKT

DOW JONES MONTH CLOSING VALUES

	JAN	FEB	MAR	APR	MAY	JUN
1950	202	203	206	214	223	209
1951	249	252	248	259	250	243
1952	271	260	270	258	263	274
1953	290	284	280	275	272	268
1954	292	295	304	319	328	334
1955	409	412	410	426	425	451
1956	471	484	512	516	478	493
1957	479	465	475	494	505	503
1958	450	440	447	456	463	478
1959	594	604	602	624	644	644
1960	623	630	617	602	626	641
1961	648	662	677	679	697	684
1962	700	708	707	665	613	561
1963	683	663	683	718	727	707
1964	785	800	813	811	821	832
1965	903	904	889	922	918	868
1966	984	952	925	934	884	870
1967	850	839	866	897	853	860
1968	856	841	841	912	899	898
1969	946	905	936	950	938	873
1970	744	778	786	736	700	684
1971	869	879	904	942	908	891
1972	902	928	941	954	961	929
1973	999	955	951	921	901	892
1974	856	861	847	837	802	802
1975	704	739	768	821	832	879
1976	975	973	1000	997	975	1003
1977	954	936	919	927	899	916
1978	770	742	757	837	841	819
1979	839	809	862	855	822	842
1980	876	863	786	817	851	868
1981	947	975	1004	998	992	977
1982	871	824	823	848	820	812
1983	1076	1113	1130	1226	1200	1222
1984	1221	1155	1165	1171	1105	1132
1985	1287	1284	1267	1258	1315	1336
1986	1571	1709	1819	1784	1877	1893
1987	2158	2224	2305	2286	2292	2419
1988	1958	2072	1988	2032	2031	2142
1989	2342	2258	2294	2419	2480	2440
1990	2591	2627	2707	2657	2877	2881
1991	2736	2882	2914	2888	3028	2907
1992	3223	3268	3236	3359	3397	3319
1993	3310	3371	3435	3428	3527	3516
1994	3978	3832	3636	3682	3758	3625
1995	3844	4011	4158	4321	4465	4556
1996	5395	5486	5587	5569	5643	5655
1997	6813	6878	6584	7009	7331	7673
1998	7907	8546	8800	9063	8900	8952
1999	9359	9307	9786	10789	10560	10971
2000	10941	10128	10922	10734	10522	10448
2001	10887	10495	9879	10735	10912	10502
2002	9920	10106	10404	9946	9925	9243
2003	8054	7891	7992	8480	8850	8985
2004	10488	10584	10358	10226	10188	10435
2005	10490	10766	10504	10193	10467	10275
2006	10865	10993	11109	11367	11168	11150
2007	12622	12269	12354	13063	13628	13409
2008	12650	12266	12263	12820	12638	11350

DOW JONES MONTH CLOSING VALUES

JUL	AUG	SEP	OCT	NOV	DEC	
209	217	226	225	228	235	**1950**
258	270	271	262	261	269	**1951**
280	275	271	269	284	292	**1952**
275	261	264	276	281	281	**1953**
348	336	361	352	387	404	**1954**
466	468	467	455	483	488	**1955**
518	502	475	480	473	500	**1956**
509	484	456	441	450	436	**1957**
503	509	532	543	558	584	**1958**
675	664	632	647	659	679	**1959**
617	626	580	580	597	616	**1960**
705	720	701	704	722	731	**1961**
598	609	579	590	649	652	**1962**
695	729	733	755	751	763	**1963**
841	839	875	873	875	874	**1964**
882	893	931	961	947	969	**1965**
847	788	774	807	792	786	**1966**
904	901	927	880	876	905	**1967**
883	896	936	952	985	944	**1968**
816	837	813	856	812	800	**1969**
734	765	761	756	794	839	**1970**
858	898	887	839	831	890	**1971**
925	964	953	956	1018	1020	**1972**
926	888	947	957	822	851	**1973**
757	679	608	666	619	616	**1974**
832	835	794	836	861	852	**1975**
985	974	990	965	947	1005	**1976**
890	862	847	818	830	831	**1977**
862	877	866	793	799	805	**1978**
846	888	879	816	822	839	**1979**
935	933	932	925	993	964	**1980**
952	882	850	853	889	875	**1981**
809	901	896	992	1039	1047	**1982**
1199	1216	1233	1225	1276	1259	**1983**
1115	1224	1207	1207	1189	1212	**1984**
1348	1334	1329	1374	1472	1547	**1985**
1775	1898	1768	1878	1914	1896	**1986**
2572	2663	2596	1994	1834	1939	**1987**
2129	2032	2113	2149	2115	2169	**1988**
2661	2737	2693	2645	2706	2753	**1989**
2905	2614	2453	2442	2560	2634	**1990**
3025	3044	3017	3069	2895	3169	**1991**
3394	3257	3272	3226	3305	3301	**1992**
3540	3651	3555	3681	3684	3754	**1993**
3765	3913	3843	3908	3739	3834	**1994**
4709	4611	4789	4756	5075	5117	**1995**
5529	5616	5882	6029	6522	6448	**1996**
8223	7622	7945	7442	7823	7908	**1997**
8883	7539	7843	8592	9117	9181	**1998**
10655	10829	10337	10730	10878	11453	**1999**
10522	11215	10651	10971	10415	10788	**2000**
10523	9950	8848	9075	9852	10022	**2001**
8737	8664	7592	8397	8896	8342	**2002**
9234	9416	9275	9801	9782	10454	**2003**
10140	10174	10080	10027	10428	10783	**2004**
10641	10482	10569	10440	10806	10718	**2005**
11186	11381	11679	12801	12222	12463	**2006**
13212	13358	13896	13930	13372	13265	**2007**

STOCK MKT

NASDAQ PERCENT MONTH CHANGES

	JAN	FEB	MAR	APR	MAY	JUN
1972	4.2	5.5	2.2	2.5	0.9	— 1.8
1973	— 4.0	— 6.2	— 2.4	— 8.2	— 4.8	— 1.6
1974	3.0	— 0.6	— 2.2	— 5.9	— 7.7	— 5.3
1975	16.6	4.6	3.6	3.8	5.8	4.7
1976	12.1	3.7	0.4	— 0.6	— 2.3	2.6
1977	— 2.4	— 1.0	— 0.5	1.4	0.1	4.3
1978	— 4.0	0.6	4.7	8.5	4.4	0.0
1979	6.6	— 2.6	7.5	1.6	— 1.8	5.1
1980	7.0	— 2.3	— 17.1	6.9	7.5	4.9
1981	— 2.2	0.1	6.1	3.1	3.1	— 3.5
1982	— 3.8	— 4.8	— 2.1	5.2	— 3.3	— 4.1
1983	6.9	5.0	3.9	8.2	5.3	3.2
1984	— 3.7	— 5.9	— 0.7	— 1.3	— 5.9	2.9
1985	12.8	2.0	— 1.8	0.5	3.6	1.9
1986	3.4	7.1	4.2	2.3	4.4	1.3
1987	12.4	8.4	1.2	— 2.9	— 0.3	2.0
1988	4.3	6.5	2.1	1.2	— 2.3	6.6
1989	5.2	— 0.4	1.8	5.1	4.3	— 2.4
1990	— 8.6	2.4	2.3	— 3.5	9.3	0.7
1991	10.8	9.4	6.4	0.5	4.4	— 6.0
1992	5.8	2.1	— 4.7	— 4.2	1.1	— 3.7
1993	2.9	— 3.7	2.9	— 4.2	5.9	0.5
1994	3.0	— 1.0	— 6.2	— 1.3	0.2	— 4.0
1995	0.4	5.1	3.0	3.3	2.4	8.0
1996	0.7	3.8	0.1	8.1	4.4	— 4.7
1997	6.9	— 5.1	— 6.7	3.2	11.1	3.0
1998	3.1	9.3	3.7	1.8	— 4.8	6.5
1999	14.3	— 8.7	7.6	3.3	— 2.8	8.7
2000	— 3.2	19.2	— 2.6	— 15.6	— 11.9	16.6
2001	12.2	— 22.4	— 14.5	15.0	— 0.3	2.4
2002	— 0.8	— 10.5	6.6	— 8.5	— 4.3	— 9.4
2003	— 1.1	1.3	0.3	9.2	9.0	1.7
2004	3.1	— 1.8	— 1.8	— 3.7	3.5	3.1
2005	— 5.2	— 0.5	— 2.6	— 3.9	7.6	— 0.5
2006	4.6	— 1.1	2.6	— 0.7	— 6.2	— 0.3
2007	2.0	— 1.9	0.2	4.3	3.1	0.0
2008	— 9.9	— 5.0	0.3	5.9	4.6	— 9.1
FQ POS	25/37	18/37	23/37	23/37	23/37	22/37
% FQ POS	68 %	49 %	62 %	62 %	62 %	59 %
AVG GAIN	3.1 %	0.3 %	0.2 %	1.1 %	1.3 %	0.9 %
RANK GAIN	1	8	10	5	4	6

NASDAQ PERCENT MONTH CHANGES

STOCK MKT

*JUL	*AUG	*SEP	*OCT	*NOV	*DEC		*YEAR
— 1.8	1.7	— 0.3	0.5	2.1	0.6	**1972**	17.2
7.6	— 3.5	6.0	— 0.9	— 15.1	— 1.4	**1973**	31.1
— 7.9	— 10.9	— 10.7	17.2	— 3.5	— 5.0	**1974**	— 35.1
— 4.4	— 5.0	— 5.9	3.6	2.4	— 1.5	**1975**	29.8
1.1	— 1.7	1.7	— 1.0	0.9	7.4	**1976**	26.1
0.9	— 0.5	0.7	— 3.3	5.8	1.8	**1977**	7.3
5.0	6.9	— 1.6	— 16.4	3.2	2.9	**1978**	12.3
2.3	6.4	— 0.3	— 9.6	6.4	4.8	**1979**	28.1
8.9	5.7	3.4	2.7	8.0	— 2.8	**1980**	33.9
— 1.9	— 7.5	— 8.0	8.4	3.1	— 2.7	**1981**	— 3.2
— 2.3	6.2	5.6	13.3	9.3	0.0	**1982**	18.7
— 4.6	— 3.8	1.4	— 7.4	4.1	— 2.5	**1983**	19.9
— 4.2	10.9	— 1.8	— 1.2	— 1.9	1.9	**1984**	— 11.3
1.7	— 1.2	— 5.8	4.4	7.4	3.5	**1985**	31.5
— 8.4	3.1	— 8.4	2.9	— 0.3	— 3.0	**1986**	7.4
2.4	4.6	— 2.4	— 27.2	— 5.6	8.3	**1987**	— 5.2
— 1.9	— 2.8	2.9	— 1.3	— 2.9	2.7	**1988**	15.4
4.2	3.4	0.8	— 3.7	0.1	— 0.3	**1989**	19.2
— 5.2	— 13.0	— 9.6	— 4.3	8.9	4.1	**1990**	— 17.8
5.5	4.7	0.2	3.1	— 3.5	11.9	**1991**	56.9
3.1	— 3.0	3.6	3.8	7.9	3.7	**1992**	15.5
0.1	5.4	2.7	2.2	— 3.2	3.0	**1993**	14.7
2.3	6.0	— 0.2	1.7	— 3.5	0.2	**1994**	— 3.2
7.3	1.9	2.3	— 0.7	2.2	— 0.7	**1995**	39.9
— 8.8	5.6	7.5	— 0.4	5.8	— 0.1	**1996**	22.7
10.5	— 0.4	6.2	— -5.5	0.4	— 1.9	**1997**	21.6
— 1.2	— 19.9	13.0	4.6	10.1	12.5	**1998**	39.6
— 1.8	3.8	0.2	8.0	12.5	22.0	**1999**	85.6
— 5.0	11.7	— 12.7	— 8.3	— 22.9	— 4.9	**2000**	— 39.3
— 6.2	— 10.9	— 17.0	12.8	14.2	1.0	**2001**	— 21.1
— 9.2	— 1.0	— 10.9	13.5	11.2	— 9.7	**2002**	— 31.5
6.9	4.3	— 1.3	8.1	1.5	2.2	**2003**	50.0
— 7.8	— 2.6	3.2	4.1	6.2	3.7	**2004**	8.6
6.2	— 1.5	0.0	— 1.5	5.3	— 1.2	**2005**	1.4
— 3.7	4.4	3.4	4.8	2.7	— 0.7	**2006**	9.5
— 2.2	2.0	4.0	5.8	— 6.9	— 0.3	**2007**	9.8
17/36	19/36	19/36	20/36	25/36	20/36		24/36
47 %	53 %	53 %	56 %	69 %	56 %		72 %
— 0.3 %	0.3 %	— 0.8 %	0.9 %	2.0 %	1.7 %		12.3 %
11	9	12	7	2	3		

* 2008 Not Included in Calculations

NASDAQ MONTH CLOSING VALUES

	JAN	FEB	MAR	APR	MAY	JUN
1972	119	125	128	131	133	130
1973	128	120	117	108	103	101
1974	95	94	92	87	80	76
1975	70	73	76	79	83	87
1976	87	90	91	90	88	90
1977	96	95	94	95	96	100
1978	101	101	106	115	120	120
1979	126	123	132	134	131	138
1980	162	158	131	140	150	158
1981	198	198	210	217	223	216
1982	188	179	176	185	179	171
1983	248	261	271	293	309	319
1984	268	253	251	247	233	240
1985	279	284	279	281	291	296
1986	336	360	375	383	400	406
1987	392	425	430	418	417	425
1988	345	367	375	379	370	395
1989	401	400	407	428	446	435
1990	416	426	436	420	459	462
1991	414	453	482	485	506	476
1992	620	633	604	579	585	564
1993	696	671	690	661	701	704
1994	800	793	743	734	735	706
1995	755	794	817	844	865	933
1996	1060	1100	1101	1191	1243	1185
1997	1380	1309	1222	1261	1400	1442
1998	1619	1771	1836	1868	1779	1895
1999	2506	2288	2461	2543	2471	2686
2000	3940	4697	4573	3861	3401	3966
2001	2773	2152	1840	2116	2110	2161
2002	1934	1731	1845	1688	1616	1463
2003	1321	1338	1341	1464	1596	1623
2004	2066	2030	1994	1920	1987	2048
2005	2062	2052	1999	1922	2068	2057
2006	2306	2281	2340	2323	2179	2172
2007	2464	2416	2422	2525	2605	2603
2008	2390	2271	2279	2413	2523	2293

NASDAQ MONTH CLOSING VALUES

JUL	AUG	SEP	OCT	NOV	DEC	
128	130	130	130	133	134	1972
109	105	111	110	94	92	1973
70	62	56	65	63	60	1974
83	79	74	77	79	78	1975
91	90	91	90	91	98	1976
101	100	101	98	103	105	1977
126	135	133	111	115	118	1978
141	150	150	136	144	151	1979
172	182	188	193	208	202	1980
212	196	180	195	201	196	1981
167	178	188	213	232	232	1982
304	292	297	275	286	279	1983
230	255	250	247	242	247	1984
301	298	280	293	314	325	1985
371	383	351	361	360	349	1986
435	455	444	323	305	331	1987
387	377	388	383	372	381	1988
454	469	473	456	456	455	1989
438	381	345	330	359	374	1990
502	526	527	543	524	586	1991
581	563	583	605	653	677	1992
705	743	763	779	754	777	1993
722	766	764	777	750	752	1994
1001	1020	1044	1036	1059	1052	1995
1081	1142	1227	1222	1293	1291	1996
1594	1587	1686	1594	1601	1570	1997
1872	1499	1694	1771	1950	2193	1998
2638	2739	2746	2966	3336	4069	1999
3767	4206	3673	3370	2598	2471	2000
2027	1805	1499	1690	1931	1950	2001
1328	1315	1172	1330	1479	1336	2002
1735	1810	1787	1932	1960	2003	2003
1887	1838	1897	1975	2097	2175	2004
2185	2152	2152	2120	2233	2205	2005
2091	2184	2258	2367	2432	2415	2006
2546	2596	2702	2859	2661	2652	2007

STOCK MKT

S&P/TSX MONTH PERCENT CHANGES

	JAN	FEB	MAR	APR	MAY	JUN
1985	8.1	0.0	0.7	0.8	3.8	— 0.8
1986	— 1.7	0.5	6.7	1.1	1.4	— 1.2
1987	9.2	4.5	6.9	— 0.6	— 0.9	1.5
1988	— 3.3	4.8	3.4	0.8	— 2.7	5.9
1989	6.7	— 1.2	0.2	1.4	2.2	1.5
1990	— 6.7	— 0.5	— 1.3	— 8.2	6.7	— 0.6
1991	0.5	5.8	1.0	-0.8	2.2	— 2.3
1992	2.4	— 0.4	— 4.7	— 1.7	1.0	0.0
1993	— 1.3	4.4	4.4	5.2	2.5	2.2
1994	5.4	— 2.9	— 2.1	— 1.4	1.4	— 7.0
1995	— 4.7	2.7	4.6	— -0.8	4.0	1.8
1996	5.4	— 0.7	0.8	3.5	1.9	— 3.9
1997	3.1	0.8	— 5.0	2.2	6.8	0.9
1998	0.0	5.9	6.6	1.4	— 1.0	— 2.9
1999	3.8	— 6.2	4.5	6.3	— 2.5	2.5
2000	0.8	7.6	3.7	— 1.2	— 1.0	10.2
2001	4.3	— 13.3	— 5.8	4.5	2.7	— 5.2
2002	— 0.5	— 0.1	2.8	— 2.4	— 0.1	— 6.7
2003	— 0.7	— 0.2	— 3.2	3.8	4.2	1.8
2004	3.7	3.1	— 2.3	— 4.0	2.1	1.5
2005	— 0.5	5.0	— 0.6	— 3.5	3.6	3.1
2006	6.0	— 2.2	3.6	0.8	— 3.8	— 1.1
2007	1.0	0.1	0.9	1.9	4.8	— 1.1
2008	— 4.9	3.3	— 1.7	4.4	5.6	— 1.7
FQ POS	15/24	13/24	15/24	14/24	17/24	11/24
% FQ POS	63 %	54 %	63 %	58 %	71 %	46 %
AVG GAIN	1.5 %	0.9 %	1.0 %	0.6 %	1.9 %	-0.1 %
RANK GAIN	3	6	4	8	2	10

S&P/TSX MONTH PERCENT CHANGES

STOCK MKT

*JUL	*AUG	*SEP	*OCT	*NOV	*DEC		*YEAR
2.4	1.5	— 6.7	1.6	6.8	1.3	**1985**	20.5
— 4.9	3.2	— 1.6	1.6	0.7	0.6	**1986**	6.0
7.8	— 0.9	— 2.3	— 22.6	— 1.4	6.1	**1987**	3.1
— 1.9	— 2.7	— 0.1	3.4	— 3.0	2.9	**1988**	7.3
5.6	1.0	— 1.7	— 0.6	0.6	0.7	**1989**	17.1
0.5	— 6.0	— 5.6	— 2.5	2.3	3.4	**1990**	— 18.0
2.1	— 0.6	— 3.7	3.8	— 1.9	1.9	**1991**	7.8
1.6	— 1.2	— 3.1	1.2	— 1.6	2.1	**1992**	— 4.6
0.0	4.3	— 3.6	6.6	— 1.8	3.4	**1993**	29.0
3.8	4.1	0.1	— 1.4	— 4.6	2.9	**1994**	— 2.5
1.9	— 2.1	0.3	— 1.6	4.5	1.1	**1995**	11.9
— 2.3	4.3	2.9	5.8	7.5	— 1.5	**1996**	25.7
6.8	— 3.9	6.5	— 2.8	— 4.8	2.9	**1997**	13.0
— 5.9	— 20.2	1.5	10.6	2.2	2.2	**1998**	— 3.2
1.0	— 1.6	— 0.2	4.3	3.6	11.9	**1999**	29.7
2.1	8.1	— 7.7	— 7.1	— 8.5	1.3	**2000**	6.2
— 0.6	— 3.8	— 7.6	0.7	7.8	3.5	**2001**	— 13.9
— 7.6	0.1	— 6.5	1.1	5.1	0.7	**2002**	— 14.0
3.9	3.6	— 1.3	4.7	1.1	4.6	**2003**	24.3
— 1.0	— 1.0	3.5	2.3	1.8	2.4	**2004**	12.5
5.3	2.4	3.2	— 5.7	4.2	4.1	**2005**	21.9
1.9	2.1	— 2.6	5.0	3.3	1.2	**2006**	14.5
— 0.3	— 1.5	3.2	3.7	— 6.4	1.1	**2007**	7.2
15/23	11/23	8/23	15/23	14/23	22/23		17/23
65 %	48 %	35 %	65 %	61 %	96 %		74 %
1.0 %	— 0.5 %	— 1.4 %	0.5 %	0.8 %	2.6 %		8.3 %
5	11	12	9	6	1		

* 2008 Not Included in Calculations

STOCK MKT

S&P/TSX MONTH CLOSING VALUES

	JAN	FEB	MAR	APR	MAY	JUN
1985	2595	2595	2613	2635	2736	2713
1986	2843	2856	3047	3079	3122	3086
1987	3349	3499	3739	3717	3685	3740
1988	3057	3205	3314	3340	3249	3441
1989	3617	3572	3578	3628	3707	3761
1990	3704	3687	3640	3341	3565	3544
1991	3273	3462	3496	3469	3546	3466
1992	3596	3582	3412	3356	3388	3388
1993	3305	3452	3602	3789	3883	3966
1994	4555	4424	4330	4267	4327	4025
1995	4018	4125	4314	4280	4449	4527
1996	4968	4934	4971	5147	5246	5044
1997	6110	6158	5850	5977	6382	6438
1998	6700	7093	7559	7665	7590	7367
1999	6730	6313	6598	7015	6842	7010
2000	8481	9129	9462	9348	9252	10196
2001	9322	8079	7608	7947	8162	7736
2002	7649	7638	7852	7663	7656	7146
2003	6570	6555	6343	6586	6860	6983
2004	8521	8789	8586	8244	8417	8546
2005	9204	9668	9612	9275	9607	9903
2006	11946	11688	12111	12204	11745	11613
2007	13034	13045	13166	13417	14057	13907
2008	13155	13583	13350	13937	14715	14467

JUL	AUG	SEP	OCT	NOV	DEC	
2779	2820	2632	2675	2857	2893	1985
2935	3028	2979	3027	3047	3066	1986
4030	3994	3902	3019	2978	3160	1987
3377	3286	3284	3396	3295	3390	1988
3971	4010	3943	3919	3943	3970	1989
3561	3346	3159	3081	3151	3257	1990
3540	3518	3388	3516	3449	3512	1991
3443	3403	3298	3336	3283	3350	1992
3967	4138	3991	4256	4180	4321	1993
4179	4350	4354	4292	4093	4214	1994
4615	4517	4530	4459	4661	4714	1995
4929	5143	5291	5599	6017	5927	1996
6878	6612	7040	6842	6513	6699	1997
6931	5531	5614	6208	6344	6486	1998
7081	6971	6958	7256	7520	8414	1999
10406	11248	10378	9640	8820	8934	2000
7690	7399	6839	6886	7426	7688	2001
6605	6612	6180	6249	6570	6615	2002
7258	7517	7421	7773	7859	8221	2003
8458	8377	8668	8871	9030	9247	2004
10423	10669	11012	10383	10824	11272	2005
11831	12074	11761	12345	12752	12908	2006
13869	13660	14099	14625	13689	13833	2007

S&P 500 1950 - 2007 BEST - WORST

10 BEST

YEARS

	Close	Change	Change
1954	36	11 pt	45 %
1958	55	15	38.1
1995	616	157	34.1
1975	90	22	31.5
1997	970	230	31.0
1989	353	76	27.3
1998	1229	259	26.7
1955	45	10	26.4
2003	1112	232	26.4
1985	211	44	26.3

MONTHS

	Close	Change	Change
Oct 1974	74	10 pt	16.3 %
Aug 1982	120	12	11.6
Dec 1991	417	42	11.2
Oct 1982	134	13	11.0
Aug 1984	167	16	10.6
Nov 1980	141	13	10.2
Nov 1962	62	6	10.2
Mar 2000	1499	132	9.7
May 1990	361	30	9.2
Jul 1989	346	28	8.8

DAYS

		Close	Change	Change
Wed	1987-Oct 21	258	22 pt	9.1 %
Wed	2002-Jul 24	843	46	5.7
Mon	2002-Jul 29	899	46	5.4
Tue	1987-Oct 20	237	12	5.3
Tue	1997-Oct 28	922	45	5.1
Tue	1998 Sep 8	1023	50	5.1
Wed	1970 May 27	73	3	5.0
Wed	2001 Jan 3	1348	64	5.0
Thu	1987 Oct 29	245	11	4.9
Thu	2000 Mar16	1458	66	4.8

10 WORST

YEARS

	Close	Change	Change
1974	69	– 29 pt	– 29.7 %
2002	880	– 268	– 23.4
1973	98	– 21	– 17.4
1957	40	– 7	– 14.3
1966	80	– 12	– 13.1
2001	1148	– 172	– 13.0
1962	63	– 8	– 11.8
1977	95	– 12	– 11.5
1969	92	– 12	– 11.4
2000	1320	– 149	– 10.1

MONTHS

	Close	Change	Change
Oct 1987	252	– 70 pt	– 21.8 %
Aug 1998	957	– 163	– 14.6
Sep 1974	64	– 9	– 11.9
Nov 1973	96	– 12	– 11.4
Sep 2002	815	– 101	– 11.0
Mar 1980	102	– 12	– 10.2
Aug 1990	323	– 34	– 9.4
Feb 2001	1240	– 126	– 9.2
Oct 1978	93	– 9	– 9.2
Apr 1970	82	– 8	– 9.0

DAYS

		Close	Change	Change
Mon	1987 Oct 19	225	– 58 pt	– 20.5 %
Mon	1987 Oct 26	228	– 21	– 8.3
Mon	1997 Oct 27	877	– 65	– 6.9
Mon	1998 Aug 31	957	– 70	– 6.8
Fri	1988 Jan 8	243	– 18	– 6.8
Mon	1962 May 28	56	– 4	– 6.7
Mon	1955 Sep 26	43	– 3	– 6.6
Fri	1989 Oct 13	334	– 22	– 6.1
Fri	2000 Apr 14	1357	– 84	– 5.8
Mon	1950 Jun 26	18	– 1	– 5.4

10 BEST

YEARS

	Close	Change	Change
1954	404	124 pt	44 %
1975	852	236	38.3
1958	584	148	34.0
1995	5117	1283	33.5
1985	1547	335	27.7
1989	2753	585	27.0
1996	6448	1331	26.0
2003	10454	2112	25.3
1999	11453	2272	25.2
1997	7908	1460	22.6

MONTHS

	Close	Change	Change
Aug 1982	901	93 pt	11.5 %
Oct 1982	992	95	10.6
Oct 2002	8397	805	10.6
Apr 1978	837	80	10.5
Apr 1999	10789	1003	10.2
Nov 1962	649	60	10.1
Nov 1954	387	35	9.9
Aug 1984	1224	109	9.8
Oct 1998	8592	750	9.6
Oct 1974	666	58	9.5

DAYS

		Close	Change	Change
Wed	1987 Oct 21	2028	187 pt	10.2 %
Wed	2002 Jul 24	8191	489	6.3
Tue	1987 Oct 20	1841	102	5.9
Mon	2002 Jul 29	8712	448	5.4
Wed	1970 May 27	663	32	5.1
Tue	1998 Sep 8	8021	381	5.0
Thu	1987 Oct 29	1938	92	5.0
Thu	2000 Mar 16	10630	499	4.9
Tue	1982 Aug 17	831	39	4.9
Tue	2002 Oct 15	8255	378	4.8

10 WORST

YEARS

	Close	Change	Change
1974	616	– 235 pt	– 27.6 %
1966	786	– 184	– 18.9
1977	831	– 174	– 17.3
2002	8342	– 1680	– 16.8
1973	851	– 169	– 16.6
1969	800	– 143	– 15.2
1957	436	– 64	– 12.8
1962	652	– 79	– 10.8
1960	616	– 64	– 9.3
1981	875	– 89	– 9.2

MONTHS

	Close	Change	Change
Oct 1987	1994	– 603 pt	– 23.2 %
Aug 1998	7539	– 1344	– 15.1
Nov 1973	822	– 134	– 14.0
Sep 2002	7592	– 1072	– 12.4
Sep 2001	8848	– 1102	– 11.1
Sep 1974	608	– 71	– 10.4
Aug 1974	679	– 79	– 10.4
Aug 1990	2614	– 291	– 10.0
Mar 1980	786	– 77	– 9.0
Jun 1962	561	– 52	– 8.5

DAYS

		Close	Change	Change
Mon	1987 Oct 19	1739	– 508 pt	– 22.6 %
Mon	1987 Oct 26	1794	– 157	– 8.0
Mon	1997 Oct 27	8366	– 554	– 7.2
Mon	2001 Sep 17	8921	– 685	– 7.1
Fri	1989 Oct 13	2569	– 191	– 6.9
Fri	1988 Jan 8	1911	– 141	– 6.9
Mon	1955 Sep 26	456	– 32	– 6.5
Mon	1998 Aug 31	7539	– 513	– 6.4
Mon	1962 May 28	577	– 35	– 5.7
Fri	2000 Apr 14	10306	– 618	– 5.7

STOCK MKT **NASDAQ 1972- 2007 BEST - WORST**

10 BEST

YEARS

	Close	Change	Change
1999	4069	1877 pt	85.6 %
1991	586	213	56.9
2003	2003	668	50.0
1995	1052	300	39.9
1998	2193	622	39.6
1980	202	51	33.9
1985	325	78	31.5
1975	78	18	29.8
1979	151	33	28.1
1976	98	20	26.1

MONTHS

	Close	Change	Change
Dec 1999	4069	733 pt	22.0 %
Feb 2000	4697	756	19.2
Oct 1974	65	10	17.2
Jun 2000	3966	565	16.6
Apr 2001	2116	276	15.0
Nov 2001	1931	240	14.2
Oct 2002	1330	158	13.5
Oct 1982	1771	25	13.3
Sep 1998	1694	195	13.0
Oct 2001	1690	191	12.8

DAYS

		Close	Change	Change
Wed	2001 Jan 3	2617	325 pt	14.2 %
Tue	2000 Dec 5	2890	274	10.5
Thu	2001 Apr 5	1785	146	8.9
Wed	2001 Apr 18	2079	156	8.1
Tue	2000 May 30	3459	254	7.9
Fri	2000 Oct 13	3317	242	7.9
Thu	2000 Oct 19	3419	247	7.8
Wed	2002 May 8	1696	122	7.8
Fri	2000 Dec 22	2517	177	7.6
Wed	1987 Oct 21	352	24	7.4

10 WORST

YEARS

	Close	Change	Change
2000	2471	– 1599 pt	– 39.3 %
1974	60	– 32	– 35.1
2002	1336	– 615	– 31.5
1973	92	– 42	– 31.1
2001	1950	– 520	– 21.1
1990	374	– 81	– 17.8
1984	247	– 32	– 11.3
1987	331	– 18	– 5.2
1981	196	– 7	– 3.2
1994	752	– 25	– 3.2

MONTHS

	Close	Change	Change
Oct 1987	323	– 121 pt	– 27.2 %
Nov 2000	2598	– 772	– 22.9
Feb 2001	2152	– 621	– 22.4
Aug 1998	1499	– 373	– 19.9
Mar 1980	131	– 27	– 17.1
Sep 2001	1499	– 307	– 17.0
Oct 1978	111	– 22	– 16.4
Apr 2000	3861	– 712	– 15.6
Nov 1973	94	– 17	– 15.1
Mar 2001	1840	– 312	– 14.5

DAYS

		Close	Change	Change
Mon	1987 Oct 19	360	– 46 pt	– 11.3 %
Fri	2000 Apr 14	3321	– 355	– 9.7
Mon	1987 Oct 26	299	– 30	– 9.0
Tue	1987 Oct 20	328	– 32	– 9.0
Mon	1998 Aug 31	1499	– 140	– 8.6
Mon	2000 Apr 03	4224	– 349	– 7.6
Tue	2001 Jan 02	2292	– 179	– 7.2
Mon	1997 Oct 27	296	– 118	– 7.2
Wed	2000 Dec 20	2333	– 179	– 7.1
Wed	2000 Apr 12	3770	– 286	– 7.1

S&P /TSX (CANADA) 1985 - 2007 BEST - WORST

10 BEST

YEARS

	Close	Change	Change
1999	8414	1928 pt	29.7 %
1993	4321	971	29.0
1996	5927	1214	25.7
2003	8221	1606	24.3
2005	11272	2026	21.9
1985	2893	493	20.5
1989	3970	580	17.1
2006	12908	1636	14.5
1997	6699	772	13.0
2004	9247	1026	12.5

MONTHS

	Close	Change	Change
Dec 1999	8414	894 pt	11.9 %
Oct 1998	6208	594	10.6
Jun 2000	10196	944	10.2
Jan 1985	2595	195	8.1
Aug 2000	11248	842	8.1
Nov 2001	7426	540	7.8
Jul 1987	4030	290	7.8
Feb 2000	9129	648	7.6
Nov 1996	6017	418	7.5
Mar 1987	3739	240	6.9

DAYS

		Close	Change	Change
Wed	1987 Oct 21	3246	269 pt	9.0 %
Fri	1987 Oct 30	3019	147	5.1
Thu	1998 Oct 15	5864	268	4.8
Tue	2000 Oct 31	9640	387	4.2
Fri	2000 Dec 08	9549	382	4.2
Tue	1998 Sep 08	5977	235	4.1
Tue	2002 Oct 15	6219	241	4.0
Wed	2001 Apr 18	8131	312	4.0
Fri	2000 Jan 17	8429	315	3.9
Wed	2001 Jan 03	8938	326	3.8

10 WORST

YEARS

	Close	Change	Change
1990	3257	– 713 pt	– 18.0 %
2002	6615	– 1074	– 14.0
2001	7688	– 1245	– 13.9
1992	3350	– 162	– 4.6
1998	6486	– 214	– 3.2
1994	4214	– 108	– 2.5
1987	3160	94	3.1
1986	3066	173	6.0
2000	8934	520	6.2
2007	13833	925	7.2

MONTHS

	Close	Change	Change
Oct 1987	3019	– 883 pt	– 22.6 %
Aug 1998	5531	– 1401	– 20.2
Feb 2001	8079	– 1243	– 13.3
Nov 2000	8820	– 820	– 8.5
Apr 1990	3341	– 299	– 8.2
Sep 2000	10378	– 870	– 7.7
Sep 2001	6839	– 561	– 7.6
Jul 2002	6605	– 540	– 7.6
Oct 2000	9640	– 738	– 7.1
Jun 1994	4179	– 301	– 7.0

DAYS

		Close	Change	Change
Mon	1987 Oct 19	3192	– 407 pt	– 11.3 %
Wed	2000 Oct 25	9512	– 840	– 8.1
Mon	1987 Oct 26	2846	– 233	– 7.6
Tue	1987 Oct 20	2977	– 215	– 6.7
Fri	2001 Feb 16	8393	– 574	– 6.4
Mon	1997 Oct 27	6599	– 434	– 6.2
Thu	1998 Aug 27	5800	– 373	– 6.0
Mon	2001 Sep 17	6908	– 437	– 5.9
Fri	2000 Apr 14	8474	– 492	– 5.5
Thu	1987 Oct 22	3108	– 138	– 4.3

BOND YIELDS

BOND YIELDS 10 YEAR TREASURY*

	JAN	FEB	MAR	APR	MAY	JUN
1954	2.48	2.47	2.37	2.29	2.37	2.38
1955	2.61	2.65	2.68	2.75	2.76	2.78
1956	2.9	2.84	2.96	3.18	3.07	3
1957	3.46	3.34	3.41	3.48	3.6	3.8
1958	3.09	3.05	2.98	2.88	2.92	2.97
1959	4.02	3.96	3.99	4.12	4.31	4.34
1960	4.72	4.49	4.25	4.28	4.35	4.15
1961	3.84	3.78	3.74	3.78	3.71	3.88
1962	4.08	4.04	3.93	3.84	3.87	3.91
1963	3.83	3.92	3.93	3.97	3.93	3.99
1964	4.17	4.15	4.22	4.23	4.2	4.17
1965	4.19	4.21	4.21	4.2	4.21	4.21
1966	4.61	4.83	4.87	4.75	4.78	4.81
1967	4.58	4.63	4.54	4.59	4.85	5.02
1968	5.53	5.56	5.74	5.64	5.87	5.72
1969	6.04	6.19	6.3	6.17	6.32	6.57
1970	7.79	7.24	7.07	7.39	7.91	7.84
1971	6.24	6.11	5.7	5.83	6.39	6.52
1972	5.95	6.08	6.07	6.19	6.13	6.11
1973	6.46	6.64	6.71	6.67	6.85	6.9
1974	6.99	6.96	7.21	7.51	7.58	7.54
1975	7.5	7.39	7.73	8.23	8.06	7.86
1976	7.74	7.79	7.73	7.56	7.9	7.86
1977	7.21	7.39	7.46	7.37	7.46	7.28
1978	7.96	8.03	8.04	8.15	8.35	8.46
1979	9.1	9.1	9.12	9.18	9.25	8.91
1980	10.8	12.41	12.75	11.47	10.18	9.78
1981	12.57	13.19	13.12	13.68	14.1	13.47
1982	14.59	14.43	13.86	13.87	13.62	14.3
1983	10.46	10.72	10.51	10.4	10.38	10.85
1984	11.67	11.84	12.32	12.63	13.41	13.56
1985	11.38	11.51	11.86	11.43	10.85	10.16
1986	9.19	8.7	7.78	7.3	7.71	7.8
1987	7.08	7.25	7.25	8.02	8.61	8.4
1988	8.67	8.21	8.37	8.72	9.09	8.92
1989	9.09	9.17	9.36	9.18	8.86	8.28
1990	8.21	8.47	8.59	8.79	8.76	8.48
1991	8.09	7.85	8.11	8.04	8.07	8.28
1992	7.03	7.34	7.54	7.48	7.39	7.26
1993	6.6	6.26	5.98	5.97	6.04	5.96
1994	5.75	5.97	6.48	6.97	7.18	7.1
1995	7.78	7.47	7.2	7.06	6.63	6.17
1996	5.65	5.81	6.27	6.51	6.74	6.91
1997	6.58	6.42	6.69	6.89	6.71	6.49
1998	5.54	5.57	5.65	5.64	5.65	5.5
1999	4.72	5	5.23	5.18	5.54	5.9
2000	6.66	6.52	6.26	5.99	6.44	6.1
2001	5.16	5.1	4.89	5.14	5.39	5.28
2002	5.04	4.91	5.28	5.21	5.16	4.93
2003	4.05	3.9	3.81	3.96	3.57	3.33
2004	4.15	4.08	3.83	4.35	4.72	4.73
2005	4.22	4.17	4.5	4.34	4.14	4.00
2006	4.42	4.57	4.72	4.99	5.11	5.11
2007	4.76	4.72	4.56	4.69	4.75	5.10
2008	3.74	3.74	3.51	3.68	3.88	4.10

* Source: Federal Reserve Bank of St. Louis, monthly data calculated as average of business days

JUL	AUG	SEP	OCT	NOV	DEC	
2.3	2.36	2.38	2.43	2.48	2.51	**1954**
2.9	2.97	2.97	2.88	2.89	2.96	**1955**
3.11	3.33	3.38	3.34	3.49	3.59	**1956**
3.93	3.93	3.92	3.97	3.72	3.21	**1957**
3.2	3.54	3.76	3.8	3.74	3.86	**1958**
4.4	4.43	4.68	4.53	4.53	4.69	**1959**
3.9	3.8	3.8	3.89	3.93	3.84	**1960**
3.92	4.04	3.98	3.92	3.94	4.06	**1961**
4.01	3.98	3.98	3.93	3.92	3.86	**1962**
4.02	4	4.08	4.11	4.12	4.13	**1963**
4.19	4.19	4.2	4.19	4.15	4.18	**1964**
4.2	4.25	4.29	4.35	4.45	4.62	**1965**
5.02	5.22	5.18	5.01	5.16	4.84	**1966**
5.16	5.28	5.3	5.48	5.75	5.7	**1967**
5.5	5.42	5.46	5.58	5.7	6.03	**1968**
6.72	6.69	7.16	7.1	7.14	7.65	**1969**
7.46	7.53	7.39	7.33	6.84	6.39	**1970**
6.73	6.58	6.14	5.93	5.81	5.93	**1971**
6.11	6.21	6.55	6.48	6.28	6.36	**1972**
7.13	7.4	7.09	6.79	6.73	6.74	**1973**
7.81	8.04	8.04	7.9	7.68	7.43	**1974**
8.06	8.4	8.43	8.14	8.05	8	**1975**
7.83	7.77	7.59	7.41	7.29	6.87	**1976**
7.33	7.4	7.34	7.52	7.58	7.69	**1977**
8.64	8.41	8.42	8.64	8.81	9.01	**1978**
8.95	9.03	9.33	10.3	10.65	10.39	**1979**
10.25	11.1	11.51	11.75	12.68	12.84	**1980**
14.28	14.94	15.32	15.15	13.39	13.72	**1981**
13.95	13.06	12.34	10.91	10.55	10.54	**1982**
11.38	11.85	11.65	11.54	11.69	11.83	**1983**
13.36	12.72	12.52	12.16	11.57	11.5	**1984**
10.31	10.33	10.37	10.24	9.78	9.26	**1985**
7.3	7.17	7.45	7.43	7.25	7.11	**1986**
8.45	8.76	9.42	9.52	8.86	8.99	**1987**
9.06	9.26	8.98	8.8	8.96	9.11	**1988**
8.02	8.11	8.19	8.01	7.87	7.84	**1989**
8.47	8.75	8.89	8.72	8.39	8.08	**1990**
8.27	7.9	7.65	7.53	7.42	7.09	**1991**
6.84	6.59	6.42	6.59	6.87	6.77	**1992**
5.81	5.68	5.36	5.33	5.72	5.77	**1993**
7.3	7.24	7.46	7.74	7.96	7.81	**1994**
6.28	6.49	6.2	6.04	5.93	5.71	**1995**
6.87	6.64	6.83	6.53	6.2	6.3	**1996**
6.22	6.3	6.21	6.03	5.88	5.81	**1997**
5.46	5.34	4.81	4.53	4.83	4.65	**1998**
5.79	5.94	5.92	6.11	6.03	6.28	**1999**
6.05	5.83	5.8	5.74	5.72	5.24	**2000**
5.24	4.97	4.73	4.57	4.65	5.09	**2001**
4.65	4.26	3.87	3.94	4.05	4.03	**2002**
3.98	4.45	4.27	4.29	4.3	4.27	**2003**
4.5	4.28	4.13	4.1	4.19	4.23	**2004**
4.18	4.26	4.20	4.46	4.54	4.47	**2005**
5.09	4.88	4.72	4.73	4.60	4.56	**2006**
5.00	4.67	4.52	4.53	4.15	4.10	**2007**

BOND YIELDS 5 YEAR TREASURY*

	JAN	FEB	MAR	APR	MAY	JUN
1954	2.17	2.04	1.93	1.87	1.92	1.92
1955	2.32	2.38	2.48	2.55	2.56	2.59
1956	2.84	2.74	2.93	3.20	3.08	2.97
1957	3.47	3.39	3.46	3.53	3.64	3.83
1958	2.88	2.78	2.64	2.46	2.41	2.46
1959	4.01	3.96	3.99	4.12	4.35	4.50
1960	4.92	4.69	4.31	4.29	4.49	4.12
1961	3.67	3.66	3.60	3.57	3.47	3.81
1962	3.94	3.89	3.68	3.60	3.66	3.64
1963	3.58	3.66	3.68	3.74	3.72	3.81
1964	4.07	4.03	4.14	4.15	4.05	4.02
1965	4.10	4.15	4.15	4.15	4.15	4.15
1966	4.86	4.98	4.92	4.83	4.89	4.97
1967	4.70	4.74	4.54	4.51	4.75	5.01
1968	5.54	5.59	5.76	5.69	6.04	5.85
1969	6.25	6.34	6.41	6.30	6.54	6.75
1970	8.17	7.82	7.21	7.50	7.97	7.85
1971	5.89	5.56	5.00	5.65	6.28	6.53
1972	5.59	5.69	5.87	6.17	5.85	5.91
1973	6.34	6.60	6.80	6.67	6.80	6.69
1974	6.95	6.82	7.31	7.92	8.18	8.10
1975	7.41	7.11	7.30	7.99	7.72	7.51
1976	7.46	7.45	7.49	7.25	7.59	7.61
1977	6.58	6.83	6.93	6.79	6.94	6.76
1978	7.77	7.83	7.86	7.98	8.18	8.36
1979	9.20	9.13	9.20	9.25	9.24	8.85
1980	10.74	12.60	13.47	11.84	9.95	9.21
1981	12.77	13.41	13.41	13.99	14.63	13.95
1982	14.65	14.54	13.98	14.00	13.75	14.43
1983	10.03	10.26	10.08	10.02	10.03	10.63
1984	11.37	11.54	12.02	12.37	13.17	13.48
1985	10.93	11.13	11.52	11.01	10.34	9.60
1986	8.68	8.34	7.46	7.05	7.52	7.64
1987	6.64	6.79	6.79	7.57	8.26	8.02
1988	8.18	7.71	7.83	8.19	8.58	8.49
1989	9.15	9.27	9.51	9.30	8.91	8.29
1990	8.12	8.42	8.60	8.77	8.74	8.43
1991	7.70	7.47	7.77	7.70	7.70	7.94
1992	6.24	6.58	6.95	6.78	6.69	6.48
1993	5.83	5.43	5.19	5.13	5.20	5.22
1994	5.09	5.40	5.94	6.52	6.78	6.70
1995	7.76	7.37	7.05	6.86	6.41	5.93
1996	5.36	5.38	5.97	6.30	6.48	6.69
1997	6.33	6.20	6.54	6.76	6.57	6.38
1998	5.42	5.49	5.61	5.61	5.63	5.52
1999	4.60	4.91	5.14	5.08	5.44	5.81
2000	6.58	6.68	6.50	6.26	6.69	6.30
2001	4.86	4.89	4.64	4.76	4.93	4.81
2002	4.34	4.30	4.74	4.65	4.49	4.19
2003	3.05	2.90	2.78	2.93	2.52	2.27
2004	3.12	3.07	2.79	3.39	3.85	3.93
2005	3.71	3.77	4.17	4.00	3.85	3.77
2006	4.35	4.57	4.72	4.90	5.00	5.07
2007	4.75	4.71	4.48	4.59	4.67	5.03
2008	2.98	2.78	2.48	2.84	3.15	3.49

* Source: Federal Reserve Bank of St. Louis, monthly data calculated as average of business days

5 YEAR TREASURY BOND YIELDS

JUL	AUG	SEP	OCT	NOV	DEC	
1.85	1.90	1.96	2.02	2.09	2.16	**1954**
2.72	2.86	2.85	2.76	2.81	2.93	**1955**
3.12	3.41	3.47	3.40	3.56	3.70	**1956**
4.00	4.00	4.03	4.08	3.72	3.08	**1957**
2.77	3.29	3.69	3.78	3.70	3.82	**1958**
4.58	4.57	4.90	4.72	4.75	5.01	**1959**
3.79	3.62	3.61	3.76	3.81	3.67	**1960**
3.84	3.96	3.90	3.80	3.82	3.91	**1961**
3.80	3.71	3.70	3.64	3.60	3.56	**1962**
3.89	3.89	3.96	3.97	4.01	4.04	**1963**
4.03	4.05	4.08	4.07	4.04	4.09	**1964**
4.15	4.20	4.25	4.34	4.46	4.72	**1965**
5.17	5.50	5.50	5.27	5.36	5.00	**1966**
5.23	5.31	5.40	5.57	5.78	5.75	**1967**
5.60	5.50	5.48	5.55	5.66	6.12	**1968**
7.01	7.03	7.57	7.51	7.53	7.96	**1969**
7.59	7.57	7.29	7.12	6.47	5.95	**1970**
6.85	6.55	6.14	5.93	5.78	5.69	**1971**
5.97	6.02	6.25	6.18	6.12	6.16	**1972**
7.33	7.63	7.05	6.77	6.92	6.80	**1973**
8.38	8.63	8.37	7.97	7.68	7.31	**1974**
7.92	8.33	8.37	7.97	7.80	7.76	**1975**
7.49	7.31	7.13	6.75	6.52	6.10	**1976**
6.84	7.03	7.04	7.32	7.34	7.48	**1977**
8.54	8.33	8.43	8.61	8.84	9.08	**1978**
8.90	9.06	9.41	10.63	10.93	10.42	**1979**
9.53	10.84	11.62	11.86	12.83	13.25	**1980**
14.79	15.56	15.93	15.41	13.38	13.60	**1981**
14.07	13.00	12.25	10.80	10.38	10.22	**1982**
11.21	11.63	11.43	11.28	11.41	11.54	**1983**
13.27	12.68	12.53	12.06	11.33	11.07	**1984**
9.70	9.81	9.81	9.69	9.28	8.73	**1985**
7.06	6.80	6.92	6.83	6.76	6.67	**1986**
8.01	8.32	8.94	9.08	8.35	8.45	**1987**
8.66	8.94	8.69	8.51	8.79	9.09	**1988**
7.83	8.09	8.17	7.97	7.81	7.75	**1989**
8.33	8.44	8.51	8.33	8.02	7.73	**1990**
7.91	7.43	7.14	6.87	6.62	6.19	**1991**
5.84	5.60	5.38	5.60	6.04	6.08	**1992**
5.09	5.03	4.73	4.71	5.06	5.15	**1993**
6.91	6.88	7.08	7.40	7.72	7.78	**1994**
6.01	6.24	6.00	5.86	5.69	5.51	**1995**
6.64	6.39	6.60	6.27	5.97	6.07	**1996**
6.12	6.16	6.11	5.93	5.80	5.77	**1997**
5.46	5.27	4.62	4.18	4.54	4.45	**1998**
5.68	5.84	5.80	6.03	5.97	6.19	**1999**
6.18	6.06	5.93	5.78	5.70	5.17	**2000**
4.76	4.57	4.12	3.91	3.97	4.39	**2001**
3.81	3.29	2.94	2.95	3.05	3.03	**2002**
2.87	3.37	3.18	3.19	3.29	3.27	**2003**
3.69	3.47	3.36	3.35	3.53	3.60	**2004**
3.98	4.12	4.01	4.33	4.45	4.39	**2005**
5.04	4.82	4.67	4.69	4.58	4.53	**2006**
4.88	4.43	4.20	4.20	3.67	3.49	**2007**

BOND YIELDS

3 MONTH TREASURY

	JAN	FEB	MAR	APR	MAY	JUN
1982	12.92	14.28	13.31	13.34	12.71	13.08
1983	8.12	8.39	8.66	8.51	8.50	9.14
1984	9.26	9.46	9.89	10.07	10.22	10.26
1985	8.02	8.56	8.83	8.22	7.73	7.18
1986	7.30	7.29	6.76	6.24	6.33	6.40
1987	5.58	5.75	5.77	5.82	5.85	5.85
1988	6.00	5.84	5.87	6.08	6.45	6.66
1999	8.56	8.84	9.14	8.96	8.74	8.43
1990	7.90	8.00	8.17	8.04	8.01	7.99
1991	6.41	6.12	6.09	5.83	5.63	5.75
1992	3.91	3.95	4.14	3.84	3.72	3.75
1993	3.07	2.99	3.01	2.93	3.03	3.14
1994	3.04	3.33	3.59	3.78	4.27	4.25
1995	5.90	5.94	5.91	5.84	5.85	5.64
1996	5.15	4.96	5.10	5.09	5.15	5.23
1997	5.17	5.14	5.28	5.30	5.20	5.07
1998	5.18	5.23	5.16	5.08	5.14	5.12
1999	4.45	4.56	4.57	4.41	4.63	4.72
2000	5.50	5.73	5.86	5.82	5.99	5.86
2001	5.29	5.01	4.54	3.97	3.70	3.57
2002	1.68	1.76	1.83	1.75	1.76	1.73
2003	1.19	1.19	1.15	1.15	1.09	0.94
2004	0.90	0.94	0.95	0.96	1.04	1.29
2005	2.37	2.58	2.80	2.84	2.90	3.04
2006	4.34	4.54	4.63	4.72	4.84	4.92
2007	5.11	5.16	5.08	5.01	4.87	4.74
2008	2.82	2.17	1.28	1.31	1.76	1.89

* Source: Federal Reserve Bank of St. Louis, monthly data calculated as average of business days

3 MONTH TREASURY BOND YIELDS

JUL	AUG	SEP	OCT	NOV	DEC	
11.86	9.00	8.19	7.97	8.35	8.20	**1982**
9.45	9.74	9.36	8.99	9.11	9.36	**1983**
10.53	10.90	10.80	10.12	8.92	8.34	**1984**
7.32	7.37	7.33	7.40	7.48	7.33	**1985**
6.00	5.69	5.35	5.32	5.50	5.68	**1986**
5.88	6.23	6.62	6.35	5.89	5.96	**1987**
6.95	7.30	7.48	7.60	8.03	8.35	**1988**
8.15	8.17	8.01	7.90	7.94	7.88	**1999**
7.87	7.69	7.60	7.40	7.29	6.95	**1990**
5.75	5.50	5.37	5.14	4.69	4.18	**1991**
3.28	3.20	2.97	2.93	3.21	3.29	**1992**
3.11	3.09	3.01	3.09	3.18	3.13	**1993**
4.46	4.61	4.75	5.10	5.45	5.76	**1994**
5.59	5.57	5.43	5.44	5.52	5.29	**1995**
5.30	5.19	5.24	5.12	5.17	5.04	**1996**
5.19	5.28	5.08	5.11	5.28	5.30	**1997**
5.09	5.04	4.74	4.07	4.53	4.50	**1998**
4.69	4.87	4.82	5.02	5.23	5.36	**1999**
6.14	6.28	6.18	6.29	6.36	5.94	**2000**
3.59	3.44	2.69	2.20	1.91	1.72	**2001**
1.71	1.65	1.66	1.61	1.25	1.21	**2002**
0.92	0.97	0.96	0.94	0.95	0.91	**2003**
1.36	1.50	1.68	1.79	2.11	2.22	**2004**
3.29	3.52	3.49	3.79	3.97	3.97	**2005**
5.08	5.09	4.93	5.05	5.07	4.97	**2006**
4.96	4.32	3.99	4.00	3.35	3.07	**2007**

BOND YIELDS

MOODY'S SEASONED CORPORATE Aaa*

	JAN	FEB	MAR	APR	MAY	JUN
1950	2.57	2.58	2.58	2.60	2.61	2.62
1951	2.66	2.66	2.78	2.87	2.89	2.94
1952	2.98	2.93	2.96	2.93	2.93	2.94
1953	3.02	3.07	3.12	3.23	3.34	3.40
1954	3.06	2.95	2.86	2.85	2.88	2.90
1955	2.93	2.93	3.02	3.01	3.04	3.05
1956	3.11	3.08	3.10	3.24	3.28	3.26
1957	3.77	3.67	3.66	3.67	3.74	3.91
1958	3.60	3.59	3.63	3.60	3.57	3.57
1959	4.12	4.14	4.13	4.23	4.37	4.46
1960	4.61	4.56	4.49	4.45	4.46	4.45
1961	4.32	4.27	4.22	4.25	4.27	4.33
1962	4.42	4.42	4.39	4.33	4.28	4.28
1963	4.21	4.19	4.19	4.21	4.22	4.23
1964	4.39	4.36	4.38	4.40	4.41	4.41
1965	4.43	4.41	4.42	4.43	4.44	4.46
1966	4.74	4.78	4.92	4.96	4.98	5.07
1967	5.20	5.03	5.13	5.11	5.24	5.44
1968	6.17	6.10	6.11	6.21	6.27	6.28
1969	6.59	6.66	6.85	6.89	6.79	6.98
1970	7.91	7.93	7.84	7.83	8.11	8.48
1971	7.36	7.08	7.21	7.25	7.53	7.64
1972	7.19	7.27	7.24	7.30	7.30	7.23
1973	7.15	7.22	7.29	7.26	7.29	7.37
1974	7.83	7.85	8.01	8.25	8.37	8.47
1975	8.83	8.62	8.67	8.95	8.90	8.77
1976	8.60	8.55	8.52	8.40	8.58	8.62
1977	7.96	8.04	8.10	8.04	8.05	7.95
1978	8.41	8.47	8.47	8.56	8.69	8.76
1979	9.25	9.26	9.37	9.38	9.50	9.29
1980	11.09	12.38	12.96	12.04	10.99	10.58
1981	12.81	13.35	13.33	13.88	14.32	13.75
1982	15.18	15.27	14.58	14.46	14.26	14.81
1983	11.79	12.01	11.73	11.51	11.46	11.74
1984	12.20	12.08	12.57	12.81	13.28	13.55
1985	12.08	12.13	12.56	12.23	11.72	10.94
1986	10.05	9.67	9.00	8.79	9.09	9.13
1987	8.36	8.38	8.36	8.85	9.33	9.32
1988	9.88	9.40	9.39	9.67	9.90	9.86
1989	9.62	9.64	9.80	9.79	9.57	9.10
1990	8.99	9.22	9.37	9.46	9.47	9.26
1991	9.04	8.83	8.93	8.86	8.86	9.01
1992	8.20	8.29	8.35	8.33	8.28	8.22
1993	7.91	7.71	7.58	7.46	7.43	7.33
1994	6.92	7.08	7.48	7.88	7.99	7.97
1995	8.46	8.26	8.12	8.03	7.65	7.30
1996	6.81	6.99	7.35	7.50	7.62	7.71
1997	7.42	7.31	7.55	7.73	7.58	7.41
1998	6.61	6.67	6.72	6.69	6.69	6.53
1999	6.24	6.40	6.62	6.64	6.93	7.23
2000	7.78	7.68	7.68	7.64	7.99	7.67
2001	7.15	7.10	6.98	7.20	7.29	7.18
2002	6.55	6.51	6.81	6.76	6.75	6.63
2003	6.17	5.95	5.89	5.74	5.22	4.97
2004	5.54	5.50	5.33	5.73	6.04	6.01
2005	5.36	5.20	5.40	5.33	5.15	4.96
2006	5.29	5.35	5.53	5.84	5.95	5.89
2007	5.40	5.39	5.30	5.47	5.47	5.79
2008	5.33	5.53	5.51	5.55	5.57	5.68

* Source: Federal Reserve Bank of St. Louis, monthly data calculated as average of business days

MOODY'S SEASONED CORPORATE Aaa BOND YIELDS

JUL	AUG	SEP	OCT	NOV	DEC	
2.65	2.61	2.64	2.67	2.67	2.67	**1950**
2.94	2.88	2.84	2.89	2.96	3.01	**1951**
2.95	2.94	2.95	3.01	2.98	2.97	**1952**
3.28	3.24	3.29	3.16	3.11	3.13	**1953**
2.89	2.87	2.89	2.87	2.89	2.90	**1954**
3.06	3.11	3.13	3.10	3.10	3.15	**1955**
3.28	3.43	3.56	3.59	3.69	3.75	**1956**
3.99	4.10	4.12	4.10	4.08	3.81	**1957**
3.67	3.85	4.09	4.11	4.09	4.08	**1958**
4.47	4.43	4.52	4.57	4.56	4.58	**1959**
4.41	4.28	4.25	4.30	4.31	4.35	**1960**
4.41	4.45	4.45	4.42	4.39	4.42	**1961**
4.34	4.35	4.32	4.28	4.25	4.24	**1962**
4.26	4.29	4.31	4.32	4.33	4.35	**1963**
4.40	4.41	4.42	4.42	4.43	4.44	**1964**
4.48	4.49	4.52	4.56	4.60	4.68	**1965**
5.16	5.31	5.49	5.41	5.35	5.39	**1966**
5.58	5.62	5.65	5.82	6.07	6.19	**1967**
6.24	6.02	5.97	6.09	6.19	6.45	**1968**
7.08	6.97	7.14	7.33	7.35	7.72	**1969**
8.44	8.13	8.09	8.03	8.05	7.64	**1970**
7.64	7.59	7.44	7.39	7.26	7.25	**1971**
7.21	7.19	7.22	7.21	7.12	7.08	**1972**
7.45	7.68	7.63	7.60	7.67	7.68	**1973**
8.72	9.00	9.24	9.27	8.89	8.89	**1974**
8.84	8.95	8.95	8.86	8.78	8.79	**1975**
8.56	8.45	8.38	8.32	8.25	7.98	**1976**
7.94	7.98	7.92	8.04	8.08	8.19	**1977**
8.88	8.69	8.69	8.89	9.03	9.16	**1978**
9.20	9.23	9.44	10.13	10.76	10.74	**1979**
11.07	11.64	12.02	12.31	12.97	13.21	**1980**
14.38	14.89	15.49	15.40	14.22	14.23	**1981**
14.61	13.71	12.94	12.12	11.68	11.83	**1982**
12.15	12.51	12.37	12.25	12.41	12.57	**1983**
13.44	12.87	12.66	12.63	12.29	12.13	**1984**
10.97	11.05	11.07	11.02	10.55	10.16	**1985**
8.88	8.72	8.89	8.86	8.68	8.49	**1986**
9.42	9.67	10.18	10.52	10.01	10.11	**1987**
9.96	10.11	9.82	9.51	9.45	9.57	**1988**
8.93	8.96	9.01	8.92	8.89	8.86	**1989**
9.24	9.41	9.56	9.53	9.30	9.05	**1990**
9.00	8.75	8.61	8.55	8.48	8.31	**1991**
8.07	7.95	7.92	7.99	8.10	7.98	**1992**
7.17	6.85	6.66	6.67	6.93	6.93	**1993**
8.11	8.07	8.34	8.57	8.68	8.46	**1994**
7.41	7.57	7.32	7.12	7.02	6.82	**1995**
7.65	7.46	7.66	7.39	7.10	7.20	**1996**
7.14	7.22	7.15	7.00	6.87	6.76	**1997**
6.55	6.52	6.40	6.37	6.41	6.22	**1998**
7.19	7.40	7.39	7.55	7.36	7.55	**1999**
7.65	7.55	7.62	7.55	7.45	7.21	**2000**
7.13	7.02	7.17	7.03	6.97	6.77	**2001**
6.53	6.37	6.15	6.32	6.31	6.21	**2002**
5.49	5.88	5.72	5.70	5.65	5.62	**2003**
5.82	5.65	5.46	5.47	5.52	5.47	**2004**
5.06	5.09	5.13	5.35	5.42	5.37	**2005**
5.85	5.68	5.51	5.51	5.33	5.32	**2006**
5.73	5.79	5.74	5.66	5.44	5.49	**2007**

BOND YIELDS

MOODY'S SEASONED CORPORATE Baa*

	JAN	FEB	MAR	APR	MAY	JUN
1950	3.24	3.24	3.24	3.23	3.25	3.28
1951	3.17	3.16	3.23	3.35	3.40	3.49
1952	3.59	3.53	3.51	3.50	3.49	3.50
1953	3.51	3.53	3.57	3.65	3.78	3.86
1954	3.71	3.61	3.51	3.47	3.47	3.49
1955	3.45	3.47	3.48	3.49	3.50	3.51
1956	3.60	3.58	3.60	3.68	3.73	3.76
1957	4.49	4.47	4.43	4.44	4.52	4.63
1958	4.83	4.66	4.68	4.67	4.62	4.55
1959	4.87	4.89	4.85	4.86	4.96	5.04
1960	5.34	5.34	5.25	5.20	5.28	5.26
1961	5.10	5.07	5.02	5.01	5.01	5.03
1962	5.08	5.07	5.04	5.02	5.00	5.02
1963	4.91	4.89	4.88	4.87	4.85	4.84
1964	4.83	4.83	4.83	4.85	4.85	4.85
1965	4.80	4.78	4.78	4.80	4.81	4.85
1966	5.06	5.12	5.32	5.41	5.48	5.58
1967	5.97	5.82	5.85	5.83	5.96	6.15
1968	6.84	6.80	6.85	6.97	7.03	7.07
1969	7.32	7.30	7.51	7.54	7.52	7.70
1970	8.86	8.78	8.63	8.70	8.98	9.25
1971	8.74	8.39	8.46	8.45	8.62	8.75
1972	8.23	8.23	8.24	8.24	8.23	8.20
1973	7.90	7.97	8.03	8.09	8.06	8.13
1974	8.48	8.53	8.62	8.87	9.05	9.27
1975	10.81	10.65	10.48	10.58	10.69	10.62
1976	10.41	10.24	10.12	9.94	9.86	9.89
1977	9.08	9.12	9.12	9.07	9.01	8.91
1978	9.17	9.20	9.22	9.32	9.49	9.60
1979	10.13	10.08	10.26	10.33	10.47	10.38
1980	12.42	13.57	14.45	14.19	13.17	12.71
1981	15.03	15.37	15.34	15.56	15.95	15.80
1982	17.10	17.18	16.82	16.78	16.64	16.92
1983	13.94	13.95	13.61	13.29	13.09	13.37
1984	13.65	13.59	13.99	14.31	14.74	15.05
1985	13.26	13.23	13.69	13.51	13.15	12.40
1986	11.44	11.11	10.50	10.19	10.29	10.34
1987	9.72	9.65	9.61	10.04	10.51	10.52
1988	11.07	10.62	10.57	10.90	11.04	11.00
1989	10.65	10.61	10.67	10.61	10.46	10.03
1990	9.94	10.14	10.21	10.30	10.41	10.22
1991	10.45	10.07	10.09	9.94	9.86	9.96
1992	9.13	9.23	9.25	9.21	9.13	9.05
1993	8.67	8.39	8.15	8.14	8.21	8.07
1994	7.65	7.76	8.13	8.52	8.62	8.65
1995	9.08	8.85	8.70	8.60	8.20	7.90
1996	7.47	7.63	8.03	8.19	8.30	8.40
1997	8.09	7.94	8.18	8.34	8.20	8.02
1998	7.19	7.25	7.32	7.33	7.30	7.13
1999	7.29	7.39	7.53	7.48	7.72	8.02
2000	8.33	8.29	8.37	8.40	8.90	8.48
2001	7.93	7.87	7.84	8.07	8.07	7.97
2002	7.87	7.89	8.11	8.03	8.09	7.95
2003	7.35	7.06	6.95	6.85	6.38	6.19
2004	6.44	6.27	6.11	6.46	6.75	6.78
2005	6.02	5.82	6.06	6.05	6.01	5.86
2006	6.24	6.27	6.41	6.68	6.75	6.78
2007	6.34	6.28	6.27	6.39	6.39	6.70
2008	6.54	6.82	6.89	6.97	6.93	7.07

* Source: Federal Reserve Bank of St. Louis, monthly data calculated as average of business days

MOODY'S SEASONED CORPORATE Baa* BOND YIELDS

JUL	AUG	SEP	OCT	NOV	DEC	
3.32	3.23	3.21	3.22	3.22	3.20	**1950**
3.53	3.50	3.46	3.50	3.56	3.61	**1951**
3.50	3.51	3.52	3.54	3.53	3.51	**1952**
3.86	3.85	3.88	3.82	3.75	3.74	**1953**
3.50	3.49	3.47	3.46	3.45	3.45	**1954**
3.52	3.56	3.59	3.59	3.58	3.62	**1955**
3.80	3.93	4.07	4.17	4.24	4.37	**1956**
4.73	4.82	4.93	4.99	5.09	5.03	**1957**
4.53	4.67	4.87	4.92	4.87	4.85	**1958**
5.08	5.09	5.18	5.28	5.26	5.28	**1959**
5.22	5.08	5.01	5.11	5.08	5.10	**1960**
5.09	5.11	5.12	5.13	5.11	5.10	**1961**
5.05	5.06	5.03	4.99	4.96	4.92	**1962**
4.84	4.83	4.84	4.83	4.84	4.85	**1963**
4.83	4.82	4.82	4.81	4.81	4.81	**1964**
4.88	4.88	4.91	4.93	4.95	5.02	**1965**
5.68	5.83	6.09	6.10	6.13	6.18	**1966**
6.26	6.33	6.40	6.52	6.72	6.93	**1967**
6.98	6.82	6.79	6.84	7.01	7.23	**1968**
7.84	7.86	8.05	8.22	8.25	8.65	**1969**
9.40	9.44	9.39	9.33	9.38	9.12	**1970**
8.76	8.76	8.59	8.48	8.38	8.38	**1971**
8.23	8.19	8.09	8.06	7.99	7.93	**1972**
8.24	8.53	8.63	8.41	8.42	8.48	**1973**
9.48	9.77	10.18	10.48	10.60	10.63	**1974**
10.55	10.59	10.61	10.62	10.56	10.56	**1975**
9.82	9.64	9.40	9.29	9.23	9.12	**1976**
8.87	8.82	8.80	8.89	8.95	8.99	**1977**
9.60	9.48	9.42	9.59	9.83	9.94	**1978**
10.29	10.35	10.54	11.40	11.99	12.06	**1979**
12.65	13.15	13.70	14.23	14.64	15.14	**1980**
16.17	16.34	16.92	17.11	16.39	16.55	**1981**
16.80	16.32	15.63	14.73	14.30	14.14	**1982**
13.39	13.64	13.55	13.46	13.61	13.75	**1983**
15.15	14.63	14.35	13.94	13.48	13.40	**1984**
12.43	12.50	12.48	12.36	11.99	11.58	**1985**
10.16	10.18	10.20	10.24	10.07	9.97	**1986**
10.61	10.80	11.31	11.62	11.23	11.29	**1987**
11.11	11.21	10.90	10.41	10.48	10.65	**1988**
9.87	9.88	9.91	9.81	9.81	9.82	**1989**
10.20	10.41	10.64	10.74	10.62	10.43	**1990**
9.89	9.65	9.51	9.49	9.45	9.26	**1991**
8.84	8.65	8.62	8.84	8.96	8.81	**1992**
7.93	7.60	7.34	7.31	7.66	7.69	**1993**
8.80	8.74	8.98	9.20	9.32	9.10	**1994**
8.04	8.19	7.93	7.75	7.68	7.49	**1995**
8.35	8.18	8.35	8.07	7.79	7.89	**1996**
7.75	7.82	7.70	7.57	7.42	7.32	**1997**
7.15	7.14	7.09	7.18	7.34	7.23	**1998**
7.95	8.15	8.20	8.38	8.15	8.19	**1999**
8.35	8.26	8.35	8.34	8.28	8.02	**2000**
7.97	7.85	8.03	7.91	7.81	8.05	**2001**
7.90	7.58	7.40	7.73	7.62	7.45	**2002**
6.62	7.01	6.79	6.73	6.66	6.60	**2003**
6.62	6.46	6.27	6.21	6.20	6.15	**2004**
5.95	5.96	6.03	6.30	6.39	6.32	**2005**
6.76	6.59	6.43	6.42	6.20	6.22	**2006**
6.65	6.65	6.59	6.48	6.40	6.65	**2007**

FEDERAL FUNDS

	JAN	FEB	MAR	APR	MAY	JUN
1990						
1991	6.75	6.25	6.00	5.75	5.75	5.75
1992	4.00	4.00	4.00	3.75	3.75	3.75
1993	3.00	3.00	3.00	3.00	3.00	3.00
1994	3.00	3.25	3.50	3.75	4.25	4.25
1995	5.50	6.00	6.00	6.00	6.00	6.00
1996	5.25	5.25	5.25	5.25	5.25	5.25
1997	5.25	5.25	5.50	5.50	5.50	5.50
1998	5.50	5.50	5.50	5.50	5.50	5.50
1999	4.75	4.75	4.75	4.75	4.75	5.00
2000	5.50	5.75	6.00	6.00	6.50	6.50
2001	5.50	5.50	5.00	4.50	4.00	3.75
2002	1.75	1.75	1.75	1.75	1.75	1.75
2003	1.25	1.25	1.25	1.25	1.25	1.00
2004	1.00	1.00	1.00	1.00	1.00	1.25
2005	2.25	2.50	2.75	2.75	3.00	3.25
2006	4.50	4.50	4.75	4.75	5.00	5.25
2007	5.25	5.25	5.25	5.25	5.25	5.25
2008	3.00	3.00	2.25	2.00	2.00	2.00

Change in overnight rate

Source: Federal Reserve Bank of New York

FEDERAL FUNDS TARGET RATE

FEDERAL RESERVE

JUL	AUG	SEP	OCT	NOV	DEC	
8.00	8.00	8.00	7.75	7.50	7.00	**1990**
5.75	5.50	5.25	5.00	4.75	4.00	**1991**
3.25	3.25	3.00	3.00	3.00	3.00	**1992**
3.00	3.00	3.00	3.00	3.00	3.00	**1993**
4.25	4.75	4.75	4.75	5.50	5.50	**1994**
5.75	5.75	5.75	5.75	5.75	5.50	**1995**
5.25	5.25	5.25	5.25	5.25	5.25	**1996**
5.50	5.50	5.50	5.50	5.50	5.50	**1997**
5.50	5.50	5.25	5.00	4.75	4.75	**1998**
5.00	5.25	5.25	5.25	5.50	5.50	**1999**
6.50	6.50	6.50	6.50	6.50	6.50	**2000**
3.75	3.50	3.00	2.50	2.00	1.75	**2001**
1.75	1.75	1.75	1.75	1.25	1.25	**2002**
1.00	1.00	1.00	1.00	1.00	1.00	**2003**
1.25	1.59	1.75	1.75	2.00	2.25	**2004**
3.25	3.50	3.75	3.75	4.00	4.25	**2005**
5.25	5.25	5.25	5.25	5.25	5.25	**2006**
5.25	5.25	4.75	4.50	4.50	4.25	**2007**

COMMODITIES

COMMODITIES

OIL - WEST TEXAS INTERMEDIATE CLOSING VALUES $ / bbl

	JAN	FEB	MAR	APR	MAY	JUN
1950	2.6	2.6	2.6	2.6	2.6	2.6
1951	2.6	2.6	2.6	2.6	2.6	2.6
1952	2.6	2.6	2.6	2.6	2.6	2.6
1953	2.6	2.6	2.6	2.6	2.6	2.8
1954	2.8	2.8	2.8	2.8	2.8	2.8
1955	2.8	2.8	2.8	2.8	2.8	2.8
1956	2.8	2.8	2.8	2.8	2.8	2.8
1957	2.8	3.1	3.1	3.1	3.1	3.1
1958	3.1	3.1	3.1	3.1	3.1	3.1
1959	3.0	3.0	3.0	3.0	3.0	3.0
1960	3.0	3.0	3.0	3.0	3.0	3.0
1961	3.0	3.0	3.0	3.0	3.0	3.0
1962	3.0	3.0	3.0	3.0	3.0	3.0
1963	3.0	3.0	3.0	3.0	3.0	3.0
1964	3.0	3.0	3.0	3.0	3.0	3.0
1965	2.9	2.9	2.9	2.9	2.9	2.9
1966	2.9	2.9	2.9	2.9	2.9	2.9
1967	3.0	3.0	3.0	3.0	3.0	3.0
1968	3.1	3.1	3.1	3.1	3.1	3.1
1969	3.1	3.1	3.3	3.4	3.4	3.4
1970	3.4	3.4	3.4	3.4	3.4	3.4
1971	3.6	3.6	3.6	3.6	3.6	3.6
1972	3.6	3.6	3.6	3.6	3.6	3.6
1973	3.6	3.6	3.6	3.6	3.6	3.6
1974	10.1	10.1	10.1	10.1	10.1	10.1
1975	11.2	11.2	11.2	11.2	11.2	11.2
1976	11.2	12.0	12.1	12.2	12.2	12.2
1977	13.9	13.9	13.9	13.9	13.9	13.9
1978	14.9	14.9	14.9	14.9	14.9	14.9
1979	14.9	15.9	15.9	15.9	18.1	19.1
1980	32.5	37.0	38.0	39.5	39.5	39.5
1981	38.0	38.0	38.0	38.0	38.0	36.0
1982	33.9	31.6	28.5	33.5	35.9	35.1
1983	31.2	29.0	28.8	30.6	30.0	31.0
1984	29.7	30.1	30.8	30.6	30.5	30.0
1985	25.6	27.3	28.2	28.8	27.6	27.1
1986	22.9	15.4	12.6	12.8	15.4	13.5
1987	18.7	17.7	18.3	18.6	19.4	20.0
1988	17.2	16.8	16.2	17.9	17.4	16.5
1989	18.0	17.8	19.4	21.0	20.0	20.0
1990	22.6	22.1	20.4	18.6	18.2	16.9
1991	25.0	20.5	19.9	20.8	21.2	20.2
1992	18.8	19.0	18.9	20.2	20.9	22.4
1993	19.1	20.1	20.3	20.3	19.9	19.1
1994	15.0	14.8	14.7	16.4	17.9	19.1
1995	18.0	18.5	18.6	19.9	19.7	18.4
1996	18.9	19.1	21.4	23.6	21.3	20.5
1997	25.2	22.2	21.0	19.7	20.8	19.2
1998	16.7	16.1	15.0	15.4	14.9	13.7
1999	12.5	12.0	14.7	17.3	17.8	17.9
2000	27.2	29.4	29.9	25.7	28.8	31.8
2001	29.6	29.6	27.2	27.4	28.6	27.6
2002	19.7	20.7	24.4	26.3	27.0	25.5
2003	32.9	35.9	33.6	28.3	28.1	30.7
2004	34.3	34.7	36.8	36.7	40.3	38.0
2005	46.8	48.0	54.3	53.0	49.8	56.3
2006	65.5	61.6	62.9	69.7	70.9	71.0
2007	54.6	59.3	60.6	64.0	63.5	67.5
2008	93.0	95.4	105.6	112.6	125.4	133.9

* Source: Federal Reserve

OIL - WEST TEXAS INTERMEDIATE CLOSING VALUES $ / bbl

COMMODITIES

JUL	AUG	SEP	OCT	NOV	DEC	
2.6	2.6	2.6	2.6	2.6	2.6	**1950**
2.6	2.6	2.6	2.6	2.6	2.6	**1951**
2.6	2.6	2.6	2.6	2.6	2.6	**1952**
2.8	2.8	2.8	2.8	2.8	2.8	**1953**
2.8	2.8	2.8	2.8	2.8	2.8	**1954**
2.8	2.8	2.8	2.8	2.8	2.8	**1955**
2.8	2.8	2.8	2.8	2.8	2.8	**1956**
3.1	3.1	3.1	3.1	3.1	3.0	**1957**
3.1	3.1	3.1	3.1	3.0	3.0	**1958**
3.0	3.0	3.0	3.0	3.0	3.0	**1959**
3.0	3.0	3.0	3.0	3.0	3.0	**1960**
3.0	3.0	3.0	3.0	3.0	3.0	**1961**
3.0	3.0	3.0	3.0	3.0	3.0	**1962**
3.0	3.0	3.0	3.0	3.0	3.0	**1963**
2.9	2.9	2.9	2.9	2.9	2.9	**1964**
2.9	2.9	2.9	2.9	2.9	2.9	**1965**
2.9	2.9	3.0	3.0	3.0	3.0	**1966**
3.0	3.1	3.1	3.1	3.1	3.1	**1967**
3.1	3.1	3.1	3.1	3.1	3.1	**1968**
3.4	3.4	3.4	3.4	3.4	3.4	**1969**
3.3	3.3	3.3	3.3	3.3	3.6	**1970**
3.6	3.6	3.6	3.6	3.6	3.6	**1971**
3.6	3.6	3.6	3.6	3.6	3.6	**1972**
3.6	4.3	4.3	4.3	4.3	4.3	**1973**
10.1	10.1	10.1	11.2	11.2	11.2	**1974**
11.2	11.2	11.2	11.2	11.2	11.2	**1975**
12.2	12.2	13.9	13.9	13.9	13.9	**1976**
13.9	14.9	14.9	14.9	14.9	14.9	**1977**
14.9	14.9	14.9	14.9	14.9	14.9	**1978**
21.8	26.5	28.5	29.0	31.0	32.5	**1979**
39.5	38.0	36.0	36.0	36.0	37.0	**1980**
36.0	36.0	36.0	35.0	36.0	35.0	**1981**
34.2	34.0	35.6	35.7	34.2	31.7	**1982**
31.7	31.9	31.1	30.4	29.8	29.2	**1983**
28.8	29.3	29.3	28.8	28.1	25.4	**1984**
27.3	27.8	28.3	29.5	30.8	27.2	**1985**
11.6	15.1	14.9	14.9	15.2	16.1	**1986**
21.4	20.3	19.5	19.8	18.9	17.2	**1987**
15.5	15.5	14.5	13.8	14.0	16.3	**1988**
19.6	18.5	19.6	20.1	19.8	21.1	**1989**
18.6	27.2	33.7	35.9	32.3	27.3	**1990**
21.4	21.7	21.9	23.2	22.5	19.5	**1991**
21.8	21.4	21.9	21.7	20.3	19.4	**1992**
17.9	18.0	17.5	18.1	16.7	14.5	**1993**
19.7	18.4	17.5	17.7	18.1	17.2	**1994**
17.3	18.0	18.2	17.4	18.0	19.0	**1995**
21.3	22.0	24.0	24.9	23.7	25.4	**1996**
19.6	19.9	19.8	21.3	20.2	18.3	**1997**
14.1	13.4	15.0	14.4	12.9	11.3	**1998**
20.1	21.3	23.9	22.6	25.0	26.1	**1999**
29.8	31.2	33.9	33.1	34.4	28.5	**2000**
26.5	27.5	25.9	22.2	19.7	19.3	**2001**
26.9	28.4	29.7	28.9	26.3	29.4	**2002**
30.8	31.6	28.3	30.3	31.1	32.2	**2003**
40.7	44.9	46.0	53.1	48.5	43.3	**2004**
58.7	65.0	65.6	62.4	58.3	59.4	**2005**
74.4	73.1	63.9	58.9	59.4	62.0	**2006**
74.2	72.4	79.9	86.2	94.6	91.7	**2007**

COMMONITIES

GOLD $US/OZ LONDON PM MONTH CLOSE

	JAN	FEB	MAR	APR	MAY	JUN
1970	34.9	35.0	35.1	35.6	36.0	35.4
1971	37.9	38.7	38.9	39.0	40.5	40.1
1972	45.8	48.3	48.3	49.0	54.6	62.1
1973	65.1	74.2	84.4	90.5	102.0	120.1
1974	129.2	150.2	168.4	172.2	163.3	154.1
1975	175.8	181.8	178.2	167.0	167.0	166.3
1976	128.2	132.3	129.6	128.4	125.5	123.8
1977	132.3	142.8	148.9	147.3	143.0	143.0
1978	175.8	182.3	181.6	170.9	184.2	183.1
1979	233.7	251.3	240.1	245.3	274.6	277.5
1980	653.0	637.0	494.5	518.0	535.5	653.5
1981	506.5	489.0	513.8	482.8	479.3	426.0
1982	387.0	362.6	320.0	361.3	325.3	317.5
1983	499.5	408.5	414.8	429.3	437.5	416.0
1984	373.8	394.3	388.5	375.8	384.3	373.1
1985	306.7	287.8	329.3	321.4	314.0	317.8
1986	350.5	338.2	344.0	345.8	343.2	345.5
1987	400.5	405.9	405.9	453.3	451.0	447.3
1988	458.0	426.2	457.0	449.0	455.5	436.6
1989	394.0	387.0	383.2	377.6	361.8	373.0
1990	415.1	407.7	368.5	367.8	363.1	352.2
1991	366.0	362.7	355.7	357.8	360.4	368.4
1992	354.1	353.1	341.7	336.4	337.5	343.4
1993	330.5	327.6	337.8	354.3	374.8	378.5
1994	377.9	381.6	389.2	376.5	387.6	388.3
1995	374.9	376.4	392.0	389.8	384.3	387.1
1996	405.6	400.7	396.4	391.3	390.6	382.0
1997	345.5	358.6	348.2	340.2	345.6	334.6
1998	304.9	297.4	301.0	310.7	293.6	296.3
1999	285.4	287.1	279.5	286.6	268.6	261.0
2000	283.3	293.7	276.8	275.1	272.3	288.2
2001	264.5	266.7	257.7	263.2	267.5	270.6
2002	282.3	296.9	301.4	308.2	326.6	318.5
2003	367.5	347.5	334.9	336.8	361.4	346.0
2004	399.8	395.9	423.7	388.5	393.3	395.8
2005	422.2	435.5	427.5	435.7	414.5	437.1
2006	568.8	556.0	582.0	644.0	653.0	613.5
2007	650.5	664.2	661.8	677.0	659.1	650.5
2008	923.3	971.5	933.5	871.0	885.8	930.3

* Source: Bank of England

GOLD $US/OZ LONDON PM MONTH CLOSE

COMMODITIES

JUL	AUG	SEP	OCT	NOV	DEC	
35.3	35.4	36.2	37.5	37.4	37.4	**1970**
41.0	42.7	42.0	42.5	42.9	43.5	**1971**
65.7	67.0	65.5	64.9	62.9	63.9	**1972**
120.2	106.8	103.0	100.1	94.8	106.7	**1973**
143.0	154.6	151.8	158.8	181.7	183.9	**1974**
166.7	159.8	141.3	142.9	138.2	140.3	**1975**
112.5	104.0	116.0	123.2	130.3	134.5	**1976**
144.1	146.0	154.1	161.5	160.1	165.0	**1977**
200.3	208.7	217.1	242.6	193.4	226.0	**1978**
296.5	315.1	397.3	382.0	415.7	512.0	**1979**
614.3	631.3	666.8	629.0	619.8	589.8	**1980**
406.0	425.5	428.8	427.0	414.5	397.5	**1981**
342.9	411.5	397.0	423.3	436.0	456.9	**1982**
422.0	414.3	405.0	382.0	405.0	382.4	**1983**
342.4	348.3	343.8	333.5	329.0	309.0	**1984**
327.5	333.3	326.5	325.1	325.3	326.8	**1985**
357.5	384.7	423.2	401.0	383.5	388.8	**1986**
462.5	453.4	459.5	468.8	492.5	484.1	**1987**
436.8	427.8	397.7	412.4	422.6	410.3	**1988**
368.3	359.8	366.5	375.3	408.2	398.6	**1989**
372.3	387.8	408.4	379.5	384.9	386.2	**1990**
362.9	347.4	354.9	357.5	366.3	353.2	**1991**
357.9	340.0	349.0	339.3	334.2	332.9	**1992**
401.8	371.6	355.5	369.6	370.9	391.8	**1993**
384.0	385.8	394.9	383.9	383.1	383.3	**1994**
383.4	382.4	384.0	382.7	387.8	387.0	**1995**
385.3	386.5	379.0	379.5	371.3	369.3	**1996**
326.4	325.4	332.1	311.4	296.8	290.2	**1997**
288.9	273.4	293.9	292.3	294.7	287.8	**1998**
255.6	254.8	299.0	299.1	291.4	290.3	**1999**
276.8	277.0	273.7	264.5	269.1	274.5	**2000**
265.9	273.0	293.1	278.8	275.5	276.5	**2001**
304.7	312.8	323.7	316.9	319.1	347.2	**2002**
354.8	375.6	388.0	386.3	398.4	416.3	**2003**
391.4	407.3	415.7	425.6	453.4	435.6	**2004**
429.0	433.3	473.3	470.8	495.7	513.0	**2005**
632.5	623.5	599.3	603.8	646.7	632.0	**2006**
665.5	672.0	743.0	789.5	783.5	833.8	**2007**

FOREIGN EXCHANGE

FOREIGN EXCHANGE

US DOLLAR vs CDN DOLLAR MONTHLY AVG. VALUES*

	JAN		FEB		MAR		APR		MAY		JUN	
	US / CDN	CDN / US	US / CDN	CDN / US	US / CDN	CDN /US	US / CDN	CDN / US	US / CDN	CDN / US	US / CDN	CDN / US
1971	1.01	0.99	1.01	0.99	1.01	0.99	1.01	0.99	1.01	0.99	1.02	0.98
1972	1.01	0.99	1.00	1.00	1.00	1.00	0.99	1.01	0.98	1.02	0.99	1.01
1973	1.00	1.00	0.99	1.01	1.00	1.00	1.00	1.00	1.00	1.00	1.00	1.00
1974	0.99	1.01	0.97	1.03	0.97	1.03	0.96	1.04	0.96	1.04	0.97	1.03
1975	1.00	1.00	1.00	1.00	1.00	1.00	1.02	0.98	1.02	0.98	1.03	0.97
1976	1.00	1.00	0.98	1.02	0.98	1.02	0.98	1.02	0.98	1.02	0.97	1.03
1977	1.02	0.98	1.05	0.96	1.06	0.95	1.05	0.95	1.05	0.95	1.06	0.94
1978	1.11	0.90	1.12	0.90	1.13	0.88	1.13	0.88	1.12	0.89	1.12	0.89
1979	1.20	0.83	1.19	0.84	1.16	0.86	1.14	0.88	1.16	0.86	1.17	0.86
1980	1.16	0.86	1.15	0.87	1.19	0.84	1.19	0.84	1.16	0.86	1.15	0.87
1981	1.19	0.84	1.20	0.83	1.19	0.84	1.20	0.84	1.20	0.83	1.20	0.83
1982	1.20	0.84	1.23	0.81	1.23	0.81	1.22	0.82	1.24	0.80	1.29	0.77
1983	1.24	0.81	1.23	0.81	1.23	0.81	1.23	0.82	1.23	0.81	1.23	0.81
1984	1.25	0.80	1.25	0.80	1.28	0.78	1.28	0.78	1.29	0.77	1.32	0.76
1985	1.33	0.75	1.38	0.72	1.37	0.73	1.37	0.73	1.37	0.73	1.36	0.74
1986	1.42	0.70	1.42	0.70	1.40	0.72	1.37	0.73	1.38	0.72	1.39	0.72
1987	1.34	0.75	1.33	0.75	1.31	0.77	1.34	0.75	1.34	0.75	1.33	0.75
1988	1.28	0.78	1.26	0.79	1.23	0.81	1.23	0.81	1.23	0.81	1.21	0.82
1989	1.18	0.84	1.20	0.83	1.19	0.84	1.19	0.84	1.21	0.83	1.20	0.83
1990	1.19	0.84	1.19	0.84	1.17	0.85	1.17	0.86	1.17	0.85	1.17	0.86
1991	1.16	0.86	1.15	0.87	1.16	0.86	1.15	0.87	1.15	0.87	1.14	0.88
1992	1.18	0.85	1.18	0.85	1.19	0.84	1.20	0.84	1.20	0.83	1.20	0.84
1993	1.27	0.79	1.25	0.80	1.26	0.79	1.27	0.79	1.27	0.79	1.28	0.78
1994	1.33	0.75	1.35	0.74	1.38	0.72	1.38	0.72	1.38	0.72	1.38	0.72
1995	1.42	0.70	1.39	0.72	1.40	0.71	1.36	0.74	1.37	0.73	1.37	0.73
1996	1.38	0.72	1.37	0.73	1.36	0.73	1.36	0.73	1.37	0.73	1.37	0.73
1997	1.35	0.74	1.37	0.73	1.38	0.72	1.40	0.72	1.38	0.72	1.38	0.73
1998	1.46	0.68	1.42	0.70	1.42	0.70	1.43	0.70	1.45	0.69	1.47	0.68
1999	1.51	0.66	1.51	0.66	1.51	0.66	1.46	0.68	1.47	0.68	1.48	0.68
2000	1.45	0.69	1.45	0.69	1.45	0.69	1.47	0.68	1.50	0.67	1.48	0.67
2001	1.50	0.67	1.53	0.65	1.57	0.64	1.54	0.65	1.55	0.65	1.52	0.66
2002	1.59	0.63	1.60	0.62	1.59	0.63	1.57	0.64	1.53	0.65	1.51	0.66
2003	1.53	0.65	1.49	0.67	1.47	0.68	1.44	0.69	1.37	0.73	1.35	0.74
2004	1.33	0.75	1.35	0.74	1.31	0.77	1.37	0.73	1.36	0.73	1.35	0.74
2005	1.24	0.80	1.23	0.81	1.21	0.83	1.25	0.80	1.26	0.79	1.23	0.81
2006	1.15	0.87	1.14	0.88	1.16	0.86	1.12	0.89	1.09	0.91	1.11	0.90
2007	1.18	0.85	1.17	0.86	1.15	0.87	1.12	0.90	1.07	0.93	1.05	0.95
2008	1.00	1.00	0.98	1.02	1.02	0.98	1.01	0.99	0.99	1.01	1.01	0.99

Source: Federal Reserve: Avg of daily rates, noon buying rates in New York City for cable transfers payable in foreign currencies

US DOLLAR vs CDN DOLLAR MONTHLY AVG. VALUES

FOREIGN EXCHANGE

JUL US / CDN	JUL CDN / US	AUG US / CDN	AUG CDN / US	SEP US / CDN	SEP CDN / US	OCT US / CDN	OCT CDN / US	NOV US / CDN	NOV CDN / US	DEC US / CDN	DEC CDN / US	
1.02	0.98	1.01	0.99	1.01	0.99	1.00	1.00	1.00	1.00	1.00	1.00	**1971**
0.98	1.02	0.98	1.02	0.98	1.02	0.98	1.02	0.99	1.01	1.00	1.00	**1972**
1.00	1.00	1.01	0.99	1.01	0.99	1.00	1.00	1.00	1.00	1.00	1.00	**1973**
0.98	1.02	0.99	1.01	0.99	1.01	0.98	1.02	0.99	1.01	0.99	1.01	**1974**
1.03	0.97	1.03	0.97	1.03	0.98	1.02	0.98	1.01	0.99	1.02	0.98	**1975**
0.98	1.03	0.98	1.02	0.97	1.03	0.97	1.03	1.00	1.00	1.01	0.99	**1976**
1.07	0.94	1.07	0.93	1.07	0.93	1.11	0.90	1.11	0.90	1.09	0.91	**1977**
1.13	0.88	1.15	0.87	1.18	0.84	1.17	0.86	1.17	0.85	1.19	0.84	**1978**
1.17	0.85	1.17	0.86	1.16	0.86	1.18	0.84	1.17	0.85	1.17	0.86	**1979**
1.16	0.86	1.16	0.86	1.17	0.85	1.18	0.85	1.19	0.84	1.19	0.84	**1980**
1.23	0.81	1.20	0.83	1.21	0.83	1.20	0.83	1.18	0.85	1.19	0.84	**1981**
1.26	0.80	1.24	0.81	1.24	0.81	1.23	0.82	1.24	0.81	1.23	0.81	**1982**
1.23	0.81	1.23	0.81	1.23	0.81	1.23	0.81	1.24	0.81	1.24	0.80	**1983**
1.31	0.76	1.30	0.77	1.32	0.76	1.32	0.76	1.32	0.76	1.32	0.76	**1984**
1.35	0.74	1.37	0.73	1.37	0.73	1.37	0.73	1.38	0.72	1.40	0.72	**1985**
1.38	0.72	1.39	0.72	1.39	0.72	1.39	0.72	1.38	0.72	1.38	0.72	**1986**
1.33	0.75	1.32	0.76	1.31	0.76	1.32	0.76	1.31	0.76	1.30	0.77	**1987**
1.21	0.83	1.24	0.81	1.22	0.82	1.22	0.82	1.19	0.84	1.19	0.84	**1988**
1.18	0.85	1.18	0.85	1.18	0.85	1.17	0.85	1.16	0.86	1.16	0.86	**1989**
1.15	0.87	1.15	0.87	1.16	0.86	1.17	0.86	1.17	0.86	1.16	0.86	**1990**
1.15	0.87	1.14	0.88	1.13	0.88	1.12	0.89	1.14	0.88	1.16	0.87	**1991**
1.18	0.84	1.19	0.84	1.25	0.80	1.24	0.81	1.29	0.78	1.27	0.79	**1992**
1.29	0.78	1.32	0.76	1.33	0.75	1.32	0.76	1.34	0.75	1.33	0.75	**1993**
1.39	0.72	1.37	0.73	1.34	0.74	1.35	0.74	1.38	0.73	1.40	0.71	**1994**
1.37	0.73	1.34	0.75	1.34	0.75	1.34	0.75	1.36	0.74	1.36	0.73	**1995**
1.38	0.73	1.37	0.73	1.36	0.73	1.34	0.75	1.35	0.74	1.37	0.73	**1996**
1.38	0.72	1.39	0.72	1.38	0.72	1.41	0.71	1.43	0.70	1.43	0.70	**1997**
1.50	0.67	1.55	0.64	1.52	0.66	1.55	0.65	1.54	0.65	1.55	0.65	**1998**
1.50	0.66	1.49	0.67	1.47	0.68	1.47	0.68	1.47	0.68	1.45	0.69	**1999**
1.48	0.67	1.47	0.68	1.50	0.67	1.53	0.65	1.54	0.65	1.50	0.67	**2000**
1.53	0.65	1.54	0.65	1.58	0.63	1.58	0.63	1.58	0.63	1.59	0.63	**2001**
1.58	0.63	1.56	0.64	1.58	0.63	1.57	0.64	1.57	0.64	1.58	0.63	**2002**
1.41	0.71	1.40	0.72	1.35	0.74	1.32	0.76	1.30	0.77	1.29	0.77	**2003**
1.32	0.76	1.32	0.76	1.27	0.79	1.22	0.82	1.19	0.84	1.21	0.83	**2004**
1.23	0.81	1.19	0.84	1.17	0.86	1.17	0.85	1.17	0.86	1.16	0.86	**2005**
1.12	0.89	1.11	0.90	1.11	0.90	1.13	0.89	1.14	0.88	1.16	0.86	**2006**
1.06	0.94	1.05	0.95	1.00	1.00	0.95	1.05	0.99	1.01	0.98	1.02	**2007**

FOREIGN EXCHANGE

U.S. DOLLAR vs EURO MONTHLY AVG. VALUES

	JAN		FEB		MAR		APR		MAY		JUN	
	EUR / US	US / EUR	EUR / US	US / EUR	EUR / US	US / EUR	EUR / US	US / EUR	EUR / US	US / EUR	EUR / US	US / EUR
1999	1.14	0.88	1.10	0.91	1.08	0.93	1.06	0.95	1.04	0.96	1.03	0.97
2000	0.98	1.02	0.96	1.04	0.96	1.04	0.91	1.10	0.93	1.07	0.95	1.05
2001	0.93	1.07	0.92	1.09	0.88	1.14	0.89	1.13	0.85	1.18	0.85	1.18
2002	0.86	1.16	0.87	1.16	0.87	1.15	0.90	1.11	0.93	1.07	0.99	1.01
2003	1.07	0.93	1.08	0.93	1.09	0.92	1.12	0.89	1.18	0.85	1.15	0.87
2004	1.25	0.80	1.24	0.80	1.23	0.81	1.20	0.84	1.22	0.82	1.22	0.82
2005	1.30	0.77	1.33	0.75	1.30	0.77	1.29	0.77	1.23	0.81	1.21	0.83
2006	1.22	0.82	1.19	0.84	1.21	0.82	1.26	0.79	1.28	0.78	1.28	0.78
2007	1.30	0.77	1.32	0.76	1.34	0.75	1.37	0.73	1.35	0.74	1.35	0.74
2008	1.48	0.67	1.52	0.66	1.58	0.63	1.56	0.64	1.56	0.64	1.57	0.64

Source: Federal Reserve: Avg of daily rates, noon buying rates in New York City for cable transfers payable in foreign currencies

US DOLLAR vs EURO MONTHLY AVG. VALUES

JUL		AUG		SEP		OCT		NOV		DEC		
EUR / US	US / EUR	EUR / US	US / EUR	EUR / US	US / EUR	EUR / US	US / EUR	EUR / US	US / EUR	EUR / US	US / EUR	
1.07	0.94	1.06	0.95	1.06	0.94	1.05	0.95	1.01	0.99	1.01	0.99	**1999**
0.93	1.08	0.89	1.13	0.88	1.13	0.85	1.18	0.87	1.15	0.94	1.07	**2000**
0.88	1.14	0.91	1.10	0.91	1.10	0.90	1.11	0.90	1.12	0.89	1.12	**2001**
0.98	1.02	0.98	1.02	0.99	1.01	0.99	1.01	0.99	1.01	1.05	0.95	**2002**
1.12	0.89	1.10	0.91	1.17	0.86	1.16	0.86	1.20	0.83	1.26	0.79	**2003**
1.20	0.83	1.22	0.82	1.24	0.81	1.27	0.78	1.33	0.75	1.35	0.74	**2004**
1.21	0.82	1.23	0.81	1.21	0.83	1.20	0.83	1.18	0.85	1.18	0.84	**2005**
1.28	0.78	1.28	0.78	1.27	0.79	1.28	0.78	1.33	0.75	1.32	0.76	**2006**
1.37	0.73	1.36	0.73	1.42	0.70	1.45	0.69	1.47	0.68	1.46	0.68	**2007**